NOVELL'S®

GroupWise® 4 Administrator's Guide

SHAWN B. ROGERS

NOVELL PRESS®

Novell Press, San Jose

Novell's GroupWise® 4 Administrator's Guide

Published by
Novell Press
2180 Fortune Drive
San Jose, CA 95131

Library of Congress Catalog Card No.: 95-81095

ISBN: 1-56884-732-7

Printed in the United States of America

10 9 8 7 6 5 4 3 2 1

Distributed in the United States by IDG Books Worldwide, Inc.

Distributed by Macmillan Canada for Canada; by Computer and Technical Books for the Caribbean Basin; by Contemporantea de Ediciones for Venezuela; by Distribuidora Cuspide for Argentina; by CITFC for Brazil; by Ediciones ZETA S.C.R. Ltda. for Peru; by Editorial Limusa SA for Mexico; by Transworld Publishers Limited in the United Kingdom and Europe; by Al-Maiman Publishers & Distributors for Saudi Arabia; by Simron Pty. Ltd. for South Africa; by IDG Communications (HK) Ltd. for Hong Kong; by Toppan Company Ltd. for Japan; by Addison Wesley Publishing Company for Korea; by Longman Singapore Publisher Ltd. for Singapore, Malaysia, Thailand, and Indonesia; by Unalis Corporation for Taiwan; by WS Computer Publishing Company, Inc. for the Philippines; by WoodsLane Enterprises Ltd. for New Zealand.

For general information on Novell Press books in the U.S., including information on discounts and premiums, contact IDG Books at 800-434-3422 or 415-655-3000. For information on where to purchase Novell Press books outside the U.S., contact IDG Books Worldwide at 415-655-3021 or fax 415-655-3295. For information on translations, contact Waterside Productions, Inc., 2191 San Elijo Avenue, Cardiff, CA 92007-1839, at 619-632-9190. For sales inquiries and special prices for bulk quantities, call IDG Books Worldwide at 415-655-3200. For information on using Novell Press books in the classroom, or for ordering examination copies, contact Jim Kelly at 800-434-2086.

John Kilcullen, *President & CEO, IDG Books Worldwide, Inc.*
Brenda McLaughlin, *Senior Vice President & Group Publisher, IDG Books Worldwide, Inc.*

The IDG Boooks Worldwide logo is a trademark under exclusive license to IDG Books Worldwide, Inc., from International Data Group, Inc.

Rosalie Kearsley, *Publisher, Novell Press, Inc.*

Novell Press and the Novell Press logo are trademarks of Novell, Inc.

Welcome to Novell Press

Novell Press, the world's leading provider of networking books, is the premier source for the most timely and useful information in the networking industry. Novell Press books cover fundamental networking issues as they emerge—from today's Novell and third-party products to the concepts and strategies that will guide the industry's future. The result is a broad spectrum of titles for the benefit of those involved in networking at any level: end-user, department administrator, developer, systems manager, or network architect.

Novell Press books are written by experts with the full participation of Novell's own technicians and are published only on the basis of final released software, never on prereleased versions. Novell Press at IDG is an exciting partnership between two companies at the forefront of the knowledge and communications revolution. The Press is implementing an ambitious publishing program to develop new networking titles centered on the current version of NetWare and on Novell's GroupWise and other popular groupware products.

Novell Press books are translated into 12 languages and are available at bookstores around the world.

Rosalie Kearsley, Publisher, Novell Press, Inc.
David Kolodney, Associate Publisher, IDG Books Worldwide, Inc.

Novell Press

Publisher
Rosalie Kearsley

Associate Publisher
David Kolodney

Market Development Manager
Colleen Bluhm

Associate Acquisitions Editor
Anne Hamilton

Communications Project Specialist
Marcy Shanti

Managing Editor
Terry Somerson

Development Editor
Ronald J. Hull

Copy Editors
Ronald J. Hull
Vicki Van Ausdall

Technical Editors
Sean Kirkby
Rick McTague

Editorial Assistant
Jean Leitner

Production Director
Beth Jenkins

**Supervisor of
Project Coordination**
Cindy L. Phipps

Supervisor of Page Layout
Kathie S. Schnorr

Production Systems Specialist
Steve Peake

Pre-Press Coordination
Tony Augsburger
Patricia R. Reynolds
Theresa Sánchez-Baker

Media/Archive Coordination
Leslie Popplewell
Kerri Cornell
Michael Wilkey

Project Coordinator
Valery Bourke

Graphics Coordination
Shelley Lea
Gina Scott
Carla Radzikinas

Production Staff
Shawn Aylsworth
Cameron Booker
Dominique DeFelice

Proofreaders
Kathleen Prata
Christine Meloy Beck
Gwenette Gaddis
Dwight Ramsey
Carl Saff
Robert Springer

Indexer
Steve Rath

Cover Design
Archer Design

Cover Photographer
Greg Whitaker

About the Author

Shawn B. Rogers is a Certified Novell Instructor for Novell GroupWise, and a senior course developer for Novell Education's GroupWise courses. He has three years' instruction experience in WordPerfect Office 4 and Novell GroupWise 4.1. He is also a Certified Novell Administrator (CNA) for GroupWise and NetWare 4, and a Certified Novell Engineer (CNE) for NetWare 4.

He lives in Spanish Fork, Utah.

To my wonderful wife, Kellie, for your strength, support, and constant encouragement.

To my son, Cameron, for always reminding me what is truly important in life.

Acknowledgments

In all fairness, three more names should appear on the front cover of this book because of their huge contributions to this project: Ron Hull (development editor), Sean Kirkby (technical reviewer), and Rick McTague (GroupWise mentor).

Ron Hull, who works for IDG Books Worldwide, Inc., took the words of a rookie author, and by using his editorial skills and his mind-reading ability, molded them into something that sounds like a real book. Throughout the process, he provided his extensive expertise, technical knowledge, and humor, while maintaining his patience.

My technical editor and reviewer, Sean Kirkby, who works for Novell as a GroupWare SWAT Engineer, provided insight, understanding, and technical knowledge of GroupWise that only comes from years of experience supporting and testing the product. Thanks Sean, for your "Corrections," "Strong Suggestions," and "Casual Suggestions." Thanks also for your personal tutelage throughout the project.

Rick McTague, who works for USConnect of Kansas City, is in my opinion one of the industry's premier GroupWise consultants and instructors. Rick provided his "real world" insights into the contents and structure of this book. Thanks, Rick, for keeping me on track with what really happens in the GroupWise world, and for your off-the-wall comments that kept me grinning well into the early morning hours.

I would also like to express special thanks to Colleen Bluhm with Novell Press, for making this project a reality, and for her tireless efforts throughout its completion.

This book is a collection of wisdom from the finest GroupWise minds in the industry. Literally hundreds of people have contributed to this book indirectly. Thanks to those people in Novell GroupWare marketing from whose documents and white papers I borrowed liberally, and to those people in GroupWise technical support who took time out of their crowded schedules to answer my questions.

Thanks also to all the people who participate in the GroupWise (GO GROUPWISE) and WPUSERS (GO WPUSERS) forums on CompuServe, those who answer technical questions on the GroupWise Internet ListServer (I've been lurking there for many months.), those who consult with me on the Novell Education courses, and those who attend the Novell classes. Your combined wisdom and experiences contributed greatly to this work. Thanks also to Morris Blackham at teltrust.com (yes, that's their real name) for his assistance with the Internet connectivity section.

Finally, thanks to all the wonderful people I work with in Novell Education. To my new team, Doug, Janene, Rose, Amy, Kim, Kevin, Jonathan, Eric, and Cheryl—thanks for your support and encouragement with this project. And, to my old team, Stan (who set my feet on the GroupWise path three years ago), Allen, Scott, Shauna, Joe, Tammy, Mary Ann, Mitchell, and Jennifer—I miss you guys.

And last, but not least, thanks to the trout in Scofield Reservoir and the birdies at Spanish Oaks golf course—for waiting. I'm back!

(IDG Books Worldwide would like to give special thanks to Patrick J. McGovern, founder of International Data Group, who made this book possible.)

Preface

You are about to enter the world of Novell GroupWise. That's a wise choice. GroupWise is the most powerful electronic messaging system on the market today — both from the end user's perspective and from the administrator's perspective.

The GroupWise client software offers several features that set GroupWise apart from other e-mail systems. Here are a few of the features that make GroupWise unique:

- A universal In Box for all message types (mail, appointments, tasks, notes, and phone messages)

- A universal Out Box for message-status tracking (telling you when your mail has been delivered, opened, deleted, etc.)

- Rules and proxies for all GroupWise client platforms

- Integrated calendaring

- Integrated task management

From an administrator's perspective, GroupWise is extremely powerful, particularly because of its adaptability. Some of the most prominent benefits that GroupWise offers system administrators are:

- A choice of centralized or distributed administration

- Automatic directory synchronization

- High-performance message transport services

- Cross-platform database message storage

- Software management and distribution

- Support for remote clients

- Shared administration with a network

- Comprehensive connectivity and gateway components

GroupWise is very flexible. It can be configured to meet the needs of small offices with fewer than ten users, or it can be designed to service large corporations with thousands of users.

In the years that I have been teaching Novell GroupWise classes and developing GroupWise course materials for Novell Education, I have come to realize a couple of things about GroupWise systems.

First, no two GroupWise systems are identical. Because of the variety of computing platforms in use, the array of network operating systems, and the many different network topologies (i.e., structural configurations), the one constant in all GroupWise systems is that they are always unique. What works extremely well for one organization is not necessarily the best solution for another.

Second, no single person knows everything there is to know about GroupWise. There are simply too many client programs, server platforms, network operating systems, gateways, network configurations, and add-on products for any individual to be an expert on all facets of GroupWise.

However, as I have analyzed this area of the electronic messaging industry, I have noticed that there is a body of knowledge and a core set of skills that *every* GroupWise system administrator must have. There are certain principles and techniques to help you get the most out of your GroupWise system (with the least amount of exasperation). These are the topics I have chosen to address in this book.

As you read the book, you should be aware that — because of limited space — I have focused more on certain issues than on others. For example, this book covers only GroupWise *administration*. It does not explain how to use all of the GroupWise client application's features. I explain only those client features that affect administrative decisions.

Furthermore, in certain parts of the book, more emphasis has been given to Novell products than to other comparable products. As you read this book, you may notice it is somewhat Novell- and NetWare-centric. This is not to say that the book is only useful if you are using other Novell products along with GroupWise. That is definitely not the case. When I explain how GroupWise components work on a general level, the concepts apply to *all* versions of the specific GroupWise component. (For example, when I discuss the Async gateway, the general concepts apply to both the OS/2 and NLM Async gateways.) However, occasionally — when I go into more detail — I focus more on the components developed for NetWare, such as the NLM message server and NLM administration server.

There are several reasons for this book's Novell and NetWare bias. If you are running GroupWise on a Novell network, the NetWare Loadable Module (NLM) servers and gateways are the recommended versions. Those Novell products not only give the best performance, they tend to be the products most frequently used for GroupWise. Furthermore, they are the products that I am personally most familiar with.

Whenever possible, I explain in the book how to set up and use GroupWise with other platforms, such as DOS and OS/2. However, when a GroupWise component is available as a NetWare Loadable Module (NLM), I always explain how to use the NLM. To compensate for the Novell and NetWare bias of the book, the accompanying CD-ROM includes a tremendous amount of technical information about GroupWise products for other computing platforms.

This book is an excellent resource for anyone working toward Certified Novell Engineer (CNE) certification for GroupWise. In many cases, the book covers the same material taught in Novell Education courses. Sometimes, the book explains concepts in greater depth than the courses — or provides information not explained in the courses. However, the hands-on experience you get in GroupWise CNE courses undoubtedly provides benefits that I could not incorporate into a book.

I firmly believe that there is no substitute for hands-on experience. The GroupWise CNE courses are designed to provide valuable hands-on experience with GroupWise administration tasks, and the GroupWise CNE exams are based on that kind of experience. I have focused in this book as much as possible on the most important principles and skills required for GroupWise administration. If you read this book in conjunction with Novell Education's GroupWise courses, you will understand GroupWise better — and you will be a more knowledgeable system administrator and a wiser GroupWise CNE.

How This Book Is Organized

Novell's GroupWise 4 Administrator's Guide is divided into nine parts. I caution you not to skip ahead to the chapters that seem to correspond to your particular organization's needs. If you do, you will miss important concepts in the earlier chapters. Most of the chapters are not designed to be read independently of the others.

Here's an overview of each part:

Part I: Fundamental GroupWise Concepts

Part I explains introductory concepts and terminology you need to understand before you begin administering a GroupWise system. You should read this part even before you break the shrink-wrap on your GroupWise software package. Chapter 3 is particularly important, because it provides a planning strategy that, if followed, will help you implement a sound GroupWise system from the start.

Part II: Small GroupWise Systems — Single Domain, Single Post Office

In Part II, I explain how to set up GroupWise as a small system that consists of only a single GroupWise post office. The concepts presented in Part II apply to GroupWise systems of all sizes, however. This part covers essential GroupWise skills, such as how to install GroupWise from disks, how to administer the GroupWise client programs, and how to set up the GroupWise post office server (OFS) process. Post office security is also discussed in depth, and detailed diagrams illustrate how the post office message store works.

Part III: Intermediate GroupWise Systems — Single Domain, Multiple Post Offices

Part III deals with more complex systems that consist of multiple post offices. Some of the key concepts I discuss are: (1) how the GroupWise message server works and (2) how to set up and run the GroupWise NLM message server. Part III also includes detailed diagrams that illustrate how messages flow through a multiple post office GroupWise system.

Part IV: Enterprise GroupWise Systems — Multiple Domains

Part IV covers large, multidomain GroupWise systems. I explain the most common GroupWise topologies, along with their advantages and disadvantages. I also discuss the pros and cons of different GroupWise administration strategies. Chapter 10 and Chapter 11 are two of the most important chapters in the entire book. Chapter 10 explains how to set up and link multiple domains, how to configure backup message servers, and how to link domains using TCP/IP. Chapter 11 explains how automatic directory synchronization works and how to troubleshoot problems that may arise with the synchronization process.

Part V: The GroupWise Async Gateway

Part V explains how gateways work, in general, and how to configure an Async gateway to connect domains together. GroupWise Async gateways play an important role in many GroupWise systems. They allow you to connect domains that cannot be connected through a network, and they allow remote users to dial in to access a GroupWise system.

Part VI: Remote Computing with GroupWise

GroupWise Remote lets users connect to a system from remote locations — either through modems or through a network. In Part VI, I explain how to configure your Async gateway to support GroupWise Remote and how to configure and use the GroupWise Remote client software.

Part VII: Using External Domains and Combining GroupWise Systems

Part VII deals with a couple of advanced, system-level administration topics: (1) how to use external domains and (2) how to combine GroupWise systems together. I have grouped these subjects in the same part of the book because an understanding of external domains is essential when you consolidate GroupWise systems.

Part VIII: GroupWise User and Database Administration

The topics covered in Part VIII are administrative issues you will be confronted with after your GroupWise system is up and running smoothly. Part VIII deals with the day-to-day tasks that administrators perform, such as moving users from one location to another, running Check GroupWise (OFCHECK) on databases, and maintaining the GroupWise directory store databases.

Part IX: Additional GroupWise Utilities, Add-On Products, and Technologies

Part IX gives you a glimpse of other useful products that are related to (or can be integrated with) GroupWise. In this part of the book, you get a sense of what can be done with a GroupWise system. I discuss technologies that allow touch-tone telephone access to a GroupWise mailbox, faxing from a desktop with GroupWise, and that enhance GroupWise communications. In the final chapter, I give you an overview of the other Novell GroupWare products on the market.

Finally, five appendices are included at the end of the book. These appendices provide some very useful information for GroupWise administrators, including: an overview of client features that affect administrative decisions, an overview of Novell Education's GroupWise courses, a procedure for setting up a GroupWise test system on a single PC, a table explaining how message queues are monitored with various message server thread settings, and a worksheet to use when you set up users for the GroupWise Remote client.

Contents at a Glance

Table of Contents

Part IX   489

Fundamental GroupWise Concepts

In a classic episode of the '70s TV show M*A*S*H, one of the characters tries to disarm a bomb that has fallen into camp. He is crouched down near the bomb with a set of instructions in his hand, and he reads out loud, "Clip the blue wire."

Snip!

Then he continues reading, "But first, make sure that you . . ."

In the GroupWise Administration Guide, which is part of the documentation that comes with the GroupWise software, the first topic is "Setting Up a Single Domain, Single Post Office System." While in theory it's possible to start out there when you initially install GroupWise, there are several preparatory steps you can take that will make the experience more enjoyable and prevent bombs from unexpectedly going off. Part I of this book is the "But first . . ." information that you should know before you pull the disks out of the box.

Chapter One, "Fundamental GroupWise Components," is a brief introduction to the concept of store-and-forward electronic messaging. This chapter introduces some of the most fundamental concepts associated with electronic messaging systems.

Chapter Two, "Introduction to GroupWise Architecture," explains the terminology and architectural components of GroupWise. You will learn about domains, post offices, and objects, and how these components fit together to make a GroupWise system.

Chapter Three, "Planning a GroupWise Implementation," is an overview of the factors that you should consider before attempting to implement GroupWise in a full-scale production environment.

Fundamental GroupWise Components

Welcome to Novell GroupWise. Soon you will have mastered the most powerful corporate messaging system available today. This chapter introduces you to the basic components of an electronic messaging system and explains some ground-level concepts you will need to understand. You will also learn some important GroupWise terms and general messaging terminology.

History of GroupWise

Novell GroupWise has evolved a great deal over the past few years. Initially, the software was part of WordPerfect Library. When I first started working for WordPerfect in 1990, the program was called WordPerfect Office v. 3.0. However, it was not until version 3.1 was introduced that WordPerfect Office caught the attention of the e-mail world—especially among companies that were using WordPerfect 5.*x*. WordPerfect Office 3.1 was a revolutionary product because it was the first e-mail package designed for PCs that had an Out Box to track the status of mail messages. WordPerfect Office 3.1 is still used at many organizations that find its capabilities sufficient for their needs.

Version 4.0 of WordPerfect Office demonstrated even more powerful capabilities. Version 4.0 was no longer merely an e-mail system but rather for the first time provided a complete corporate messaging system. In addition to traditional electronic mail, WordPerfect Office v. 4.0 offered powerful calendaring and workflow features, along with several new kinds of messages (such as Appointments, Tasks, and Notes). The system's administration program was also dramatically enhanced, allowing for enterprise-wide administration from a central location. At that time, the WordPerfect Office client software became available for DOS, Windows, Macintosh, and UNIX clients. Then, when WordPerfect Corporation merged with Novell in 1994, WordPerfect Office v. 4.1 was renamed Novell GroupWise.

Even though the product is now called Novell GroupWise, its heritage from WordPerfect Office is still apparent. For example, in the DOS version of GroupWise the executable filename for the message server is CS.EXE. That filename only makes sense if you know that the same software was called the Connection Server in WordPerfect Office. Likewise, the input directory in GroupWise (where the message server picks up messages) is named WPCSIN, which stands for WordPerfect Connection Server Input. The keystrokes used in GroupWise also reflect its roots in WordPerfect Office. Knowing the origin of the GroupWise filenames, directories, executable files, and keystrokes will make the product much easier for you to understand. I'll give you the background on the filenames and directories in GroupWise as they come up.

E-Mail Fundamentals

GroupWise, like some other e-mail systems, is based on a concept called *store-and-forward architecture*. Messages are stored in directories or databases and then forwarded to locations that can be accessed by the messages' recipients. Store-and-forward e-mail systems have five basic components:

- ▶ Client (sometimes called the user agent)

- ▶ Message store

- ▶ Directory store

- ▶ Message transfer agent (MTA)

- ▶ Administration agent

The *client* is the part of an e-mail program that the end user sees. The end user utilizes the client to read incoming mail and to send out messages to other e-mail users. The client often performs other functions as well, including message management, spell checking, and personal calendaring.

The *message store* is the place where messages are physically stored in an e-mail system. The client software often interacts directly with the message store by placing messages into the message store's directories or databases.

The *directory store* is the place where the addressing information for users and other objects in the GroupWise system is stored. The directory store provides the information for the address book in the client program.

The *message transfer agent* (also referred to as the *message transport agent* or *MTA*) acts like a mail carrier. It picks up messages from one message store and deposits them in another. Sometimes the message transfer agent places messages directly into a message store. At other times the message transfer agent hands off the message to a different message transfer agent that will continue to process the message.

The *administration agent* coordinates the activities of the users, the client, the message store, and the message transfer agent and manages the directory store, which is a list of the users in the system. In addition, the system administrator uses the administration agent to determine where to locate the message stores. The system administrator also uses the administration agent to move the client software to the proper location and to give the message transfer agent detailed instructions about when and where to deliver messages.

THE CLIENT

Figure 1.1 illustrates the end user's perception of e-mail. When most people think of e-mail, they envision the client, which is the software interface for the end user. The client is the software you use to send and receive messages and to perform other tasks, such as organizing messages. As far as the typical end user is concerned, the e-mail client delivers messages directly between e-mail users.

F I G U R E 1.1

E-Mail from the Perspective of an End User

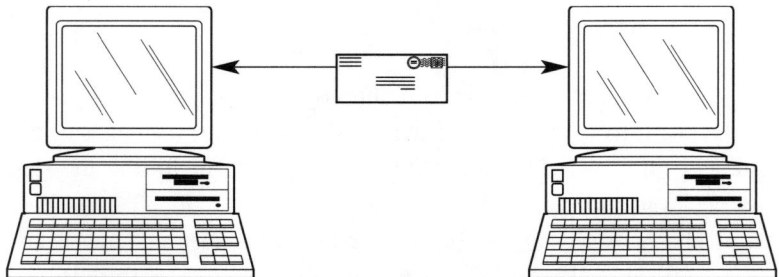

Although the client is the most recognizable part of an e-mail system, it is only a small part of the big picture. In addition to the client's end-user interface, e-mail systems are comprised of directories, databases, executable processes, connectivity processes, the network itself, hardware components, and administration tools.

The client program can have a number of different incarnations. For example, the GroupWise client is available for Microsoft Windows, Macintosh, DOS, and UNIX systems. There are also *remote clients,* which allow users to retrieve and send messages even when the users are not connected to the network where their messages are stored.

The GroupWise client software provides you with access to the most functional electronic messaging system available today. With the GroupWise client, you can send and receive mail, schedule meetings, manage tasks, maintain your personal calendar, organize your incoming and outgoing messages, and perform a wide variety of other useful tasks.

THE MESSAGE STORE

Every store-and-forward e-mail system has a message store. As the name suggests, a message store is the place where messages are physically stored. This is typically a shared location, such as a network volume. E-mail correspondents use the client to access their messages, which are held in the message store. Figure 1.2 shows how message storage works.

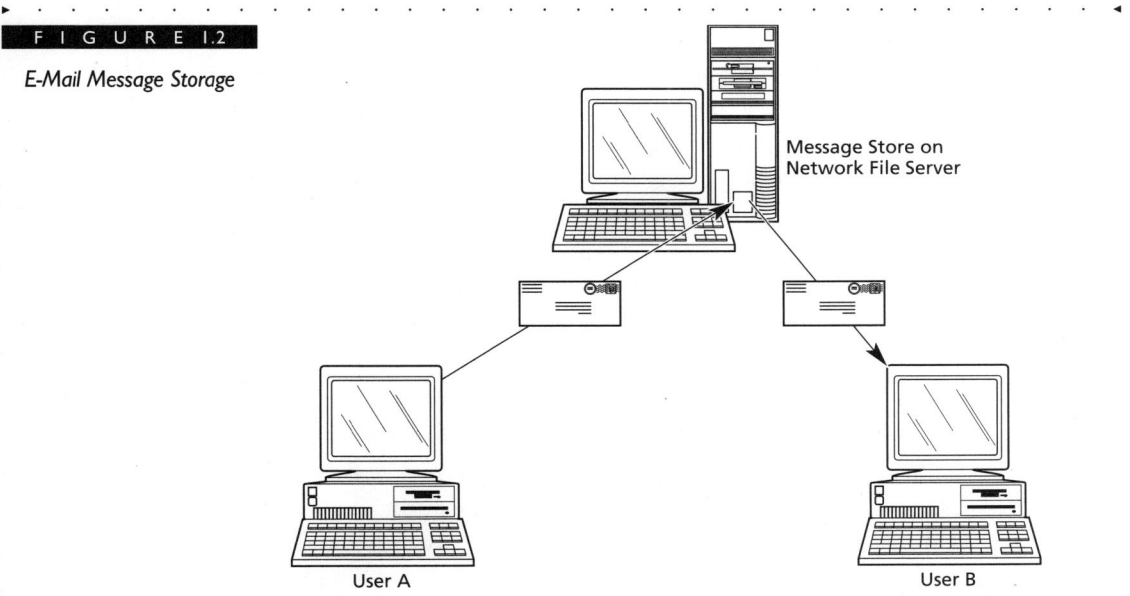

E-Mail Message Storage

Message Store on
Network File Server

User A

User B

Here's a simple analogy to help you understand how the message store works. Suppose you create a file in WordPerfect and save it in your network user directory at work. You then tell a coworker to check out the file you just put on the network. Voilà! That's electronic mail in its simplest form. In this analogy, WordPerfect performs the function of a client program, and your network directory serves as the message store. Now you see the *store* element of store-and-forward architecture.

There are two different types of message storage that e-mail systems use—database message storage and file-based message storage. An e-mail message system such as WordPerfect Office 3.1 is said to use file-based storage because it stores its messages as individual files in directories. A system that uses database message storage stores many messages together in one large database or in multiple databases. Novell GroupWise uses both database message storage and file-based message storage. GroupWise stores its messages in databases. However, it also uses a file-based storage method to store file attachments when their size exceeds a certain limit.

Because users need to access their personal messages, the message store must be accessible to every e-mail user. That means the message store databases and directories have to be located on file servers that all end users can access.

The message store concept is the key to the *cross-platform functionality* of GroupWise. The message store is not associated with any particular client platform. Therefore, users can access their messages from any version of the client. I have a PC and a Macintosh at my desk, and I often have both machines running GroupWise at the same time. If I open and read a message in the Mac client, the Windows client running on the PC notices the message has been read and updates the display to reflect that change. It makes no difference to the message store which client software I use to read the message.

When the message store is located in a platform that is different from the client's platform, the system needs to implement some form of network-level connectivity. For example, if a DOS client accesses a message store on a UNIX machine, you will need some form of connectivity between DOS and UNIX that allows the different computing platforms to communicate.

While on the subject of the message store, I should tell you a little about message security. The GroupWise message store databases are encrypted with a proprietary encryption scheme. The messages are secure and cannot be accessed by intruders. The messages are coded with the encryption technology during transit and storage. As long as GroupWise users protect their mailboxes with passwords and do not tell others their network login passwords, their messages are completely private and secure.

THE DIRECTORY STORE

E-mail systems have to have some way to keep track of their users and resources. They do this by maintaining a list of users and addresses called a *directory store*. A directory store is a database that contains information about every individual in a system. Because e-mail systems are usually part of large networks, the directory is often copied (or *replicated*) in many different locations so that all users can access its information. The directories are updated by a process called *directory synchronization*, which I will explain in more detail later on.

THE MESSAGE TRANSFER AGENT

Previously, I made an analogy between an e-mail message and a file created with WordPerfect and then copied to a network directory. In that analogy, WordPerfect was the client program.

Suppose instead that WordPerfect were used to save the file to a location on the user's hard drive, and the user then used a file-management program to move the file from the hard drive to a network directory. In that case, the file manager would serve as a message transfer agent (MTA), because it transfers the file from one location to another. If the recipient could not access the sender's network directory, the MTA would copy (or forward) the message to a network directory that the recipient could access. This is the *forward* element of store-and-forward architecture.

In an e-mail system, the MTA's job is to move messages to locations (namely, message stores) where the recipients have access to them. In GroupWise, the client places messages in directories (or *message queues*) that are monitored by the GroupWise server processes (MTAs), and the GroupWise servers then move the files to locations that the recipients can access.

In Figure 1.3, User A wants to send a message to User B, but they do not share the same message store. When User A sends the message, it is placed in a holding queue on User A's file server. The MTA picks up the message from the holding queue and forwards it to a message store on a file server that can be accessed by User B. In the figure, you will notice that the MTA is not associated with a specific computer. The MTA process could be running on a file server, or it could be running on a dedicated computer in a network that has access to both file servers.

FIGURE 1.3

The Message Transfer Agent

File Server

File Server

MTA Process

User A

User B

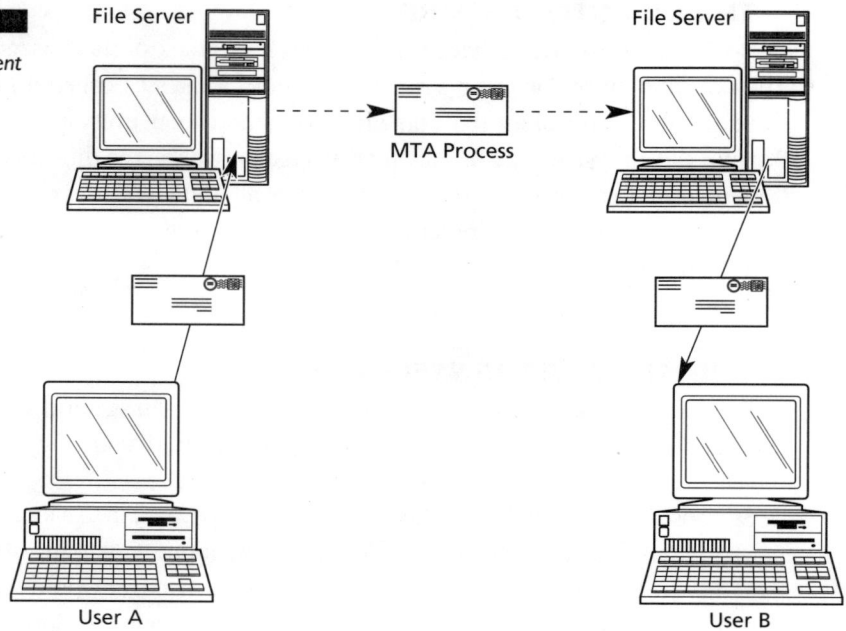

There are several processes that can act as MTAs in GroupWise:

▸ Post office server

▸ Message server

▸ GroupWise gateways

I introduce these terms here only so that you will recognize them later on when I discuss them at greater length.

ADMINISTRATION AGENT

The final basic component of an e-mail system is the administration agent. As a system administrator, you may be required to set up your system, add and remove users, perform system maintenance and troubleshooting, or expand your system.

The software that allows you, the system administrator, to control the e-mail system is called the administration agent. In GroupWise, you use the GroupWise Administration program (*GroupWise Admin*) to perform many of the administration tasks. You will use the administration agent to set up, administer, maintain, and expand the system. Here are some of the specific tasks you will use the administration agent for:

- Adding, deleting, and moving users

- Setting user preferences

- Managing client software

- Controlling system security

- Troubleshooting the system

- Running system diagnostics

- Maintaining the directory store

- Maintaining the message store

The GroupWise administration agent has two basic components: the GroupWise Admin program and the administration server. GroupWise Admin lets you perform administrative tasks like the ones listed above. The administration server, on the other hand, processes the administrative messages that are generated by GroupWise Admin. For example, if you add a new user to a specific location in the system, the administration server notifies other parts of the system about the new user.

How the Pieces Fit Together

Figure 1.4 gives you an overview of how the basic components of a store-and-forward e-mail system work together to deliver a message:

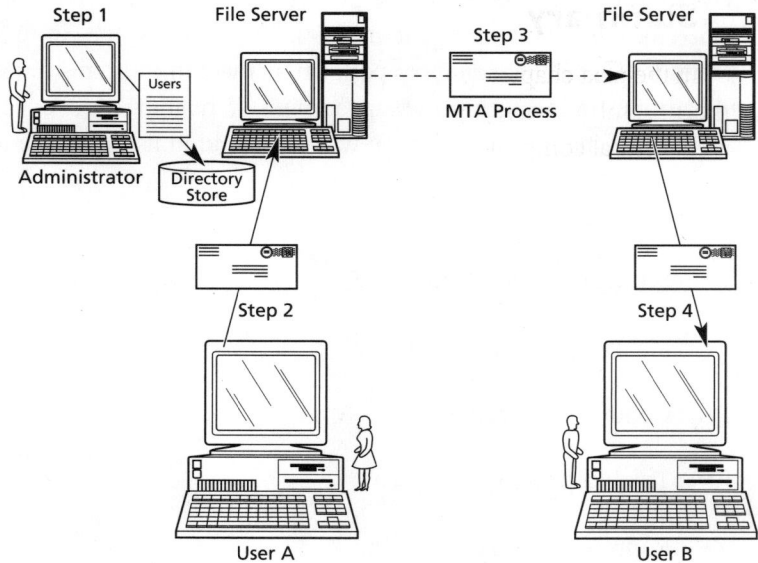

FIGURE 1.4

A Simple E-Mail Process

1 • The e-mail system administrator uses the administration agent to add User A and User B to the system. The users' information is added to the directory store.

2 • User A uses the e-mail client to create and send a message. The user may access the directory store from within the client's address book to address the message.

3 • The message transfer agent (MTA) moves the message to a message store that User B can access.

4 • User B uses the client program to read the message, which the client retrieves from the message store.

Summary

In the next chapter, you will learn about the structure of GroupWise, and I will tie in the general processes discussed in Chapter 1 with an overview of the particular architectural components of a GroupWise system.

Introduction to GroupWise Architecture

In Chapter 1, you were introduced to the five main components of an e-mail system. Now I will explain how those five components interact in GroupWise. You will also learn key GroupWise terminology, and you will get some background information on the architectural components of GroupWise. The concepts you learn in this chapter will be expanded upon throughout the book. I will explain the more technical details of each component later on.

Store-and-Forward Architecture

As I mentioned in Chapter 1, Novell GroupWise is based on a *store-and-forward architecture*. This simply means that the system uses a file-copying procedure to move messages from one place to another. Messages are copied to a certain location and are then picked up and forwarded to their destinations by one or more message transfer agents (MTAs). Depending on where a message's recipients are located, the message may be stored and forwarded many times before it reaches its final destination.

In Figure 2.1, User A creates and sends a message using the client software. The message is copied to User A's file server. That file server contains User A's message store, where a copy of the message is saved for User A's future reference. An MTA process then picks up the message and moves it to the recipient's file server, placing it in User B's message store. User B then uses the client software to read the message held in the message store. This example is a very simple illustration of how store-and-forward architecture works. In a large e-mail system, the process of copying and forwarding a single message may be repeated several times before the message reaches its final destination in a recipient's message store.

Understanding the GroupWise store-and-forward architecture is essential for administering and troubleshooting GroupWise systems. Throughout this book, you will see diagrams of message flows. These diagrams show you how messages move through a GroupWise system and are stored in databases. By using these diagrams, you will be able to troubleshoot problem areas and bottlenecks in your GroupWise system.

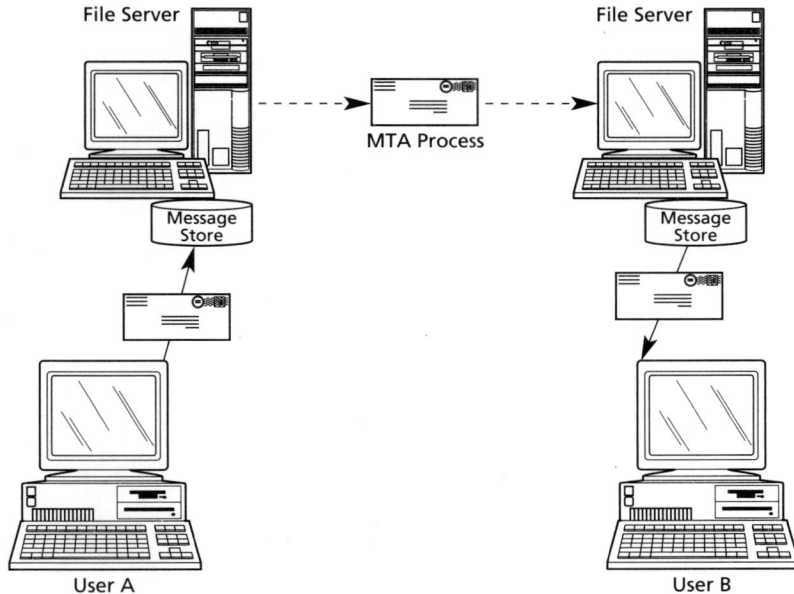

FIGURE 2.1

Store-and-Forward
Messaging

GroupWise uses *domains, post offices,* and *objects* to implement its store-and-forward architecture. Collectively, these three components make up a GroupWise system.

GroupWise Domains

A real-world postal system, such as the one shown in Figure 2.2, has many different components. In a given community, you might find a regional postal facility where regional administrative offices are located, along with a maintenance shop for the region's postal trucks. Even though the regional facility administers and coordinates the activities of the local post offices, that facility itself probably does not provide postal services directly to individuals in the community. The facility instead acts as a central routing hub for messages entering and leaving the region, and it forwards mail to the appropriate local post offices. When the regional facility receives mail from its own local post offices, it either routes the mail to other post offices within the region or else sends it on to a different regional office.

FIGURE 2.2

A Regional Postal System

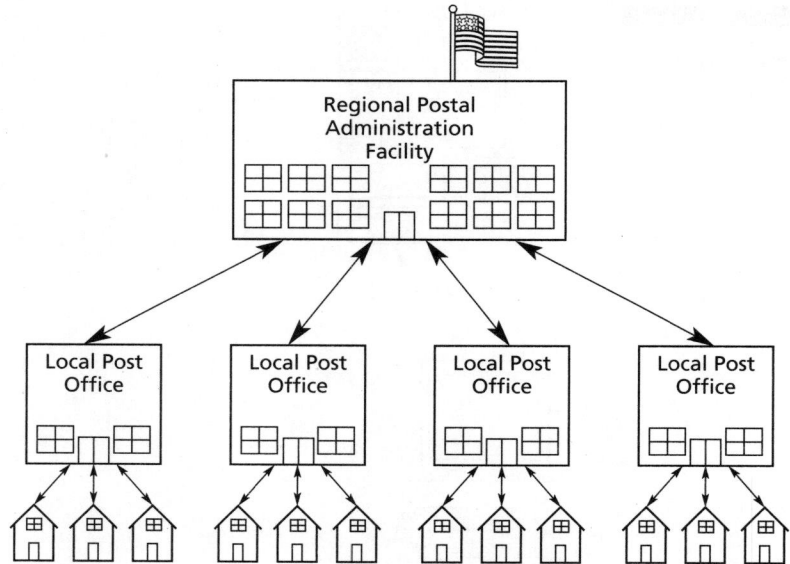

A GroupWise *domain* is conceptually very similar to such a regional postal facility. See Figure 2.3. The domain is where administration of a GroupWise system takes place. Physically, the domain is a directory structure on a file server, and the directory contains a set of executable programs, databases, and message-queue subdirectories. The GroupWise Admin agent is located in the domain subdirectory. Like the regional postal facility, the GroupWise domain contains post offices. Users in the GroupWise system are organized into post offices within domains. (We'll take a look at the physical aspects of domains in Chapter 4.)

The domain also acts as a message hub. It receives incoming messages from other domains in the GroupWise system, and it routes them to the appropriate post offices. When the domain receives a message from one of its own post offices, it checks the message to see if it should deliver the message to another post office in the domain or if it should route the message to another domain in the system. It then moves the message to the proper location.

FIGURE 2.3

A Simple GroupWise System

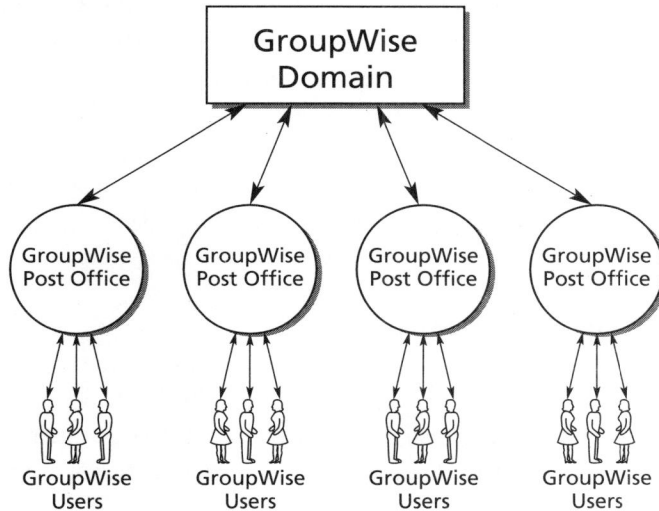

There are four types of domains in a GroupWise system:

▸ Primary

▸ Secondary

▸ External

▸ Foreign

PRIMARY DOMAINS

Each GroupWise system contains one primary domain. This domain has administrative privileges in all other domains in the system. Returning to the postal service analogy, the primary domain could be compared to a state postal facility where the administrative offices of state-level personnel are located. The primary domain, like other domains, contains a *domain database*. The domain database in the primary domain is the most important file in the entire GroupWise system. That file contains all of the address information and network-linking information for all of the domains, post offices, and users in the system.

The primary domain database is a GroupWise system's master database. All secondary domain databases—and ultimately all post office databases—are built using the information contained in the primary domain database. It is critical that you implement a backup strategy for backing up the domain database (called WPDOMAIN.DB) for the primary domain. Database backup strategies will be explained in Chapter 19.

Except for the functions associated with the primary domain's administrative privileges, the primary domain performs essentially the same role as the secondary domains.

SECONDARY DOMAINS

Once a primary domain has been created, secondary domains are used to expand the GroupWise system. A secondary domain has administrative control over its own post offices, but it has no administrative control over any of the other secondary domains or over the primary domain. The secondary domains can be compared to a regional postal facility in the postal service analogy. A secondary domain has administrative control over only those post offices associated with that domain, just like the regional postal facility controls only those post offices in its region.

In terms of their physical properties, secondary domains are virtually identical to primary domains. Secondary domains also have domain databases (also called WPDOMAIN.DB). The information in the secondary domain database is obtained from the primary domain databases. Secondary domain databases should also be backed up regularly. Backing up is not quite as crucial as in the case of the primary domain database, however. If a secondary domain database is corrupted or destroyed, it can always be rebuilt from the information stored in the primary domain database. Primary domain databases cannot be rebuilt from secondary domain databases.

There are two key differences between primary and secondary domains. First, the primary domain can manipulate any object within its domain or in any secondary domain, whereas a secondary domain can only manipulate objects within its post offices. This is a difference in administrative abilities. Second, when changes are made to a system using GroupWise Admin (such as adding objects or creating post offices), the primary domain communicates those changes to all of the secondary domains. This is a difference in directory synchronization responsibilities.

EXTERNAL DOMAINS

There are two types of external domains: GroupWise 4.x external domains and WordPerfect Office 3.1 external domains. External domains are used to connect your GroupWise system to other systems. By using a GroupWise 4.x external domain, your system can communicate with different GroupWise systems maintained by other companies or by other departments within your own company. That means users in your system can communicate with all other users on any GroupWise system without having to take any extra steps. From the user's standpoint, all users in other GroupWise systems are part of the same big system. Returning to the postal service analogy, an external domain is comparable to a regional postal facility in a different state. Although the postal facilities of two different states have very similar operations and must constantly exchange messages, neither has administrative authority over the other.

WordPerfect Office 3.1 external domains permit GroupWise 4.1 systems to connect with WordPerfect Office 3.1 systems, allowing WordPerfect Office users to exchange e-mail with GroupWise users. By using External 3.1 domains, a company can gradually convert from WordPerfect Office to GroupWise without any interruption in the ability to exchange messages. For more information about connecting WordPerfect Office 3.1 systems to GroupWise 4.1 systems, see the TechTip document entitled "Connecting Office 3.1 and GroupWise 4.1," (31TO41.TT) on the CD-ROM that comes with this book.

FOREIGN DOMAINS

Foreign domains are used to connect with electronic messaging systems other than GroupWise or WordPerfect Office systems. For example, you can use a foreign domain to connect with a system that is running Lotus cc:Mail. You can think of foreign domains as the equivalent of international postal facilities in my postal service analogy.

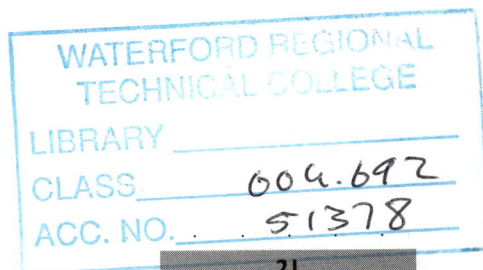

Components of a GroupWise Domain

A GroupWise domain consists of several key components that enable the domain to perform a variety of tasks. Those components are:

- ► GroupWise Admin program

- ► Domain database

- ► Message server

- ► Domain message queues

- ► Gateways

These components work together to carry out the administrative and message-delivery duties that are performed by the domain. Figure 2.4 shows the domain components. Notice the geometric shape that corresponds to each component. You will see these shapes used to represent the various components throughout this book.

Post offices are also components of a domain to the extent that a domain always has administrative authority over their functions. Moreover, a post office cannot exist without a corresponding domain. However, I will discuss post offices separately in the next main section because they have their own components and their own distinct characteristics.

▶ · ◀

FIGURE 2.4

Components of a Domain

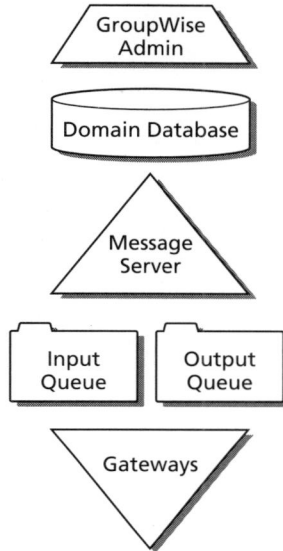

GroupWise
Admin

Domain Database

Message
Server

Input
Queue

Output
Queue

Gateways

GROUPWISE ADMIN—THE ADMINISTRATION AGENT

In the postal system analogy, the regional facility housed the administrative offices for the whole region. Likewise, all of the administration in GroupWise is done at the level of the domain. The domain directory contains the GroupWise Admin program, depicted in Figure 2.5. The GroupWise Admin program is a DOS-based application, and its executable file is usually named AD.EXE. A UNIX version of GroupWise Admin is also available. (If you're running GroupWise on NetWare 4.1, many GroupWise administration tasks can also be performed with the Windows-based NWAdmin program if you have installed the GroupWise NWAdmin Integration Module. See Chapter 20 for more information about the integration module.)

FIGURE 2.5

A GroupWise Admin Screen

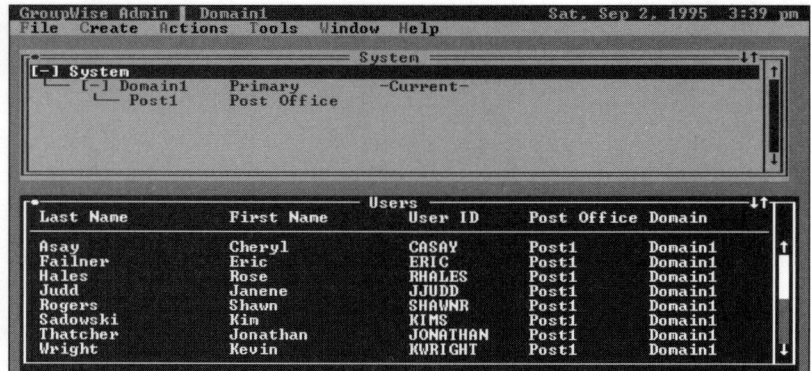

You use GroupWise Admin to create domains, post offices, and objects in GroupWise. You can also perform many other useful tasks using GroupWise Admin. I will tell you more about those tasks later on.

The server process associated with GroupWise Admin is the *administration server,* often called the *ADS process.* The administration server is responsible for informing post offices and domains about changes that have been made to the GroupWise system. For example, when a user is added to a domain, the ADS processes in the other domains update the databases in those domains to reflect the new user information. ADS processes keep all of the address books in a system current. I will discuss ADS processes in more depth in Chapter 11.

THE DOMAIN DATABASE

As I previously mentioned, domain database files (called WPDOMAIN.DB) are the most important files in any GroupWise system. A domain database contains the *directory* for the system. In other words, the domain database is the *directory store* for the GroupWise system. This terminology is a little confusing because "directory" is a common DOS term, but it has a completely different meaning in GroupWise. In GroupWise, the directory is basically an address book, similar to your personal address book or a telephone book. The directory contains the addresses of all the GroupWise users in the system. In addition to containing the user addresses, WPDOMAIN.DB database files contain other essential information, including information on how the system is configured and how the components link together.

Now you can see why the primary domain database is such an important file. Think of it this way: If your copy of the phone book were destroyed, it would be an inconvenience, but you could always get another copy. That problem would be analogous to the situation if one of the secondary domains' databases were destroyed. However, what would happen if the phone company's database were destroyed? That disaster is basically what you would face (obviously on a smaller scale) if your system's primary domain database were destroyed. I can't emphasize enough how important it is to back up your primary domain database frequently. (Also, make sure you don't forget the password for a domain database after you have chosen it. A forgotten password for a domain is just as bad as a total loss of that database. You have no way to repair a database if you have forgotten its password.)

THE GROUPWISE MESSAGE SERVER—THE DOMAIN MTA

The *message server* is the GroupWise MTA associated with a domain. Going back to our postal system analogy, the message server would be the equivalent of the trucks and employees that move the mail. The message server has two main purposes: (1) It transfers messages between post offices within a domain, and (2) it routes messages to other domains or gateways. The function of gateways will be explained later in this chapter.

Only very small GroupWise systems can do without a message server. A GroupWise system that is comprised of a single post office and one domain does not require a message server. In that case, the message delivery is handled either by the client program or by the post office server. You will learn more about the post office server later in this chapter.

In most cases, GroupWise systems need to have a message server for each domain. Message servers are necessary when:

► the system has only one domain, but that domain contains a gateway;

► the system has only one domain, but that domain has two or more post offices; or

► the system has more than one domain.

These three cases cover just about all GroupWise systems.

I will discuss message servers throughout the book. For now, just remember that message servers are associated with domains, and they route messages between post offices within a domain, as well as to other domains in the system.

DOMAIN MESSAGE QUEUES

When a user in one GroupWise domain sends a message to a user in another GroupWise domain, the message is temporarily copied to a directory where it awaits processing by the message server or by some other MTA. Such a directory, commonly called a *message queue directory,* is part of the domain's directory structure. Message queues are similar to the mail holding bins at the regional postal facility in my analogy. There are two types of message queue directories—input queues and output queues. Message queue directories will be discussed in more detail later, when I explain how messages move through the GroupWise system.

GATEWAYS

A GroupWise *gateway* is a collection of executable processes and directories that connects a GroupWise system to other GroupWise systems or to other kinds of e-mail systems. A gateway is basically an interpreter. It translates information between various formats and protocols so a GroupWise domain can communicate with a foreign e-mail system. The most common gateway in GroupWise systems is the Async gateway, which sends and receives information via modem across telephone lines. Other gateways allow GroupWise to communicate with different systems, such as cc:Mail or the Internet.

Gateways fall into two categories—conversion gateways and passthrough gateways. A *conversion gateway* converts a GroupWise message into a different messaging format. An example of a conversion gateway is the cc:Mail gateway. This gateway converts GroupWise messages to cc:Mail format.

A conversion gateway is like a language interpreter. If I speak only English and need to communicate with someone who speaks only Japanese, I could consult an interpreter who speaks both languages and who could translate from English to Japanese, as well as from Japanese to English. This is basically the same way a conversion gateway works.

A *passthrough gateway* encapsulates GroupWise messages and transfers them to another location using a non-GroupWise transfer mechanism. Another passthrough gateway at the other end unencapusulates the messages, which are then processed by the GroupWise system as regular GroupWise messages. An example of a passthrough gateway is an SMTP gateway.

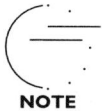

> **NOTE**
>
> **Some gateways perform both conversion and passthrough functions. GroupWise gateways reside at the domain level. I discuss Async gateways in Part V: The GroupWise Async gateway. Other types of GroupWise gateways will be discussed in Part IX.**

The GroupWise Post Office

At the next level below domains in the GroupWise structure are *post offices,* which are located on file servers. A post office's functions are managed by the domain to which it is assigned. A post office may be located on the same file server as its respective domain; however, most often a post office will be located on a file server that is connected to the domain's file server and that can be accessed by a particular group of users. GroupWise post offices are comparable to your local community post office. Each GroupWise user is assigned to a single post office.

A post office is often associated with a specific workgroup within an organization. For example, a large company's human resources department might have its own post office. When you plan your GroupWise system, you should try to organize the post offices according to existing workgroups, taking into account the file servers that those groups commonly access. Thinking through the organization of post offices in your system can help to isolate message traffic within individual groups, and in this way you can minimize the impact of GroupWise on overall network traffic.

A GroupWise post office consists of the following components:

► Post office database

► Message store

► Post office server

▶ Input and output queues

▶ Client software

These components work together to perform all of the duties of a GroupWise post office. See Figure 2.6.

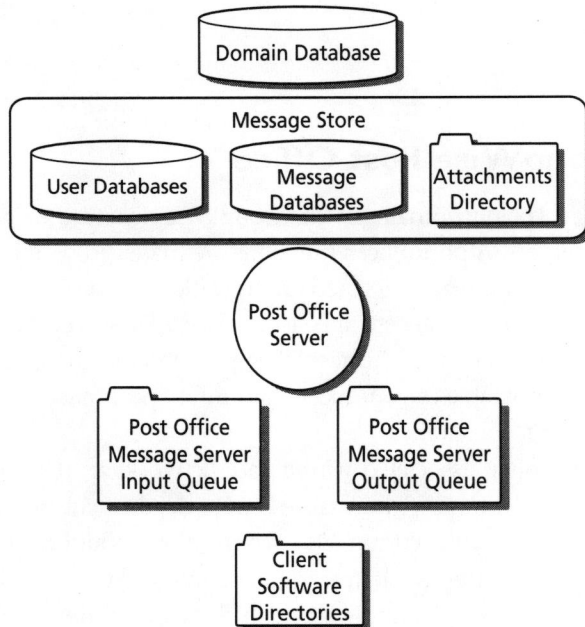

FIGURE 2.6

Components of a GroupWise
Post Office

Domain Database

Message Store

User Databases   Message Databases   Attachments Directory

Post Office Server

Post Office Message Server Input Queue

Post Office Message Server Output Queue

Client Software Directories

The *post office database* is where information is stored about users in the system. It is a post office's version of a directory store. You can think of the post office database as analogous to the listing of national ZIP codes that your local post office maintains. The database, like a ZIP code list, tells the post office where a particular message should be directed.

Real-world post offices often have mailboxes (usually called post office boxes) where individuals can go to pick up their mail. The *message store* is like a post office box. It is a place within the post office where individual users' messages are kept. Of course, most people prefer not to pick up their mail at the post office. That is why real-world post offices also have mail carriers who deliver the mail directly to homes and businesses. In GroupWise, the *post office server* performs a similar function by delivering messages to individual users.

The GroupWise post office *input and output queues* are like the two kinds of mailboxes you see at real-life post offices, where you can deposit mail according to whether it is local or destined for someone outside the area.

Finally, the GroupWise client software gives users the tools to send messages through the system just like a real-world post office provides the materials (for example, stamps and envelopes) you need in order to send mail.

THE POST OFFICE DATABASE

The post office contains a GroupWise directory database named WPHOST.DB. (The filename is a carryover from WordPerfect Office, where post offices were called hosts.) A post office's database contains addressing information for all of the users in a GroupWise system to whom that post office can send messages. As shown in Figure 2.7, the address book information that users see comes from the post office database. When users open their address books, they are actually reading an index of the WPHOST.DB file. The information in the post office database comes from the domain database.

FIGURE 2.7

Addressing Information Flow

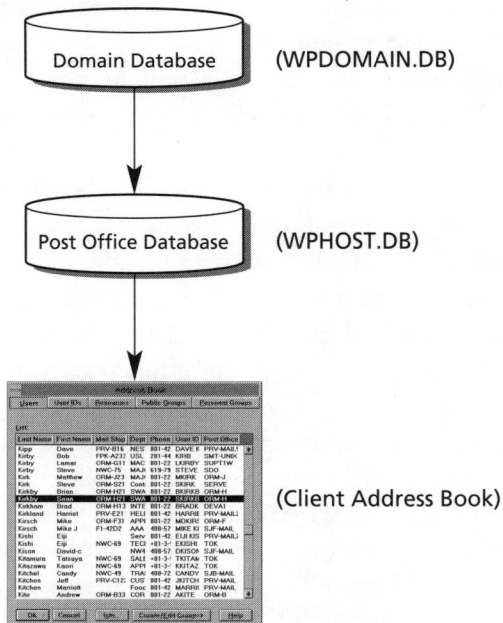

Figure 2.7 shows the flow of directory information from the primary domain database to the user.

THE MESSAGE STORE

In GroupWise, a post office's main function is message storage. Post offices contain the subdirectories and databases that hold users' messages. There are two different kinds of databases found in a post office message store: *user databases* and *message databases*. In addition, a post office message store contains a file attachments directory.

Figure 2.8 shows how the message store databases and the OFFILES subdirectories work together and how they relate to the information the user sees using the GroupWise client. There are three parts of a GroupWise message—the header information, the text of the message itself, and the file attachments (although not all messages include file attachments). Use Figure 2.8 to visualize the role of each database and how it relates to the different parts of a message as you read the following sections.

*How Message Information
Is Stored*

GroupWise Message Store

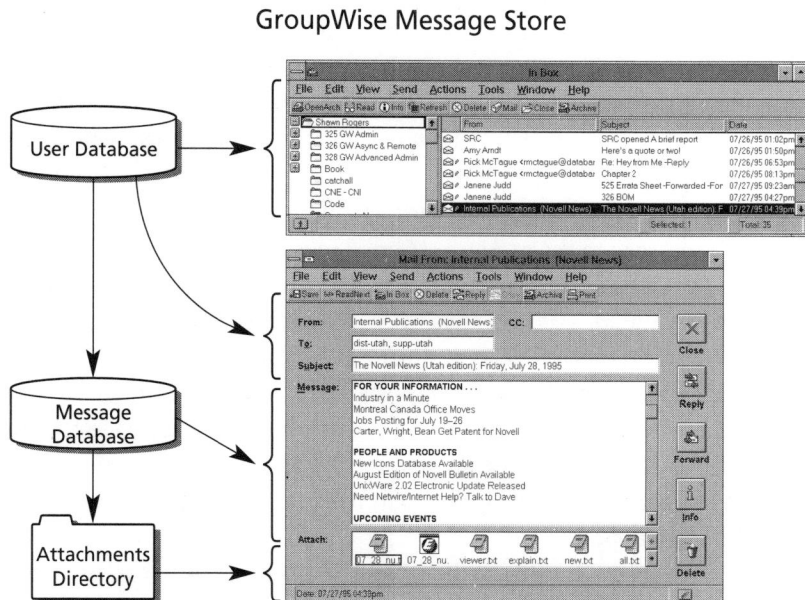

To understand how the message store databases work together, you need to understand the concept of *pointers*. Pointers are entries in a GroupWise database that point to the location of the various parts of a message. Pointers in user databases indicate where message text is stored in a message database. Pointers in message databases specify where file attachments can be found in the OFFILES subdirectories. Pointers are illustrated in Figure 2.8.

User Databases

User databases do not contain messages. However, they do store message header information, as well as information that indicates where complete messages are stored in message databases. When a GroupWise user runs the client application and opens the In Box or the Out Box, the user sees the information that is stored in the user database. The header information you see in the client application—i.e., the data in a message's To:, From:, CC:, BC:, Date:, Subject:, and Attach: fields—comes from the user database. User databases contain pointers that specify the location of message text, which is stored in the message database.

Message Databases

Messages are stored in message databases. Each user in a GroupWise post office is assigned to a specific message database. There can be up to 25 message databases in a post office, which means that many users within a post office may need to share a single message database. All messages created by a user go to that user's message database. In other words, all messages in a user's Out Box are stored in a single message database. The recipients of that user's messages who are members of the sender's post office access the message in the sender's assigned message database.

Messages coming into the post office from other post offices or domains are stored in these same message database files. However, even though an incoming message might have several recipients in a single post office, the message will be added to only one of the message databases in that post office. All of the recipients in that post office who use other message databases for outgoing messages will access the message stored in that single message database via pointers added to their user databases. Note that a message is not created separately for each recipient. It is only stored once in each post office's message store.

Here's an example to help you understand how the user and message databases interact. Suppose I send a message to 12 users in my post office. That message is stored in the message database to which I am assigned. (Many other users in my post office share the same message database.) GroupWise places a pointer in each of the recipients' user databases pointing to the message file in my assigned message database. Likewise, GroupWise places a pointer in my own user database pointing to the message. Therefore, a message is stored only one time per post office, regardless of how many users in the post office I designate as recipients.

When a user deletes a message from the In or Out Box, that user is really only deleting the pointer to the message (unless that user's pointer is the only one still pointing to the message, in which case the entire message is deleted). In the example above, the message that I sent to 12 other users will not be deleted from the message database until I delete the message from my Out Box and all of the 12 recipients delete the message from their In Boxes.

Note how the use of databases conserves the amount of disk space used by the message store. Even though I send the message to 12 users, that message is stored only once in the message store. Similarly, if the message were to contain file attachments, those files would also be stored only once in the message store.

The Attachments Directory

To prevent message databases from growing too large, messages and file attachments that exceed 2 kilobytes (2K) are stored in the post office's attachments directory. These files are encrypted with proprietary encryption technology and cannot be viewed by standard document viewers. Nor can they be opened in other programs. For added security, the filenames of those files do not reflect the files' origins or contents. Files in the attachments directory are just as secure as messages stored in the databases.

When a message or file attachments go into the file attachments directory, GroupWise places pointers in the message database pointing to that location. A single GroupWise message may contain up to 99 file attachments. File attachment size is limited only by the amount of available disk space in the post office message store.

THE POST OFFICE SERVER AND MESSAGE QUEUES

In GroupWise, post offices use an MTA called the *post office server* (also commonly referred to as the *OFS process*). The post office server is the workhorse of the GroupWise system. Its main job is to deliver messages within the post office.

The post office server also creates and delivers *status messages*. One of the distinguishing characteristics of GroupWise is its ability to track what happens to a message after the message has been sent. A GroupWise user can look in the Out Box to see whether an e-mail message has been delivered yet, whether the recipient has opened the message, and whether the recipient has deleted the message. Different kinds of status messages will appear depending on the type of GroupWise message sent. For example, a status message for an appointment might indicate that the appointment was Accepted, Declined, or Delegated.

In a well-organized GroupWise system, the post office server does most of the message processing. Some of the post office server's duties can also be performed by the client program. As the administrator, you can adjust the amount of work that the client does in relation to the post office server. This setting is called the *threshold,* which I will discuss at greater length in Part II. For now, just remember that the post office server handles delivery of messages after a specified threshold has been exceeded.

When a user sends a message that exceeds the threshold, the post office server places the message in that user's message database and adds pointers to the user databases of both the sender and the recipients of the message. After the message is placed in the message database and the pointers are added to the message databases, the post office server places a Delivered status on the message.

When a user sends a message that is destined for a user in a different post office or a different domain, the post office server places the outgoing message in the appropriate message server input queue so that the message server can proceed with the delivery of the message.

Finally, the post office server is responsible for monitoring the message server's output queue for messages that come into the post office. When a post office receives a message from a message server, the post office server adds the message to the appropriate message database and updates each recipient's user database.

CLIENT SOFTWARE LOCATION

Each post office stores the client software accessed by the users associated with that post office. The client software can be configured to run either from the network or from the workstation's hard drive. Many administrators prefer to have users run the client software from the network. Placing the client software on the network makes it easier to update the client, and it also leaves more free disk space at the user's workstation. I will tell you more about client software administration in Chapter 5.

GroupWise Objects

The most fundamental component of the GroupWise architecture is the *object*. Objects are located in GroupWise post offices. There are four kinds objects in GroupWise: user objects, resource objects, nicknames, and groups. Every object in a GroupWise system is given a unique address that reflects the object's domain name, post office name, and object ID. (An object ID can be either a name or a number, up to 32 characters long. However, long IDs can be cumbersome.)

Using GroupWise Admin, you can assign an object a specific level of *visibility*. You can configure an object to be visible in all address books in a system, in address books only within a certain domain, in address books only in a specific post office, or in no address books at all in the system.

USER OBJECTS

User objects are the GroupWise users themselves. GroupWise users are defined with the GroupWise Admin program. Many of the settings you will need to establish as a GroupWise administrator can be determined at the user level. Those settings include user preferences, user threshold settings, and visibility.

The ability to assign a specific visibility level to a GroupWise object is especially useful for user objects. If you have a user whose address should not be available to all users in the system, you can limit that user's visibility to the post office level. Other users will nevertheless be able to send messages to the object by using *explicit addressing,* which I will discuss later in this chapter.

Choosing a visibility setting is like deciding whether or not you want your telephone number to be listed. If your telephone number appears in a phone book, anybody with the phone book can look up your number and call you. This is like system-level visibility in GroupWise—anybody with access to the address book can send you a message. However, if you decide to have an unlisted telephone number, you might only give out your number to certain people you know. This is like domain-level visibility, where only people in your domain can see your address. If you want to keep an even lower profile, you might give your telephone number only to your closest friends and family. This is like post office-level visibility, where only people in your post office see your address. Finally, if you don't tell anyone your phone number, that is like setting the visibility level to None.

RESOURCES

A *resource* is an item that GroupWise users can schedule or reserve through the GroupWise client. Some typical resources include conference rooms, company cars, and video equipment.

Resources are assigned to a specific user who then becomes the *resource owner*. When a GroupWise user wishes to schedule a resource, the user places the resource's object ID in the To: line of the appointment message. The resource owner, who is responsible for the resource's schedule, will receive a request for the resource in his or her In Box. The resource owner can then accept or decline the request for the resource. GroupWise users can use the client to run a *busy search* on a resource to determine its availability within a given time frame. Like user objects, resources can be assigned different levels of visibility in the system.

NICKNAMES

A *nickname* is an alternate name that can be used to address an object in the system. An object can have more than one nickname, but the nickname must be unique within a post office.

For example, assume it is Pam Smith's responsibility to sign up her company's employees for training classes. The GroupWise administrator could give Pam the nickname SCHEDULER. All users in the system would then send messages about signing up for classes to SCHEDULER, and those messages would show up in Pam's In Box. She might then use *rules* to move all of those messages to a particular folder or to automatically reply to them. See Appendix A for an explanation of the GroupWise rules feature.

You can also use nicknames to further control the visibility of objects in a system. You can control the visibility of an object at the level of post offices, domains, or a system. Suppose, however, that you want an object to be visible to some but not all post offices with a domain. You can use a nickname to do that. For example, what if you have a resource—let's say a company car—that should only be visible to users in two out of six post offices in a domain? Remember—you should not assign the same object to two different post offices. (See discussion later under "Absolute Addresses.") If you give the car domain visibility, all post offices in the domain will see the car as a resource. Instead, you could make the car a resource in one of the two post offices and make the car visible only in that post office. Then you could create a nickname for the car in the other post office and limit the visibility of the nickname to that post office. In that case, the object would be visible in only two of the six post offices in the domain. Additional nicknames could be used to make the car visible in more post offices.

GROUPS

A *group* is a list of objects (i.e., users, resources, nicknames, or other groups) that the administrator sets up as a single addressable object. The purpose of having groups is to allow GroupWise users to send a message to all users in a particular group simply by entering a single group name on the message's To: line.

GroupWise has two kinds of groups: *public groups* and *personal groups. Public groups* are established by the system administrator. These groups are typically departments or divisions in the company. Public group information is stored in domain databases. *Personal groups* are set up by individual users. Personal group information is stored in user databases.

EXECUTABLE PROCESSES ASSOCIATED WITH OBJECTS

The two executable processes associated with user objects are the client software and Notify.

The client software is the user's interface with the GroupWise system. Through the client (also called the *user agent*) the user creates, receives, and manages GroupWise items. See Chapter 1 for a more detailed discussion of the client.

Notify (which has the filename NOTIFY.EXE) is a separate GroupWise executable process that informs GroupWise users when an item has arrived in their In Boxes. Whenever a message arrives for a user, Notify generates an on-screen message to that effect. (I hate being interrupted every time I get a message, so I think the executable filename ANNOY.EXE would be more fitting.) Notify runs at the workstation level, and users can change its configuration at their workstations. Users can decide which types of messages they want to be notified about or whether they want to receive any notification at all.

GroupWise Addressing

Now that you are familiar with the main architectural components of GroupWise, I want to take a minute to discuss addressing syntax in GroupWise. There are three important terms that will come up often when you are working with GroupWise: simple addressing, absolute addressing, and explicit addressing.

SIMPLE ADDRESSES

Simple addressing is the standard default method of addressing in GroupWise. When you use a simple address, you only enter an object's ID in the message's To: line. For example, if Mary Ann's GroupWise object ID is MARYANN, you would just enter MARYANN in the To: field. Simple addressing requires objects in the system to have unique object IDs. When simple addressing is used, GroupWise uses the directory store to determine Mary Ann's location in the system.

ABSOLUTE ADDRESSES

Every object in a GroupWise system has its own unique address, which is an *absolute address*. That address consists of the object's domain, post office, and object ID. The syntax is simply each of these components separated by a period:

```
domain.post office.object id
```

For example, suppose that user object Amy is located in the Sales post office, which is located in the domain named Headqtrs. Amy's absolute address would be:

```
HEADQTRS.SALES.AMY
```

If you want to use absolute addressing to send a GroupWise message, you need to use the above syntax in the To: field. When you select an object ID from the address book, GroupWise inserts the absolute address in the To: field.

You should decide how to name each object before you begin setting up GroupWise. When you are naming objects, bear in mind that shorter names make addressing easier. As you set up your GroupWise system, there are a few basic rules that you should keep in mind to make addressing easier. First, every object in a post office needs to have its own unique ID name. Although unique object ID names are really only necessary within each post office, it is a good idea to keep object names unique throughout a system. While GroupWise can handle identical object IDs, some mail systems cannot. Having more than one object with the same name can lead to problems if you connect your GroupWise system to other systems.

For example, it is possible to have several users with the object ID name JSMITH in your GroupWise system, as long as each JSMITH is associated with a different post office. But when those users try to communicate with friends via the Internet, they will all have the same Internet address—e.g., JSMITH@ACME.COM. Now you have a problem because GroupWise doesn't have any way to determine which JSMITH should get the message.

Second, every post office in a domain must have its own unique name. Again, it is a good idea to have unique post office names throughout your system, even though that is not absolutely necessary as long as all post offices within each domain have different names.

Third, every domain in the GroupWise system must have a unique name.

You should decide on a naming procedure during the planning stage. What appears to be a clever name at first may end up being a problem down the road. Two years from now, the primary domain name JOESDOM1 may not make much sense if Joe has left your company. And domain names are not easy to change. If you want to change a domain name that has already been established, you have to create a new domain with the desired name, re-create the post office structure, import all of the users, and then move all of the mail. GroupWise administrators who have gone through this process will attest that it is not a simple task, and it is bound to take more than a few hours. I will talk about changing domain and post office names in more detail in Chapter 18.

EXPLICIT ADDRESSING

Explicit addressing is different from absolute addressing. An explicit address defines the exact path that a message takes from a sender to a recipient. It includes the pathway from the sender's domain to the recipient's domain, and it includes every gateway, domain, and post office that the message must pass through on the way. In other words, from the sender's point of view, an explicit address reflects the complete path the message must take to get to the recipient.

The syntax for explicit addressing should look something like this:

```
domain:domain.post office.object id
```

or

```
domain:gateway:domain.post office.object id
```

Note that domains and gateways are separated by colons.

Suppose user KWRIGHT's post office is located in the SALES domain, and user JTHATCHER resides in the PAYROLL post office in the ACCT domain. KWRIGHT would use the following syntax to send a message to JTHATCHER with explicit addressing:

```
SALES:ACCT.PAYROLL.JTHATCHER
```

> **As an administrator, you can use messages with explicit addresses to troubleshoot problems in your system. You can explicitly address a message to be routed through each domain in your system to check the domain links and message-delivery speed.**
>
> **TIP**

Directory Synchronization

Directory synchronization simply means that changes made to the GroupWise system are replicated in all locations throughout the system. For example, if an administrator of a secondary domain adds ten new users, that change needs to be reflected in the primary domain database and in all of the users' address books in the system. GroupWise provides automatic directory synchronization to all primary and secondary domains by means of the administration server (also called the ADS process). When someone makes a change anywhere in a primary or secondary domain, the message server broadcasts that change automatically to all domains and post offices in the system and the administration server in each domain updates the databases. When an administrator makes a change in one part of the system, there is no need to take any further action to update the rest of the system. The administration server takes care of everything.

I will say more about directory synchronization in Chapter 11. For the moment, just remember that directory synchronization means that the GroupWise administration server replicates changes automatically throughout GroupWise systems.

Centralized and Distributed Administration

The terms *centralized administration* and *distributed administration* are often used to describe multidomain GroupWise systems. The structure of GroupWise allows almost all object administration tasks to be accomplished using the primary domain's administration program. For example, an administrator in the primary domain can add, delete, and change users in all secondary domains in the system. Referring back to our earlier postal system analogy, this would be like an administrator in the state administration office making administrative changes that affect a particular regional administration office. Handling all administration tasks from the primary domain is called *centralized administration*.

Distributed administration means that administrative tasks are performed at the level of the secondary domains. Remember: An administrator of a secondary domain only has administrative rights to users in that domain. That administrator cannot make changes to the primary domain or any other secondary domains.

There are some tasks that cannot be done at the level of the primary domain, such as creating post offices in secondary domains. Furthermore, sometimes the type of connection between domains limits the primary domain administrator's ability to make certain changes in secondary domains. You will learn more about these exceptions later in the book.

Summary

This chapter introduced you to the structural components that comprise GroupWise systems. You also learned some basic GroupWise terminology. In the next chapter, I discuss the issues you need to consider before you implement GroupWise at your organization.

Planning a GroupWise Implementation

In Chapters 1 and 2, you learned about the basic components of e-mail systems, in general, and about the components of GroupWise systems, in particular. Before you can effectively install GroupWise, however, you need to analyze your organization's needs and goals, and you need to develop a strategy for implementing GroupWise. Chapter 3 gives you a method for evaluating your organization so you can determine the best way to implement GroupWise to suit its needs. Once you have developed a strategy, you should test your proposal with a *pilot program*. In Chapter 3, you will learn how to use a pilot program before you go ahead with a full-scale implementation. Finally, I will discuss some training strategies at the end of the chapter so that before implementation you can make sure the people at your organization will have adequate training to use and maintain your GroupWise system.

A good plan starts with setting realistic expectations. In many companies today, someone in management will suggest that electronic messaging would be a useful asset. Often that person makes the suggestion after attending a seminar, a luncheon, or a computer trade show. After evaluating the different messaging options available, a manager may decide on GroupWise (usually because of the many features that make GroupWise superior to other LAN-based e-mail systems on the market). Once this decision has been made, it becomes your responsibility as the administrator to design, implement, and support the new system.

By meeting with management, users, and vendors and by becoming familiar with GroupWise, you can assess the messaging needs of your organization. There are many different issues to consider as you design a GroupWise system.

The fact that GroupWise is truly a *messaging system* means that the system can be used to send many types of messages, such as e-mail, appointments, tasks, and phone messages. By spending time meeting with different groups in the company you can determine, for example, if sharing calendar information is a higher priority than connecting to the Internet. You will need to find out how the system will be used most frequently. Network security is another issue that affects the design of a GroupWise system. Because of the nature of some departments' functions, certain parts of an organization may require higher network security than others.

How do you go about discovering a company's messaging priorities? A survey is a good place to start. A survey can help you find answers to these questions:

▶   What do the users want from their electronic messaging system?

▶ What are management's expectations with regard to increasing productivity by implementing GroupWise?

▶ Will a Business Process Re-engineering (BPR) consultant's evaulation be necessary? (See "Workflow Evaluation" below)

▶ How will GroupWise be used to solve process problems electronically?

▶ Does the physical network layer dictate certain design requirements?

These questions can seem overwhelming, especially when you consider that the original suggestion was simply "Let's get e-mail." Unfortunately, a successful implementation of a messaging system is not as simple as buying a box of software at a local computer store and installing it on a network file server. The purpose of this chapter is to help you work through and organize these issues into a design strategy that will make your implementation of GroupWise a success.

If you are a network administrator, you probably already have answers to most of the network-related questions I will ask you to think about in Chapter 3. But it's a good idea to read this chapter anyway so that you start thinking about your network from a GroupWise perspective.

If you are a consultant implementing GroupWise for a client, this chapter will help you develop a blueprint you can follow as you proceed with the implementation. If you think about the right issues in advance, you will be better prepared to address your client's needs, and you will be able to tell your client exactly what hardware and software the implementation requires.

A First Look at GroupWise Planning

By taking the time to plan your GroupWise implementation, you can ensure that your system's overall structure will be effective and efficient from the start. You will ultimately save time if you plan ahead because it is far less time-consuming to make detailed plans than it is to fix design problems after a GroupWise system has already been implemented. A carefully designed implementation of GroupWise will also make maintenance and expansion of the system much easier.

Understanding the following axiom will help you start off your GroupWise design on the right foot: *Implementation is from the top down, but planning is from the bottom up.*

Figure 3.1 illustrates what that axiom means. The first step in physically implementing GroupWise is to run the GroupWise Administration program (GroupWise Admin) and create a domain. You then create a post office (or post offices), and finally you add users. This is what I mean by implementing GroupWise from the top down. You implement GroupWise from the top of its hierarchy—i.e., domains—to the bottom level—i.e., individual objects.

FIGURE 3.1

GroupWise Planning Axiom

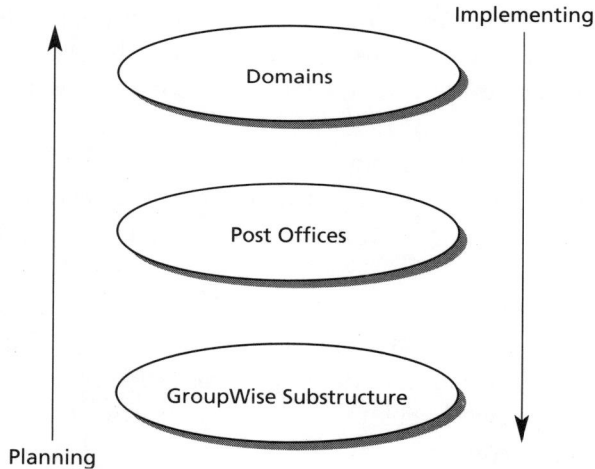

Planning involves exactly the opposite approach. When you plan a GroupWise system, you begin your analysis at the bottom by examining what I call the GroupWise *substructure.* You then take what you learned in the initial planning stage and use that information to decide where to create post offices and how to group users. Finally, you move up to domain planning—the process of deciding how many domains you need, where they should be located, and how they should connect together.

The planning process is analogous to a three-tiered cake, as illustrated in Figure 3.2.

FIGURE 3.2

GroupWise Planning

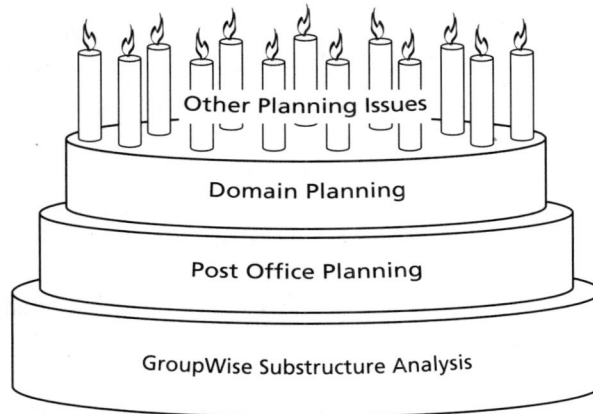

Other Planning Issues

Domain Planning

Post Office Planning

GroupWise Substructure Analysis

The bottom layer of the planning cake involves analysis of the GroupWise substructure. This analysis includes examination of the existing network, identification of e-mail performance goals, investigation of the organization and its users, and appraisal of the current e-mail systems.

The middle layer is post office planning. At this stage, you decide how you should organize users into post offices. You must take into consideration the features of GroupWise, the workflow in the organization, the computing platforms in use, and the possibility of a need for remote access to the system.

The top layer is domain planning. When you plan your system's domains, you need to consider what the workflow of departments (and other organizational units) is like, how the GroupWise system administration will be handled, where you might want to locate remote sites, what level of GroupWise message server performance you need, and what type of message server platforms you will want.

The candles on the cake correspond to planning decisions about (1) connectivity to other e-mail products, such as Lotus cc:Mail and Microsoft Mail; (2) connectivity to foreign systems, such as to the Internet; (3) additional GroupWise components or modules that the organization may need, such as the Telephone Access Server; and (4) the amount of money you want to spend on the system.

You may ask, "What about the icing on the cake?" That's your performance bonus for successfully planning and implementing the GroupWise system. I will discuss each phase of the planning process in this chapter (with the exception of how you might plan to use your bonus). This chapter should help you answer these common questions:

▶ What is the most logical way to group users in post offices?

▶ How many users should there be in each post office?

▶ How many post offices should there be in each domain, and in which domains should they be located?

▶ How many domains does the system need, and where should they be located?

▶ How should the domains be connected?

▶ What platforms should message servers and post office servers use?

▶ Which network components need to be upgraded before implementing GroupWise?

▶ Does the network layout need to be adjusted before implementing GroupWise?

These types of questions will come up again in Part III and Part IV, where I will give you answers to problems involving more complex systems.

Planning Phase 1:
Analyzing the GroupWise Substructure

The initial, bottom layer of my GroupWise planning cake involves examining the foundation upon which GroupWise will run: cabling schemes, network operating systems, file servers, wide area network connections, and various other connectivity requirements (e.g., for connecting to the Internet). See Figure 3.3.

FIGURE 3.3

*GroupWise Substructure
Analysis*

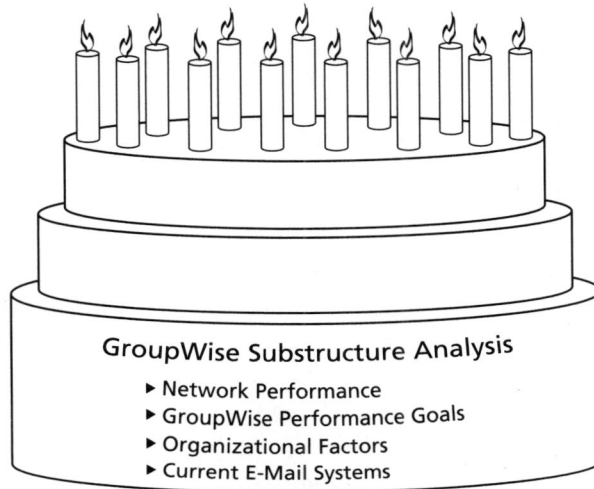

GroupWise Substructure Analysis

▸ Network Performance
▸ GroupWise Performance Goals
▸ Organizational Factors
▸ Current E-Mail Systems

Analysis of the GroupWise substructure falls into four categories:

▸   Network performance

▸   GroupWise performance goals

▸   Organizational factors

▸   Current e-mail systems

EVALUATING NETWORK PERFORMANCE

A network performance evaluation focuses on how your network works now and what led you to consider implementing a GroupWise system. When you evaluate current performance, you should look at the network as a complete entity. Look for bottlenecks and other kinds of problems. Also, try to estimate the impact GroupWise will have on the network once the system is in place. There are many software packages, such as Novell's LANalyzer, that can help you analyze the network's performance.

Your analysis of the network can be divided into four focus areas:

▸ Network architecture

▸ File servers

▸ Current performance levels

▸ Users

Network Architecture

A solid understanding of the existing network structure will be extremely important as you design your GroupWise system. You will need to have a detailed schematic diagram or map of the network. This diagram should indicate the location of the file servers, the type of cabling and the cabling scheme, the location of routers, and the type of WAN connections. You will use this diagram to help make decisions about the location of domains and post offices in your system.

File Servers

Your network schematic should show the number of file servers, as well as their locations. You should take a look at each file server and document its current configuration. Find out the exact version of the network operating system running on each server. Also, check each server's processor speed, the amount of free disk space, and how much RAM it has. These specifications will help you determine which servers can house domains and post offices and which ones can handle GroupWise NetWare Loadable Modules (NLMs). NLMs are programs that *hook into* the Novell network operating system and load directly on the file server. The GroupWise servers and some GroupWise gateways are available in NLM versions.

Current Performance Levels

Check the current usage statistics for the file servers and routers. Are the file servers and routers operating well under capacity, near capacity, or beyond recommended capacity? If the file servers are operating at or near their limits, hardware modifications (e.g., adding more RAM or disk storage) would be recommended prior to installing GroupWise.

Users

You need to determine how users are currently set up on the network. How are users physically connected? Does the grouping of users in the network design make sense? Are the users *segmented* (that is, on the same cable segment) according to department? Do the users log in to file servers that are nearby? How many users log in to each server? Which servers do the users access most often? These issues will help you determine where post offices should be located.

GROUPWISE PERFORMANCE GOALS

The next thing you should try to determine is what level of performance your organization expects from its GroupWise system. Performance goals should be evaluated in terms of message delivery time and system reliability. If your organization expects messages to be delivered in a matter of seconds, the system you design will be quite different from the system you would set up for an organization that could tolerate an average delivery time of ten minutes. You also need to determine how much system down time the organization can reasonably be expected to handle.

Message-Delivery Time

Acceptable message-delivery time is often very hard to calculate. Here are some questions to consider that will help you determine an acceptable message-delivery time for your organization:

▶ What do the users expect from an e-mail system?

▶ Has the organization used a different e-mail system before GroupWise? If so, what kind of delivery speed are the users accustomed to?

▶ Will the users tolerate a slowdown in message-delivery time during peak message transfer periods?

As a general rule, message-delivery time decreases in direct proportion to the amount of money an organization is willing to spend. If an organization invests in high-end computers and high-performance GroupWise servers, it will get fast message delivery. If an organization is not willing or able to invest in high-end machines and servers, it will find that its message-delivery time is longer.

System Reliability

As a general rule, e-mail users expect their e-mail system to work properly at all times. If the system is not reliable, they won't use it. I've worked with several companies whose users don't use e-mail simply because they don't trust it to handle important messages. Instead, they use less-efficient modes of communication such as faxes, interoffice mail, and voice mail.

Dissatisfaction among users tends to have a snowball effect in an organization. Before you know it, even formerly devoted e-mail users get discouraged with the system because nobody reads their messages even when the system is working.

GroupWise is an exceptionally reliable e-mail system. Since I started using GroupWise at work in early 1994, I can count on one hand the number of times the system has gone down. Unlike other systems, GroupWise does not need to go down for system maintenance (except in very rare and unusual circumstances).

When you analyze an organization's expectations in relation to system reliability, consider these questions:

▸ At what times during the day will users want to use their e-mail the most?

▸ Will users need 24-hour access to their e-mail?

▸ If the e-mail system goes down, what effect will that have on users' ability to perform their jobs?

This last question is particularly important. If e-mail is the most important tool users have for doing their jobs effectively, they will quickly come to mistrust a system that goes down regularly. You may discover that some domains that rely heavily on e-mail will need backup message servers configured in case the primary message server goes down. Some departments may want their message stores backed up nightly as an additional precautionary measure to prevent loss of data.

Understanding what kind of system reliability the users expect will help you decide which hardware and software components to use. You may decide to recommend redundant hard drives for the network file servers that house the message store, or you may decide to recommend setting up a backup message server. Some GroupWise server platforms are inherently more reliable than others. For example, the NLM or OS/2 server processes are faster and more dependable than the DOS server pack.

ORGANIZATIONAL ANALYSIS

Organizational considerations are probably the hardest factors to evaluate. However, if you can get a grasp on them as you plan your GroupWise system, you will be able to explain to others why you have made certain choices, and you may even be able to sway the opinion of those who disagree with your decisions.

Your organizational analysis will help you take into account many of the external considerations that can influence the implementation of a GroupWise system. Consider the following factors:

- ▶ The skill level of the users

- ▶ The skill level of support personnel

- ▶ The skill level of the administrators

- ▶ General attitude toward the GroupWise implementation (for example, are people excited about it? Apathetic? Apprehensive?)

Skill Level of Users

The existing skill levels of an organization's e-mail users will help you decide how much training will be needed after GroupWise has been implemented. Find out the answers to these questions before you roll out GroupWise:

- ▶ How familiar are the users with electronic messaging? Is e-mail an entirely new concept to them?

- ▶ What resources are available to help them learn how to use GroupWise?

- ▶ Will educational literature alone be sufficient, or will they need training classes?

The answers to these questions will help you decide the best method for bringing users up to speed on GroupWise. If users are well-versed in electronic messaging, the built-in tutorial and on-line help may provide enough training to make those users GroupWise experts. At the end of this chapter, I discuss some of the training resources that are available.

Skill Level of Support Personnel

One of the biggest nightmares faced by help desk employees is a large-scale implementation of a software program that they have never seen before. Untrained help desk personnel will be frustrated if they don't receive adequate training prior to the implementation, and their frustration will be apparent to the rest of the GroupWise users, who are likely to become frustrated, too. Evaluate the following issues to decide how much training your organization's support department and information systems personnel should receive prior to and during the GroupWise implementation:

▸ Do the support personnel know how to use GroupWise?

▸ What training will they require so they can answer questions about the GroupWise client software?

▸ How much GroupWise administrative work will they need to do, and will they require administration-level training?

▸ Do training resources exist internally or will you need to contact someone to provide training?

I know from my own experience that training both end users and administrators is essential for a successful GroupWise implementation. Novell did not use GroupWise prior to the merger with WordPerfect. Soon after the merger was announced, it became clear that this situation would quickly change. Novell's personnel needed training, and they needed it fast. Six e-mail administrators from Novell attended a weeklong training seminar on GroupWise administration. Right after that, they implemented GroupWise in a test department. The training experience was one of the key factors that contributed to Novell's successful transition to GroupWise.

General Attitudes

If you can gauge the attitudes of the people who will be affected by the implementation of GroupWise, you will be better prepared to handle objections and opposition. Unfortunately, company politics often influence your chances of pulling off a successful GroupWise implementation.

I'm a firm believer that GroupWise can win over die-hard fans of other e-mail systems—but first they have to be persuaded to give the new system a fair chance. Often a short demonstration of the many innovative features GroupWise offers can make users excited about using GroupWise.

Goals of Organizational Analysis

Thinking about the issues discussed earlier can help you as you make the following decisions about your implementation of GroupWise:

- whether you will need to obtain utilities to convert existing e-mail messages;

- whether you will need an API gateway to import and export users and to convert existing messages (see Part VIII);

- whether connections to other e-mail systems need to be maintained and for how long;

- which end-user training programs you will recommend;

- who you will recommend as help desk and support personnel;

- how much training you will recommend for the GroupWise administrators;

- which perceptions about GroupWise you need to change in order for the implementation to be successful.

Other things to consider during your organizational analysis are how your relationship with other software vendors will be affected, whether you should anticipate opposition to a new system, and whether you can count on having the necessary resources to support GroupWise once it has been implemented.

CURRENT E-MAIL SYSTEMS

I recently assisted with the conversion of a large organization's e-mail system to GroupWise. The organization had been using two different e-mail packages—one for its Macintosh users and one for its PC users. One employee had over 2,000 messages neatly organized into folders in her Macintosh e-mail program. These messages were critical messages that tracked the progress of many different projects currently in progress in her department. As you can imagine, she was not very excited about the prospect of saving each of those messages to disk. Needless to say, she opposed the transition to GroupWise. You should consider these issues before implementing GroupWise in a company where other e-mail systems are currently used:

► Do the e-mail users have a lot of messages stored in an e-mail system?

► If they do, how can they retain those messages? Can those messages be moved directly into GroupWise, or will they need to be saved to disk?

► How much opposition will be generated by the decision to move to GroupWise?

► Do users maintain their schedules in a software program?

► Can the schedules be moved easily into GroupWise or will they need to be reentered manually?

These can be some of the most difficult problems to deal with during a GroupWise implementation. If users have many messages in an existing e-mail program, you can often find a creative solution. In the example I gave above, we were able to find a way to connect GroupWise to the Macintosh system, and the user was able to forward her messages to her GroupWise mailbox. Even though the process was not automatic and took some time to complete, it was an acceptable solution.

Sometimes the GroupWise Application Programming Interface (API) gateway can be used to build custom translation programs that will import information from one application to another. In other cases, saving messages from another e-mail system to disk and re-creating schedules from scratch are the only practical solutions. If you know in advance that these issues will come up, you can be prepared to overcome objections and find the optimal solutions.

Planning Phase 2:
Grouping Users into Post Offices

The second level of the planning cake involves post office planning, as shown in Figure 3.4. One of the most critical decisions that you will have to make when you implement GroupWise is how to group users into post offices.

FIGURE 3.4

Post Office Planning

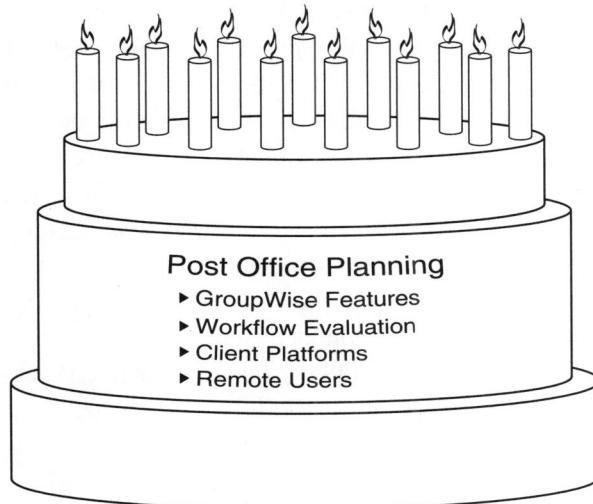

Post Office Planning
▸ GroupWise Features
▸ Workflow Evaluation
▸ Client Platforms
▸ Remote Users

IMPORTANT

If you can identify groups of people that send messages to each other frequently, you can place those users into the same post office. That way, you will isolate GroupWise traffic and greatly reduce the impact of GroupWise on your network traffic.

In a well-organized GroupWise system, most e-mail traffic is isolated within post offices. This minimizes GroupWise-generated network traffic and results in the best performance of the GroupWise system. Isolating traffic within post offices also allows users to take full advantage of GroupWise client features (e.g., the proxy feature).

When planning post offices, you should evaluate these factors:

- ▸ GroupWise features

- ▸ Workflow

- ▸ Client platforms

- ▸ Remote users

GROUPWISE FEATURES

When you group users into post offices, you need to take into consideration the following features of GroupWise: proxy, rules, file attachments, security, and resources. (See Appendix A for a detailed description of these features.) The following case study will help you see how these features affect grouping of users.

The management employees of BrightSmiles, Inc.—a modeling company—frequently send messages to each other about candidates for modeling assignments. Because many careers are affected by management's decisions, e-mail messages must be kept very secure. It should not be possible for the rest of the company to see the messages under any circumstances. Often these confidential messages are accompanied by head shots, which are transmitted in the form of large file attachments. Management is concerned that its e-mail system's performance may be adversely affected by the large size of the messages' attachments. Management also wants its assistants to be able to view all of the managers' calendars. However, the names of these managers should not appear in any other address book in the GroupWise system.

A well-organized grouping strategy can help an administrator meet many of this company's needs. One solution would be to group these managers and their assistants into their own GroupWise post office. The system administrator could establish a policy requiring all users to set passwords on their mailboxes. By using the proxy feature, managers could grant their assistants *read-only proxy access* to their appointments, tasks, and notes. Without knowing management's passwords, other users are not able to see anything in the managers' mailboxes. By setting the visibility of the managers' user objects to "Post Office," the names of these managers would not appear in any other address books outside their own post office. Finally, because management shares the same post office message store, the large file attachments would only need to be stored one time on a single company file server. This is one of the main advantages of the store-and-forward architecture of GroupWise systems. This setup conserves disk space and improves message delivery performance. These issues will be discussed in greater detail in Parts III and IV.

WORKFLOW EVALUATION

The workflow evaluation is perhaps the most important aspect of the middle layer of the planning process. Simply put, workflow is how people work together. Ask yourself who talks to whom the most. You should look at the communication flow within a company, and you should group workers who communicate most frequently into post offices. For example, if your Accounting Department communicates with Shipping every day, message flow would be greatly enhanced by combining those two departments into one post office.

Usually, a survey of managers in a company will provide answers to questions about company workflow and bring other related issues to the surface. Sometimes, companies bring in an outside Business Process Re-engineering (BPR) consultant to analyze corporate communications.

Obviously, there cannot be one scheme that fits all situations, and I am not going to attempt the impossible here by trying to list all of the possibilities. But I will suggest a sensible methodology for designing your GroupWise system.

Client Platforms

GroupWise client applications are implemented at the post office level. End users expect to be able to use GroupWise on the computing platform they use at work. Before you implement GroupWise at an organization, you need to know which computing platforms are in use within the organization. Find out the answers to these questions before you begin your implementation:

- ▸ What computing platforms does the organization currently use?

- ▸ How many users have IBM-compatible PCs?

- ▸ How many are running only DOS-based applications?

▸ How many are running Windows?

▸ Are there any UNIX users?

▸ Are there any Macintosh users?

If you know which computing platforms the end users utilize everyday, you will have a good idea which GroupWise clients they need. I'll discuss installation of GroupWise clients in the next chapter.

REMOTE USERS

After an organization has been using GroupWise for a while, eventually some users will ask, "How can I get my GroupWise messages at home or while on the road?" GroupWise Remote is a very useful component that can be added to a GroupWise system to handle those situations.

You should consider the need for GroupWise Remote at the outset, while you are organizing users into post offices. Often, companies have groups of users that work away from the main offices and cannot connect to the corporate network. A typical example is a field sales force that has sales reps located throughout the country. If you can group the remote users into a post office, you will minimize the impact of GroupWise Remote on the overall GroupWise system.

To determine if an organization will need the capabilities offered by GroupWise Remote, ask yourself these questions:

▸ Are there any employees who work at home on their computers?

▸ Does the company have a sales force that is not connected to the network?

▸ Does the company have users who travel frequently and need to stay in touch with the office?

If you answered "yes" to any of these questions, your organization should consider implementing a GroupWise system that can support GroupWise Remote. If the potential exists for using GroupWise Remote, you should plan for it from the beginning. (See Part VI for more on GroupWise Remote.)

Planning Phase 3:
Planning Domains

As shown in Figure 3.5, the top layer of the GroupWise planning cake involves grouping post offices into domains.

Domain Planning

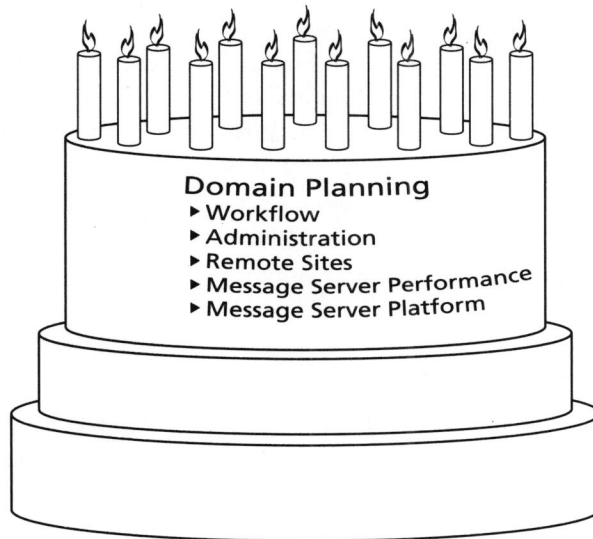

Domain Planning
- ▸ Workflow
- ▸ Administration
- ▸ Remote Sites
- ▸ Message Server Performance
- ▸ Message Server Platform

These are the main factors to consider:

▸   Department or business-unit workflow

▸   Administration

▸   Location of remote sites

▸   Message server performance

▸   Message server platforms

DEPARTMENT OR BUSINESS-UNIT WORKFLOW

Your analysis of department or business-unit workflow will be an analysis of communications among departments, business units, and even individual companies. Because the size of GroupWise systems can vary enormously, the messaging system will have to be designed to match the flow of information within the particular organizational structure.

The sharing of information needs to be analyzed between departments. For example, if Accounting always needs to generate an invoice after Shipping fills an order, those two departments would fit nicely together in one domain.

Communication between business units depends on the employees' daily routines and business goals. You should find out how members of business units communicate with other departments. If you can detect a relationship based on established procedures, then this might suggest that you should group those units in a common domain.

Like all other planning issues, an entire book could be written on just this topic. Business Process Re-engineering (BPR) consulting firms can offer some direction as you analyze communications and workflow within an enterprise.

ADMINISTRATION

As mentioned in Chapter 2, the domain level is where administration of GroupWise systems takes place. The number of available GroupWise administrators and their level of expertise will be a deciding factor as you determine how many domains your system should have. To fully grasp the issues involved in creating domains, you will need a greater understanding of the role of domains in GroupWise systems. Part IV will deal with the subject of multiple-domain administration in greater detail.

The ability of the system administrator to delegate administrative duties to separate domains is a key feature of GroupWise. Planning the administration of a GroupWise system involves taking into account the organization's personnel, system maintenance issues, and managerial concerns.

The likelihood that you will find qualified e-mail system administrators depends on where you are located and the type of industry you work in. The duties of e-mail system administrators are numerous and varied. Traditionally, network administrators are given the additional responsibility of e-mail system administration. This may work in smaller companies (50–500 users) with server-based e-mail systems. It most certainly is not a good idea at large companies (500 plus users) that have enterprisewide GroupWise messaging systems. In general, one person working a full 40-hour week can handle a system with up to about 1,000 users if that person is dedicated solely to GroupWise administration. Of course, if one administrator has to answer every end user's question (and those questions can be complicated), then the size of the system a single administrator can handle will be smaller. If you plan your system properly, you can prevent your organization's help desk from being overwhelmed with calls related to e-mail.

Maintenance of the system includes directory store database maintenance, message store maintenance, and software updates. Weekly, monthly, and event-driven maintenance will be discussed in Part VII.

LOCATION OF REMOTE SITES

Many GroupWise implementations involve connecting the GroupWise system with company sites in different locations. GroupWise can be configured to communicate with remote locations, but often additional GroupWise components and hardware are needed. Find out the answers to these questions before you start implementing GroupWise in an organization that may need GroupWise Remote:

▶ Does the organization have satellite offices in other areas?

▶ Are there offices in other states or countries?

▶ Are those offices connected to the main network?

▶ What kind of network link is available between sites?

▶ Are other connection types possible besides modem access?

▶ How much network traffic currently passes through the WAN links?

▶ Does the organization expect to connect with other organizations that use GroupWise?

How you answer these questions will influence both the cost of the implementation and the configuration of GroupWise domains and post offices in the system.

MESSAGE SERVER PERFORMANCE

Message server performance is a complex issue that requires thorough knowledge of how the message server works. The issue of message server performance also requires an understanding of how GroupWise messages are processed, how directory synchronization occurs in a GroupWise system, and how primary and secondary domains work together. These issues will be dealt with in depth in Parts III and IV. For now, I will give you some preliminary advice to keep in mind during the planning of your system.

Basically, you don't want delivery of administrative messages (that is, directory-synchronization messages) to take up all of the message server's time. The task of transferring users' business-related messages (which form the bulk of the message server's responsibility) should not take a backseat to the delivery of regular administrative messages (which are automatically given higher priority by the message server). You can avoid that problem by wisely choosing which domain will be the primary domain in a system. Refer to Part IV for a more complete discussion of the different types of domains.

If a message server becomes bogged down with regular GroupWise messages, you will need to add another message server to the system in order to balance the load between the two message servers. Because there can only be one message server per domain, you would in fact need to add another domain, along with post offices and objects. You could end up having to shuffle post offices and users around. That task can be a tedious—if not arduous—process. I explain how to optimize message server performance in the next section.

MESSAGE SERVER PLATFORM

Planning for efficient message server performance is really a matter of planning for growth of the GroupWise system. When trying to decide how many post offices should be in a domain, a major consideration should be which message server platform will be used. Table 3.1 will give you a general idea of how many post offices and users a domain can handle given a specific message server platform. Of course, there are several other factors that come into play, such as the type of network operating system that is being used, the kind of computer that will run the message server process, the number of messages the users send, the size and number of file attachments that users transmit, and the level of message delivery performance that is desired. The numbers in this table provide general guidelines based on observations by GroupWise consultants who have implemented GroupWise in a variety of network configurations. With the proper configurations, these numbers can be quite a bit higher (especially for systems using NLM and UNIX message servers). As they say in the TV car commercials, your actual mileage may vary.

T A B L E 3.1	MESSAGE SERVER PLATFORM	NUMBER OF POST OFFICES	USERS PER POST OFFICE
Message Server Platforms	DOS message server	2–4	50–100
	OS/2 message server	3–5	100–150
	NLM message server	4–6	100–250
	UNIX message server	4–6	100–250

In summary, when you plan the domains in a system, your analysis should proceed in the following order of priority:

1 • Department and business-unit workflow analysis

2 • Administration analysis

3 • Message server platform analysis

Other Planning Issues: Connectivity, Add-On Components, and Cost

If the three layers of the planning cake represent the planning phases discussed earlier in this chapter, the candles on the cake correspond to four ancillary issues, as illustrated by Figure 3.6.

Other Planning Issues

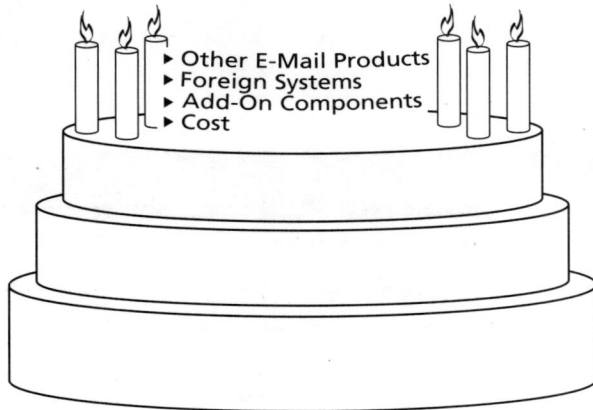

▶ Other E-Mail Products
▶ Foreign Systems
▶ Add-On Components
▶ Cost

Those additional issues are:

▶ Connectivity to other e-mail products

▶ Connectivity to foreign systems

▶ GroupWise functionality (add-on components)

▶ Cost

Each of these issues should be carefully analyzed to ensure that you meet your organization's messaging objectives.

CONNECTING GROUPWISE TO OTHER E-MAIL PRODUCTS

A GroupWise implementation is usually done gradually over a period of time. Often an organization needs to maintain e-mail communication between two different e-mail systems during the GroupWise implementation. Sometimes departments will refuse to change e-mail systems, and you will need to make sure they can still communicate with the rest of the company. In these situations, you need to know what steps to take to guarantee reliable communication between different e-mail systems.

Before you begin a GroupWise implementation, make sure you know how you would answer these questions:

▶ Does the organization currently use other electronic messaging products? Which ones?

▶ Will it continue to use these products after GroupWise is implemented, or will GroupWise be used exclusively?

If GroupWise will be used in conjunction with other systems, you need to know which products will have to be purchased to allow GroupWise users to communicate with the other system. GroupWise can connect to many different e-mail systems through gateways, but these gateways are additional components that must be purchased separately. In order to use the components, you will have to have extensive knowledge of how the interconnecting systems work.

Once you know which gateways you need, you should determine how administration tasks will be performed across gateways. In many cases, administration tasks must be performed in both systems. In those cases, some administrative redundancy is inevitable. For example, when you add a user to the GroupWise system, someone may have to add that same user to the interconnecting systems. In some cases, however, the gateway will be able to automatically synchronize the directories of the interconnecting systems.

Before beginning a GroupWise implementation, you should know which hardware and software components will be needed to link the different systems, how much the components will cost, and what skills will be needed by the administrators linking the systems. Knowing these things in advance will prevent unpleasant surprises during the implementation.

CONNECTING GROUPWISE TO FOREIGN SYSTEMS

GroupWise gateways put the whole world right at your doorstep. In a typical work week, I use GroupWise to send numerous e-mail messages to people outside the system who are on the Internet. I have no idea which e-mail program they are using to read my messages, and they have no idea that my messages come from a GroupWise system. I can also send GroupWise messages to users of on-line services via the Internet.

Before you begin a GroupWise implementation, you should be aware of any foreign networks or e-mail systems that are already connected to the organization's system or which may be connected in the future. You should find out if the organization's existing network has access to the Internet, and if the organization will want to send and receive GroupWise messages through the Internet.

EVALUATING GROUPWISE FUNCTIONALITY (ADD-ON COMPONENTS)

Evaluation of functionality means analyzing the kind of tasks your organization wants GroupWise to perform. You need to determine whether the standard version of GroupWise is adequate or whether the organization would benefit from additional GroupWise modules or special features.

In a very simple implementation, GroupWise can serve as a powerful e-mail, calendaring, and scheduling package. However, you can design more complex implementations that can handle remote users, faxing, paging, telephone access, routing of forms, list server functions, and many other capabilities.

You should be aware of the level of functionality that your organization desires. Consider how you might use each of the following:

▸ Electronic faxing

▸ Automatic paging

▸ Project-based message forums

▸ Telephone access for messages and calendar items

▸ Automated form routing

▸ Electronic bulletin board list server functions

▸ Workflow application programming

Many additional features can be added to a GroupWise system to increase its usefulness to an organization. For example, users can send faxes directly from GroupWise if a GroupWise Fax/Print gateway is installed. Users can also send messages to other users' pagers if the GroupWise Pager gateway is installed. Ask yourself the following questions to see if GroupWise can be used to meet your organization's special needs:

▸ Will users need to send faxes directly from their desktop PC? Will they need to receive faxes?

► Will some users want to be paged when certain types of messages appear in their In Boxes?

► Will users want to listen to their e-mail via telephone?

► Would groups working on specific projects profit from having common message areas that contain message threads that pertain to their projects?

► Will electronic forms be used to route and store information?

It is always a good idea to ask people at your organization whether they think they can use the various GroupWise add-on features that are available. Often people don't realize they need something until they know it is available. (Before Thomas Edison came along, few people would have said they needed light bulbs.) If you tell your organization about all of GroupWise's capabilities during the planning stage, you will be able to implement all of the necessary features from the very beginning, or you can at least design the system to accommodate features that might become necessary later on.

Answering all of the questions above will assist you in developing a logical plan for customizing GroupWise. Your answers will help you as you determine:

► which GroupWise clients need to be supported (see Chapter 5);

► whether to implement GroupWise Remote and which remote clients you need (see Part VI);

► whether Async gateways need to be implemented and, if so, where to locate them (see Part V);

► whether you will need additional hardware to implement GroupWise;

► whether you need to have gateways that connect your system with other messaging systems (see Part IX);

► whether any additional hardware and software are necessary for you to connect to other systems;

▸ whether you need to obtain additional hardware or software to provide faxing, paging, and telephone access capabilities (see Part IX).

ANALYZING COSTS

After analyzing all of the factors to be considered during the planning process, you should be able to estimate the cost of implementing your GroupWise system. Here are some factors to consider as you estimate implementation costs:

▸ Hardware and software upgrades

▸ GroupWise components

▸ GroupWise mailbox licenses

▸ Training and consulting

Hardware and Software Upgrades

After analyzing your organization's needs, you should be able to estimate the costs of file server upgrades. You will be able to tell how many processor upgrades and how much memory and disk space you will need. You should also be able to judge whether the users' machines will have to be upgraded to run the client applications. Finally, you should be able to determine whether network operating systems and workstation operating systems need to be upgraded.

GroupWise Components

The questions you ask yourself during the planning phases will help you to know whether you should recommend specific GroupWise components. You should also have an idea of how many message servers and gateways you will need to purchase and which client platforms the users should have.

GroupWise Licenses

GroupWise is licensed on a *per mailbox* basis. That number is basically equal the number of users in the GroupWise system. For the end user, the advantage of this licensing policy is that one user can legally use as many different client platforms as desired with one license. For example, in a typical week, I use the Windows client, the DOS client, the Macintosh client, and the Windows Remote client to access my mailbox. I only need one license to run all four of those clients.

Training and Consulting

Thorough planning should give you a general idea of how much training and consulting the organization will need to facilitate the transition to a GroupWise system.

Cost analysis involves balancing different factors. You will have to decide what level of performance is required and what level is merely wished for. If you have an unlimited budget for new hardware and the most expensive software, you can build a high-performance GroupWise system. With super-fast file servers, tons of memory, high-speed network links, and enormous disk capacity running multithreaded 32-bit operating systems, you can build a GroupWise system that practically delivers messages before you send them. Most GroupWise administrators, however, have to face reality and learn how to deal with 386 computers with 2MB of RAM running Windows on top of DOS on overcrowded networks.

GroupWise is flexible; it can provide exceptionally high performance when cost is not a factor, but it can also provide very good performance even when the best equipment is not available.

Preparing to Implement a GroupWise System

During your initial analysis, all of the issues raised in this chapter may not be resolved completely, but you should be able to make some fairly accurate projections. However, even the most thorough analysis can't prevent all of the surprises you might encounter when you roll out a new system. The best way to double-check your analysis and to uncover surprises before they happen is to run a *pilot program,* where you actually test a small-scale GroupWise system at your organization.

There are two different approaches to running pilot programs. The first is to set up GroupWise in a lab environment where you try to simulate a full-scale system. The second approach is to implement GroupWise in a single department of the organization—as kind of test market. The best way to run a pilot program is probably to use a combination of both methods, initially testing the system in a lab and then trying it out in a department.

SETTING UP A GROUPWISE LAB

Setting up GroupWise in a lab environment gives system administrators extremely valuable experience. It is a good way to get the roll-out team up to speed on GroupWise administration and troubleshooting issues.

In a lab environment, you can use the GroupWise Applications Programming Interface (API) gateway to send messages through the system to simulate various levels of GroupWise network traffic. This helps identify problem spots that may arise during the implementation. Learning to use the API gateway early in the process will also help you automate administration of the GroupWise system later.

NOTE

The API gateway is a programming tool and requires some custom program development to be useful in this situation.

A lab will need to be able to simulate a variety of GroupWise configurations. For example, a good lab might have three or four file servers with various hardware configurations and operating systems. The lab should also be equipped with some modems and phone lines to test gateways and GroupWise Remote.

The lab must be able to test the file server, message server, and hardware configurations that are most likely to be found in the organization. The lab should also be able to test out the GroupWise clients on a variety of typical end user workstation configurations.

After you have completed the analyses discussed earlier in this chapter, try to determine what hardware would best approximate the real-world environment of your organization. Assemble a couple of typical file servers and find two or three typical end user machines and put them together in a lab environment. Run the clients on each of the workstations to get a feel for the client performance. Set up the API gateway and pump messages through the lab system to find out how much the message server machines can handle before performance becomes unacceptable. These tests will prove to be invaluable.

ROLLING OUT GROUPWISE TO A TEST DEPARTMENT

Rolling out GroupWise to a test department will give you a more accurate prediction of what the full scale roll-out will be like. This approach will help you identify potential problems with message traffic levels and with your system's configuration. More important, it will uncover the needs of the end users. You will quickly be able to identify the users' most common problems and concerns, and you will be prepared to address those during the full-scale roll-out.

You should be sure to involve training and help desk personnel with the GroupWise testing. Those people are the ones who will be dealing directly with the users' problems and who often will be called on to provide creative solutions.

Trainers will be a useful resource for identifying the most common questions and concerns of the users. Have the trainers develop a training program that addresses the questions and concerns that come up during the testing.

When you select a test group, you should pick a group that is representative of the whole organization. If possible, choose a group that will generate traffic through potential weak spots in the network. For example, if there is a department that is divided into two halves that work at different sites, you might want to use that department to test the ability of the WAN link to handle the traffic.

If your system will incorporate GroupWise Remote, you should choose a test group that includes remote users. You should set up the Async gateway and have the remote users communicate with the other users in the system.

WHAT THE PILOT PROGRAM SHOULD TEST

You should organize the pilot program to evaluate these factors:

► The amount of network traffic that GroupWise will generate

► The ability of the existing network to handle demands generated by the GroupWise processes, especially if it uses the NLMs

► Potential conflicts with existing programs and processes in the system

► The speed of message delivery

► The amount of training that users will need

You are bound to be surprised by the GroupWise usage patterns you see. Be sure to overestimate the amount of network traffic and allow for growth. You will undoubtedly find that usage increases as users become more familiar with GroupWise.

TRAINING RESOURCES

I firmly believe that if you don't pay attention to the training needs of your organization, you won't be able to pull off a successful a roll-out. Many organizations adopt the "ask-a-neighbor" approach to training. Although that approach sometimes works, more often it causes a lot of frustration and wastes a lot of time. There is, however, a much better way. Novell has developed a complete set of training resources to help employees quickly become productive GroupWise users. You will find a complete listing of these resources in Appendix B. Here's a quick overview:

End User Training   Novell Education offers a beginning GroupWise client course designed to acquaint GroupWise end users with the basics of GroupWise.

Help Desk and Support Personnel Training   In addition, Novell offers a CNA (Certified Novell Administrator) program for GroupWise administrators.

Administrator Training   Novell also offers a CNE (Certified Novell Engineer) program for GroupWise, which is targeted towards administrators and system integrators.

Summary

In this chapter you learned a planning strategy that will help you implement a sound GroupWise system. In Part II I take you through the steps for implementing a small system.

Small GroupWise Systems

Single Domain, Single Post Office

In Part II, I will explain how to set up a small GroupWise system. Although this part of the book focuses primarily on a simple GroupWise system, the concepts introduced here apply to GroupWise systems of all sizes. Every GroupWise administrator should have a good understanding of the concepts presented in Part II. In Part II, I will discuss the GroupWise installation process, GroupWise client applications, and post office management issues.

Part II Scenario

Fairbanks and Hunt Accounting is a small partnership specializing in tax preparation and planning for technical companies. They are centralized in a single office, employing 15 CPAs and 35 support staff members, including secretaries, researchers, and paralegals. Every desk has a computer on it. The partners, who have read articles about GroupWise in mass market computer journals, have recently realized the potential of GroupWise to improve productivity and give them a better return on their computing investment.

The typical workstation at Fairbanks and Hunt is a low-end 486 machine with 8MB of RAM. Most workers rely heavily on Windows applications, especially the word processing and spreadsheet components of PerfectOffice. They don't have an internal e-mail system yet.

The company owns a single NetWare 3.11 file server running a single segment LAN to which everyone connects. Their computer reseller, who is under contract, supports and maintains the file server.

Think about how you would handle the GroupWise implementation in this scenario as you read Part II. I will give you a possible solution to this scenario at the end of Part II.

Installing GroupWise and Configuring a GroupWise System

The scenario at the beginning of Part II involves a typical small office environment in which a relatively simple installation of GroupWise would meet the company's electronic messaging needs. Chapter 4 addresses the issues this type of simple installation presents for a GroupWise administrator.

As you learned in Chapter 2, a basic GroupWise system at a minimum must have the following components:

- A domain

- A post office

- User objects

- At least one version of a GroupWise client

In addition, all but the very smallest GroupWise systems need a message transfer agent (MTA) to handle message processing. If a GroupWise system contains a gateway or multiple post offices or domains, it has to have a message server. If a GroupWise system consists of a single domain and one post office with no gateways, a GroupWise post office server is strongly recommended (but it is not an absolute requirement).

NOTE

> **GroupWise servers are sold in a message server pack, which contains all of the GroupWise servers (message server, post office server, and administration server). These servers are not available separately.**

Chapter 4 outlines the administrative tasks you need to perform in order to set up a GroupWise system on a network. This chapter walks you through the creation of a GroupWise infrastructure—domains, post offices, and user objects—and explains what needs to happen at each step of the way. I will describe in detail the directory structures, databases, and executable processes associated with both domains and post offices.

Chapter 5 deals with the client software, which is the final component you need for a basic GroupWise system.

NOTE

Appendix C provides instructions for setting up a GroupWise test system on an individual PC. You will need GroupWise 4.1 for Windows Client/Administration to create the test system. Using a test system gives you hands-on experience with the concepts you will learn in Part II.

Initial GroupWise Installation

After you have completed the analysis discussed in Chapter 3, you should be ready to implement a GroupWise system in a small organization. Although administrators usually do not relish the thought of poring over lifeless software documentation, the documentation that comes with GroupWise Client/Admin is an excellent resource for you during an initial GroupWise installation. Make sure you have the following documentation:

▶ *GroupWise Installation Guide*

▶ *GroupWise Administration Guide*

PREPARATION

Before you begin installing GroupWise, you should decide where to locate the domain (or domains) and post office directory structures. At Fairbanks and Hunt Accounting, the company described in Part II's introductory scenario, the decision about where to locate the domain and post office would be simple because the company has only one file server. Both the domain and post office directory structures would have to be installed on that file server.

After you determine where to locate the directory structures, you should next decide on a convention for naming the domain and post office. Consider the possibility that the system might later need to be expanded to include multiple post offices and domains.

Here is some advice to keep in mind as you prepare for the installation:

▶ Make the names of domains and post offices short and simple. The names should reflect the identity of the groups belonging to the domains or post offices, but they should not be cumbersome for the administrator to use.

▶ Do not locate the post office in a subdirectory of the domain directory. Putting the post office there makes management of network rights much more difficult.

▶ Although the names of domains and post offices need not be identical to their respective directories' names, it is helpful if they are at least similar to the directory names. For example, you could create a post office named Advertising that is located in the directory J:\ADVERT.

▶ Use the worksheet in the *GroupWise Installation Guide* to record your post office and domain names.

INSTALLATION

The *GroupWise Installation Guide* explains the procedure for actually installing the software. It is simply a matter of inserting the diskettes and then running INSTALL. You will start by entering the name of the directory where you want the files to be installed. Remember—the directory that you enter in the Install To: field becomes your domain directory.

When you run the installation program, you will be prompted for the files you want to install. See Figure 4.1.

The following files can be installed during the installation process:

▶ GroupWise Admin files

▶ Office 3.1 Compatibility files

▶ Windows client

▶ DOS client

F I G U R E 4.1

GroupWise Installation

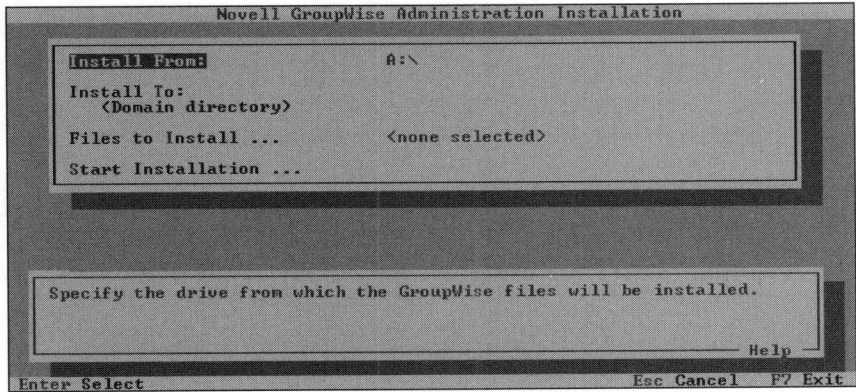

```
                        Novell GroupWise Administration Installation

     ┌─────────────────────────────────────────────────────────────────────┐
     │ Install From:                    A:\                                  │
     │                                                                       │
     │ Install To:                                                           │
     │    <Domain directory>                                                 │
     │                                                                       │
     │ Files to Install ...             <none selected>                      │
     │                                                                       │
     │ Start Installation ...                                                │
     └─────────────────────────────────────────────────────────────────────┘

     ┌─────────────────────────────────────────────────────────────────────┐
     │ Specify the drive from which the GroupWise files will be installed.   │
     │                                                                       │
     │                                                              Help ─   │
     └─────────────────────────────────────────────────────────────────────┘
      Enter  Select                                    Esc  Cancel   F7  Exit
```

NOTE

The GroupWise Client/Admin packs for DOS and Windows have to be purchased separately. Both come with the DOS version of GroupWise Admin. If you need both versions of the client, the software can be installed during the same GroupWise Admin installation session if you have both sets of client disks. The message server pack, all gateway programs, and the files for Macintosh and UNIX clients must be installed separately.

The Windows client and DOS client files need to be first installed at the domain level and then copied (you will sometimes hear the term *pushed*) to the post office. The client directories in the domain serve as a storage location (or *archive*) for the client files. GroupWise users never directly access the client files stored in the domain. Therefore, if you have limited disk space, you can delete the client files from the domain after they have been copied to the post offices.

Once you have successfully installed the files, the next step is to run GroupWise Admin (AD.EXE) from the domain directory.

Creating the Initial Domain, Post Office, and User Objects

When the diskette installation is complete, the directory should contain all of the executable program files and subdirectories necessary for GroupWise to operate. However, the directory still lacks a domain database file (WPDOMAIN.DB). Remember—the WPDOMAIN.DB file in the primary domain is the master database for the whole GroupWise system. The first domain you create in a GroupWise system will always be the primary domain.

ASSISTED SETUP

The first time you run GroupWise Admin, the program detects the absence of a domain database file and automatically launches the Assisted Setup routine. Figure 4.2 shows you what your screen should look like when that routine begins. The Assisted Setup routine only kicks in when you create the initial domain (which will be the primary domain). You can exit the Assisted Setup routine after you have created the primary domain, or you can continue to use Assisted Setup while you are creating post offices, installing client software, and adding users. Assisted Setup will not run again after it is used to create the first domain. It cannot be used to set up any of the secondary domains.

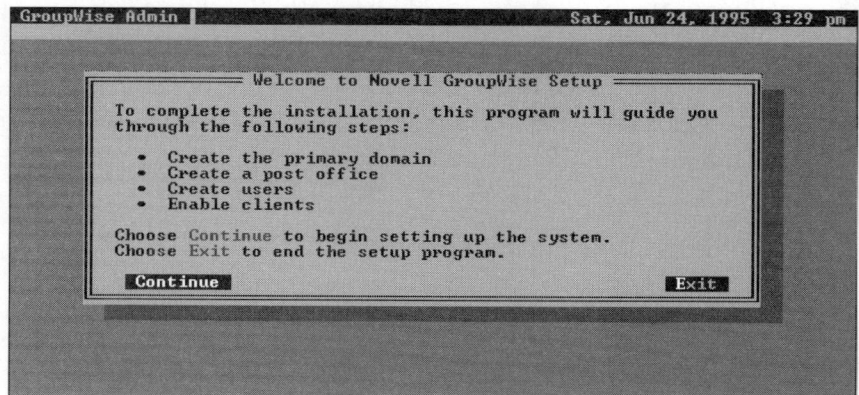

FIGURE 4.2

Assisted Setup Introductory Screen

```
GroupWise Admin                              Sat, Jun 24, 1995  3:29 pm

        ═══════════ Welcome to Novell GroupWise Setup ═══════════
         To complete the installation, this program will guide you
         through the following steps:

            •  Create the primary domain
            •  Create a post office
            •  Create users
            •  Enable clients

         Choose Continue to begin setting up the system.
         Choose Exit to end the setup program.

            Continue                                    Exit
```

The first thing Assisted Setup asks for is the name of the primary domain and the name of its directory. Once you have entered that information, Assisted Setup will create the domain database. It will then prompt you for the time zone (e.g., Pacific, Mountain, Central, or Eastern) where the domain is located. It will also ask you for the dates when daylight saving time begins and ends in your area, if applicable. You will then be asked to confirm the language. Because rules for sorting lists vary from language to language, this option lets you choose the sorting rules of a specific spoken language to be used in the lists displayed in GroupWise Admin. Finally, you will be asked to confirm the network type.

Next, Assisted Setup will ask you for the name of the first post office and its directory path. Assisted Setup will then create the post office directory structure and the post office database file, WPHOST.DB.

Assisted Setup will then ask you to choose the client files to be copied from the domain to the post office. The client files copied to the post office are the files that the users will need to access in order to run GroupWise.

The next step is to add user objects. You can add users manually with the help of Assisted Setup or you can elect to proceed with the next step. If you will be importing users from a network directory or from an import file, you should not add users with Assisted Setup.

The final step in the Assisted Setup routine is to enable the GroupWise clients. This is actually just an instruction screen that gives details about how to enable the clients. This step is not carried out in GroupWise Admin. You should choose the View Summary option to review the configuration of your domain and post office, and then you will have the option to choose Done to exit GroupWise Admin, or you can choose Admin to proceed with GroupWise Admin.

At this point, the following tasks should be complete:

► You have successfully installed the GroupWise software from the diskettes.

► You have created the initial domain (which will be the primary domain), the first post office, and some user objects.

DOMAIN DIRECTORY STRUCTURE AND FILES

After the initial software installation and the creation of the first domain, the domain directory structure should look like Figure 4.3.

▶ · ◀

FIGURE 4.3

Domain Directory Structure

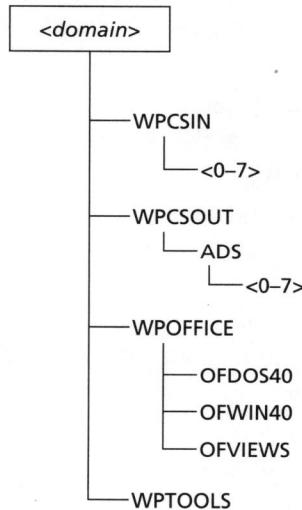

```
                        ┌─────────────┐
                        │  <domain>   │
                        └──────┬──────┘
                               │
                               ├──WPCSIN
                               │     └──<0–7>
                               │
                               ├──WPCSOUT
                               │     └──ADS
                               │          └──<0–7>
                               │
                               ├──WPOFFICE
                               │     ├──OFDOS40
                               │     ├──OFWIN40
                               │     └──OFVIEWS
                               │
                               └──WPTOOLS
```

Table 4.1 briefly describes the domain directory and its subdirectories. You will notice that many of the directory names and filenames have been carried over from WordPerfect Office. (Words in angle brackets indicate that the name is variable. Names in parentheses indicate former WordPerfect Office names from which current directory names have been derived.)

TABLE 4.1

The Domain Directory and Subdirectories

DIRECTORY	PURPOSE
<domain>	Contains the domain database file (WPDOMAIN.DB), the GroupWise Admin executable file (AD.EXE), and other files necessary for administrative tasks.

T A B L E 4.1	DIRECTORY	PURPOSE
The Domain Directory and Subdirectories (continued)	WPCSIN\<0–7 > (WordPerfect Connection Server Input)	Acts as the input queue for the domain's message server. Messages coming into a domain from other domains in the system are temporarily stored in this directory's subdirectories to await message transfer by the message server.
	WPCSOUT\ADS\<0–7>	Acts as the input queue for the administration server on the domain level. This directory is created the first time that the administration server runs. (The administration server is discussed in Chapter 11.)
	WPOFFICE (WordPerfect Office)	Contains the subdirectories that house the DOS and Windows client files.
	WPOFFICE\OFDOS40 (WordPerfect Office \ Office for DOS 4.0)	Contains the DOS client files in uncompressed format.
	WPOFFICE\OFVIEWS (WordPerfect Office \ Office Views)	Contains subdirectories that hold the view files for the DOS and Windows clients. (A *view* is a template for creating GroupWise messages within the GroupWise client.)
	WPOFFICE\OFWIN40 (WordPerfect Office \ Office for Windows 4.0).	Contains the Windows client files in compressed format.
	WPTOOLS (WordPerfect Tools)	Contains files used to perform maintenance tasks for the GroupWise system, as well as files used to convert WordPerfect Office 3.1 information into GroupWise. The key file in this directory is the Check GroupWise utility, OFCHECK.EXE, which is used to manage GroupWise databases. The Check GroupWise utility is discussed in Chapter 19.

Figure 4.4 depicts and Table 4.2 explains the key files contained in the domain directory:

FIGURE 4.4

Domain Files

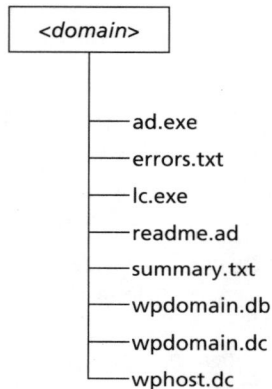

```
<domain>
        ad.exe
        errors.txt
        lc.exe
        readme.ad
        summary.txt
        wpdomain.db
        wpdomain.dc
        wphost.dc
```

TABLE 4.2

Domain Directory Files

FILENAME	FUNCTION
AD.EXE	The GroupWise Administration program.
ERRORS.TXT	This is a reference file for GroupWise administrators. It contains descriptions of the error messages generated by GroupWise clients, GroupWise Admin, and GroupWise server processes.
LC.EXE	A launcher application used by GroupWise Admin to run other administrative-executable programs.
README.AD	The GroupWise Admin README file. It contains a listing of the rights to the GroupWise directories that are needed by users and GroupWise processes. It also contains information about installing GroupWise on networks other than Novell networks.

TABLE 4.2	FILENAME	FUNCTION
Domain Directory Files (continued)	SUMMARY.TXT	A text file summary of the actions performed during the Assisted Setup routine.
	WPDOMAIN.DB (WordPerfect Domain Database)	The domain database. This file contains the GroupWise directory (address book) and linking information for links to post offices and other domains.
	WPDOMAIN.DC	A template file used when creating domain database files.
	WPHOST.DC	A template file used when creating post office databases.

The domain MTA (or message server) has not been installed yet. The message server has its own installation routine. Message server files may be installed in a domain subdirectory, or they may be installed elsewhere, depending on the message server platform that is used.

The domain is the core of the GroupWise system and should only be accessible to certain authorized people. As administrator, you will need full access rights to the domain and its subdirectories. However, you should limit network rights in the domain to administrative personnel, and you should create a secret domain password. In order to set a password in GroupWise Admin, select File, Setup, Environment, and then Password.

Don't forget the domain password! Forgetting the password on a domain database is just as bad as losing the entire database. There is no way to access the domain if you forget the password.

POST OFFICE DIRECTORY STRUCTURE AND FILES

Figure 4.5 shows the post office directory structure immediately after the Assisted Setup routine. Table 4.3 gives brief descriptions of the subdirectories. Once again, you will notice that most names have been carried over from WordPerfect Office.

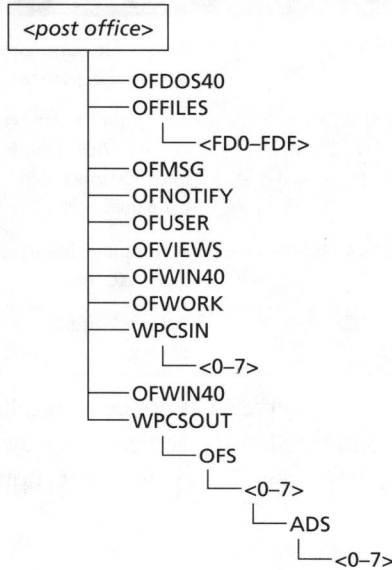

```
<post office>
    ├── OFDOS40
    ├── OFFILES
    │       └── <FD0–FDF>
    ├── OFMSG
    ├── OFNOTIFY
    ├── OFUSER
    ├── OFVIEWS
    ├── OFWIN40
    ├── OFWORK
    ├── WPCSIN
    │       └── <0–7>
    ├── OFWIN40
    └── WPCSOUT
            └── OFS
                    └── <0–7>
                            └── ADS
                                    └── <0–7>
```

DIRECTORY	PURPOSE
<post office>	Contains the post office database, WPHOST.DB.
OFDOS40 (Office for DOS 4.0)	Contains the DOS client files.
OFFILES (Office Files)	Contains file attachments and messages that exceed 2K. This is one of three message store directories.
OFMSG (Office Message)	Contains the message databases named MSGxx.DB, where xx represents databases xx.DB, where xxx represents the users' three-character IDs. This is also a message store directory.
OFNOTIFY (Office Notify)	Contains Notify program files.

	DIRECTORY	PURPOSE
TABLE 4.3 *The Post Office Directory* *(continued)*	OFUSER (Office User)	Contains the user databases named USER*xxx*.DB, where *xxx* represents the users' three-character IDs. This is also a message store directory.
	OFVIEWS (Office Views)	Contains the views for the Windows and DOS clients. (A *view* is a template for creating GroupWise messages within the GroupWise client.)
	OFWIN40 (Office for Windows 4.0)	Contains the Windows client files.
	OFWORK (Office Work)	Holds messages set for delayed delivery. It is also used to process messages for GroupWise Remote users who choose the network connection option. (GroupWise Remote is explained in Chapter 15.)
	WPCSIN\<0–7> (WordPerfect Connection Server Input)	Temporarily stores messages addressed to other post offices or domains while the messages await processing by the domain message server. This is a message server input queue.
	WPCSOUT\OFS\<0–7> (WordPerfect Connection Server Output)	Stores messages coming into the post office before they are processed by the post office server. This is a message server output queue.
	WPCSOUT\ADS\<0–7> (WordPerfect Connection Server Output)	Acts as the post office level administration server input queue. It is used for administrative updates to the WPHOST.DB file. This directory is created the first time you run the administration server. The administration server is discussed in Chapter 11.

NOTE This table does not contain directories for the Macintosh or UNIX client files. Those files are installed with separate installation routines. They can be installed to the domain or to the post office, according to the needs of the organization.

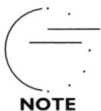

Figure 4.6 and Table 4.4 show the files that are stored in the post office directory:

Post Office Files

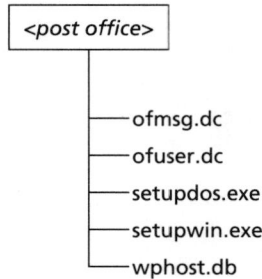

```
<post office>
        |
        |----ofmsg.dc
        |----ofuser.dc
        |----setupdos.exe
        |----setupwin.exe
        |----wphost.db
```

Post Office Files

FILENAME	DESCRIPTION
OFMSG.DC	A template file used to create message databases.
OFUSER.DC	A template file used to create user databases.
SETUPDOS.EXE	The DOS client setup program.
SETUPWIN.EXE	The Windows client setup program.
WPHOST.DB	The post office database file. It contains the GroupWise system's directory (address book) information that is accessed by the users within the post office.

Unlike the domain, the post office directory structure should be accessible to GroupWise users, who will need to have some network rights there. However, the rights that individual users need will depend on the message-delivery strategy and security strategy that you implement and on the client platforms that are used in the post office. The specific rights necessary for different message-delivery methods will be discussed in Chapter 6.

ADDING USERS TO A POST OFFICE

The last step you need to complete when you set up the infrastructure of a basic GroupWise system is to assign users to the post office. There are several methods for adding users to post offices:

▸ User objects can be added manually in GroupWise Admin.

▸ User information can be imported from a WordPerfect Office Notebook file or ASCII text file.

▸ User objects can be imported from the Novell NetWare bindery or from a NetWare 4.1 file server's context, Banyan STDA, IBM LAN Server, and LAN Manager (see the supporting documentation for more on how to import user information).

▸ User objects can be imported from other databases or e-mail systems via the API gateway.

When creating user objects, you are required to add information to the following fields:

▸ Domain.PO

▸ User ID

▸ Visibility

Domain.PO   The domain and post office that the user belongs to.

User ID   The user's ID that GroupWise uses to address and deliver messages. It needs to be unique within the post office.

Visibility   Determines what address books within the GroupWise system will display this user's information. System visibility is the default.

Novell recommends that you also add information to these fields:

▸ First name

▸ Last name

▸ Network ID

NOTE

NetWare 4.1 requires a typeless, fully qualified name in the Network ID field. See Chapter 20 for information on integrating GroupWise with NetWare 4.1.

The Acct ID fields and the Gateway Access fields are used in conjunction with GroupWise gateways. The Expire Date field is used if you want the user to have only temporary access to GroupWise. Once the expiration date has passed, the user is not able to log in to the post office. Expired records will not be automatically deleted, however, in case the expiration date needs to be extended.

The rest of the fields are useful for informational purposes only. They tend to make the address book more helpful to the GroupWise users. You can also define up to ten custom fields. The process for defining custom fields is explained in the *GroupWise Administration Guide*.

Summary

After reading this chapter, you should be familiar with the steps you need to follow to set up a basic GroupWise system. However, at this point, the users still have no way to access the system.

Chapter 5 explains how to set up and administer the GroupWise client applications.

Enabling the Client Software

In the previous chapter, you learned how to set up the infrastructure of a simple GroupWise system. That system included a single domain, a single post office, and user objects. Before you have a fully functional GroupWise system, however, you need to complete one more step. You need to enable the client software so that the GroupWise users can send and retrieve messages. Chapter 5 explains how to set up the various kinds of GroupWise clients.

If you are setting up a test system on a single PC, you can implement the steps explained this chapter by referring to the directions in Appendix C.

In Chapter 2, I mentioned that the GroupWise message store is not limited to any particular computing platform. This feature of the message store makes possible the cross-platform capabilities you have with GroupWise. GroupWise clients are available in DOS, Windows, Macintosh, and UNIX versions. I will not say any more about the UNIX client in this chapter. If you want more information on that subject, you can refer to the CD-ROM that comes with this book. (See the files named UNIXCLNT.IE and UNIXFACT.WPD on the CD-ROM.) GroupWise remote clients are available in DOS, Windows, and Macintosh.

In this chapter I will tell you how an administrator should set up the client software at a small company like the one I described in the scenario at the beginning of Part II. The company in that scenario, Fairbanks and Hunt Accounting, runs mostly Windows applications. Also, you will recall that Fairbanks and Hunt uses PerfectOffice. Therefore, shared code management will be a factor. In addition to explaining how to set up the Windows client at a small organization such as Fairbanks and Hunt, I will explain how to set up the DOS and Macintosh client applications.

Client Installation Options

Each of the three client programs I discuss in this chapter can be run either from a network or from a GroupWise user's local hard drive.

SETTING UP THE CLIENT TO RUN FROM THE NETWORK

To set up the GroupWise client to run from the network, you need to install the client in the post office and make sure it is accessible to the users. In other words, you install the program and verify that the users have the necessary network rights to run it.

There are a couple of distinct advantages to having users run the client from the network. First, it is easy to update the software after the installation because you only need to update it on the network. Second, it saves disk space on the local hard drives.

One disadvantage is that loading GroupWise from a network usually takes longer than from a local hard drive. Another drawback of running the client from the network is that it increases network traffic because users load the program across network wire.

SETTING UP THE CLIENT TO RUN FROM A WORKSTATION

You can install the GroupWise client files to the local workstation's hard drive. When you install the client to the local hard drive, you can customize the installation to meet the user's needs. You can perform a default installation of all the client files, you can customize the installation so that only the desired files are installed to certain directories, or you can perform a "bare bones" installation that only installs the minimum files required for the client to run.

The advantages of running the client from a workstation's hard drive are: (1) It can reduce network traffic because the program is not running on the network, and (2) it can improve performance of the GroupWise client application.

The main disadvantage of running the client from a workstation's hard drive is that an administrator cannot easily update all of the client files. Furthermore, in the case of the Windows client software, installation to the workstations' hard drives makes shared code management more complicated. I will explain what I mean by "shared code management" later in this chapter.

NOTE

When GroupWise is running from the workstation's local hard drive and the GroupWise client gets updated in the post office client directory on the network, the workstation will detect that a newer version of the client has been installed to the post office and will prompt the user to update the client on the workstation.

GroupWise Windows Client

As you learned in Chapter 4, the Windows client files are stored as compressed files at the domain level. If the GroupWise users are going to run the Windows client from a network, the Windows client files must be decompressed at the post office level.

> **If you want users to run the Windows client *only from their hard drives*, don't decompress the client files at the post office level. Likewise, if you want users to run the Windows client *only from the network*, decompress the files at the post office level and then delete the compressed files. This will prevent users from installing the client on their hard drives. If you want users to have a choice between either a workstation installation or a local installation, decompress the Windows client files in the post office OFWIN40 subdirectory and leave the compressed files in the OFWIN40\SETUP post office subdirectory.**

TIP

DECOMPRESSING THE WINDOWS CLIENT IN THE POST OFFICE

You use the SETUPWIN.EXE program (located in the post office directory) to decompress the client software. When you decompress the client in the post office, you will need to run SETUPWIN with the /A option. (*A* stands for "Administrator.") When you run SETUPWIN /A, you will see the options shown in Figure 5.1, which depicts a GroupWise network installation screen.

FIGURE 5.1

Network Installation

```
┌─────────────────────────────────────────────────────────────┐
│ ▢              GroupWise Server Install                      │
├─────────────────────────────────────────────────────────────┤
│                                                               │
│   ┌──────────────────┐   Installs all GroupWise files to a   │
│   │ Standard Install │   hard drive.                         │
│   └──────────────────┘   Disk space required:   17 M         │
│                                                               │
│   ┌──────────────────┐   Allows you to select which files to │
│   │  Custom Install  │   install and to specify the          │
│   └──────────────────┘   destination locations.              │
│                          Disk space required:   12 M to 18 M │
│                                                               │
│   ┌──────────────────┐   Installs files for minimal          │
│   │     Minimum      │   operation.                          │
│   └──────────────────┘   Disk space required:   12 M         │
│                                                               │
│          ┌──────────┐        ┌──────────┐                     │
│          │   Exit   │        │   Help   │                     │
│          └──────────┘        └──────────┘                     │
└─────────────────────────────────────────────────────────────┘
```

SETUPWIN /A must be run from a Windows workstation. As the administrator, you should log in to the file server from a Windows workstation. Then, make sure you have supervisory rights to the post office directory. Also, verify that the drive mappings from this workstation to the post office directory are the same mappings that the GroupWise users will use. The drive mapping to the network's shared code directory is especially important. (*Shared code* is a core set of files shared by many Novell applications. It is explained at length later in this chapter.)

If a copy of shared code for other Novell applications, such as WordPerfect for Windows or PerfectOffice, already exists on the file server, you should use the Custom installation option so that you can install the GroupWise shared code to the existing network shared code directory.

SETUPWIN /A decompresses the client files in the *<post office>*\OFWIN40\SETUP directory. SETUPWIN /A does not enable the local workstation to run GroupWise. It does not create a program group or icons, and it does not set up configuration files, such as a .BIF file or .INI files.

SETTING UP THE WINDOWS WORKSTATIONS

Once you have decompressed the GroupWise client at the post office level, either the administrator or the GroupWise users must run the SETUPWIN program while in Windows to set up the client at the individual workstations. When you run SETUPWIN to enable the client at the workstation level, you do not use the /A option.

NOTE

If the client files are not decompressed at the post office level, users can still run SETUPWIN, but they won't have the option to do a workstation installation. They will have to install the client to their hard drives.

The recommended hardware requirements for the Windows client are a 486/33 with 8MB RAM. The amount of required hard disk space depends on the installation method you use.

When the administrator or users install GroupWise by running SETUPWIN, they will be presented with the installation options illustrated in Figure 5.2.

FIGURE 5.2

Installation Screen

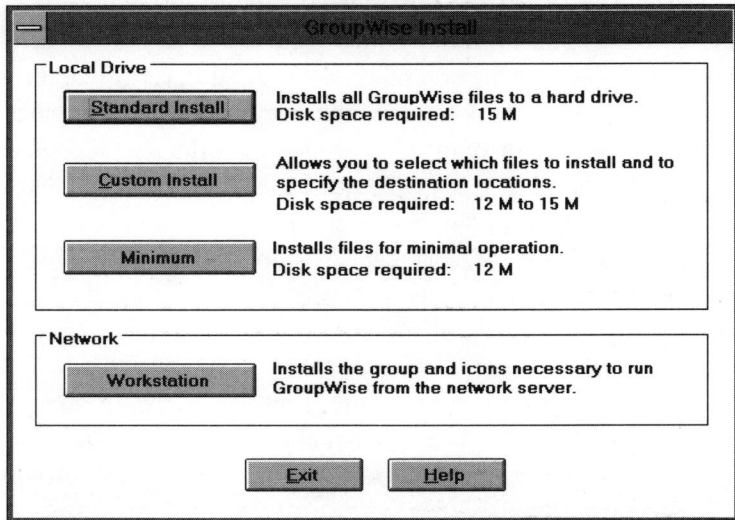

GroupWise Install

Local Drive

Standard Install   Installs all GroupWise files to a hard drive.
Disk space required: 15 M

Custom Install   Allows you to select which files to install and to
specify the destination locations.
Disk space required: 12 M to 15 M

Minimum   Installs files for minimal operation.
Disk space required: 12 M

Network

Workstation   Installs the group and icons necessary to run
GroupWise from the network server.

Exit   **Help**

Standard Install   Configures the client to run from the hard drive, and places the program files in default locations. It also sets up the program group and GroupWise icons. A standard installation requires 18MB of disk space.

Custom Install   Configures the client to run from the local hard drive, and gives the user the choice of which files to install and where to install them. It also sets up the program group and GroupWise icons.

Minimum   Installs only the files that are absolutely necessary to run GroupWise. A minimum installation installs the GroupWise program files, the shared program files (shared code), the Outside In viewers (used to view file attachments), and the TrueType font files. It does not install other components such as the Speller, Thesaurus, QuickFinder, and help files. The Minimum option also sets up the program group and GroupWise icons. The minimum installation option requires 11MB of hard disk space.

Workstation   Configures the client to run from the network. This option creates a program group and GroupWise icons, and it sets up the necessary configuration files. This option uses no disk space.

NOTE

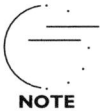

The term "workstation installation" is misleading. The term refers to setting up a GroupWise user's workstation to run the client program from the post office client directory on the file server. However, when you perform a workstation installation, you do not copy the client files to the workstation's hard drive. Rather, you set up the client application so that it can be run at the workstation from the post office client directory.

All of these installations will give the user the option of running the QuickTour, a demonstration program that can be run after the installation is complete. The main menu of QuickTour is shown in Figure 5.3. I strongly recommend that new GroupWise users take advantage of QuickTour. The program takes about ten minutes to go through, and it is an excellent way to familiarize them with GroupWise.

FIGURE 5.3

QuickTour Screen

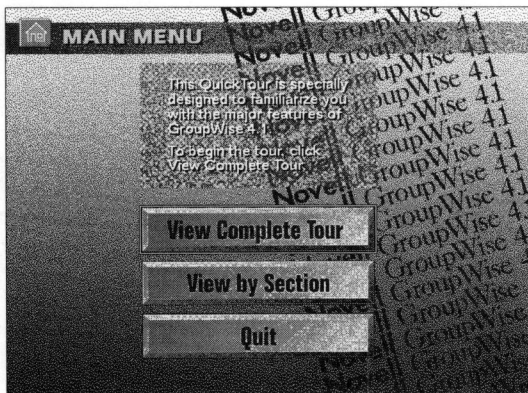

HOW THE WINDOWS CLIENT WORKS

The top portion of the Windows client screen is shown in Figure 5.4.

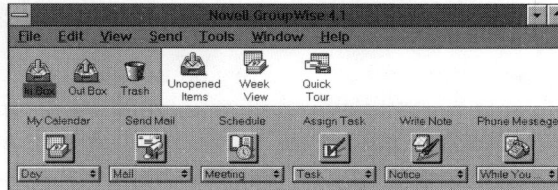

The Windows client uses three main types of files: GroupWise program files, shared code files, and configuration files. When you opt for standard installation, the GroupWise program files are stored in the OFWIN40 directory, the shared code files are stored in the WPC20 directory, and the configuration files are installed in various other locations, such as the Windows directory.

GroupWise Files (OFWIN40 Directory)

These files are specific to GroupWise. The files in this directory include the GroupWise Windows client executable file (OFWIN40.EXE) and its supporting files. (The name OFWIN40 is derived from WordPerfect Office 4.0 for Windows, a precursor of GroupWise.)

Shared Code Files (WPC20 Directory)

Shared code files (also known as PerfectFit Technology) are files and executable programs that are used by several Novell applications, such as WordPerfect 6.1 for Windows, Quattro Pro for Windows, and Presentations for Windows. Shared code includes Dynamic Link Library (DLL) files that are common to those Novell/WordPerfect applications that are written to run with Windows. The Speller, Thesaurus, and QuickFinder are examples of shared code programs.

At the end of this chapter, I discuss some techniques for managing shared code and for troubleshooting shared code problems.

Configuration Files

The main GroupWise configuration file is the Binary Initialization File, commonly known as the ".BIF" file. It replaces the .INI files used in previous versions of GroupWise. There are two kinds of .BIF files for Novell applications—the network .BIF controlled by the system administrator and the private .BIFs controlled by the individual users. The network administrator can establish user preferences in the .BIF and choose to override settings in users' private .BIFs. The .BIF files are shared by the Novell/WordPerfect applications that use shared code. The .BIF file will be discussed in more detail in the section on shared code at the end of this chapter.

Environment files are another type of configuration file. These files have the .ENV file extension. The environment files contain startup switches, which are read when the program is launched. The Windows client uses the OF_OF_.ENV file, which is stored in the *<post office>*\OFWIN40 directory. The shared code files also have an environment file: SH_SH_.ENV. The switches stored in the shared code environment file are *session specific*. That means the switches are stored in memory when the first Novell/WordPerfect application is loaded, and they affect any subsequent Novell/WordPerfect programs that are loaded during that session.

The startup switches used by the Windows client are the same as those used by the DOS client. I will say more about the startup switches a little later in this chapter.

The GroupWise DOS Client

Figure 5.5 shows a view of the DOS client.

FIGURE 5.5

GroupWise DOS Client

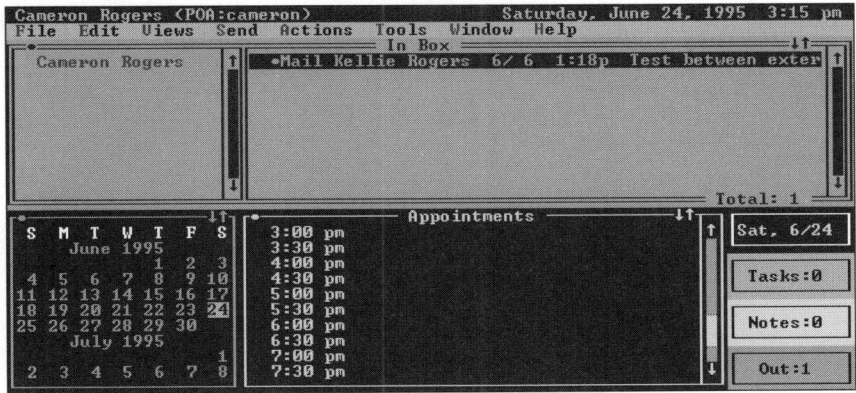

The GroupWise client for DOS is a highly functional client with a character-based user interface. There are several reasons why the DOS client is handy to have around.

> It's fast on 386 and low-end 486 computers or on machines with limited RAM.

> It's easy to run from the command line.

> It takes less disk space than the Windows client.

As I explained earlier, the DOS client is decompressed at the domain and post office levels. The administrator or the users run the SETUPDOS application from the post office directory to set up the individual workstations.

RUNNING SETUPDOS.EXE

You can run SETUPDOS.EXE from the post office to set up the DOS client on workstation computers. SETUPDOS performs these tasks:

> modifies the path information in the AUTOEXEC.BAT file;

> modifies files and buffers settings in the CONFIG.SYS file, if necessary;

> configures Notify, if desired;

> copies the DOS client files to the local drive, if desired;

> allows for the conversion of WordPerfect Office 3.x data, such as calendar and schedule items, if the organization is changing over from WordPerfect Office 3.x.

As an administrator, you should run SETUPDOS a couple of times so that you can answer users' questions. For the most part, however, the setup routine for the DOS client is easy enough that you could simply print out an instruction sheet and distribute it to the GroupWise users in the system.

Startup Switches Used by the DOS and Windows Clients

Technically, both the Windows GroupWise client and the DOS GroupWise client are DOS-based applications. They share many common startup switches. As an administrator, you should know how to use the startup switches in Table 5.1. These are the switches you will typically use for troubleshooting. You will often see these switches in environment files.

TABLE 5.1	STARTUP SWITCH	DESCRIPTION
Startup Switches	**/HOME-***directory* or **/PH-***directory*	Points to the user's post office. It is used extensively for testing and troubleshooting. (The /HOME switch only works with the Windows client. The /PH switch works with both the Windows and DOS clients.) Example: OF.EXE/PH-J:\POST1
	/D-*directory*	Instructs GroupWise to write temporary files to a specific directory. This is often helpful for testing and troubleshooting. Example: *OFWIN /D-C:\TEMP*
	/@U-*user ID*	Lets you specify a user ID to log in as a certain user. The switch is intended to allow a user to log in to his or her GroupWise mailbox from someone else's computer. It is often used by administrators for troubleshooting purposes. Example: OFWIN /@U-MARY The command OFWIN /@U-? will prompt for the user ID when GroupWise is launched.
	/NT-*network type*	Specifies the network type. See the GroupWise Reference manual for the values that correspond with different network operating systems. The number for Novell NetWare is 1. Example: /NT-1 specifies a Novell NetWare network.

T A B L E 5.1	STARTUP SWITCH	DESCRIPTION
Startup Switches *(continued)*	/NI-*directory* (Windows client only)	Lets you specify the location of the public .BIF file.
	/PI-*directory* (Windows client only)	Lets you specify the location of the private .BIF file.
	/WPC-*directory* (Windows client only)	Lets you specify the location of the shared code files.

For a complete list of startup switches, see the GroupWise Reference manual for the type of client you are using.

Startup switches can be located:

▸ In an environment file (.ENV)

▸ In a DOS environment variable

▸ On the command line

If duplicate switches exist, the following rules apply:

▸ .ENV files overrule the Windows Registration database (REG.DAT file). This rule applies to only the Windows client.

▸ .ENV variables overrule switches in an environment file.

▸ Command line switches overrule switches found anywhere else.

Macintosh GroupWise Client

Figure 5.6 shows you the Macintosh GroupWise client's screen.

FIGURE 5.6

Macintosh Client

You have two options for setting up the Macintosh client. You will recall from Chapter 4 that there is no option for installing Macintosh client software at the domain level. However, you can install the Macintosh client from an installation folder on the network, or else you can install from the diskettes directly to the Macintosh workstation's hard drive.

Creating an installation folder makes installation easier and less time-consuming, especially if you plan to have users do the installation themselves. I recommend that you create an OFMAC40 directory in each post office directory to serve as the installation folder. This gives users easy access to the installation folder. After you create the folder, drag the contents of each client diskette into the folder.

Although it is possible to run the Macintosh client software from the post office, the program is really intended to be a local client. If you nevertheless decide to allow Mac users to run the client from the post office, you must give the users more rights to the post office directory than are normally required for the Windows or DOS client.

NOTE

The README.AD file, installed to the domain directory during GroupWise installation, contains a complete listing of the network rights required by each client application for the post office directories. You will find here a list of the additional rights needed by the Macintosh client.

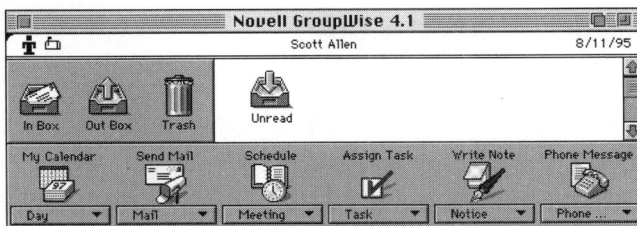

The Macintosh users may wish to install the Macintosh client on a network drive if they do not have sufficient disk space on the startup disk.

Managing Shared Code

A complete discussion of shared code would be beyond the scope of this book. However, I'll give you a thumbnail explanation of shared code here and then refer you to some resources you can consult for more information.

The textbook definition of "shared code" is: a core set of program files and dynamic link libraries (DLLs) that are used by Novell Applications Group products (including WordPerfect) and that are written to run with Microsoft Windows. See Figure 5.7.

F I G U R E 5.7

Shared Code

GroupWise
Files

C:\OFWIN40

WPWin 6.1
Files

C:\WPWIN

C:\WPC20

Shared Code
Files

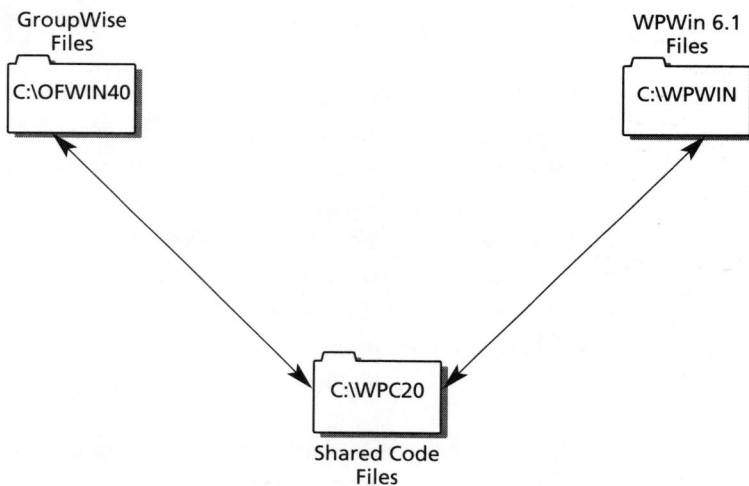

Shared code allows applications to share functionality, which reduces their disk space and memory requirements. Shared code also helps to provide a common look and feel among Novell Applications Group products. The Speller, Thesaurus, File Manager, QuickFinder, and Macro facility are all examples of shared code applications. If these shared code components are loaded by one Novell application, the next Novell application loaded will use the code already stored in memory.

If GroupWise is the only Novell application you use, shared code management won't be an issue. However, if you use GroupWise along with other Novell applications (such as WordPerfect), you will need a basic understanding of how shared code works and how different versions of shared code can affect your programs. When managing shared code, the biggest challenge to an administrator is keeping track of the different versions of shared code.

SHARED CODE VERSIONS

There are two major versions of shared code used by Novell applications—version 1.x and version 2.x. Programs that run using shared code 1.x cannot run using shared code 2.x, and vice versa. Shared code 1.x applications include WordPerfect 5.x for Windows and WordPerfect Office 4.0. A document containing a complete list of Novell applications and their corresponding shared code versions can be found in SCVERS.TT on the accompanying CD-ROM.

Within the two main versions, there are sub-versions. For example, programs that use shared code 2.x may ship with shared code sub-version 2.1, 2.2, or 2.3.

IMPORTANT

Within each main version, a program written for a lower version of shared code—for example shared code 2.1—can use later versions of shared code—such as version 2.3. However, programs written for a higher version of shared code will *not* run properly with older versions of the shared code.

PREVENTING SHARED CODE PROBLEMS

The easiest way to avoid problems with shared code is to make sure you do not copy an older version of shared code over a newer version. Installation programs automatically check the date on already-installed code, and they never write over newer code. However, it is not uncommon for administrators to copy older code over newer code accidentally when they are attempting to consolidate shared code into one directory.

Shared code for a certain application may contain files specific to that application, as well as shared files. For example, GroupWise ships with Software Compatibility Corporation (SCC) Outside In viewer files, which are used to view file attachments. These files are specific to GroupWise but are nevertheless installed in the shared code directory.

TIP

If a new shared code version is released with a product that you support, don't delete the old shared code files in the shared code directory before loading the new code.

Instead of deleting old shared code before loading a newer version of the shared code, you should install the latest shared code in the same directory and let the installation program *blend* the shared code files together. If you delete the contents of the shared code directory before installation, you may delete the application-specific files that will not be replaced by the shared code that ships with the product you are installing. For example, suppose you already have GroupWise on the network and you decide to install WordPerfect 6.1 for Windows. If you delete the contents of the shared code directory used by GroupWise, the WordPerfect installation will not replace the GroupWise viewer files that were deleted.

If you are supporting multiple Novell Applications Group products on the network, Novell recommends that you use a multiproduct shared code directory. The best way to create a multiproduct shared code directory is to install the programs in *layers* from oldest to newest, allowing each successive program you install to overwrite the files in the shared code directory.

This procedure ensures that the newest shared code is being used, that all supplementary files for each application are installed, and that a valid set of configuration files exists.

TROUBLESHOOTING PROBLEMS WITH SHARED CODE

When troubleshooting shared code problems, it is crucial that you know which version of shared code is running. The first Novell Applications Group product loaded during a Windows session will determine which version of shared code is in use. That application will load its own version of shared code into memory, along with the startup switches contained in its SH_SH_.ENV file. When you launch another Novell application, that program recognizes that shared code has already been loaded into memory, and it *hooks* into that shared code. This can mean trouble when the two programs load shared code from different locations, when the shared code is not the exact same version, or when the switches in the SH_SH_.ENV file are different.

For example, suppose I launch Windows and run WordPerfect for Windows 6.1 from the network. Then I load GroupWise from my hard drive. GroupWise will try to use the shared code that is stored in memory. There's no problem if the shared code version is the same *and* if the shared code for both programs comes from the same location. But if the programs run shared code from different locations, the first program to load controls which version of shared code will be used. When that happens, you may notice some of these problems occurring:

▶ Programs may not launch correctly and will generate shared code error messages, such as "File not found."

▶ Programs may run, but features and preferences may disappear and reappear at random.

Occasionally, programs that load shared code may load the code without your knowing it. For example, if PerfectOffice has placed the Desktop Application Director (DAD) in your Windows startup group, shared code will be loaded into memory whenever you run Windows. GroupWise Notify is another application that is often loaded at startup. When troubleshooting shared code problems, check the Windows Task List to make sure that a shared code application is not already running.

An important skill you need to troubleshoot shared code problems is the ability to find where configuration files point to shared code. Here are some locations where you might find pointers to shared code.

Windows REG.DAT File   When a program is installed that uses shared code, the install process writes the location of the shared code to the Windows Registration database. Run REGEDIT /V, locate the SHWin20 entry, and check the field labeled Preferred to make sure that the path is pointing to the correct location.

.ENV Files   .ENV files are environment files that store startup switches for Windows-based programs. Startup switches pointing to the location of shared code can be included in .ENV files. .ENV switches will override the information stored in REG.DAT.

.ENV Variables   An environment variable stored in the AUTOEXEC.BAT file or in a login script will override switches stored in the REG.DAT file and in the .ENV file.

Command Line   The /WPC startup switch used on the command line will override all other locations of shared code pointers. You should use this switch from the command line only when you are troubleshooting.

BINARY INITIALIZATION FILE (BIF)

A Binary Initialization File (BIF) is a configuration file that is shared by Novell Applications Group applications that are written for Windows. The .BIF file stores application preferences. There are two kinds of .BIF files: the public .BIF stored on the network for network installations of Novell applications, and the private .BIF file, usually stored in the Windows directory. The public .BIF is the master .BIF stored on the network. It stores configuration values that are common for all users. The private .BIF is stored in the user's Windows directory (or in another directory that can be specified with a switch). The filename for the private .BIF is WPCSET.BIF. Private .BIFs store individual users' preferences and settings.

Occasionally, users get strange error messages when they launch applications. Or sometimes applications fail to load at all. While not always the case, these problems may result from corruption of a .BIF file. If you encounter a problem relating to shared code (or receive related error messages) and cannot find a solution, locate the user's WPCSET.BIF and rename it WPCSET.OLD. Then try to launch the program again. The program will create a new WPCSET.BIF file. If it loads correctly, you've probably found the answer to your problem. If the problem still occurs, rename the WPCSET.OLD file WPCSET.BIF again and continue troubleshooting. Each time a new WPCSET.BIF file is generated, the user will have to reset many of his or her application preferences.

SHARED CODE TROUBLESHOOTING CHECKLIST

Here's a troubleshooting checklist to help you figure out shared code problems:

1 • Find out where the shared code for each program loads from.

2 • If you maintain a common shared code directory on the network for multiple Novell applications, make sure you install the programs in order from oldest to newest. This ensures that all supplemental files for each application are located in the shared code directory and that the latest versions of the shared DLLs are being used.

3 • Use the /WPC switch from the command line to override any other pointers that may be correct. If the program loads correctly with the /WPC switch, you will know that there must be an incorrect pointer somewhere.

4 • Find a four leaf clover, throw salt over your shoulder, and then cross your fingers.

NOTE

Using the /WPC switch from the command line is recommended as a troubleshooting option only. It is not recommended that this be used as a permanent fix to a shared code problem.

Here are some tips for finding out where shared code is loading from:

1 • Run REGEDIT /V and check the SHWin2x entry. Make sure the Preferred statement points to the right location for the shared code.

2 • Click on Help, About... from within the Novell application to check the location and version of shared code that has been loaded into memory.

3 • Make sure programs that use shared code have not been loaded without your knowledge (for example, from the Windows startup group). Run the Windows Task List to make sure no programs have been loaded that you aren't aware of.

4 • Check the SH_SH_.ENV file for a /WPC switch pointing to a shared code location.

5 • Check the OF_OF_.ENV file in the post office directory for startup switches.

6 • Check the program's icon properties for a /WPC switch in the command line.

The accompanying CD-ROM contains a utility program developed by the GroupWise support team. This utility, GSC.EXE, should be copied to the hard drive and then executed from within Windows. It will locate and identify shared code problems and recommend methods for solving them. This utility should be in every GroupWise administrator's bag of tricks.

NOTE

The file on the CD-ROM is GSC41.EXE. This is a self-extracting zipped file that decompresses into GSC.EXE and several supplemental files. Copy these files to a directory on your hard drive, and then run GSC.EXE from Windows.

The following documents contained on the CD-ROM that comes with this book will help you prevent and troubleshoot shared code problems:

- ▸ BIF_OVER.TT — A Binary Information File (.BIF) overview written by the GroupWise support team.

- ▸ SHCODE.TT — An overview of shared code written by the GroupWise support team.

- ▸ GPFTROUB.TT — The GroupWise support team's suggestions for troubleshooting General Protection Faults with the GroupWise Windows client.

Summary

In this chapter, you learned about the GroupWise client programs and how they are implemented. You also learned about managing shared code, and I showed you some techniques for preventing shared code problems.

Chapter 6 will discuss GroupWise post office in depth. I will give you a detailed explanation of the post office message store and post office servers.

Managing a GroupWise Post Office

In Chapter 6, I cover a wide variety of topics on the subject of GroupWise post office administration.

As a GroupWise administrator, you will need to understand how post office security works. It will be important for you to know which settings in GroupWise provide the highest level of security for users' mailboxes. In this chapter, you will learn the differences between high-security and low-security settings.

A GroupWise administrator also needs a solid understanding of the post office message store. In Chapter 6, I explain exactly how messages are stored in a post office. I also present detailed diagrams here that will help you visualize message delivery in a post office.

Finally, I discuss the advantages of implementing a post office server. The post office server handles message delivery within a post office so that the client does not have to do all of the work. This chapter explains how to use threshold settings to balance the workload between the post office server and the client. I use diagrams to illustrate how message delivery works within a post office when a post office server is used instead of the client.

When you initially install GroupWise and create your system's first post office, there are two important default settings that you should be aware of. First, post office security is set by default at Low. As you will see in this chapter, the low-security setting is not very secure unless the users in the post office use passwords for their mailboxes. Second, the post office message delivery mode is automatically set at *Server Never*. That default setting means that the client software handles all message delivery within the post office. The Server Never setting also prevents mail from being delivered outside of the post office. This setting would only be useful in a system that consists of a single GroupWise domain with one post office. I will discuss these default settings in this chapter and tell you how you can change them.

Post Office Security

When you add a user to a GroupWise system, GroupWise Admin creates a unique *user record* for that user. The user record contains information about that user's GroupWise user ID and network login ID. The user record distinguishes that user from all other users in the post office. When users run the GroupWise client and open their mailboxes, the system scans the user records to determine which mailboxes to open. Ideally, GroupWise identifies users by automatically detecting their network login IDs and matching those IDs with users in a given post office.

If for some reason GroupWise cannot find a user's network ID to determine whose mailbox to open, it will return a "Network ID Not Found" error message. To get around that problem, a startup switch can be used to specify the network ID to be used. The /LA-*network login ID* switch (where *network login ID* is the user's network login ID) tells the GroupWise Windows client to use a specific network ID to identify which mailbox should be opened. (The /@N-*network login ID* switch is used for the DOS client.)

You can tell GroupWise to identify the mailbox based on a GroupWise user ID rather than the network login ID. The switch /@U-*user ID* (where *user ID* is the user's GroupWise user ID) tells GroupWise to open the mailbox that corresponds to a GroupWise user ID instead of a network ID.

A more common use of the switch /@U-*user ID* is to gain access to a mailbox from a workstation that has been logged into in someone else's name. For example, if I'm at a workstation that has been logged into the network under another person's name, I can run GroupWise with the /@U-*user ID* switch to access my personal GroupWise mailbox. Obviously, this switch can be abused if mailboxes have not been protected with security settings and passwords.

The post office security setting determines the circumstances in which a user's mailbox can be accessed. GroupWise has two security settings: Low and High. See Figure 6.1. When the security is set to Low, GroupWise becomes very trusting. When it encounters the /@U-*user ID* switch, it assumes that the person using the switch is really the user identified by the user ID. When GroupWise security is set to High, GroupWise becomes more wary. It makes the person using the switch go to greater lengths to prove access to the mailbox is warranted.

Post Office Security Setting

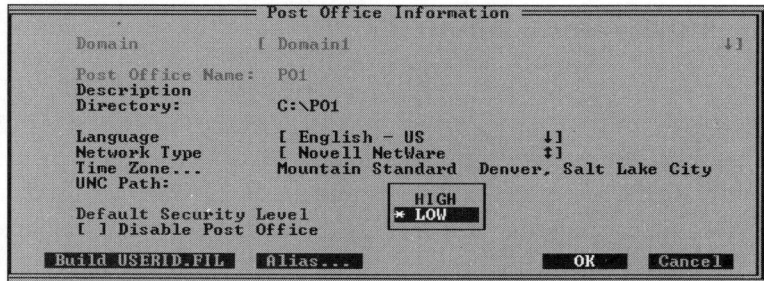

```
═════════════════════════ Post Office Information ═════════════════════════
   Domain              [ Domain1                                         ↓]

   Post Office Name:    P01
   Description
   Directory:           C:\P01

   Language            [ English - US             ↓]
   Network Type        [ Novell NetWare           ↕]
   Time Zone...         Mountain Standard  Denver, Salt Lake City
   UNC Path:
                                          ┌─────────┐
                                          │  HIGH   │
   Default Security Level                 │▪ LOW    │
   [ ] Disable Post Office                └─────────┘

   ▐ Build USERID.FIL ▌   ▐ Alias... ▌              ▐  OK  ▌   ▐ Cancel ▌
```

LOW SECURITY

When the post office security is set to Low, the /@U-*user ID* switch will let anyone access the mailbox, *unless* the mailbox's owner has used a password to protect the mailbox.

For example, suppose Mike—a GroupWise user—logs in to NetWare with his network user name, MIKE. If he launches GroupWise without the /@U-*user ID* switch, GroupWise checks the network login ID, matches his network ID (MIKE) with his mailbox, and opens that mailbox.

Suppose Mike sits next to Cindy and, for some reason, he would like to read the contents of Cindy's mailbox. He knows that her GroupWise ID is CINDY, so he launches GroupWise with the /@U-CINDY switch. If the post office security level is Low, GroupWise would let him into Cindy's mailbox. As far as GroupWise is concerned, he is Cindy. He has complete access to her mailbox, and he can do anything he wants in GroupWise as Cindy. He can even send mail in her name.

Suppose instead that Cindy is a cautious GroupWise user and wants to protect her mailbox. Therefore, she goes into GroupWise preferences and sets a password for her mailbox. Now Mike is out of luck. If he tries to run GroupWise with the /@U-CINDY switch, GroupWise will require Mike to enter Cindy's password before he can get into her mailbox. In effect, by setting a password, Cindy has made her mailbox high security, even though the rest of her post office is set at low security.

In summary, if post office security is low, anybody can get into other people's mailboxes with the /@U-*user ID* switch unless passwords have been set on mailboxes. A password on a mailbox gives that mailbox high security.

HIGH SECURITY

If the post office security is set to High and no password has been set on a mailbox, only the owner of the mailbox can gain access to that mailbox. Under those circumstances, access will be granted only if GroupWise can validate the owner's identity by querying the network. If the network detection fails, even the true owner of the mailbox may be denied access. If post office security is set to High, the /@U-*user ID* switch cannot provide access to a mailbox that has no password.

If a mailbox *has* a password and security is set at High, GroupWise handles the /@U-*user ID* switch differently. In that case, GroupWise will allow access if the person using the switch is able to enter the correct password.

Suppose that Mike's and Cindy's post office security is set to High, and Cindy has not protected her mailbox with a password. Mike, who is as nosy as ever, wants to know what's in Cindy's mailbox. He tries to run GroupWise with the /@U-CINDY switch. GroupWise would recognize that the request for access was not coming from Cindy's workstation, and it would deny access because Cindy has not set a password on her mailbox. (The actual response GroupWise gives is "GroupWise Error [D01B] Access to GroupWise has been denied.")

If, instead, Cindy had set a password for her mailbox and Mike was able to enter that password, GroupWise would allow Mike to access Cindy's mailbox from his workstation.

There's one other possible scenario you should be aware of as you deal with GroupWise security settings. When users set passwords for their mailboxes, they get a check-box option called *Password Applies Only to Other Users*. See Figure 6.2. When a user selects this option, GroupWise does not ask for a password if the network query validates the user's identity. If the network query does not confirm the user's identity, it will prompt the user for the mailbox password.

FIGURE 6.2

Set Password Dialog Box

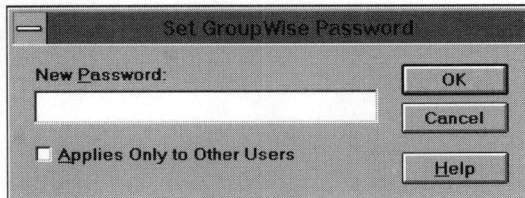

Set GroupWise Password

New Password:

[   ]   OK

                           Cancel

☐ Applies Only to Other Users
                           Help

Suppose that Cindy doesn't want to be asked for her mailbox password every time she runs the GroupWise client, so she selects the *Password Applies Only to Other Users* option when she chooses her password. Now when someone tries to access Cindy's mailbox, GroupWise simply checks to make sure that the workstation is logged in under Cindy's name. If it is, GroupWise will open the mailbox. In this scenario, Mike could gain access to Cindy's mailbox if he were able to log in to the network as Cindy.

The most secure GroupWise setting (assuming post office security has been set to High) is to leave the *Password Applies Only to Other Users* option unselected. While Cindy would need to enter her password every time she runs GroupWise, this setting would prevent others from accessing her mailbox—even if they were able to log in to the network as her. If Cindy were to leave her workstation unattended while she was still logged in to the network, someone else would be required to enter her password in order to access her mailbox.

Table 6.1 summarizes post office security settings. This table describes the various security settings when the *Password Applies Only to Other Users* option has been selected.

| TABLE 6.1

Post Office Security Settings	POST OFFICE SECURITY	RESULT OF NET-WORK AUTO-DETECTION	PASSWORD SET	RESULT WHEN I@U-*USER ID* SWITCH IS USED
	Low	ID not validated	No	Access granted to everybody.
	Low	ID validated	No	Access granted to everybody.
	Low	ID not validated	Yes	Password must be entered before access is granted.
	Low	ID validated	Yes	People at other workstations must enter password before access is granted.
	High	ID not validated	No	Access denied.
	High	ID validated	No	Access granted.
	High	ID not validated	Yes	Password must be entered before access is granted.
	High	ID validated	Yes	Access is granted without prompting for password.

If you decide to set your post office security to High, you should encourage users to set passwords for their mailboxes. This may seem like an unnecessary precaution, but if the network ID validation should fail for some reason, users who have not set passwords would be denied access to their own mailboxes. If you should ever encounter that problem as an administrator, you have the following three options:

▸ Set passwords for those users by using GroupWise Admin, and run the Check GroupWise program (often called OFCHECK or OFCHECK.EXE) with the Reset User Preferences option selected. See Chapter 19 for more information on OFCHECK.

▸ Temporarily set the post office security to Low so the users can enter GroupWise and set their own passwords.

▸ Figure out why network detection is not working and resolve that problem.

The bottom line is this: Encourage users who are concerned about security to use common sense. Tell them to make their network and GroupWise passwords obscure, and stress how important it is to keep passwords confidential. Suggest that they do not to leave their workstations unattended while they are logged in. If they follow these rules, their mailboxes will remain secure.

The Post Office Message Store

In Chapter 2, I gave you an overview of how the message store works. Figure 2.8 showed the databases and directories where the different parts of a typical GroupWise message are stored. You will recall that a post office message store consists of user databases, message databases, and a file attachments directory. These three components work together to store the GroupWise messages in a post office. One big advantage of having messages stored in databases is that a specific message only needs to be stored one time in the network. The message is stored in the form of a record in a database (unlike file-based e-mail systems, where messages are stored in an individual file or files). All recipients of that message have pointers to the message. This means that even though a message may be delivered to 50 users in the post office, the message and its file attachments are only stored once.

Now that you know more about a post office's physical structure and properties, I will discuss the message store's directories and databases in more detail.

USER DATABASES

The post office contains a subdirectory called OFUSER (which stands for "Office User"—a name carried over from WordPerfect Office). An example of an OFUSER subdirectory is shown in Figure 6.3. This directory contains a database for every user assigned to a post office. Those user databases are also commonly referred to as the users' mailboxes. The naming convention for a user database is USER*xxx*.DB, where *xxx* is the user's *file ID*. The file ID is usually *hashed* (generated by an algorithm), but it can be controlled by the administrator. If you, as the administrator, want to assign specific file IDs, you can use a WordPerfect Office Notebook file or an ASCII file to import the information.

F I G U R E   6.3

User Databases in the OFUSER Subdirectory

user1dw.db	23552	6/24/95	4:16:00pm
user22p.db	23552	6/24/95	4:16:48pm
user6id.db	23552	6/24/95	4:16:26pm
user6rw.db	27648	6/24/95	4:15:44pm
user77u.db	23552	6/24/95	4:16:56pm
user8k3.db	23552	6/24/95	4:15:52pm
usercby.db	23552	6/24/95	4:16:18pm
userepw.db	23552	6/24/95	4:17:28pm
usergfe.db	23552	6/24/95	4:16:08pm
useri5w.db	23552	6/24/95	4:17:20pm
userlkv.db	23552	6/24/95	4:16:38pm
usernyh.db	23552	6/24/95	4:17:36pm
userrn9.db	23552	6/24/95	4:17:12pm
users3a.db	23552	6/24/95	4:17:44pm
uservu5.db	23552	6/24/95	4:17:04pm
userx6r.db	25600	6/24/95	4:17:48pm

User databases are not automatically created when you create user objects in GroupWise Admin. A user database is created for a user when one of two events takes place: (1) the first time that the user runs the client, or (2) the first time a message is sent to that user.

User databases contain the header information for messages. The header information includes the data in the To:, From:, CC:, BC:, and Subject: fields, as well as the date and time the message was created. The user databases do not contain the actual messages. Along with message header information, user databases also contain pointers to the actual messages, which are stored in message databases. When GroupWise users run the client software and open their In Box, Out Box, or Trash, they see a list of the messages headers from their user databases. When a user opens a message in the In Box, Out Box, or Trash, the user accesses the message records in the message databases and the file attachments in the attachments directory.

MESSAGE DATABASES

Another component of a post office's structure is the OFMSG subdirectory. (OFMSG is another carryover from WordPerfect Office. It's short for "Office Message.") An example of an OFMSG subdirectory is shown in Figure 6.4. This subdirectory contains the message databases. The message databases in a post office are named MSG*xx*.DB, where *xx* represents numbers from 0–24. There are usually 25 message databases in a post office. Each user in the post office is assigned to a specific message database (e.g., MSG16.DB) for the messages that he or she *sends*. As new users are added to a post office, GroupWise assigns users to message databases in a way that keeps the size of the message databases roughly balanced.

F I G U R E 6.4

Message Databases

msg15.db	40960	6/24/95	4:17:48pm
msg23.db	36864	6/5/95	3:42:58pm
msg24.db	36864	5/18/95	9:01:26pm
msg4.db	36864	6/6/95	1:02:38pm
msg7.db	36864	5/18/95	7:56:28pm

Here is an example of how the message store works. Suppose GroupWise user Kellie sends a message to 50 users in her post office. That message is stored as a record in the message database assigned to Kellie. Kellie and the 50 recipients of the message receive pointers in their user databases directing them to the message in Kellie's message database. Even though all of the messages Kellie sends are stored in one message database, all of the users in the post office will be able to read the messages stored in that database. Another way to think about this is that all messages in a specific user's Out Box are stored in the message database assigned to that user.

Also, because there are only 25 message databases, several users are often assigned to the same message database.

Understanding how message databases function will be very helpful as you troubleshoot users' problems. If some users in a post office can't access the messages in their Out Box, but most of the users in the post office aren't having any difficulty, it's possible that the users experiencing problems are all assigned to the same message database. Or, if messages sent from certain individuals cannot be accessed by the recipients, that could also indicate a problem with a specific message database. If so, that message database may need to be repaired.

Because there are only 25 message databases to handle all of the messages sent by all of the users in a post office, message databases can grow very large. To prevent message databases from becoming too huge and unwieldy, large messages and file attachments are stored in a different part of the message store—the attachments subdirectory.

THE ATTACHMENTS SUBDIRECTORY

Messages and file attachments that exceed 2K in size are stored in the attachments subdirectory. The attachments subdirectory in the post office is named OFFILES (another carryover from WordPerfect Office, where the directory name was "Office Files"). See Figure 6.5. Messages and files are stored in the OFFILES subdirectory as individual files. They are not stored in databases. These files are encrypted with the GroupWise encryption technology. The files cannot be viewed with standard document viewers, and they cannot be opened in other programs. They are every bit as secure as the messages stored in the databases. For added security, filenames for the files in this directory do not reflect the files' contents or origins.

OFFILES Directory

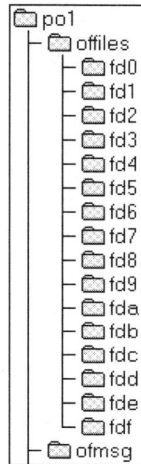

```
📁 po1
  └ 📁 offiles
      ├ 📁 fd0
      ├ 📁 fd1
      ├ 📁 fd2
      ├ 📁 fd3
      ├ 📁 fd4
      ├ 📁 fd5
      ├ 📁 fd6
      ├ 📁 fd7
      ├ 📁 fd8
      ├ 📁 fd9
      ├ 📁 fda
      ├ 📁 fdb
      ├ 📁 fdc
      ├ 📁 fdd
      ├ 📁 fde
      └ 📁 fdf
  └ 📁 ofmsg
```

When a message or file goes into the OFFILES directory, GroupWise places a pointer in the appropriate message database indicating that the message or file is being stored in OFFILES.

MESSAGE FLOW WITHIN A POST OFFICE

It's time for one of those message flow diagrams I have been promising you. This diagram should help you better understand how the user databases, message databases, and the file attachments directory work together.

In the following diagram, Figure 6.6, a user sends a message to three other users in the post office. This is a very basic example of GroupWise message flow, in that the client software handles all of the delivery of messages. You will see that message flows become much more complex later when I add the post office server and message server components to them.

FIGURE 6.6

*Message Flow in Server
Never Mode*

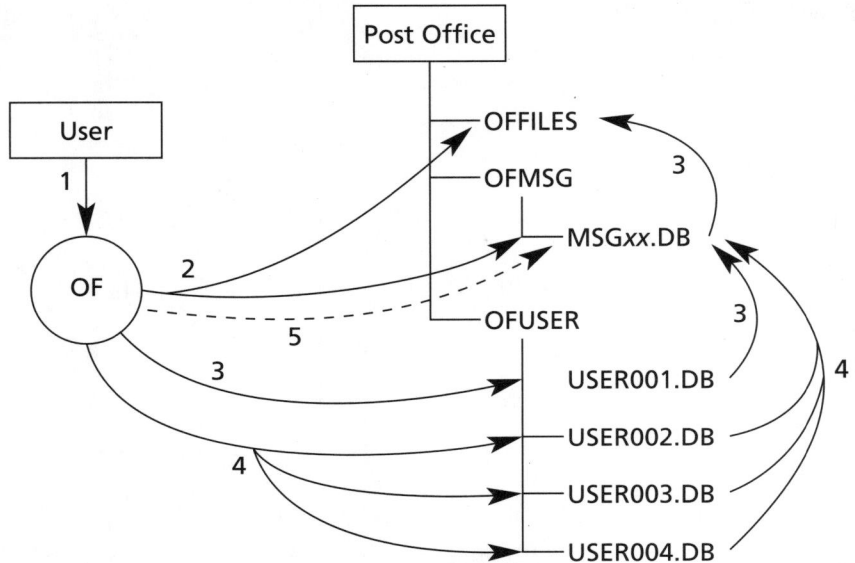

Here is what the message flow diagram shows:

1 • The GroupWise user runs the client and sends a message to three recipients in the user's own post office. The message contains a file attachment that exceeds 2K in size. (In the figure, the sender's user database is USER001.DB.)

2 • The client places the message in the message database to which the sender has been assigned, and the client places the attachment in the OFFILES directory.

3 • The client places a pointer in the sender's user database (USER001.DB) pointing to the message in the message database and a pointer in the message database pointing to the attachment in the OFFILES directory. (These pointers allow the sender to see the message by looking in the Out Box.)

4 • The client places a pointer in each of the recipients' user databases pointing to the message in the sender's message database.

5 • The client updates the message database, changing the status of the message to *Delivered.* (Broken lines in message flow diagrams represent message status updates.) The sender can verify that the message has been successfully delivered by checking the Out Box to see if the status has changed.

When a recipient opens the message, GroupWise places an *Opened* tag in the message database. When the sender checks the status of the message by looking in the Out Box, the tags in the message database tell the client what the current status is. There are separate tags for each recipient so the sender can tell who has read the message and who hasn't.

NOTE

Figure 6.6 only shows the subdirectories and databases mentioned in Steps 1–5. It does not show all of the subdirectories and files in a post office. Also, the user databases are named 001–004 for the sake of convenience only. The actual 3-character ID will either be an imported file ID, or it will be a value generated by GroupWise Admin and assigned to a specific user when that user's GroupWise account is created. In Figure 6.6, the arrows on the right illustrate the pointers in the user databases that point to the message database. In subsequent message flow diagrams, I will not include those arrows.

What happens when one of the recipients deletes the message? When a message is deleted, it goes to the Trash. The message in the Trash keeps a pointer to the message in the message database. When the user empties the Trash, that user's pointer to that message is deleted, and the user will no longer be able to access that message. However, the message itself remains in the message database until (1) all recipients delete the message and empty that message from their Trash, *and* (2) the sender deletes the message from the Out Box and empties the Trash. When all of the pointers to that message have been deleted, the message itself will be deleted from the message database, along with any file attachments that are associated with that message.

GroupWise users also have an option of archiving messages. When a message is *archived,* it is moved from the post office message store to a location on the user's hard drive or to a personal directory on the network. The location of the archive directory can be set in the GroupWise client preferences or in GroupWise Admin. When a message is archived, the message record, file attachments, headers, and pointer information are extracted from the post office message store and saved in an archive file.

As far as the post office message store is concerned, archiving a message is the same as deleting the message. The user's pointer to the archived message is removed from the message database. Users can *unarchive* messages from their archive directory back to the post office message store. Additional information about archiving will be discussed in Chapter 19.

You will notice in Figure 6.6 that sending a message to many recipients within a post office places a heavy burden on the client program. When the client has to do all of this work, the user's machine is tied up. The user cannot do other things with the computer until the message delivery process is finished. This process can happen very quickly if there are only a few recipients, but it can take a long time when a message is sent to a lot of people. That's when a post office server becomes necessary to take some of the load off the client program.

The Post Office Server

The post office has its own GroupWise server process that handles the delivery of messages: the post office server. The post office server is commonly known as the *OFS process*. The post office server is a component of the GroupWise Message Server Pack, which must be purchased separately from the GroupWise client and GroupWise Admin programs. The post office server is the workhorse of the GroupWise system. It handles the majority of the message delivery tasks within a GroupWise post office.

The Message Server Pack is available in four versions: DOS, OS/2, NLM, and UNIX. The DOS message server is the least powerful of the four versions, but the DOS version can be extremely useful in low message-traffic situations, especially if you are looking for reliable performance at a low cost.

The OS/2, NLM, and UNIX message servers are more powerful, multithreaded message servers that work very well for high-traffic, -performance GroupWise implementations. I will tell you more about message servers from time to time throughout this book.

The letters OFS usually appear in the filename of the post office server's executable file. For example, the NLM post office server's filename is NGWOFS.NLM.

Depending on the platform you have chosen, the OFS process runs either on the post office file server (as in the case of the NLM or UNIX versions) or on a dedicated workstation. The post office server has these main jobs:

▸ Delivering local messages

▸ Creating status messages

▸ Running users' *rules*

▸ Processing *busy search* requests

Depending on the message delivery mode, explained later in this chapter, OFS will place messages into the message store and add pointers to the message store databases. It is also in charge of creating status messages. Rules and busy searches are explained in Appendix A. You should study the message flow graphics in this chapter to understand the role that OFS plays in message delivery.

POST OFFICE MESSAGE QUEUE DIRECTORIES

The post office server uses message queue directories in order to deliver messages effectively. The post office message queue directories, shown in Figure 6.7, are OFWORK, WPCSIN, and WPCSOUT. These directories are temporary holding places for messages that are destined for users both within the post office and throughout the GroupWise system.

FIGURE 6.7

Message Queue Directories

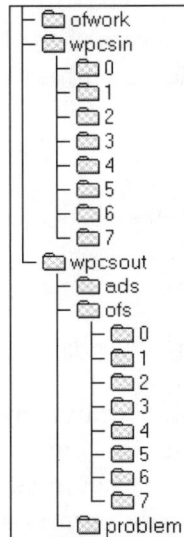

```
├─ 📁 ofwork
├─ 📁 wpcsin
│   ├─ 📁 0
│   ├─ 📁 1
│   ├─ 📁 2
│   ├─ 📁 3
│   ├─ 📁 4
│   ├─ 📁 5
│   ├─ 📁 6
│   └─ 📁 7
└─ 📁 wpcsout
    ├─ 📁 ads
    ├─ 📁 ofs
    │   ├─ 📁 0
    │   ├─ 📁 1
    │   ├─ 📁 2
    │   ├─ 📁 3
    │   ├─ 📁 4
    │   ├─ 📁 5
    │   ├─ 📁 6
    │   └─ 📁 7
    └─ 📁 problem
```

OFWORK   This is a message queuing directory that has two special functions. It handles requests from GroupWise Remote clients, as well as messages sent using the delayed delivery option.

WPCSIN   This is the message server input queue. The GroupWise client or the post office server places messages in WPCSIN that are destined for other post offices or domains in the system. The messages will be held in WPCSIN until the message server picks them up for processing. This subdirectory will be discussed in upcoming chapters that discuss the domain message server.

WPCSOUT   This is the message server output queue. WPCSOUT has a subdirectory called OFS. The message server places messages coming into the post office in the WPCSOUT\OFS subdirectory. The GroupWise client also places messages in the WPCSOUT\OFS subdirectory when the Application Threshold is exceeded or the message delivery mode is Server Always. I explain the application Threshold in the next subsection.

MESSAGE DELIVERY MODES

As you already know, the post office server can be set up to take the load off the client software. This is accomplished by configuring the message delivery mode for the post office. The three delivery modes are *Server Never, Server Always,* and *Use Application Thresholds.* See Figure 6.8.

Server Never

Because Groupwise doesn't ship with a message server pack included, Server Never is the default message delivery mode setting. When you choose Server Never for the delivery mode, the GroupWise client program handles all delivery of messages in the post office. This mode is practical only in very small implementations of GroupWise (with no more than about 25 users). This is the delivery mode depicted in Figure 6.6.

Server Always

When Server Always is selected as the delivery mode, the post office server handles all database updating and message delivery within the post office message store. The client simply queues the message to the post office server, and the server does the rest.

F I G U R E   6.8

*Message Delivery Mode
Selection*

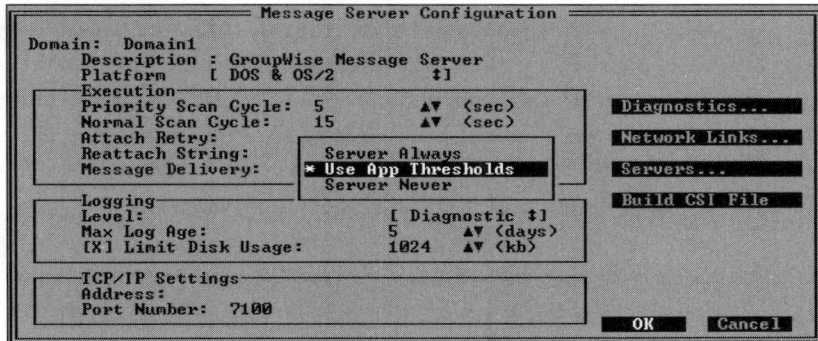

```
══════════════════ Message Server Configuration ══════════════════
Domain:  Domain1
     Description : GroupWise Message Server
     Platform   [ DOS & OS/2      ↕]
    ┌Execution
    │ Priority Scan Cycle:   5         ▲▼ (sec)          ┌──────────────────┐
    │ Normal Scan Cycle:    15         ▲▼ (sec)          │ Diagnostics...   │
    │ Attach Retry:                                      └──────────────────┘
    │ Reattach String:      ┌─────────────────────┐      ┌──────────────────┐
    │ Message Delivery:     │  Server Always      │      │ Network Links... │
    │                       │* Use App Thresholds │      └──────────────────┘
    │                       │  Server Never       │      ┌──────────────────┐
    ┌Logging                └─────────────────────┘      │ Servers...       │
    │ Level:                        [ Diagnostic ↕]      └──────────────────┘
    │ Max Log Age:                  5   ▲▼ (days)        ┌──────────────────┐
    │ [X] Limit Disk Usage:      1024   ▲▼ (kb)          │ Build CSI File   │
    ┌TCP/IP Settings                                     └──────────────────┘
    │ Address:
    │ Port Number:   7100                              ┌──────┐  ┌────────┐
                                                       │  OK  │  │ Cancel │
                                                       └──────┘  └────────┘
```

IMPORTANT

GroupWise users can alter their own user databases in many ways. Some of these alterations include adding information to their personal calendars, creating personal notes, changing preferences, and creating rules. When Server Always is selected, the post office server handles these changes, even though the GroupWise user is the only actual "recipient." Because these activities are not handled directly by the GroupWise client, there will be a delay before the GroupWise user notices changes. That delay is often a source of frustration for users, and it is a major drawback to using the Server Always setting.

Use Application Thresholds

This setting allows you to determine how much work is done by the GroupWise client program and how much is done by the post office server. A value of 5 for the Application Threshold means that the client program will handle delivery of a message if there are five or fewer recipients. The threshold setting is a "less-than-or-equal-to" setting. If there are six or more recipients, the post office server handles it. The setting is also an "all-or-nothing" setting. When Application Threshold is set to 5, and there are seven recipients of a message, the post office server delivers it to all seven. The client does not deliver the message to the first five and then leave the other two to be delivered by the post office server.

Here's a simple analogy. I recently had a party and invited 20 guests. I could have delivered all of the invitations by hand, but it would have taken me over an hour to do it. However, had there been only four, I would have delivered them myself. In this case, my own tolerance threshold was set to 4. Therefore, instead of delivering them personally, I gave all of the invitations to the postal service to deliver.

GroupWise Admin lets you set different Application Thresholds for individual users, post offices, or domains. You can identify those users with high-performance computers and set their threshold settings to a higher value than the Application Threshold for the rest of the post office. Creating custom threshold settings allows you to have the client application handle the extra message delivery workload created by certain users, and it takes some of the burden off the post office server. An individual user's threshold setting overrides the post office setting. Similarly, the post office Application Threshold setting overrides the domain setting.

When you determine the Application Thresholds for post offices, you should try to balance two considerations: (1) the message delivery load you will place on the post office server, and (2) the level of performance your users demand from the GroupWise client.

Table 6.2 summarizes the processes that are used in each of the message delivery modes.

TABLE 6.2 *Message Delivery Duties*	DELIVERY MODE	CLIENT	POST OFFICE SERVER (OFS)
	Server Never	Handles all message delivery	Not used
	Server Always	Not used in message delivery	Handles all message delivery
	Use Application Thresholds	Handles all message delivery if the number of recipients is less than or equal to the threshold value	Handles all message delivery if the number of recipients exceeds the threshold value

Application Threshold = 0

The default Application Threshold setting is 0. This is Novell's recommended setting if you are using a 32-bit multithreading post office server platform (NLM, OS/2, or UNIX). This setting gives you the best client performance, and the additional workload can easily be handled by the high-performance post office servers.

If you are using the DOS post office server, a good rule of thumb to follow when you set Application Thresholds is to start at 2 and move up from there until you find the best threshold setting for a post office.

You might think that setting the Application Threshold to 0 would have the same effect as choosing Server Always (that is, making the post office server do all of the work), but that's not the case.

With Application Threshold set to 0, the client program still handles certain tasks such as (1) placing messages in message databases; (2) placing file attachments in the OFFILES directory; and (3) adding pointers to the senders' user databases. In that case, the post office server only takes care of placing the appropriate pointers in the recipients' user databases. This is the major advantage that Application Threshold = 0 has over the Server Always setting. When a user does something that affects his or her user database, the user does not experience a delay in the operation of the client application.

Also, whenever you select any Application Threshold, users must have certain network rights. They need to have Read, Write, and Create (RWC) rights in the OFUSER and OFMSG directories, and they need Read, Write, Create, and Erase (RWCE) rights in the OFFILES directory.

> **This assumes that the users are running the DOS or Windows client on a Novell NetWare network. For the rights required for the Macintosh client and for rights required for other network operating systems, refer to the README.AD file located in the domain directory.**

NOTE

However, if you choose Server Always for the delivery mode, the client passes *all* delivery tasks to the post office server—including placing messages in message databases and adding pointers to the senders' user databases. The main advantage of this configuration is that fewer post office directory rights need to be granted to the users in the system. With Server Always, the users only need Read (R) rights to the OFMSG, OFUSER, and OFFILES directories. The network directories therefore remain more secure.

Because of the delay users experience with the Server Always setting, I recommend that you only use this setting when a post office absolutely requires maximum network security.

MESSAGE FLOW WHEN THE APPLICATION THRESHOLD IS EXCEEDED

When the Application Threshold is exceeded, the post office server handles some of the message delivery tasks. Therefore, the message flow is somewhat different from what you saw in Figure 6.6. Refer to Figure 6.9. Again, assume that the user sends the message to three recipients, and the message includes a file attachment that exceeds 2K in size.

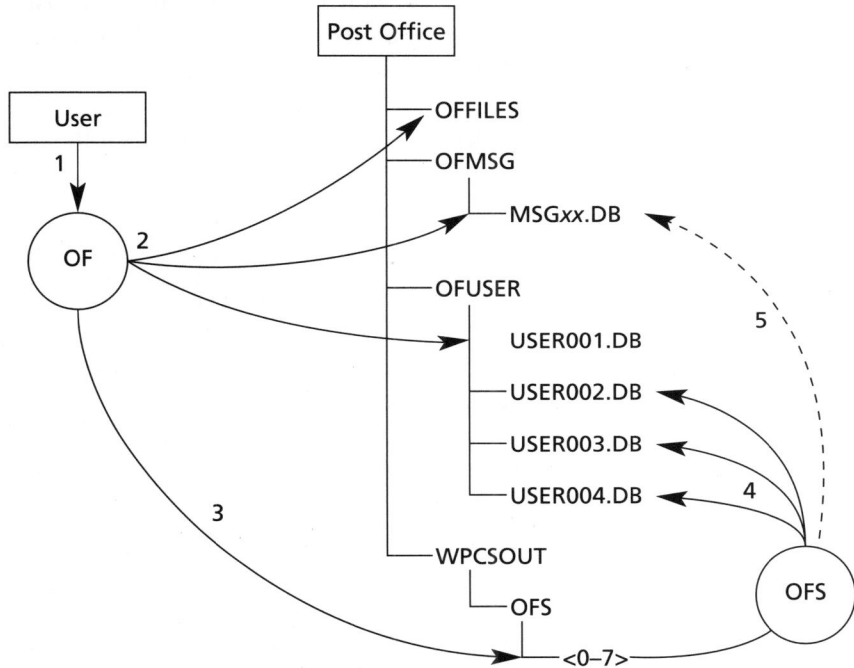

F I G U R E 6.9

Message Flow with Post Office Server Configured and Application Threshold Exceeded

Here is what Figure 6.9 shows:

1 • The sender creates the message in the client application.

2 • The client puts the message in the message database, places a pointer in the sender's user database to the message in the message database, places file attachments or messages over 2K in the attachments directory, and places a pointer in the message database to the information in the attachments directory.

3 • The client places a message containing a list of the message recipients in the post office server (OFS) queue.

4 • The post office server sees the message in the OFS\<0–7> directory and places pointers in the recipients' user databases.

5 • OFS places a *Delivered* status message in the message database.

NOTE

To simplify the illustration, the pointers from the user databases to the message database and OFFILES directory have been omitted. The broken line indicates delivery of a status message.

Figure 6.10 shows the message delivery process when the delivery mode is set to Server Always.

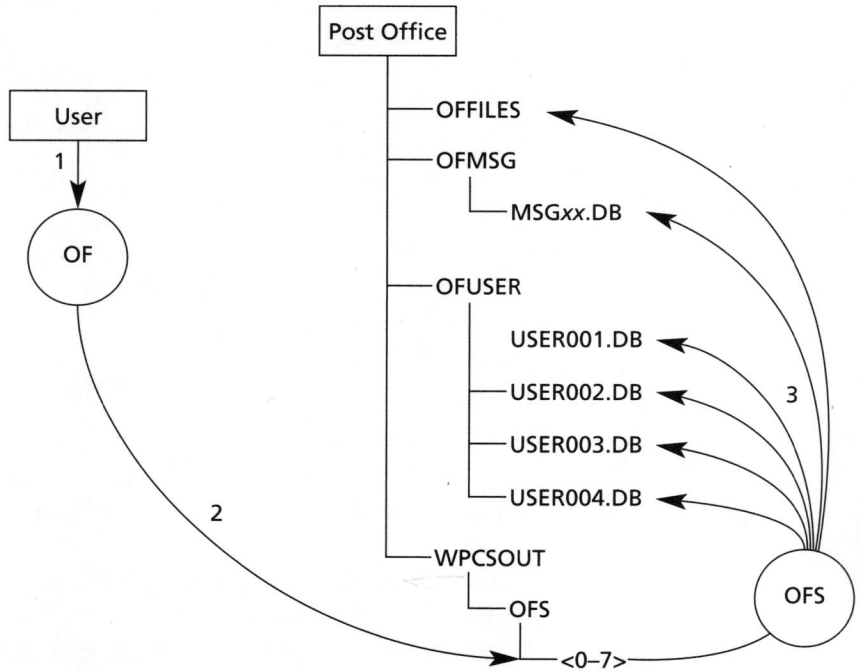

F I G U R E 6.10

Message Flow when Delivery Mode Is Server Always

Here is what you see in Figure 6.10:

1 • The sender creates the message in the client application.

2 • The client writes the entire message to the WPCSOUT\OFS\<0–7> subdirectory (the post office server queue).

3 • The post office server places the message in the message database and the file attachments in the OFFILES directory, and it places pointers in the sender's and all recipients' user databases.

Summary

In this chapter, you learned how to configure post office security settings. You also learned how the message store works and how messages are delivered in a single post office system.

Solution to Part II Scenario

The scenario for Part II involved a small accounting firm with a single file server. That firm obviously would want to implement a single domain, single post office GroupWise configuration.

Now I will tell you how Fairbanks and Hunt's consultant implemented their GroupWise system. The GroupWise domain and post offices were configured in separate volumes on the file server. The Windows client was installed at the domain level and copied to the post office. Once the client software had been enabled at the post office level, the domain copy of the client software was removed to conserve disk space. The client software could be easily reinstalled if necessary or if the company received software updates.

The consultant used the NetWare bindery import function to set up all 50 users in a single post office. (See "Adding Users to a Post Office" in Chapter 4.) Public groups were established so that the users could easily address GroupWise messages to groups of users.

The Windows client was enabled at the post office, giving users the choice of running the GroupWise client either from the network or from their local hard drives. When the consultant ran SETUPWIN /A on the post office level, he chose the Custom Install option and installed the GroupWise shared code to the PerfectOffice shared code directory on the network. This procedure guaranteed that the users who run PerfectOffice and GroupWise from the network will always access the same shared code. He also wrote up an instruction sheet for users who decide to run GroupWise from their local drives. The instruction sheet advised those users to locate PerfectOffice's shared code on their hard disks and install the GroupWise shared code to the same directory.

To help users quickly learn how to use the client, users were asked to run the QuickTour after the client installation was complete.

To provide efficient message delivery, the firm purchased the GroupWise Message Server NetWare Loadable Module (NLM) pack. The Post Office Server NLM was installed and configured on the NetWare file server. The message delivery mode was set to Use Application Threshold=0. This setting makes it the client's responsibility to update the sender's user database, the message database, and the OFFILES directory. It gives the post office server the job of delivering messages to all of the recipients in the post office. In this way, the client's performance is optimized.

OTHER CONSIDERATIONS

Server RAM Depending on the current server utilization levels, it may be necessary to add more RAM to the server. Novell recommends that 8MB of RAM be allocated for all of the message server components. However, because this is a single post office system, the Message Server NLM and the Administration Server NLM are not necessary. Only the Post Office Server NLM is required.

Disk Space The system administrator should plan on at least 5MB of disk space per user in the post office. However, Novell suggests that 10MB be allocated for each user if possible. The system administrator should monitor the amount of disk space that is used by the GroupWise message store.

Workstations All workstations should be Windows-capable machines with a recommended 8MB of RAM. If all workstations cannot meet this requirement, the firm should consider purchasing the DOS client for the low-end machines.

On-Site Administration An on-site administrator should be chosen to help end users as needed. The administrator should be familiar with the basics of e-mail culture and courtesy. He or she should also be familiar with NetWare tasks, such as running SYSCON and using drive mappings. The administrator should also learn how to use the Check GroupWise utility (discussed in Chapter 19).

Intermediate GroupWise Systems

Single Domain, Multiple Post Offices

Part II showed you how to set up a GroupWise system with only one post office. I introduced you to the issues presented by an initial installation of GroupWise software, and I explained how to set up the first domain and post office and how to add users. You also learned how to enable the client software. Finally, I discussed how the post office server works and how messages move through a single–post office GroupWise system—with and without a post office server.

As an organization grows, it will eventually become necessary to expand the GroupWise system. As a rough rule of thumb, another GroupWise post office should be created once an existing post office exceeds 250 users. This is a very general rule, and many factors play into the decision to add post offices. Some of the factors to consider are the number of file servers that users log into, the amount of traffic generated in the single post office, and the rate at which the organization is growing. In theory, the maximum number of GroupWise users a single post office can handle is over 65,000. In a normal work environment, however, 250 users (give or take a hundred or so) is a manageable size for a post office.

Part III will show you how to set up a GroupWise system for an organization that needs more than one post office but still requires only a single domain.

Part III Scenario

Orton Consulting is a small management consulting firm consisting of 250 employees. There are eight different departments within the firm:

- Accounting and Finance

- Curriculum and Training

- Software Development

- Publications

- Marketing and Advertising

- Sales

▶ Human Resources

▶ Corporate Quality

Two Novell NetWare 3.12 file servers more than adequately meet their network needs. Orton uses matching Pentium servers with 64MB of RAM and 5GB of hard disk space. Most workstations in the company are Windows-capable. One hundred users from Accounting and Finance, Curriculum and Training, Software Development, and Publications log in to the domain ORTONA. The directory of MIS also considers ORTONA its home. The other departments primarily use ORTONB. They are excited about the new functionality Novell GroupWise will soon be giving them, but want to make sure they set it up optimally.

Their network is represented in Figure III.1:

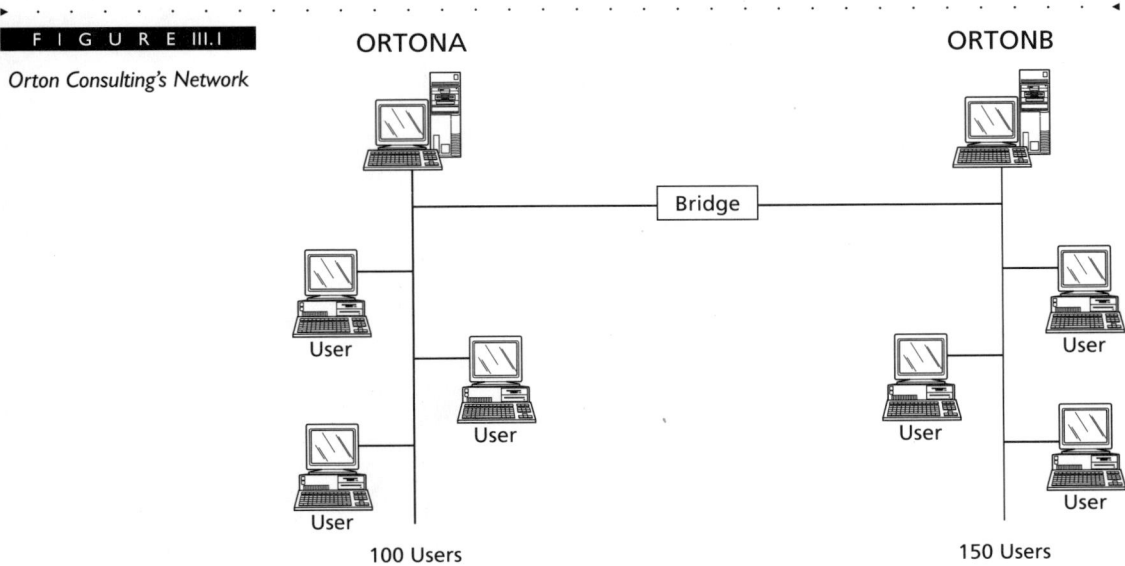

FIGURE III.1

Orton Consulting's Network

ORTONA   ORTONB

Bridge

User   User

User   User

User   User

100 Users   150 Users

CHAPTER 7

Implementing a Multiple Post Office GroupWise System

Figure 7.1 shows an abstract model of a single domain, multiple post office system. As you can see, each post office has its own set of users. Keeping in mind the concepts discussed in Part II, you can see that users in one post office can send messages to other users in the same post office by letting either the client or the post office server handle message delivery. But, until a domain-level MTA is established, users in different post offices cannot send messages to each other. The domain-level MTA that allows post offices to communicate is the *message server.*

NOTE

GroupWise treats gateways like post offices. Adding a gateway to a single post office system is just like adding another post office. An MTA is required to communicate between the post office and the gateway. If a gateway needs to be added to a single post office system for any reason (e.g., for connecting to the Internet or for supporting GroupWise Remote users) that system needs to have a message server. I will explain more about gateways in Chapter 14.

F I G U R E 7.1

A Single Domain, Multiple Post Office System

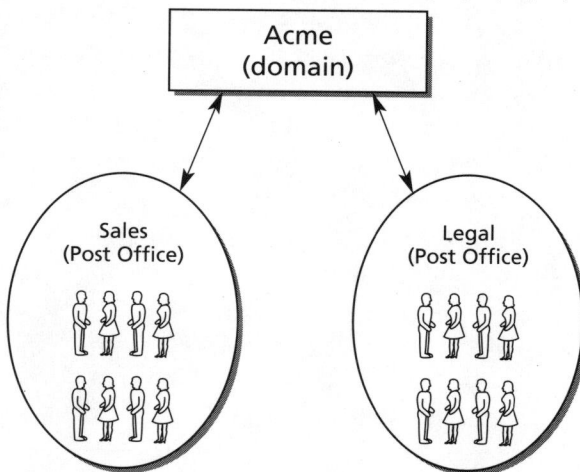

What Is a Message Server?

The word *server* can be used in many different ways in the computer industry. Understanding what this word means in GroupWise terminology is critical. A GroupWise server is not a physical server like a network file server. A GroupWise server is a program that moves messages from place to place. The server program gains access to the GroupWise system in much the same way that users do. Most administrators set up their GroupWise servers with a network user account that has the rights and permissions needed to read and write files in the various GroupWise directories. GroupWise servers often run on a dedicated workstation in the network or, as in the case of the NetWare NLM GroupWise servers, directly on a NetWare file server.

In GroupWise, the entire server system is often referred to as the *message server.* However, there is also a specific component of the GroupWise Server Pack that is called the message server. Usually, you can tell from the context which meaning is intended. In this book, I will make it clear which specific component of the GroupWise server system I am referring to — the administration server, the post office server, or the message server. *Message server* will therefore normally refer to the particular GroupWise server that functions on the domain level and that transfers messages between post offices and domains. You can think of it as the domain server because it services all the post offices in the domain, and it is installed and configured on the domain level.

In Chapter 5, I made an analogy between GroupWise and a real-world postal system. I said that a GroupWise post office is similar to the local post office in your community, and I compared GroupWise domains to regional postal facilities. A regional facility acts as a hub that routes mail sent between local post offices. Suppose that a regional postal facility went on strike. Your local post office could still deliver mail to all users in its area, but there would be no mechanism to handle the delivery of mail directed to other local post offices. This is similar to the way GroupWise works. Without a domain message server, messages cannot be sent between users in different post offices.

In Chapter 6, you learned how the post office server works. It functions on the post office level and places messages into users' mailboxes and into the post office message store. The message server does not handle final delivery of any messages. It is a point-to-point delivery agent. Think of the message server like the mail trucks that deliver messages between each post office in a region. The post office server is comparable to the mail carriers who actually deliver letters to the recipients.

Deciding When Multiple Post Offices Are Necessary

As a GroupWise system grows, it eventually becomes necessary to create additional post offices. The decision about when you should expand a single post office system into a multiple post office system depends on several factors:

- The organization's structure

- The network structure and the arrangement of file servers

- GroupWise performance considerations

MAKING THE POST OFFICE STRUCTURE FIT THE ORGANIZATION

In most GroupWise implementations, it makes sense to pattern the GroupWise system after the organizational structure and the way the network infrastructure has been laid out. You should organize post offices to group users who work together (e.g., users in the same department). In the Part III scenario, there are two file servers, and all of the users in the company either log in to one file server or the other. In that case, it would make sense to have two post offices so that the existing network does not need to be modified and so that GroupWise traffic is divided between each server.

As you plan additional post offices, you need to ask these questions:

- How will all of the users be split between the post offices?

- Will users be grouped by organizational units or by physical proximity?

- Which users will need to proxy for others? See Appendix A for an explanation of the proxy feature.

- What are the current network limitations?

▸ Are there any GroupWise visibility concerns? For example, are there any resources in one post office that should not be available to users in another post office? See Chapter 2 for an explanation of visibility.

▸ What is the current volume of message traffic?

For additional planning considerations, see Chapter 3.

MAKING THE POST OFFICE STRUCTURE FIT THE NETWORK

Network limitations often dictate where you need to locate post offices. Users need access to the file server that houses their post office. However, it may not be feasible for all users to access a single file server. Therefore, you should create post offices on file servers that are regularly used by specific departments or groups of users.

Suppose that an organization has three file servers, and 100 users have been assigned to each file server. The file servers are on the same network cable, but users have access only to the file server that they log into. In this situation, the network structure calls for three post offices—one on each file server. The only other option would be to grant additional login and network rights in more than one file server for some of the users.

Message traffic is another important factor. Generally, message traffic tends to be higher among users in the same department than it is among users in different departments. (From my own experience, I know that I send about 60 percent of my messages to users in my department.) Post offices can and should be used to isolate GroupWise traffic. In many situations, it makes sense to give individual departments their own post offices.

GROUPWISE PERFORMANCE CONSIDERATIONS

As you consider the location of post offices and begin to plan for their implementation, you should evaluate these factors:

▸ The size of the message store

▸ The number of network routers and their locations

▸ The message delivery mode

Remember that post offices contain GroupWise message stores. You should evaluate the capacity of each server in order to determine which servers can house post offices. As a rough rule of thumb, allow an average of 5–10MB of file server disk space per user for message storage needs. Of course, some users will not need that much space and others will require more. For example, I usually have over 300 messages in my mailbox—many of which contain file attachments. Granted, a good number of those messages have been received by other users in my post office, so they have been stored only once in the message store. Nevertheless, based on the amount of disk space my messages occupy in the archive directory on my hard drive, I'm sure that my own mailbox takes up at least 15–20MB of the file server's disk space.

Another consideration is that GroupWise performance will be affected by the number of network routers the client executable has to go through. The speed of the network link between the CPU and the post office message store has a direct impact on GroupWise client efficiency. For example, when there are two routers between a workstation and the file server where the corresponding post office resides, the client has to update databases across those two routers while the user waits to regain control of the workstation. This is particularly a problem when there is a slow WAN link (fewer than 10 megabits per second) between the client and the message store. Whenever possible, try to avoid GroupWise configurations that require the client to go through routers to reach the message store.

Creating Additional Post Offices Using GroupWise Admin

Up to this point, I haven't said very much about GroupWise Admin. In Part II, I showed you how to use the Assisted Setup program in GroupWise Admin to create an initial domain and post office and to add users. The Assisted Setup program only guides you the first time you run GroupWise Admin. After that, you are on your own to navigate your way through the various GroupWise Admin menus you need to use in order to perform administration tasks.

Because the domain directory serves as the archive directory for the GroupWise software, you don't need the GroupWise diskettes to create a post office. When you create a post office, GroupWise Admin pushes the client software and other GroupWise files across the network to the post office directory. Therefore, the file server that houses the domain must have a physical network connection to the file server that houses the post office.

The two menus in GroupWise Admin that you will use extensively to build your system are the Create menu and the Actions menu. The Create menu gives you options for creating domains, post offices, gateways, and user objects. The Actions menu allows you to make changes to them after they have been created.

The procedure for creating a new post office is quite simple:

1 • Make sure that the machine running GroupWise Admin has a drive mapping to the file server and volume where the new post office will be located.

2 • Run AD.EXE.

3 • Choose the Create menu option.

4 • Choose Post Office.

You will see the dialog box shown in Figure 7.2.

FIGURE 7.2

Post Office Information Dialog Box

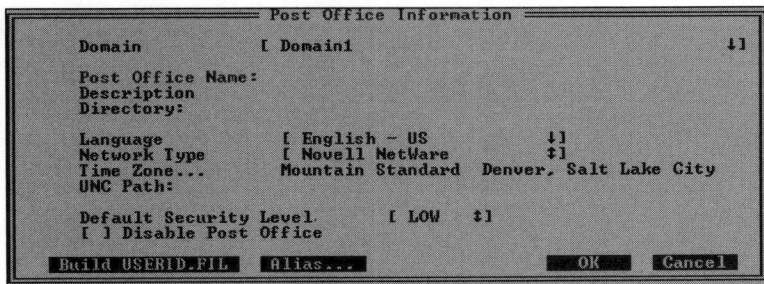

```
═════════════════════════ Post Office Information ═════════════════════════
 Domain              [ Domain1                                          ↓]

 Post Office Name:
 Description
 Directory:

 Language            [ English - US          ↓]
 Network Type        [ Novell NetWare        ↕]
 Time Zone...        Mountain Standard  Denver, Salt Lake City
 UNC Path:

 Default Security Level.      [ LOW   ↕]
 [ ] Disable Post Office

   Build USERID.FIL     Alias...                    OK      Cancel
```

The fields you must add information to are:

► Post Office Name

► Directory

▸   Language

▸   Network Type

▸   Time Zone

After you have made these selections, the Select Client Software dialog box will appear. The client software stored in the domain can then be copied to the new post office. Obviously, if the client software was deleted from the domain or was never installed there (for example, if the DOS client software was not installed in the domain), then you will not be able to copy that software from the domain. The Select Client Software dialog box is shown in Figure 7.3.

F I G U R E 7.3

Select Client Software
Dialog Box

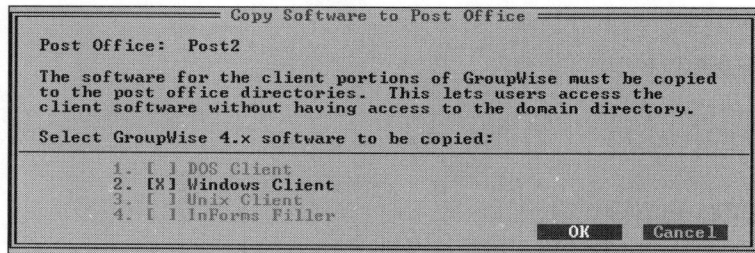

```
══════════════ Copy Software to Post Office ══════════════
Post Office:   Post2

The software for the client portions of GroupWise must be copied
to the post office directories.  This lets users access the
client software without having access to the domain directory.

Select GroupWise 4.x software to be copied:

          1.  [ ] DOS Client
          2.  [X] Windows Client
          3.  [ ] Unix Client
          4.  [ ] InForms Filler
                                              OK        Cancel
```

If you select *None,* you can copy the software from the domain to the post office later by using the Software Management option under the Tools menu in GroupWise Admin.

Once you have created a second post office, a multiple post office GroupWise structure will be in place (see Figure 7.1). You can use one of the methods outlined in Chapter 4 to add users. However, until you install and configure the message server, the users will not be able to send messages between the post offices.

How the Message Server Works

As I mentioned at the beginning of this chapter, the message server works at the level of the domain. Every domain in a GroupWise system must have its own message server, and a domain will never have more than one active message server. (A separate message server license is required for each domain.) As you learn about how the message server works, it is important to keep in mind that the message server processes many different types of messages—such as e-mail messages, appointments, busy searches, and administrative messages.

The GroupWise message server performs these duties:

▸ It receives messages from the post offices within the domain and delivers those messages to the next destination indicated by the address (i.e., to another post office or gateway within the domain, or to another domain). See Figure 7.4.

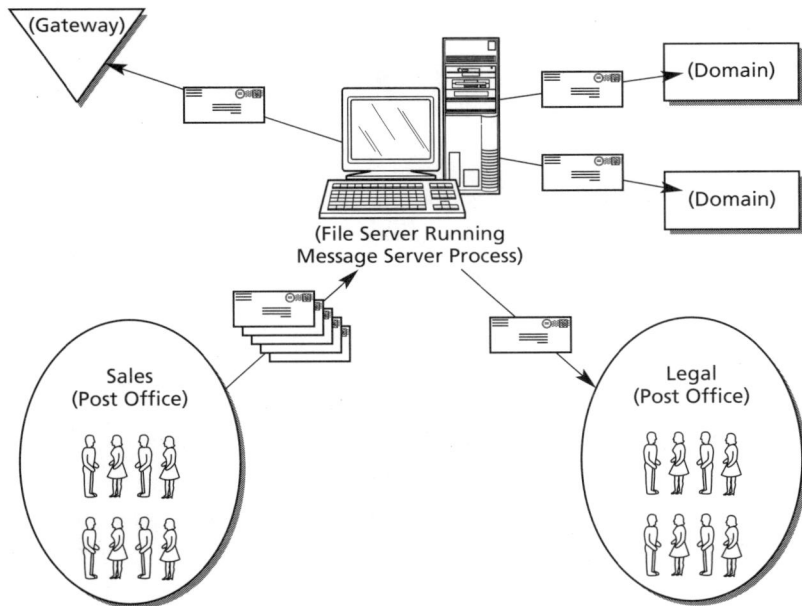

FIGURE 7.4

Message Server Functions

▸ It receives messages from other domains and delivers those messages to (1) the appropriate post office or gateway within the domain or (2) other domains. See Figure 7.5.

*Message Server Routing
Messages from Another
Domain*

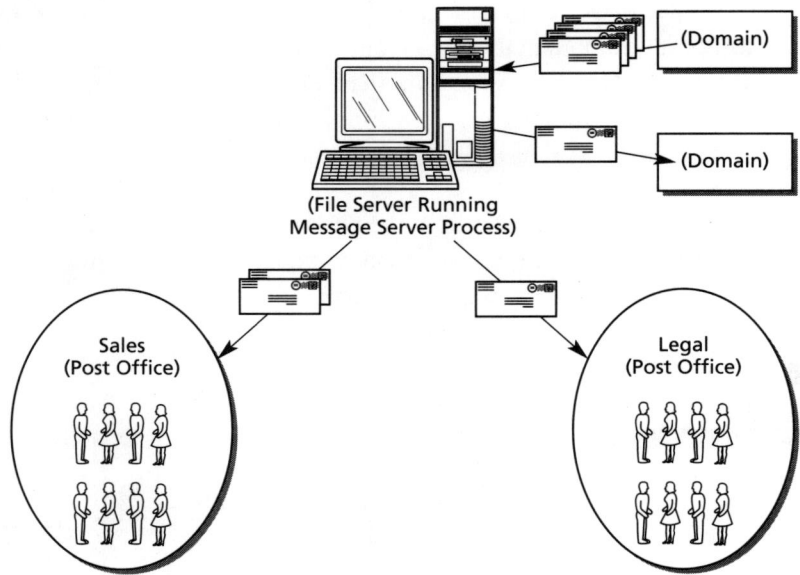

(Domain)

(Domain)

(File Server Running
Message Server Process)

Sales
(Post Office)

Legal
(Post Office)

▶ It receives messages from the gateways in the domain and routes these messages to the appropriate destinations—either to a post office within the domain or to another domain. See Figure 7.6.

▶ It routes administrative messages to their proper destinations. The processing of administrative messages will be discussed in Part V.

In message flow diagrams later in this chapter and throughout the book, you will see exactly how message servers perform each of these duties.

The message server's other duties include logging message statistics, controlling message routing, and performing related tasks.

When the message server is running, it acts as a lookout that watches over the input queues. It constantly scans (*polls*) these queues for messages that need to be processed. When it finds messages that are waiting to be delivered, it forwards them to their next location. Depending on the message server platform in use, the message server may also launch (or *spawn*) other processes, such as the post office server, the administration server, or the gateway programs.

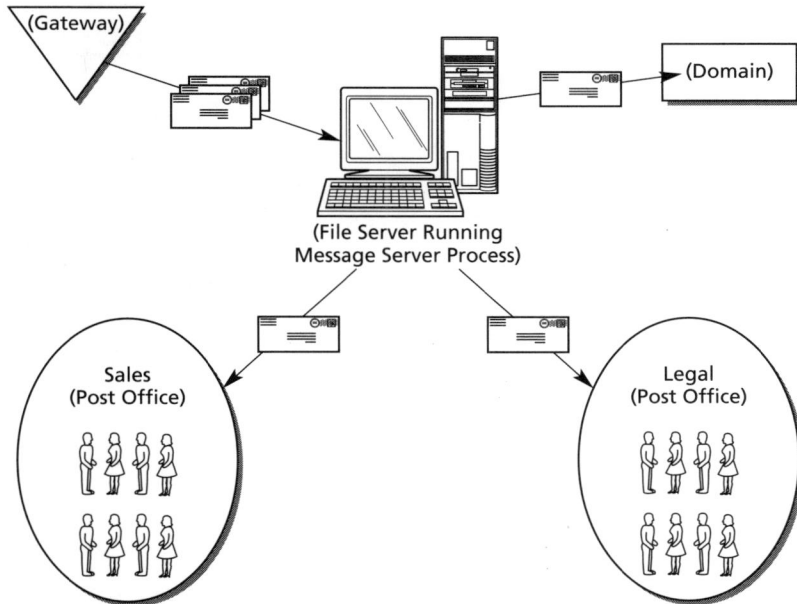

FIGURE 7.6

Message Server Routing Messages from Gateway

MESSAGE SERVER QUEUES

The message server uses input and output queues to perform its duties. Figure 7.7 shows the message server input queues used in a GroupWise system that consists of a single domain and two post offices. (There are also message server queues in the domain structure, but they are only used for messages leaving the domain and messages coming into the domain. They are not used for normal message delivery in a single domain system. The domain-level message server queues will be discussed in Part IV.)

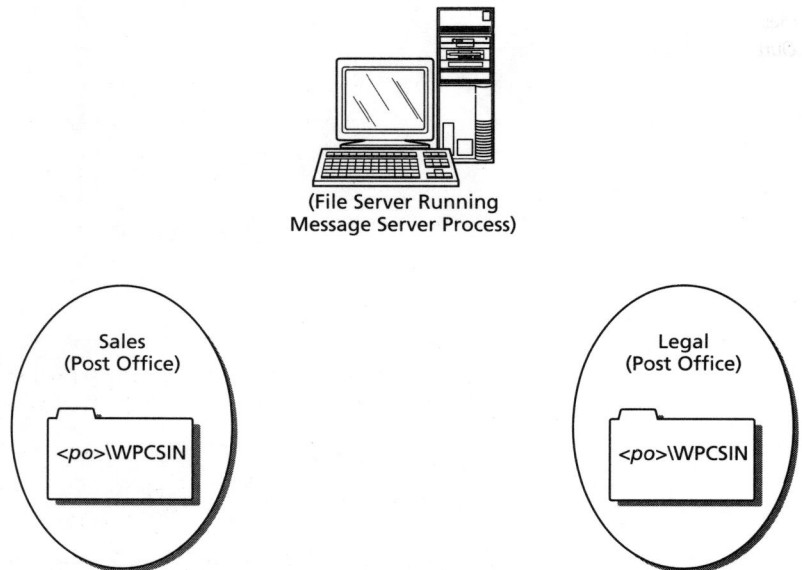

F I G U R E 7.7

Message Server Input Queues

(File Server Running Message Server Process)

Sales (Post Office)

<po>\WPCSIN

Legal (Post Office)

<po>\WPCSIN

The message server input queue is WPCSIN. The post office-level processes (the client and the post office server) place messages into the WPCSIN directory structure for the message server to process. (WPCSIN stands for "WordPerfect Connection Server Input"—a carryover from WordPerfect Office, where the message servers were called *connection servers*.)

The message server works according to the store-and-forward architecture described earlier in this book. It constantly polls message input queues and processes the messages it finds in them. When it finds a message, it reads the addressing information and forwards the message to the appropriate message output queues, shown in Figure 7.8. Note that the message server does not directly update any post office databases; it only sends messages to the post office server, which then updates the message store.

FIGURE 7.8

*Message Server
Output Queues*

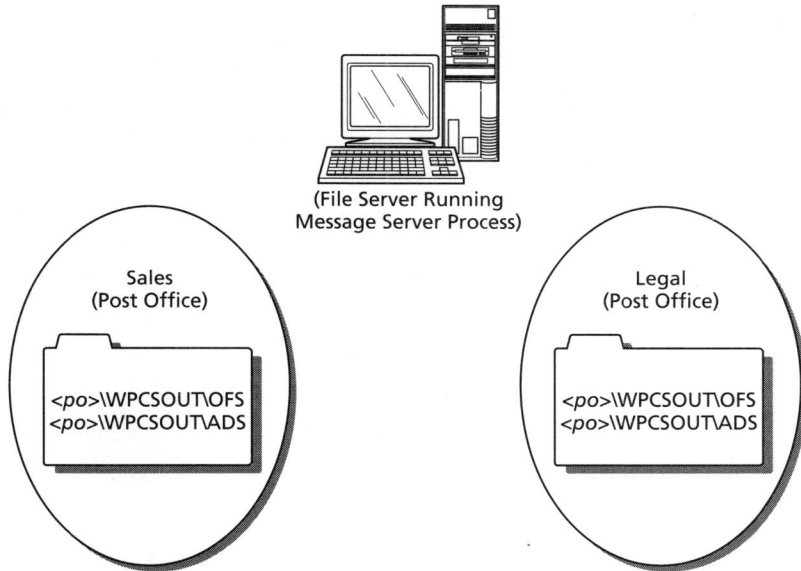

(File Server Running
Message Server Process)

Sales
(Post Office)

<po>\WPCSOUT\OFS
<po>\WPCSOUT\ADS

Legal
(Post Office)

<po>\WPCSOUT\OFS
<po>\WPCSOUT\ADS

The message server output queue at the post office level is WPCSOUT\OFS. The message server process places messages destined for users in a post office into the WPCSOUT\OFS directory. Those messages are then processed by the post office server. (WPCSOUT stands for "WordPerfect Connection Server Output".) The message flow diagrams at the end of this chapter provide you with more detailed information about how these queues work together.

Installing and Configuring the Message Server

The message server is available for these platforms:

- Novell NetWare NLM

- UNIX

- OS/2

- DOS

Later in this chapter in the section entitled "Overview of GroupWise Message Server Platforms," I will tell you about the key features and benefits of each platform. Even though the message server software varies depending on the platform, the responsibilities of the message server processes are always the same. All versions of the message server use the same kind of input and output queues. The only real differences stem from the way they have to operate on each different platform and from their hardware and software requirements. Performance does vary depending on the message server platform you are using.

As mentioned previously, the message server is sold in a *message server pack,* which is comprised of three GroupWise servers:

- The message server

- The post office server

- The administration server

The message server's program name is different for each platform, but it usually has either *CS* or *MS* in it. The post office server program typically has *OFS* somewhere in its name. The administration server program name often contains the letters *ADS*. Table 7.1 shows the executable filenames that are associated with the DOS, OS/2, and NLM message server packs.

	PLATFORM	MESSAGE SERVER	POST OFFICE SERVER	ADMINISTRATION SERVER
TABLE 7.1 *Message Server Pack Filenames*	DOS	CS.EXE	OFS.EXE	ADS.EXE
	OS/2	MSOS2.EXE	OFSOS2.EXE	ADSOS2.EXE
	NLM	NGWMS.NLM	NGWOFS.NLM	NGWADS.NLM

Each message server pack has its own installation process. The installation program for the NLM and DOS message server packs runs from a DOS workstation. The installation for UNIX and OS/2 message servers can only be run from workstations using those two platforms, respectively. Refer to the specific platform's instructions regarding its particular requirements. The NLM message server will be discussed further in Chapter 8.

CREATING NETWORK ACCESS ACCOUNTS FOR GROUPWISE SERVERS

If your GroupWise system consists of multiple post offices on more than one file server, your message server will need network access rights to the directories on each file server that houses a post office. This applies to all network operating systems. *Access accounts* should be used to allow the message server to log in to the file servers. An access account is a user account you create on each file server. All of the access accounts in your system must have the same user name and password. The access accounts must also include the following rights in the domain and post office directories:

- Create files or directories
- Erase files or directories
- Read or execute files
- Scan for files
- Write to files

Make sure the access accounts have multiple concurrent logins on the file servers.

NOTE The terminology used here applies primarily to Novell NetWare, but the concepts apply to any network operating system you may be using. If you are running a non-NetWare network, you will need to use the rights that are equivalent to these NetWare rights. Refer to the README.AD file in the domain directory for a list of network rights for various network operating systems.

Here is an example of how access accounts can be used. Suppose a domain has two post offices that reside on two different file servers. The system administrator creates an access account called GWUSER and assigns the password GWISE. This same access account and password must be created on both of the file servers in the domain. This will allow the message server to log in to each server to process messages.

In multiple domain systems, access accounts must include rights to all of the other domain directories. This enables the message server to deliver messages to all domains. If you are running a NetWare 4.1 system, you can create access accounts in all of the domains by creating a user in one of the Organizations or Organizational Units with a file server housing a GroupWise domain. Grant that user the necessary rights to each file server. Then, create an alias for that user in each Organization or Organizational Unit with a file server housing a domain or post office.

NOTE This access account should reject system-generated workstation messages. On a Novell NetWare network, the appropriate command is CASTOFF ALL.

CONFIGURING THE MESSAGE SERVER USING GROUPWISE ADMIN

Once you have installed the message server, it must be configured using GroupWise Admin. You configure the message server by editing the domain. Follow these steps to enable and configure the message server:

1 • When you open GroupWise Admin, highlight the appropriate domain in the list of domains.

2 • Choose Actions, and then choose Edit.

3 • Select Message Server Configuration, and the dialog box shown in Figure 7.9 will then appear.

FIGURE 7.9

*Message Server
Configuration Dialog Box*

```
═══════════════════ Message Server Configuration ═══════════════════
Domain:  Domain1
   1. Description  : GroupWise Message Server
   2. Platform     [ NLM          ‡]
 ┌─3. Execution─────────────────────────────────────┐   Diagnostics...
 │    Priority Scan Cycle:  5        ▲▼  (sec)       │
 │    Normal Scan Cycle:    15       ▲▼  (sec)       │   Network Links...
 │    Attach Retry:         600      ▲▼  (sec)       │
 │    Reattach String:                              │   Servers...
 │    Message Delivery:   [ Use App Thresholds  ‡]  │
 ┌─4. Logging───────────────────────────────────────┐   Build CSI File
 │    Level:                   [ Normal     ‡]      │
 │    Max Log Age:             7     ▲▼ (days)       │
 │    [X] Limit Disk Usage:    1024  ▲▼ (kb)         │
 ┌─5. TCP/IP Settings───────────────────────────────┐
 │    Address:                                      │
 │    Port Number:  7100                            │
 └──────────────────────────────────────────────────┘   OK    Cancel
```

4 • Select the message server platform that you will use.

5 • Set the Execution option, including the desired message delivery mode.

6 • Set the desired Logging Level options.

7 • Choose Build CSI File.

8 • You will receive a prompt that asks Save MS Configuration File Before Building? Answer Yes.

9 • Choose OK.

The Build CSI File option notifies the message server of the changes. If the message server is running, it will automatically restart the message server process to conform to the new configuration.

NOTE

Only the DOS message server actually uses the WPDOMAIN.CSI file located in the domain directory. However, the Build CSI File option notifies all message server platforms of the updated configuration. Exiting GroupWise Admin also causes the updated configuration to be sent to the message server.

The various options you can choose when you configure the message server are described in Table 7.2.

TABLE 7.2	OPTION	DESCRIPTION
Message Server Configuration Options	Priority Scan Cycle	This field sets the intervals, in seconds, at which the message server scans the high-priority input queues for messages. The high-priority message queues are the WPCSIN\<0–3> subdirectories. The smaller the interval, the faster messages are routed. However, a faster scan cycle increases network traffic.
	Normal Scan Cycle	This field sets the intervals, in seconds, at which the message server scans the normal priority input queues. The normal priority message queues are the WPCSIN\<4–7> subdirectories. The smaller the interval, the faster messages are routed. However, a faster scan cycle increases network traffic.
	Attach Retry	This option sets the time interval, in seconds, the message server waits before attempting to unblock a post office, gateway, or domain that has gone down.
	Message Delivery	Allows you to choose the message delivery modes. The options are Server Always, Server Never, and Use Application Threshold.
	Logging Level	This option sets the amount of information that will be written to the log file. The higher the level, the more information will be written to the log file. However, writing information increases the processing that the message server's CPU must do and increases disk space usage. The settings you can choose—from lowest to highest—are Off, Normal, Verbose, or Diagnostic. (For the DOS message server, the settings are None, Low, Medium, and High.)
	Max Log Age	Lets you set how many days the log files remain on the disk before they are automatically deleted.

TABLE 7.2	OPTION	DESCRIPTION
Message Server Configuration Options	Limit Disk Usage	Lets you set the amount of disk space that can be used by the log files.
(continued)	TCP/IP Settings	You will use this option when you connect domains with TCP/IP connections. I will explain TCP/IP connections in Part IV.

Remember that the default GroupWise message delivery mode is Server Never. This mode will not work in a multiple post office or multiple domain GroupWise systems. You must choose either Application Threshold (which is the most common) or Server Always.

Notice that although you may select Application Threshold as the delivery mode in this dialog box, you don't actually provide the threshold value here. The threshold setting can be set at the domain, post office, or user level by following the steps below.

To set a specific value for the application threshold, go to the main GroupWise Admin screen and highlight the domain, post office, or user. Then follow these steps:

1 • Choose Actions.

2 • Choose GroupWise 4.*x* Options.

3 • Choose Environment.

4 • Choose Additional Environment Options.

5 • Select Threshold, and enter the desired value.

The domain level threshold governs all users in the domain unless the threshold value has been changed at the post office level, in which case the post office threshold value governs. Likewise, the post office threshold value governs all users in the post office, unless that value is changed at the user level, where the user setting governs.

If you have 50 users in a post office with Pentium computers, 50 users with 486 computers, and 50 users with 386 computers, you may want to set higher thresholds for the Pentium users, lower thresholds for the 486 users, and even lower thresholds for the 386 users. Those settings would help balance message processing so that the load would be divided more equitably between the client software and post office servers.

Overview of GroupWise Message Server Platforms

The configuration of the message server will depend on the platform in use. The DOS and OS/2 message servers are run from dedicated workstations. The NLM message server runs on a Novell NetWare 3.1x or 4.x file server. Refer to the specific message server package for your platform to get more specific information on configuring and running the message server process. Here's an overview of each message server platform.

NETWARE NLM MESSAGE SERVER PACK

The NLM message server pack is typically the best option for GroupWise systems running on Novell networks. The NetWare NLM message server programs run with NetWare 3.1x and 4.x file servers. This message server provides very high-performance message delivery.

The NLM message server is a native 32-bit application, and it makes full use of the multithreading capabilities of the network operating system. Because the NLM message server runs directly on the file server, a separate dedicated workstation is not required. All GroupWise servers can run on a single file server if desired. However, for best performance, the post office server should run on the file server that houses the post office.

The main advantage of the NLM-based GroupWise servers is that they run on the same machine where the message queues are located. Therefore, you don't have the across-the-wire network traffic that is characteristic of the other message server platforms.

The NLM message server supports TCP/IP transport between domains. I explain how to set up and run the NLM message server in Chapter 8. TCP/IP links will be discussed in Chapter 10.

OS/2 MESSAGE SERVER PACK

The message server for an OS/2 platform is a powerful message server that provides much higher performance than the DOS message server. It is often used in non-Novell network environments and in environments where the NLMs are not practical. Like the NLM message server, this server supports TCP/IP connections between GroupWise domains.

The OS/2 message server is a native 32-bit application, and it makes full use of the multithreading capabilities of the OS/2 operating system. It uses a separate pair of threads for each message server input queue (WPCSIN). One of the threads handles high-priority messages; the other handles all other message priorities. Threads are also used in other areas, such as logging, queue maintenance, and user interface. The administrator has the ability to define additional threads if desired.

All of the GroupWise OS/2 servers (message server, post office server, and administration server)·can run from the same OS/2 workstation. The OS/2 message server features an OS/2 Presentation Manager interface, complete with online help and pull-down menus.

UNIX MESSAGE SERVER

The UNIX message server is available for the following kinds of UNIX systems:

- SunOS

- Data General (DG) Aviion

- HP 9000 (700 and 800 series)

- IBM RS6000

- SVR4 (System 5, Release 4)

- SCO UNIX

- Solaris 2

The UNIX message server is used in UNIX-based GroupWise domains. Like the NLM version, it is a high-performance message server. The UNIX message server takes advantage of the multithreading capability of UNIX, and it is a native 32-bit application.

DOS MESSAGE SERVER

The DOS message server is a very functional message server, but not one that should ordinarily be used in a high-performance environment. Its main benefit is that is very easy to configure and use. It does require a dedicated workstation to run on, but that workstation can be a low-end computer (e.g., a 386).

The DOS message server excutable file, CS.EXE, handles domain-level message routing. It can also spawn other MTA processes, such as the post office servers, gateway servers, and administration server. However, because the DOS message server does not have multitasking or multithreading capabilities, it can only do one thing at a time. When a post office server for one of the post offices is processing messages, no processing can be done for other post offices, for gateways, or for the domain.

The DOS message server is a very capable server, but you will typically want to use it in GroupWise implementations where high-speed message delivery is not a concern or where the resources that can be dedicated to a GroupWise system are very limited. Nevertheless, it is a very good training tool because it can be run on most DOS-based workstations.

Message Flow Between Post Offices in the Same Domain

As I mentioned earlier, message flow is the same for all message server platforms. Figures 7.10 and 7.11 illustrate how messages move from one GroupWise post office to another within the same domain. Pay close attention to how the message server handles delivery between the two post offices.

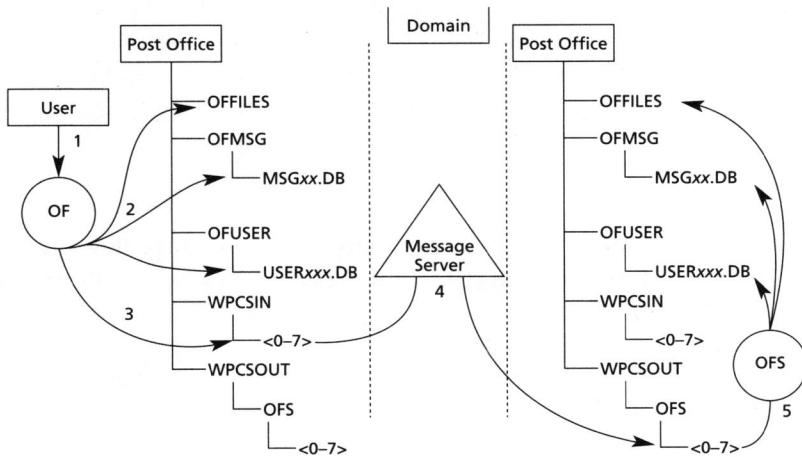

FIGURE 7.10

Post Office-to-Post Office Message Flow in the Same Domain

In Figure 7.10 and in all future diagrams in this book, I assume that an Application Threshhold setting is in use.

NOTE

Here is the path, as illustrated in Figure 7.10, that a GroupWise message takes from one post office to another in the same domain:

1 • The GroupWise user creates a message intended for a single recipient located in another post office within the same domain.

2 • The client places the message in the sender's mailbox. The client inserts the message in the message database, adds pointers to the sender's user database, and places file attachments in the OFFILES directory (if necessary).

3 • The client puts a copy of the message in the post office message server input queue (WPCSIN\<0-7>).

4 • The message server (MS) scans the input queue and detects the message. It reads the message's address and recognizes that the message is destined for a recipient in a post office within the domain. It then places the message in the recipient post office's message server output queue (WPCSOUT\OFS\<0–7>).

5 • At the recipient post office, the post office server (OFS) detects the message, reads the address information, and completes the delivery of the message to the appropriate mailbox. The post office server adds the message to the message database, inserts a pointer in the recipient's user database, and places file attachments in the OFFILES directory.

NOTE

To reduce the complexity of the message flow diagrams, I will show the processing of status messages in separate illustrations throughout the book.

Figure 7.11 illustrates the path of a status message that is created when a message is sent to another post office within a domain.

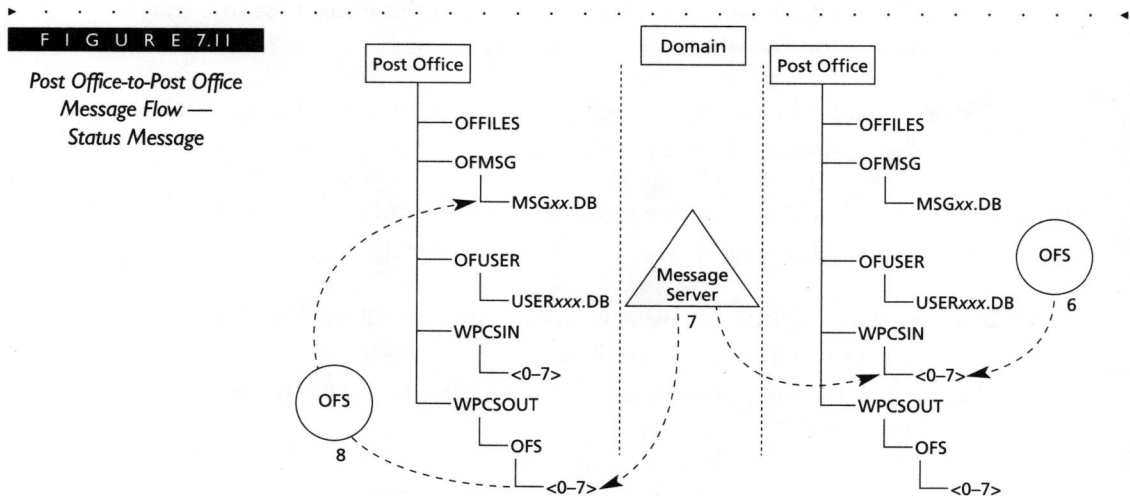

FIGURE 7.11

*Post Office-to-Post Office Message Flow —
Status Message*

The process illustrated in Figure 7.11 is a continuation of the process depicted in Figure 7.10. The steps that follow the delivery of the original message are:

1 • The post office server generates a *Delivered* status message addressed to the originating post office, and it places the status message in the message server input queue (WPCSIN\<0–7>).

2 • The message server scans the input queue and detects the message. It reads the status message's address and places the status message in the original sender's post office message server output queue (WPCSOUT\OFS\<0–7>).

3 • The post office server detects the status message in the message server output queue and updates the message record in the message database with the status.

Notice that two separate post office server (OFS) processes are involved—one for the sender's post office and one for the recipient's post office—but only one message server process is involved. Furthermore, no domain-level input or output queues are used in this process. They would only be used if for some reason the destination post office were closed. In that case, the message would be stored at the domain level in the WPCS\MSLOCAL\MSHOLD directories until the recipient's post office was open again.

Summary

If you have set up a single PC test system according to the instructions in Appendix C, you can continue that process by creating a second post office, by adding more users, and by installing a DOS message server. You should then be able to send messages between users in different post offices in a single domain.

The following documents on the CD-ROM contain additional information relating to this chapter:

▶ DOSMSRVR.IE GroupWise 4.1 DOS Message Server Instant Expert Guide

▶ NLMMSRVR.IE GroupWise 4.1 NLM Message Server Instant Expert Guide

▶ UNIXMSRV.IE GropuWise 4.1 UNIX Message Server Instant Expert Guide

In the next chapter, I will tell you how to set up, configure, and optimize an NLM message server in a single domain system that has multiple post offices. If you do not plan to use an NLM message server platform in your GroupWise system, make sure you at least read the section entitled "Optimizing NLM Performance," which explains the options available in the Message Server Configuration screen that apply to all message server platforms.

GroupWise NLM Message Servers

This chapter focuses on NetWare Loadable Module (NLM) message servers. I have devoted a whole chapter to NLM message servers for several reasons:

▸ The GroupWise NLM message server provides the best performance in a Novell NetWare 3.1x and 4.x environment.

▸ Since the introduction of the NLM Message Server Pack, it has become the most widely used message server platform.

▸ I believe that it is essential for a GroupWise administrator to understand the GroupWise NLMs, especially if an organization has made a long-term commitment to GroupWise. Future Novell GroupWare products will most likely build upon the NLM concept.

What Is an NLM?

A NetWare Loadable Module (NLM) is a program that is loaded directly on a NetWare file server. NLMs can be loaded and unloaded from server memory while the network file server is running.

The NetWare file server allocates a portion of memory to the NLM when the NLM is loaded. The NLM uses this memory to perform a task and then returns control of the memory to the operating system when the NLM is unloaded.

One of the most critical things to remember about using NLMs, in general, is that you should be sure to keep them updated. New versions of NLMs are frequently released to improve performance and fix problems. New NLMs are posted on bulletin boards and other Novell Online services.

For hints on how to keep your NLMs and utilities updated, refer to the GroupWise Tech Tip document, FINDPTCH.TT, "Locating GroupWise and NetWare Patch Files," on the CD-ROM.

What Is a UNC Path?

GroupWise NLMs use Universal Naming Convention (UNC) paths. The GroupWise NLM servers must be able to access the domain and post office directories without using DOS and DOS drive designators, such as X:. The syntax for finding a domain or a post office directory on a particular network file server is UNC.

UNC syntax specifies an absolute location on the file server. The syntax is as follows:

```
\\server\volume\directory\subdirectory
```

where server stands for the name of the server, volume stands for the name of the volume, and so on. The syntax should not be confused or interchanged with the standard NetWare syntax, which is:

```
server/volume:\directory\subdirectory
```

IMPORTANT

You should define the UNC path for *each* domain and post office in your system if you are using the NLM message server pack.

When UNC entries are used in GroupWise, they are distributed throughout the GroupWise system so that every domain database has the same information regarding every other domain in the system. This sharing of the UNC field is possible because it represents an absolute location on the network. The DOS drive letter is a relative location because the drive mappings can vary from workstation to workstation.

TIP

To identify the UNC path of your current drive and directory, type the TRUENAME command at the DOS command prompt if you are using MS-DOS 5.0 or above.

GroupWise NLM Overview

In a GroupWise system running the NLM message server, you must be familiar with these types of NLMs:

▸ NetWare NLMs used by GroupWise NLMs, which are installed when NetWare is installed

▸ GroupWise message server NLMs, including the NLM message server, the NLM post office server, and the NLM administration server

▸ GroupWise NLMs that supplement the GroupWise message server NLMs

NETWARE NLMS USED BY GROUPWISE

The following NLMs are copied to the SYS:\SYSTEM directory when NetWare is installed on a file server. They have to be on the file server in order for the GroupWise NLMs to work, and they must be the most recent versions.

These NLMs are sometimes referred to as *dependency NLMs* because the GroupWise NLMs need them in order to run. See Table 8.1.

TABLE 8.1 Dependency NLMs	NLM	NAME	DESCRIPTION
	CLIB.NLM	C Libraries	General routines and functions used by many NLMs.
	STREAMS.NLM	Network Protocol Streams	A common interface that allows the operating system to access different network protocols.
	TLI.NLM	Transport Level Interface	An NLM used at the server console to provide Transport Level Interface (TLI) communication services. It requires STREAMS.NLM and CLIB.NLM. This NLM is only needed if the message server connects to other message servers via TCP/IP.
	NWSNUT.NLM	NLM User Interface Utility	A utility that gives GroupWise servers the standard NetWare user interface of windows and lists.

TABLE 8.1	NLM	NAME	DESCRIPTION
Dependency NLMs *(continued)*	AFTER311.NLM	NetWare 3.11 Forward Compatibility Support	A compatibility NLM required for GroupWise servers running on NetWare 3.1x file servers.
	SNMP.NLM (optional)	Simple Network Management Protocol	A standard management protocol that provides control and monitoring of network software that provides control and hardware.
	TCPIP.NLM (optional)	TCP/IP Network Protocol	An NLM that allows NetWare file servers to transmit and receive TCP/IP network packets.

IMPORTANT

If you are running the GroupWise NLMs on NetWare 3.x, make sure you are using CLIB version 3.12h or higher. If you are running the GroupWise NLMs on NetWare 4.02, make sure you are using CLIB version 4.1 or later. For NetWare 3.x and 4.02, you should install DHANDFX.NLM. For NetWare 4.02, CSEMFIX.NLM should also be installed.

GROUPWISE NLMS

A GroupWise NLM is an executable program that is loaded directly on the file servers where a GroupWise post office or domain is located. The GroupWise NLMs are the ideal message server and post office server platform when Novell NetWare is the network operating system because of their highly efficient interaction with the file server, GroupWise databases, and GroupWise message queue directories.

You should bear in mind that GroupWise NLMs will not function properly unless the supporting NetWare NLMs have been installed and loaded. When the first GroupWise NLM is loaded, it will automatically load all of the supporting NetWare NLMs.

The GroupWise NLMs that ship with the NLM Message Server Pack include these programs:

▸ Post office server NLM

▸ Message server NLM

▸ Administration server NLM

▸ Bindery synchronization NLM

There are other GroupWise utilities that integrate GroupWise with NetWare—such as the GroupWise NetWare Administration snap-in module, which is available from NetWire and other Novell online services. The snap-in module provides some GroupWise administrative capabilities from the NetWare Administration program. Those utilities will be discussed later in this book.

Post Office Server NLM   You learned about the GroupWise post office server in Chapter 6. Among other things, the post office server is responsible for delivering messages within a post office and for creating messages regarding the status of delivered mail. The post office server NLM program is called NGWOFS.NLM.

Message Server NLM   I discussed the message server in Chapter 7. The message server is a GroupWise MTA that moves messages between other GroupWise servers. The message server will move messages between post offices within the same domain and to other domains. The GroupWise message server NLM is named NGWMS.NLM.

Administration Server NLM   I have not said much about the administration server so far. It takes care of directory synchronization, creating administrative messages that are sent to other domains. The administration server makes sure that administrative changes in one domain are carried out in all of the other domains in a GroupWise system. I will discuss the administration server at length in Part IV. For now, simply remember that the GroupWise administration server NLM is NGWADS.NLM.

Bindery Synchronization NLM   NetWare 3.x stores the user directory and user information in the NetWare bindery. When a change is made to the NetWare bindery, the bindery synchronization NLM updates the information in GroupWise. For example, if a new user is added to the bindery, the bindery synchronization NLM automatically adds that user to GroupWise. This NLM is often used in NetWare environments where network changes occur frequently. The bindery synchronization NLM is NGWBDS.NLM.

Supplemental GroupWise NLMs   Some NLMs installed along with the GroupWise NLM Server Pack support the operation of the main GroupWise message server NLMs. Table 8.2 describes each of those NLMs:

	NLM	DESCRIPTION
TABLE 8.2 *Supplemental GroupWise NLMs*	NGWMSIP.NLM	Supports TCP/IP.
	NGWUTIL.NLM (GroupWise 4.1 only)	Loads utility NLMs called NGWUTILx.NLM (see below).
	NGWUTIL3.NLM (GroupWise 4.1 only)	Required when running GroupWise 4.1 on NetWare 3.1x. (It is automatically loaded by NGWUTIL.NLM. It is not required for GroupWise 4.1a or above.)
	NGWUTIL4.NLM (GroupWise 4.1 only)	Required when running GroupWise 4.1 on NetWare 4.x. (It is automatically loaded by NGWUTIL.NLM. It is not required for GroupWise 4.1a or above.)
	NGWLIB.NLM	Stores the function libraries for all GroupWise NLMs.

Installing the NLM Message Server Pack

Each message server pack has its own installation routine. The NLM Message Server Pack is installed from a DOS workstation that has access to the file server where the GroupWise domain is located. The administrator needs administrative rights to the domain directory and to the SYS:\SYSTEM directory on that file server.

The NLM Message Server Pack requires NetWare 3.1x or 4.x, 7MB RAM (if all GroupWise servers are loaded on one file server), and all NetWare supporting NLMs (see above).

Follow these steps to install the NLM Message Server Pack:

1 • Log in to the file server as the administrator (or equivalent).

2 • Insert the NLM message server disk into the workstation disk drive, and type **A:INSTALL**.

The installation screen shown in Figure 8.1 will appear.

3 • Verify that the drive to the SYS:\SYSTEM option displays the correct drive letter for the drive mapped to the SYS:\SYSTEM directory.

NOTE

In most NetWare environments, drive Z is mapped to the SYS: volume by default. However, if this is not correct in your system and you do not change the drive letter for this option, the installation will fail.

F I G U R E 8.1

GroupWise NLM Message Server Installation Screen

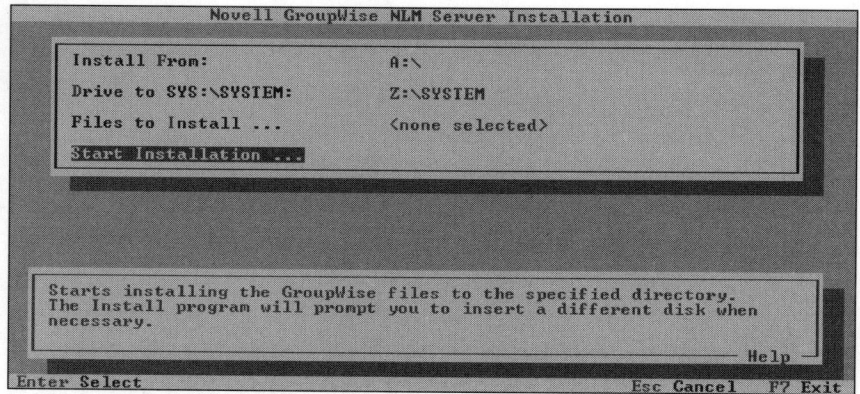

4 • Select the files to install and then choose F10.

5 • Choose Start Installation.

The GroupWise message server NLMs, the supplemental NLMs, and the startup file templates will be installed to the SYS:\SYSTEM directory.

Configuring the Message Server in GroupWise Admin

After the files are installed, you need to configure your GroupWise domain to use the NLM message server. Follow these steps to configure a GroupWise domain for GroupWise NLM servers:

1 • Run AD.EXE.

2 • Highlight the domain and choose Actions and then Edit.

3 • Choose Message Server Configuration. The screen shown in Figure 8.2 will appear.

F I G U R E 8.2

*Message Server
Configuration Screen*

```
┌─────────────────────── Message Server Configuration ────────────────┐
│ Domain:  Domain1                                                     │
│     1. Description : GroupWise Message Server                        │
│     2. Platform    [ NLM              ‡]                             │
│    ┌─3. Execution─────────────────────────────────┐                 │
│    │ Priority Scan Cycle:   5       ▲▼ (sec)      │  Diagnostics... │
│    │ Normal Scan Cycle:    15       ▲▼ (sec)      │                 │
│    │ Attach Retry:        600       ▲▼ (sec)      │  Network Links..│
│    │ Reattach String:                             │                 │
│    │ Message Delivery:    [ Server Never      ‡]  │  Servers...     │
│    │                                              │                 │
│    ┌─4. Logging────────────────────────────────┐  │  Build CSI File │
│    │ Level:                  [ Normal     ‡]    │                    │
│    │ Max Log Age:              7     ▲▼ (days)  │                    │
│    │ [X] Limit Disk Usage:  1024     ▲▼ (kb)    │                    │
│    │                                            │                    │
│    ┌─5. TCP/IP Settings────────────────────────┐                    │
│    │ Address:                                   │                    │
│    │ Port Number:  7100                         │    OK    Cancel    │
└─────────────────────────────────────────────────────────────────────┘
```

4 • Change Message Server Platform to NLM.

5 • Change the Message Delivery Mode to either Use App Thresholds or Server Always to enable the message server.

6 • Check the network links to verify that UNC paths are properly configured. Edit the links if necessary.

DEFINING THE ADMINISTRATOR OF A DOMAIN

You can use GroupWise Admin to specify a domain administrator who will receive GroupWise messages in his or her In Box when certain errors occur. Those GroupWise messages may be generated by the message server, the post office server, or the administration server. You can choose a domain administrator when you view the Domain Information screen in GroupWise Admin. The dialog box for setting the domain administrator is shown in Figure 8.3.

FIGURE 8.3

Domain Administrator
Information Dialog Box

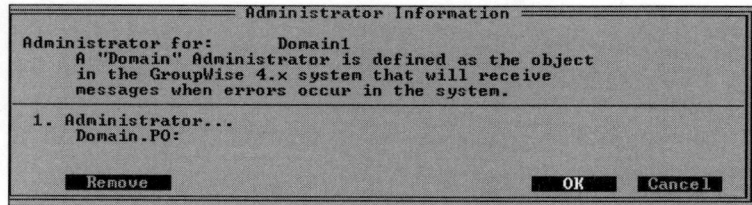

```
═══════════════════════ Administrator Information ═══════════════════════
Administrator for:        Domain1
      A "Domain" Administrator is defined as the object
      in the GroupWise 4.x system that will receive
      messages when errors occur in the system.

   1. Administrator...
      Domain.PO:


        Remove                                      OK     Cancel
```

Creating Network Access Accounts for the GroupWise Servers

If a domain contains multiple file servers, you must use access accounts to provide the GroupWise servers access to each file server. The access account was explained in Chapter 7.

All of the access accounts must have the same user name and password. The access accounts must also include the following rights in the domain and post office directories:

► Create files or directories

► Erase files or directories

► Read or execute files

► Scan for files

► Write to files

Make sure the access accounts have multiple concurrent logins on the file servers.

In multiple domain systems, access accounts must include rights to all of the other domain directories that the domain has a direct link with. This enables the message server to deliver messages to all domains. In NetWare 4.1 systems, you can create access accounts in all of the domains by creating a user in one of the Organizations or Organizational Units with a file server housing a GroupWise domain. Grant that user the necessary rights to each file server. Then, create an alias for that user in each Organization or Organizational Unit with a file server housing a domain or post office.

Editing the Startup Files

The GroupWise NLMs use startup files that contain switches necessary for the NLMs to load properly. They can also be used to customize the operation of the GroupWise servers and optimize performance. Startup file templates for each of the GroupWise servers are installed during the message server installation. These files are in ASCII format and must be edited before you can use them. When you view the text of the files, semicolons (;) indicate comment lines or disabled switches. These files are listed in Table 8.3.

TABLE 8.3	FILE	DESCRIPTION
Startup Files	STARTUP.MS	The message server startup file
	STARTUP.ADS	Administration server startup file
	STARTUP.OFS	Post office server startup file
	STARTUP.BDS	Bindery synchronization startup file

I explain the most common switches for each NLM server process and give examples of the servers' startup files below.

Running the NLMs

After you have installed the NLMs, configured the message server options in GroupWise Admin, created network access accounts for each file server, and edited each of the appropriate startup files, you are ready to run the NLMs on your system.

The GroupWise NLMs are loaded like any other NetWare NLM. To run an NLM, you must be able to access the NetWare prompt either by using the file server console or by running RCONSOLE from a network workstation.

You should use the startup files when you load the NLMs. The syntax for loading an NLM with a startup file is as follows:

```
LOAD NLM filename @startup filename
```

where *NLM filename* is the name of the NLM and *startup filename* is the name of the startup file.

RUNNING THE MESSAGE SERVER NLM

Follow these steps to load the message server NLM on your file server:

1 • With the file server running, access the file server console or use RCONSOLE to access the server prompt.

2 • Use the following syntax to load the NLM:
```
LOAD NGWMS @STARTUP.MS
```

NOTE
> **The startup filename does not have to be STARTUP.MS. It can be any valid filename. I recommend that you use startup filenames that appropriately describe the startup file. For example, if you have a domain named Headquarters and a post office named Sales, the message server startup file might be named HEADQTRS.MS, and the post office server startup file might be named SALES.OFS.**

The most common startup switches for the NLM message server are explained in Table 8.4.

TABLE 8.4	SWITCH	DESCRIPTION
NLM Message Server Startup Switches	/HOME	Points the server to the source of configuration information and, in most cases, to input and output queues. (It is always required.)
	/USER	Specifies the NetWare user account that will be used to access other file servers. (On NetWare 4.x systems, you should use the full distinguished name.)
	/PASSWORD	Specifies the password for the user account indicated by the /USER switch.
	/HELP	Prints a list of the startup switches to the console screen.

TABLE 8.4	SWITCH	DESCRIPTION
NLM Message Server Startup Switches (continued)	/WORK	Points to the directory where the message server can create work directories and files. (This switch is required for the message server NLM.)
	/FAST0	Forces the message server to monitor the 0 and 1 priority directories separately.
	/FAST4	Forces the message server to monitor the 2 and 3 priority directories separately from the 4–7 priority directories.
	@	Points to a file that the GroupWise NLM should look to for startup switches that would normally be included as parameters to the LOAD command.

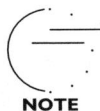

NOTE

The NLM message server requires that you create the same user account and password on all remote file servers to which the NLM needs access. You specify the user account and password using the /USER and /PASSWORD command line switches when the NLM is loaded. *If you are running the NLM message server on a NetWare 4.x file server, you must use the full distinguished name with the /USER switch.*

A portion of the STARTUP.MS file is shown here:

```
; STARTUP.MS sample startup file for the Message Server NLM.
; Replace the values in the square brackets with your own
    values.
; Do not place your values in square brackets.
; Place a semicolon in front of those switches you are not
    using.
; Be sure to save in ASCII format.
; See the Message Server Guide for more information.
; All optional switches have been disabled.

; Points the NLM to the domain directory. This switch is
    required.
/home=vol:[\domain directory]
; Points the NLM to the Message Server Directory. This switch
    is required.
```

```
; The default is the \WPCS\ directory.
;/work=vol:[\message server directory]

; Provides the NLM with the remote file server's NetWare user
    ID.
; /user-[Novell user ID]

; Provides the NLM with the remote file servers's NetWare
    password.
; /password-[Novell password]

; Displays the startup switch help screen
   ; /help
```

The GroupWise message server NLM supports TCP/IP connections between domains. The required startup switches for TCP/IP connections are found at the end of the STARTUP.MS file. Linking domains with TCP/IP connections will be discussed in Part IV.

RUNNING THE POST OFFICE SERVER NLM

The post office server is loaded in the same way as the message server. However, some of the startup switches are different. Follow these steps to load the post office server NLM:

1 • With the file server running, access the file server console or use RCONSOLE to access the server prompt.

2 • Use the following syntax to load the NLM:

```
LOAD NGWOFS @STARTUP.OFS
```

The most common startup switches for the post office server are shown in Table 8.5.

	SWITCH	DESCRIPTION
T A B L E 8.5 *Common Post Office Server Startup Switches*	/HOME	Points the NLM to the post office directory. (This is the only required switch for the post office server.)
	@	Points the NLM to the startup file.
	/CPU	Sets the NLM's CPU utilization threshold level. (This switch is used to ensure that the NLM does not dominate your file server's CPU.)
	/PRIORITY	Controls how many threads are used for high-priority items. (The default is two, which includes high-priority items such as busy searches and priority messages.)

A portion of the post office server startup file is shown below:

```
; Points the NLM to the post office directory. This switch is
    required.
/home=[server\vol:]\[post office directory]
; Provides the NLM with the remote file server's NetWare user
    ID.
; /user-[Novell user ID]

; Provides the NLM with the remote file servers's NetWare
    password.
; /password-[Novell password]

; Displays the startup switch help screen
; /help

; PERFORMANCE SWITCHES
; Sets the CPU Utilization threshold level.
;/cpu-[percentage]
; Sets how many threads are dedicated to high priority
    processing
;/priority-[threads]
; Sets how many threads the NLM spawns. The default is 4.
;/threads-[number]
```

Threads

When working with the GroupWise NLMs, you often come across the term *threads*. Threads are processes or paths of execution that run in the network operating system. They allow separate processes to be run simultaneously on the server.

When a post office server NLM is loaded, it initiates the threads requested with the / threads switch. Each thread contains the code to perform the NLM's function. The more threads the NLM uses, the more it dominates the file server's CPU at the expense of other network applications.

Although threads may be initiated by the same program, each thread operates independently of the others. For example, one thread may process a message while another thread polls the post office directories.

The post office server users two types of threads—high priority and normal priority. High-priority threads process items such as busy searches and other items placed in the high-priority directory's WPCSOUT\OFS\<0–3>. (A *busy search* is a GroupWise client function that a GroupWise user performs when trying to find an available time to schedule an appointment with other users. For more information about busy searches, see Appendix A.) Normal-priority threads process everything not processed by the high-priority threads (messages placed in the WPCSOUT\OFS\<4–7>).

RUNNING THE ADMINISTRATION SERVER NLM

I have not said a great deal about the administration server yet. It will be discussed in depth in Part IV. However, because you can run the administration server NLM just like any other NLM, I will briefly describe the use of the administration server NLM here. Follow these steps to run the administration server NLM:

1 • With the file server running, access the file server console or use RCONSOLE to access the server prompt.

2 • Use the following syntax to load the NLM:

```
LOAD NGWADS @STARTUP.ADS
```

The most common startup switches for the administration server NLM are described in Table 8.6.

	SWITCH	DESCRIPTION
TABLE 8.6 *Common Administration* *Server Startup Switches*	@	Points the NLM to the location of the startup file.
	/HOME	Points the NLM to the domain directory. (It is a required switch.)
	/USER	Sets the network user ID for accessing remote file servers. (When any domains or post offices reside on remote file servers, you must set up an identical access account on each server to give the administration server access.)
	/PASSWORD	Sets the password for accessing remote file servers.

See the *GroupWise NLM Message Server Reference Manual* for a complete listing of the startup switches for each GroupWise server.

Other NLM Loading Considerations

As an administrator, you should be familiar with the following tasks related to GroupWise NLMs:

▸ Using startup files instead of command line switches

▸ Unloading the GroupWise NLMs

▸ Loading the NLMs through the AUTOEXEC.NCF file

▸ Loading multiple copies of GroupWise NLMs

▸ Optimizing NLM performance

▸ Setting Scan Cycle and Attach Retry

▸ Adjusting Logging Levels

▸ Manipulating message server threads

USING STARTUP FILES

When you install the NLM Message Server Pack, generic server startup files are installed in the SYSTEM directory. These files contain all the available switches for their respective NLMs. These files must be edited prior to use. Some of the advantages of using startup files are:

▸ Startup files eliminate the need for long strings of startup switches when using the LOAD command.

▸ Startup files can include comment lines to indicate exactly what each switch does.

▸ Startup files can be edited on the GroupWise server's screen.

NOTE

When a startup file requires a reference to a directory, such as a domain directory, you cannot use DOS drive letters. You must use the NetWare syntax to specify the server, volume, and directory—for example, USA\SYS:DOMAIN1\WPCS.

UNLOADING THE GROUPWISE NLMS

Some common GroupWise NLMs are loaded to support all GroupWise server NLMs. For example, the NGWLIB.NLM contains common library routines used by all GroupWise NLMs. These NLMs, along with the required NetWare dependency NLMs, are not always unloaded when all the GroupWise server NLMs are unloaded. Here are some rules to follow when unloading GroupWise NLMs:

▸ NLMs must be unloaded in the same sequence in which they were loaded.

▸ Use the F7 (exit) function to exit a GroupWise server NLM instead of using the unload command.

▸ These GroupWise files must be unloaded manually:

  ▸ NGWLIB.NLM

  ▸ NGWMSIP.NLM

> ▸ NGWUTIL3 (if running GroupWise 4.1 and
>   NetWare 3.1x)

> ▸ NGWUTIL4 (if running GroupWise 4.1 and
>   NetWare 4.x)

NOTE

Some of the dependency Novell NLMs, such as CLIB and STREAMS, may be used by other applications. You may not want to unload them.

LOADING THE NLMS THROUGH AUTOEXEC.NCF

Once you have tested the GroupWise NLMs on your system, you can edit the file server's AUTOEXEC.NCF file to include the necessary NetWare and GroupWise NLMs. This will allow them to be loaded as part of the NetWare file server's startup sequence.

LOADING MULTIPLE COPIES OF A GROUPWISE NLM

It may occasionally be necessary to load multiple copies of a GroupWise NLM on the same file server. Suppose that you have a single domain, dual post office system on two file servers. One file server contains the domain directory structure and a post office, and the other file server houses the other post office. Suppose also that the file server that contains only the post office is not capable of running the post office server. In that case, the file server that holds the domain could run the message server NLM and two post office server processes. (Note that this would not be advisable, because the OFS process would be polling the post office directories across the network wire, thus eliminating one of the key advantages of the NLM servers.)

To run multiple NLMs, you would have to run the NLM twice using separate startup files that point to different post offices and different work directories.

OPTIMIZING NLM PERFORMANCE

As I mentioned earlier, the main reason for implementing the GroupWise servers on the NLM platform is to eliminate network input/output by placing the process on the same computer that holds the message store and message queue directories. Data can be written to and read from a file or database much faster on a local disk drive than across the network.

The post office server derives the greatest benefit. The post office server NLM can perform its tasks without generating a single packet of network traffic if it is running on the file server that houses the post office. This is because the post office server does all of its work with the directories and databases that are in the post office directory structures. It does not poll directories or write to databases located in the domain or in other post offices.

Here are some other settings that can be adjusted to improve a GroupWise server's performance:

▸ Scan Cycle and Attach Retry

▸ Logging Level

▸ Message Server Threads

Each of these settings can be configured in the Message Server Configuration dialog box, shown in Figure 8.2.

Scan Cycle and Attach Retry

The Scan Cycle and Attach Retry settings are configured in GroupWise Admin using the Message Server Configuration screen. You can use these settings to balance network traffic against idle time.

Even when message load is light, the message server can create a lot of network traffic just scanning its input queues. That unnecessary traffic can be minimized by setting the scan cycle to a higher number. However, if the scan cycle is set too high, important messages could end up waiting a long time to be picked up by the message server. The default is every 5 seconds for high-priority messages, and every 15 seconds for normal-priority messages.

Attach Retry can also be used to optimize NLM performance. If this setting is too low and a file server is unreachable, the message server can create excess network traffic trying to reestablish the connection. However, you do not want the message server to ignore an available file server because it is waiting too long before it makes another attempt to connect. You want to adjust this setting so that you strike a balance. The default is 600 seconds (or 10 minutes).

Logging Level

The logging level can have a big impact on the message server's performance. It requires a lot of processing time to write everything that the server does to a log file and to the screen. When a system has proven itself to be stable, the logging levels on all the servers should be lowered at least to the *Normal* setting.

Message Server Threads

The message server NLM makes full use of the multithreading capabilities of NetWare 3 and NetWare 4 operating systems. By default, the message server allocates two threads for each of its input queues. However, this may create a bottleneck under some circumstances.

For example, if a domain has a lot of GroupWise Remote users, their requests for data from their mailboxes are routed to the post office server as priority 1 message files. With only one thread to handle both priority 1 and priority 0 message files, you will see a much slower response to busy searches when a lot of GroupWise Remote requests come in.

The /FAST0 switch causes the message server to give both priority queues their own thread. The busy search performance will still be affected, but a busy search will never have to wait for a lot of GroupWise Remote requests to be processed first.

A similar circumstance can affect the delivery of priority 4 (normal priority) messages. In this case, an abundance of priority 2 (Admin) messages can delay the processing of normal priority messages. If a lot of Admin functions such as moving users and purging trash are holding up normal priority messages, you can use the FAST/4 switch.

This switch allocates one thread to service the priority 2 and 3 queues and a separate thread to service the 4 through 7 queues.

Appendix D contains a table that shows how the threads will handle the various message server input queues with the various thread settings.

> **NOTE**
>
> **The extra threads should only be used if necessary. The NetWare operating system uses a great deal of memory and processing time to manage CPU usage for each thread.**

Threads are also used in other areas, such as logging, queue maintenance, and the user interface.

Summary

In this chapter, you learned how to set up the NLM message server, how to configure it, and how to optimize its performance. I will tell you more about the message server's duties throughout the book.

The following documents on the CD-ROM contain additional information relating to this chapter:

▸ NLMMSRVR.IE   *GroupWise 4.1 NLM Message Server Instant Expert Guide*

▸ NLMTROUB.WPD   *GroupWise 4.1 NLM Message Server Trouble-shooting Guide*

In Part IV, I explain the issues involved in planning and implementing multiple domain GroupWise systems.

Solution to Part III Scenario

Orton would be better off with two post offices, one on each server. Separate post offices would keep the impact of e-mail traffic across their bridge at a minimum. While the company could get by with a single post office, the only additional "costs" of having two post offices would be the resources needed to run an extra OFS process on the second server and the file server disk space for the post office message store. (Because the Message Server Pack is licensed per domain, an additional Message Server Pack for the second post office's OFS process would not need to be purchased.)

Assuming ORTONA is less busy than ORTONB, GroupWise Admin should be based at ORTONA. Another reason for locating GroupWise Admin there is because ORTONA houses the MIS directory. ORTONA will run three processes: (1) the domain message server, which handles deliveries between post offices; (2) the post office server for Post Office A; and (3) the administration server. ORTONB will only run the post office server for Post Office B.

Orton will need these GroupWise components:

- One GroupWise Client/Admin Pack for Windows (includes five maibox licenses)

- 245 Additional mailbox licenses

- One NLM Message Server Pack

Implementation Considerations

- The administrator should create a public group for each of the eight departments.

- In addition to the other GroupWise servers, the administrator should consider using the bindery synchronization NLM.

▶ Because GroupWise Admin itself is capable making administrative updates in both post offices, the administration server would probably be unnecessary. However, the administrator would have to make sure both post offices are open when administrative changes are made.

▶ DOS message servers could be used if price were an issue, but it would take longer for messages to be delivered. It would also add to network traffic and require dedication of two low-end workstations

I strongly recommend the NLM platform for Novell NetWare networks because it allows for easier administration, better performance, less maintenance, and minimal impact on the network. In addition, the NLM provides room for future growth.

Enterprise GroupWise Systems

Multiple Domains

In Part III, I explained how to set up a GroupWise system that consists of a single domain and multiple post offices. In Part IV, I will show you how to set up and configure a multiple domain GroupWise system. I will also discuss the key issues you will encounter when you administer a multiple domain system.

A multidomain GroupWise system is often referred to as an *enterprise* GroupWise system. GroupWise is very scalable. It can easily be adapted for use by large, multinational corporations. Creating enterprise systems is simply a matter of setting up multiple GroupWise domains and connecting them together.

The following scenario involves a large company that plans to implement GroupWise. This company will be used for the scenarios in Parts IV through VII of this book.

Company Description

North Central andWestern Allied Caregivers (NoCWACs) is a major health insurance provider that serves the intermountain western region of the United States. NoCWACs is based in Denver, Colorado, and serves customers in Colorado, Utah, Idaho, Wyoming, and Montana. Although it is headquartered in Denver, NoCWACs has fairly large regional offices in Salt Lake City, Utah, and Butte, Montana. The two regional offices employ about 200 people each.

In Denver, NoCWACs employs approximately 2,200 people in a complex that consists of three buildings. Building A houses administrative personnel (including the NoCWACs executive suites), Human Resources, and Payroll. Building B houses the Claims Department. Building C houses the Customer Service Department, the Information Systems Department, and the Publications Department. Figure IV.1 represents the physical layout of the NoCWACs headquarters:

FIGURE IV.I

*Layout of NoCWACs
Headquarters*

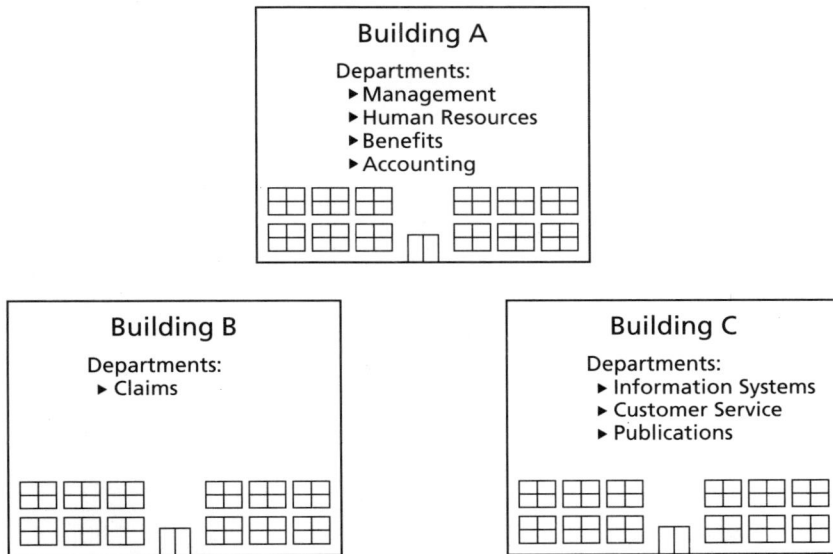

NoCWACs Headquarters

Building A

Departments:
▶ Management
▶ Human Resources
▶ Benefits
▶ Accounting

Building B

Departments:
▶ Claims

Building C

Departments:
▶ Information Systems
▶ Customer Service
▶ Publications

A description of the personnel employed by NoCWACs is shown in Table IV.1.

T A B L E IV.I

NoCWACs Employees

BUILDING	DEPARTMENT	NUMBER OF	OCCUPATIONS
A	Management	250	Executives, Administrative Assistants, Receptionists.
A	Human Resources	150	Hiring, Personnel Management.
A	Benefits	100	Employee Benefits Management.
A	Accounting and Payroll	100	Billing, Payroll, Collections.
B	Claims	1200	Central Claims Office Employees. (Handle claims processing for all client claims in excess of $5,000.)
C	Information Systems	50	Technical Employees. (Handle all computing and networking issues for the Denver site, including a help desk staff of 20 people.)
C	Customer Service	350	Customer Service Employees. (Provide 24-hour customer assistance, including general questions, complaints, and physician referrals.)
C	Publications	20	Editors and Writers. (Create and distribute a health issues newsletter, as well as the internal company newsletter.)

Networking Environment

Buildings A, B, and C are located in the same business park. The three buildings are connected by 56 Kbps frame relay links, which are currently running at about 75 percent capacity. Future plans call for upgrading links between buildings, possibly to T-1 connections—but that is at least a year away.

BUILDING A

Building A has four NetWare 4.1 file servers. The file servers are described in Table IV.2.

TABLE IV.2 *File Servers for Building A*	SERVER NAME	SPECIFICATIONS	FUNCTION	NUMBER OF USERS
	ADMIN	NetWare 4.1 Pentium processor 2GB disk space	Used by management and staff	250
	HR	NetWare 4.1 486/66 processor 1GB disk space	Shared by HR and Benefits Departments	250
	ACCOUNT1	NetWare 3.12 486/66 processor 500MB disk space	Used by the Accounting Department staff	100
	ACCOUNT2	NetWare 4.1 Pentium processor All disk space reserved for secure data and databases	A secure file server that holds payroll information and other secure data	30 members of the Accounting Department staff attach to this server

BUILDING B

Building B also has four file servers. They are described in Table IV.3.

TABLE IV.3

File Servers for Building B

SERVER NAME	SPECIFICATIONS	FUNCTION	NUMBER OF USERS
CLAIMS1	NetWare 3.12 486/66 processor 2GB disk space	General purpose file server	300
CLAIMS2	NetWare 3.12 486/66 processor 2GB disk space	General purpose file server	500
CLAIMS3	NetWare 3.12 486/66 processor 2GB disk space	General purpose file server	400
CLAIMS4	NetWare 4.1 486/66 processor 500MB disk space	Secure file server that stores claims master database	All Claims Department employees attach to this server

BUILDING C

Building C has three file servers, which are described in Table IV.4.

TABLE IV.4

File Servers for Building C

SERVER NAME	SPECIFICATIONS	FUNCTION	NUMBER OF USERS
CS1	NetWare 4.1 486/66 processor 500MB disk space	General purpose file server	350
IS1	NetWare 4.1 Pentium processor 1GB disk space	General purpose file server	50
IS2	NetWare 4.1 486/66 processor 500MB disk space	Used by Information Systems Department for testing and applications archival	50 Information Systems employees

Part IV Scenario

You are a member of the NoCWACs Information Systems (IS) team. You have been asked to lead a task force charged with implementing GroupWise company-wide. Management has determined that the implementation should take place in three stages.

Stage One   The first stage of the implementation will be to plan and install GroupWise at the company headquarters.

Stage Two   The second stage involves connecting the regional offices to the main GroupWise system.

Stage Three   The third stage involves implementing support for GroupWise Remote for all of the insurance agents employed by NoCWACs. Rumors have been circulating that NoCWACs—the largest health insurer in the Rocky Mountain region—will soon be branching into other areas of insurance coverage.

Conditions

During your analysis of the company headquarters, you discovered the following conditions:

▶ NoCWACs management must be able to assign proxy rights to their assistants.

▶ There are three conference rooms in Building A that should be set up as resources—but only management can be allowed to schedule these rooms.

▶ The Information Systems team is wary of increasing the network traffic across the links between the buildings. The team fears that GroupWise might overload the connections between buildings.

▶ Building B is a three-story building—the largest building in the business park. The employees work on all three floors. Five IS employees are assigned to Building B to support the claims processors. The Claims Department has a high rate of employee turnover. Their network administrators have requested that they be in charge of administering GroupWise in their building.

▸ The Customer Service Department works three shifts. During the day there are 200 employees at work; 100 employees work in the evening; and 50 employees work the night shift. The department has a total of only 200 workstations because the evening and nighttime employees share their workstations with the day shift employees.

▸ Most of the workstations in the company are 486/33 (or faster) IBM-compatible machines running Windows.

▸ The 20 employees in the Publications Department run Macintosh Power PCs. They have a strong bias against PCs and Windows.

CHAPTER 9

Multiple Domain GroupWise Systems

Novice GroupWise administrators often ask the following questions at GroupWise training classes and forums:

▸ How many domains should my GroupWise system have?

▸ How many post offices should I have in my domains?

▸ How many users should be in each post office?

▸ What is the best way to link domains?

Invariably, the answer to all of these questions must be, "It depends." There are too many factors involved to permit off-the-cuff answers. As they say, there's an exception to every rule—and that maxim certainly holds true in the area of multiple domain GroupWise systems.

It is impossible to give quick answers because GroupWise can so easily be customized and scaled to both small and large networking environments. As you implement GroupWise, you will discover ways to make it work better for you. Implementing GroupWise will be a continuous process of setting up your system a certain way, trying it out, and then deciding which strategic decisions to stick with and which to change. Just when you think your system's perfect, a new technology will come along that you'll want to try out.

This chapter discusses several strategies for setting up GroupWise in large local-area-network (LAN) and wide-area-network (WAN) environments. Three common GroupWise architectures will be discussed: simple, star, and ring.

NOTE

A GroupWise architecture is not a specific option that you can select using GroupWise Admin. An architecture is a system's structure that results from linking all of the domains together. The domain links can be reconfigured at any time to change the architecture.

Planning a Multiple Domain GroupWise System

When you are implementing a multiple domain GroupWise system, you must decide whether multiple domains are necessary, which architecture should be used, which file servers should run the GroupWise server processes, and which domain should be the primary domain.

Not every GroupWise system needs multiple domains. Here are some issues to consider as you determine whether your system needs more than one domain:

▸ Which sites need to be connected by GroupWise?

▸ Are those sites connected by a network? If so, what kind of physical network connection do they have (e.g., 56 kilobits per second lines, T1, etc.)?

▸ Which departments or business units at each site need to communicate internally only?

▸ Which departments or business units at each site need to communicate with other groups at the same site?

▸ Which departments or business units need to communicate with groups at other sites?

▸ Is a qualified GroupWise administrator available to administer the GroupWise system at each site or can someone adequately manage the GroupWise system remotely?

▸ How many users are there at each site?

▸ What kind of hardware is available for the message servers? Is that hardware already working at or near its capacity?

Typically, in an environment with separate physical locations (e.g., offices in different cities) you will want to have at least one domain at each site. This is especially true if the sites are connected by a slow network link, such as a 56 kilobits per second (Kbps) link or a T1. By creating a domain at each site, you can reduce the amount of traffic across the slow network link.

As you plan your system, you should be aware of the differences between sites that house only post offices and sites where both domains and post offices are located. The main difference lies in the performance of administrative tasks. Because administrative tasks are performed at the domain level and not at the post office level, sites that house only post offices must be administered from somewhere else. Another difference is that you can connect two domains using gateways, but you need a physical network connection to connect post offices to domains. Furthermore, you can connect domains using the TCP/IP transport protocol. That mode of connection is not currently available to connect post offices to domains. These factors will influence your decision about where to locate post offices and domains.

If you decide to have a domain at each site, you should be aware of the additional system requirements necessitated by each domain. Each domain requires additional disk space for the domain databases and files (20–25MB). Also, each domain requires hardware and memory resources for its message server. (If you are using the NLM message server, you will only need to be concerned about having adequate memory resources.) Finally, you will need to obtain a message server license for each additional domain.

Suppose your company has two sites—one in New York and one in Dallas—which are connected by a 56 Kbps data line. You have three options to consider as you set up the GroupWise system.

▸ You could set up one domain and a single post office that includes all of the users at both locations.

▸ You could set up a single domain and create two post offices—one in each location.

▸ You could create a separate domain and post office at each location.

Option 1: Single Post Office for All Users   One option would be to have a single post office—for example, one post office located on a file server in New York. However, that setup would be inefficient. Whenever users in Dallas run the client, the client program would have to read and write to mailbox databases in New York across the 56 Kbps line, as illustrated in Figure 9.1. This would generate a lot of traffic on the 56 Kbps line. Furthermore, the users in Dallas would undoubtedly be frustrated with the system because the client would operate very slowly there.

Option 2: Post Offices at Both Sites   Another option would be to have one domain, but two post offices—one in New York and one in Dallas. This configuration would avoid client-generated traffic on the 56 Kbps line, and it would provide better client performance than the first option. However, when a system has multiple post offices, a message server is required. The message server could run in either New York or Dallas, but it would have to poll the message server input queues (WPCSIN) in both post offices. The message server would therefore generate constant polling traffic on the 56 Kbps line, as shown in Figure 9.2. In addition, the message server would have to transfer interdomain messages across the 56 Kbps line. To decrease the traffic, you might lengthen the time between polling scans. However, a longer time span would delay delivery of messages because they would not be detected in the WPCSIN directory as quickly. In any event, system performance would be adversely affected—either by the increased message traffic or by the longer polling interval. Nevertheless, although this option may not be an ideal arrangement, it is a reasonable solution when it would not be feasible to implement message servers in two locations (because of the expense, the additional hardware resources required, a lack of qualified administrators, or for some other reason).

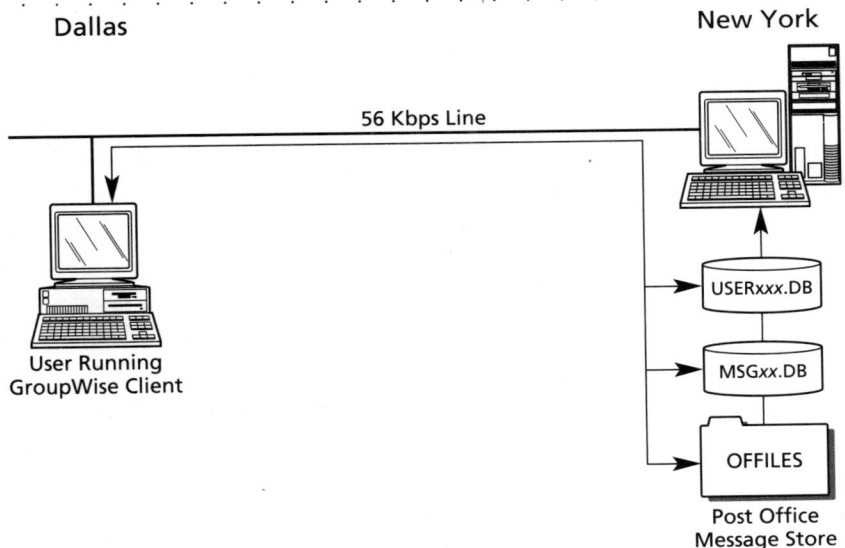

FIGURE 9.1

Single Post Office Spanning Multiple Sites

Dallas

New York

56 Kbps Line

User Running
GroupWise Client

USERxxx.DB

MSGxx.DB

OFFILES

Post Office
Message Store

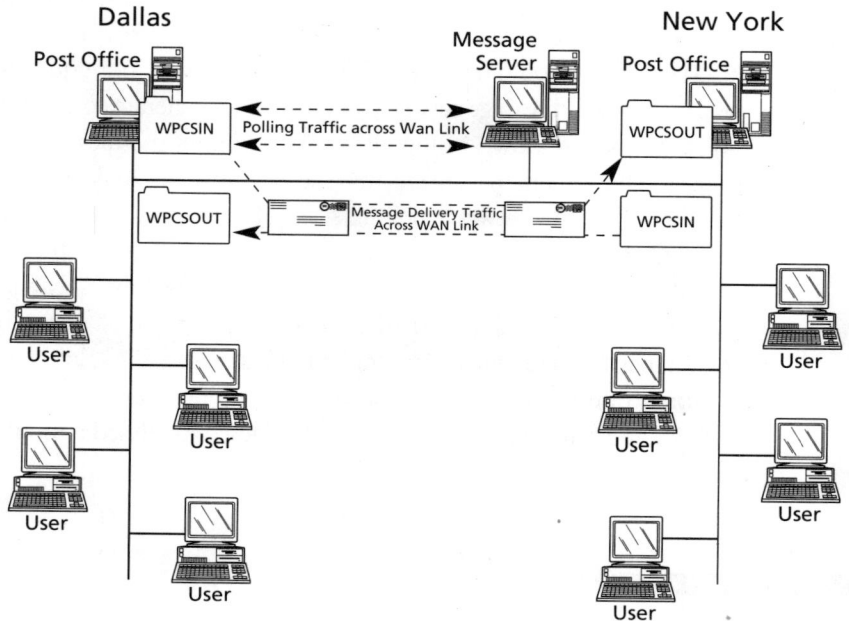

F I G U R E 9.2

*Single Domain with Post
Offices at Separate Sites*

Option 3: Domains at Both Sites   Usually, the best solution would be to set up a separate domain at each site. This arrangement requires message servers at both sites, but the only traffic across the 56 Kbps line would be the messages sent between the domains. Each message server would deliver messages directly to the other domain's input queues, as shown in Figure 9.3.

You will notice that there is no polling traffic across the WAN link with this design. The message servers only poll the domain directories, post offices, and gateways in their own domains.

As a general rule, you should break a GroupWise system into separate domains whenever a slow link is involved. All post offices in a domain should be reachable through relatively high-speed links.

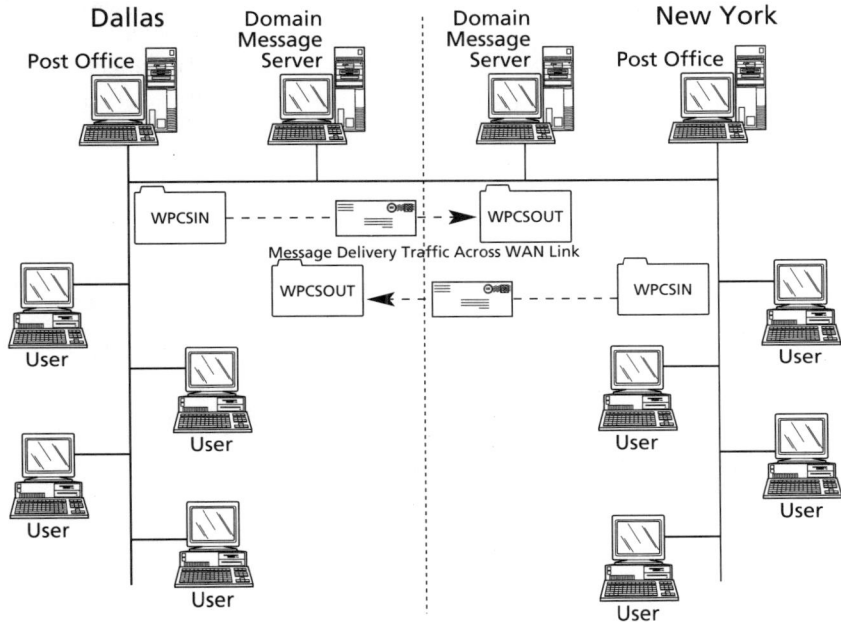

FIGURE 9.3

Domains Located at Separate Sites

GroupWise System Architectures

There are many different architectures for multidomain GroupWise systems. This section shows you three basic configurations that are commonly used for GroupWise implementations:

▸ Simple

▸ Star

▸ Ring

Each architecture has its own strengths and weaknesses. Sometimes it makes sense to use a combination of different architectures. You should remember that once you have decided to use a specific architecture, that decision does not have to be final. Your system will probably evolve over time. You can try out different designs and make modifications as you try to find the best arrangement for your organization.

The different architectures result from the different ways that domains can be linked. There are two different kinds of links you will see when domains are in the same local area network (LAN) or wide area network (WAN)—direct links and indirect links. (A third type of link is a *gateway link*, which is typically used only when domains cannot be connected with a network connection.) A *direct link* means that the message server for one domain has direct network access to the other domain's directory structure. An *indirect link* means that a domain's message server cannot directly access the other domain's directory structure, but it can nevertheless send messages to that domain by routing them through other domains in the system. (I explain these link types in more detail in Chapter 10.)

The architecture you use should be determined by the physical structure of your network—its WAN links, routers, and network segments. The goal is to match the GroupWise domain links as closely as possible to the physical path that messages will take to get from one domain to another.

SIMPLE ARCHITECTURE

In a simple architecture, every domain is directly linked to every other domain in the system, as shown in Figure 9.4. This architecture is sometimes referred to as a *mesh*). The simple architecture provides the most efficient message delivery because it requires the fewest number of message server transfers (sometimes called *hops*) for any message, assuming that all domains are on the same LAN.

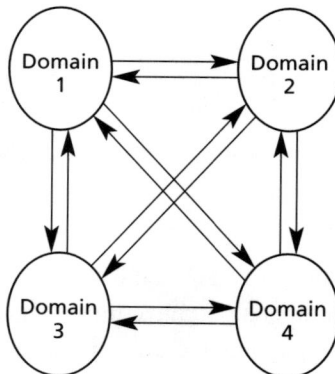

FIGURE 9.4

Simple Architecture

If you have more than one physical site and several domains at each site, you should consider using the simple architecture at each site, connecting only one domain at each site to the other site. See Figure 9.5. That way, only one domain transfers all messages to the other site. This strategy is especially useful when the WAN link between sites is slow.

FIGURE 9.5

Simple Architecture for Two Sites

Site 1

Site 2

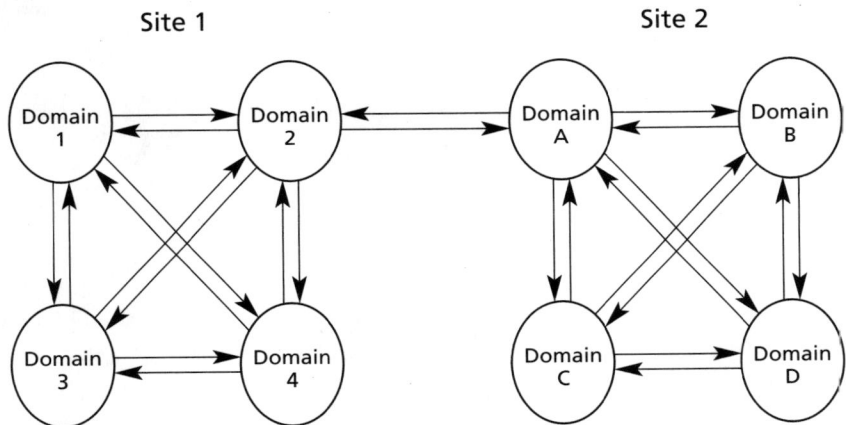

The simple architecture is recommended if your system uses NLM message servers. Usually, the simple architecture works best—especially when the network operating system supports virtually unlimited connections (for example, NetWare 4.1).

STAR ARCHITECTURE

The star architecture is a popular, and often highly efficient, configuration for large GroupWise implementations. This architecture uses one domain as a hub, and every other domain in the system links directly to the hub, as shown in Figure 9.6. Each domain links indirectly to every other domain in the system through the hub.

In a star architecture, the hub domain should almost always be the primary domain. This allows for the most efficient directory synchronization. Furthermore, centralized administration can be done from the hub domain. For example, that domain could serve as a central location for adding and removing users.

FIGURE 9.6

GroupWise Star
Configuration

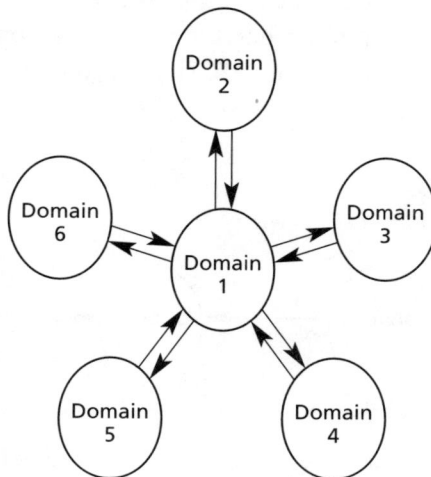

Usually the hub domain does not contain any post offices or objects. Having post offices in the hub domain diminishes the performance of the entire system because the message server in the hub would need to use its resources to monitor those post offices in addition to handling all of the messages sent between domains.

Occasionally, it makes sense to use the hub domain to house gateways for a system. As a general rule, it is best to install gateways in domains that generate the majority of gateway traffic. However, when domains generate relatively equal amounts of gateway traffic—for example, when a system supports many GroupWise Remote users spread throughout the system—an Async gateway in the hub domain can provide efficient message processing. Likewise, if GroupWise users receive messages from foreign systems, such as the Internet, installing gateways in the hub domain ensures that only one domain transfer occurs when foreign messages reach the system.

TIP

If you use the star architecture and your system connects to the Internet, an SMTP gateway in the hub domain can provide efficient message-processing for users in every domain.

Generally, though, when gateways are installed in the hub domain, that domain's message server must service all message queues for the gateways. If the gateways don't generate a lot of traffic, then there isn't much impact on message delivery performance. However, if the gateways handle a large volume of messages, having the gateways in the hub would hinder message delivery performance for messages between domains. If that is the case, you should consider creating a dedicated domain to hold the gateways. This configuration is shown in Figure 9.7.

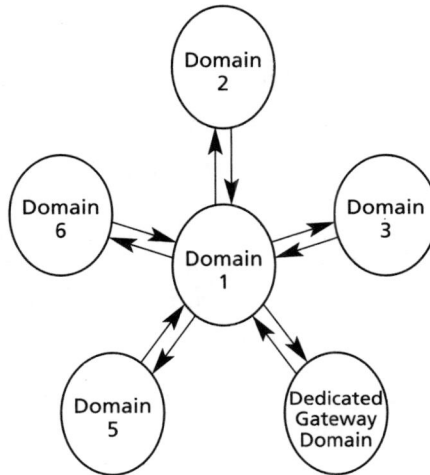

Remember that in a star configuration, the message server in the hub domain handles all traffic between all domains in the system. The message server in the primary domain should therefore be running on a high-performance computer. I recommend using the NLM message server on a high-performance NetWare file server. The OS/2 message server would be a good alternative.

The major disadvantage to the star architecture is that a problem with the hub domain can disable the whole system. If you use the star architecture, you should seriously consider having a backup message server. (I discuss backup message servers in detail in Chapter 10.)

You should also consider using *transfer pull directories* on the hub server. Normally, the hub domain's message server *pushes* (i.e., distributes) messages to each secondary domain's message servers. With transfer pull directories, each secondary domain's message server *pulls* (picks up) its messages from the hub. In the primary domain's administration program, the links between the primary and each secondary domain are defined as separate directories on the hub. In each secondary domain's admininistration program, the link to the hub is then defined as a transfer pull directory. The secondary domain's message server periodically checks this directory for messages. Thus, the hub never has to contact other domains to deliver mail; instead, the other domains contact the hub. Transfer pull directories can help control traffic on slow or high-cost links between domains. They are also useful if the network operating system limits the number of simultaneous server attachments allowed.

RING ARCHITECTURE

The ring architecture is the least common of the architectures discussed here, but it may be more appropriate for some wide-area-network (WAN) configurations than the other architectures. In a ring architecture, shown in Figure 9.8, each domain connects directly to two other domains, so that all of the domains together form a ring. This architecture is more resilient than the star configuration. If the message server for one domain goes down, the other domains can still communicate with each other. The disadvantage of the ring architecure is that every domain can potentially cause some disruption of message flow. In a star architecture, only the hub domain can cause problems for the entire system.

Ring Architecture

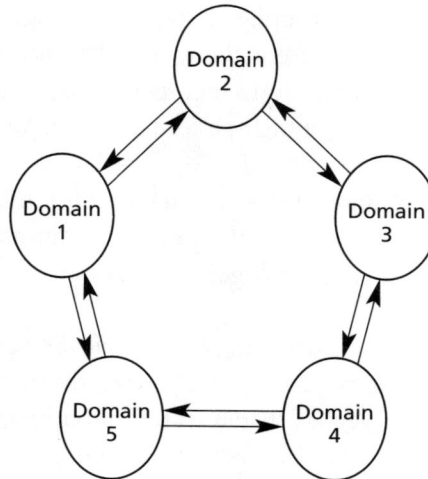

Choosing the Primary Domain

The decision about which domain to use as the primary domain is critical. The primary domain should be located so that it can be easily accessed by the GroupWise system's administrators, and it should have a direct network connection to every other domain in the system, if possible.

The primary domain is the central point from which directory synchronization messages are distributed. For this reason, the primary domain needs to have the highest performance of any domain in the system. If possible, it should be located on a high-performance file server, and the GroupWise administrator should have easy access to the domain database and directory structure.

CHANGING A SECONDARY DOMAIN TO A PRIMARY DOMAIN

Your decision about the primary domain is not irreversible. A secondary domain can be made into the primary domain. To change the primary domain, you need to have access to GroupWise Admin for the old primary domain. When you are in GroupWise Admin for that domain, follow these steps to designate a new primary domain:

1 • Make sure that no administrative processes occur during the reorganization by disabling all administration servers in the system and by making sure that no secondary domains are running GroupWise Admin. Also, check the Pending Operations option under the Actions menu for the domain.

2 • Highlight the secondary domain that is to become the new primary domain.

3 • Select Actions, and then select Edit.

4 • Change the domain type from Secondary to Primary.

5 • When you are asked whether to change the domain type, answer Yes.

6 • Specify the location of the new primary domain database and choose OK.

The secondary domain will then become the primary domain, and the domain that was previously the primary domain becomes a secondary domain.

IMPORTANT

Make sure that no administrative processes, such as adding or renaming users, occur while you are creating a new primary domain. All directory synchronizations must go through the primary domain. If administrative changes are made during the designation of a new primary domain, the directory synchronization messages will be sent to the wrong domain and those changes will not reach the rest of the system.

GroupWise Administration Strategies

There are two methods of performing GroupWise administration: centralized administration and distributed administration. It is best to use a combination of the two methods in some situations. The method you use will depend on these factors:

- ▶ Where the domains are located

- ▶ Whether the domains are connected with a physical network connection or with a gateway (asynchronous) connection

- ▶ Whether each domain has a qualified GroupWise administrator

- ▶ Whether a single administrator has direct access to every domain in the system

The important thing to remember about the administration strategies I discuss in this section is that these strategies only pertain to *administration of objects*. There are some GroupWise administrative tasks that must be done in specific domains, such as creating post offices and rebuilding databases. (You will recall that an administrator of a primary domain has administrative rights for all secondary domains in the system, but an administrator of a secondary domain has administrative rights only for that domain.) The administration methods I discuss here do not apply to those types of tasks but, instead, to administrative tasks involving objects (e.g., user objects and resources).

CENTRALIZED ADMINISTRATION

In centralized administration, the primary domain's administrator manages the objects in all domains in the system, as shown in Figure 9.9. That administrator is responsible for adding, deleting, modifying, and moving objects in all domains.

F I G U R E 9.9

Centralized Administration

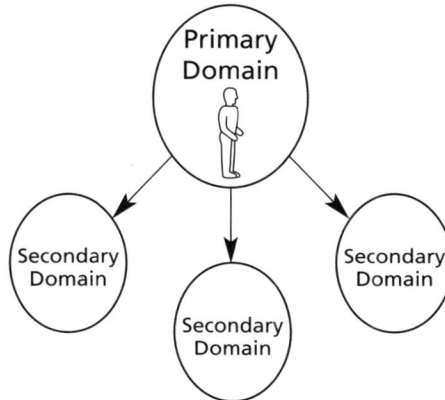

In centralized administration, the administrator uses the primary domain's administration program to perform tasks. Administrative tasks are carried out through a *request/confirm/replicate* process, as illustrated in Figure 9.10.

F I G U R E 9.10

*Request/Confirm/Replicate
Model*

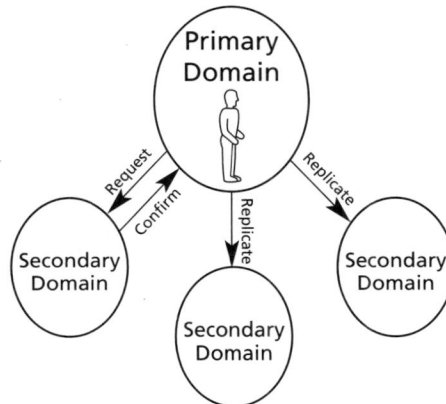

Suppose you are the administrator for a primary domain and you need to add a user to a secondary domain. Here are the steps you would take:

1 • Run GroupWise Admin from the primary domain.

2 • Highlight the post office in the secondary domain and add the user by selecting Create, and then choosing User.

3 • The primary domain creates an administrative message, which it sends to the secondary domain. The message requests that the secondary domain's administration server add the user. This is the *request* portion of the centralized administration model.

4 • The secondary domain's administration server verifies that there aren't any duplicate users in the domain, and it then adds the user.

5 • The secondary domain sends the primary domain a message indicating that the requested change has been made. This is the *confirm* portion of the model.

6 • The primary domain then sends a message to all other domains to inform them of the change. This is the *replicate* portion of the model.

The GroupWise administration server is the agent through which object administration takes place. The administration server operates just like any other GroupWise server—using the store-and-forward messaging process I explained earlier. I explain how the administration server operates in Chapter 11.

DISTRIBUTED ADMINISTRATION

In distributed administration, an administrator is assigned to each domain in a GroupWise system, as shown in Figure 9.11.

FIGURE 9.11

Distributed Administration

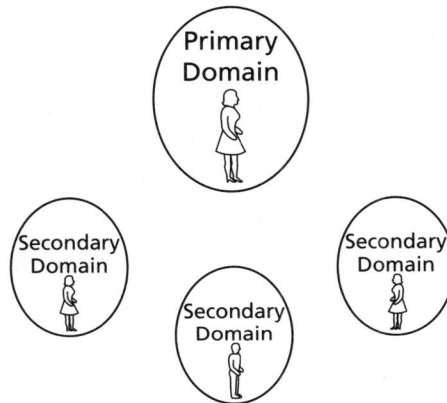

Objects are added, deleted, edited, and moved in a secondary domain using the secondary domain's administration program. An important point to remember is that the primary domain still has administrative rights to make changes to all secondary domains. However, as a policy, the primary domain administrator lets secondary domain administrators make changes in the secondary domains.

The distributed administration model lacks two of the elements of centralized administration. Instead of a request/confirm/replicate process, the secondary domain simply makes changes and then distributes information about the changes to the other domains. This replication process is accomplished by sending a message to the primary domain, which then sends information about the changes to all of the other secondary domains' admininstration servers.

Summary

In this chapter, you learned strategies for implementing multidomain GroupWise systems. You also learned how to perform some object-administration tasks in those systems. The next chapter discusses the actual steps involved in creating a multiple domain system and how message servers handle messages sent between the domains.

CHAPTER 10

Setting Up a Multiple Domain System

In Chapter 9, I explained how to decide when multiple domains are needed. I also described the various architectures that you can use to implement an enterprise-wide GroupWise system, as well as strategies for administering a large system.

You will recall that GroupWise architectures are formed by linking domains together—either directly or indirectly. This chapter explains how to set up and configure direct and indirect links between domains.

After reading this chapter, you will know how to set up a multiple domain GroupWise system and how to enable multiple domains to communicate with each other.

Creating Additional Domains

The first domain you create in a system will always be the primary domain. All domains created after the primary domain are secondary domains (with the exception of external and foreign domains, which will be discussed later). However, if you later decide to make one of the secondary domains the primary domain, you can easily make that conversion. See "Changing a Secondary Domain to a Primary Domain" in Chapter 9.

Once you have decided to add a domain to your system—and you have identified the file server that will hold the domain—the process for creating another domain is very simple:

1 • Make sure that the computer running GroupWise Admin for the primary domain has network access to the file server that will hold the secondary domain.

2 • Run GroupWise Admin for the primary domain.

3 • Choose Create.

4 • Choose Domain. The Create Domain dialog box, shown in Figure 10.1, will appear.

FIGURE 10.1

Create Domain Dialog Box

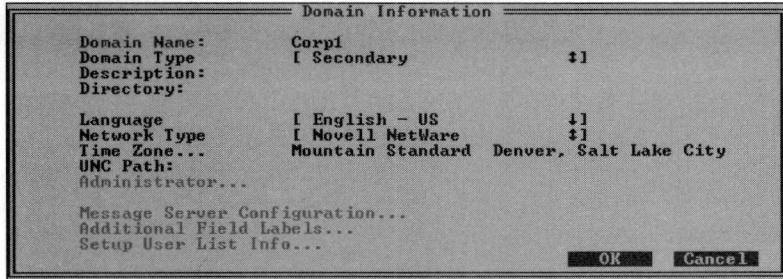

```
================================= Domain Information =================================
    Domain Name:        Corp1
    Domain Type         [ Secondary                          ↕]
    Description:
    Directory:

    Language            [ English - US                       ↕]
    Network Type        [ Novell NetWare                     ↕]
    Time Zone...        Mountain Standard   Denver, Salt Lake City
    UNC Path:
    Administrator...

    Message Server Configuration...
    Additional Field Labels...
    Setup User List Info...
                                               ███ OK ███   ███ Cancel ███
```

5 • Fill in the required fields:

  ▸ Domain Name

  ▸ Domain Path

  ▸ Time Zone

  ▸ UNC Path (This field is only necessary if you will be using the NLM message server.)

6 • Choose OK.

7 • When prompted, select the software to be copied to the secondary domain. The options for copying software are shown in Figure 10.2.

FIGURE 10.2

Copy Software Dialog Box

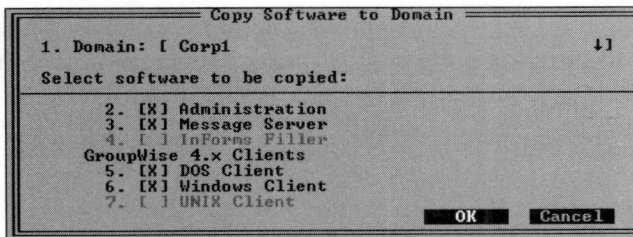

```
============================ Copy Software to Domain ============================
   1. Domain: [ Corp1                                            ↕]

   Select software to be copied:

        2. [X] Administration
        3. [X] Message Server
        4. [ ] InForms Filler
     GroupWise 4.x Clients
        5. [X] DOS Client
        6. [X] Windows Client
        7. [ ] UNIX Client
                                        ███ OK ███   ███ Cancel ███
```

The options in the Copy Software dialog box can be used to copy the GroupWise Admin program, the DOS message server software, and any client platform (except Macintosh) from the primary domain to the new secondary domain.

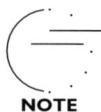

> **NOTE**
>
> **NLM message server files are installed (by default) to the SYS:SYSTEM directory of the file server running the message server process, and the OS/2 message server files are installed to the hard drive of an OS/2 workstation.**

The above steps will create the secondary domain database (WPDOMAIN.DB) and the domain directory structure and files. You will not be able to create the secondary domain's post offices from the primary domain's GroupWise Admin program, however. You must run GroupWise Admin for the secondary domain to create those post offices.

Even though the domain structure will be in place after you have completed the steps above, the domains will not be able to communicate with each other until the message server links have been defined between the domains. See the section "Linking Domains Together," later in this chapter.

Review of Domain Directory Structure

The secondary domain directory structure is identical to the primary domain structure. The secondary domain has a domain database (WPDOMAIN.DB), which is constructed when the domain is created. The information in the secondary domain database is taken from the primary domain database. Because the secondary domain database is built from the information contained in the primary domain database, it can easily be rebuilt if it becomes damaged.

> **IMPORTANT**
>
> **You should implement a backup strategy for your primary domain database. See Chapter 19. Secondary domains can be rebuilt from the primary domain database, but the primary domain database *cannot* be rebuilt from the secondary domain databases.**

The secondary domain also contains archive file directories for the client software that will be copied to the post offices in the domain.

Secondary domains also need to have message servers. Even if a secondary domain has only one post office, a message server will be required so that the domain can communicate with the primary domain and other secondary domains.

Secondary domains also usually contain the GroupWise Admin program. Keeping GroupWise Admin in a secondary domain allows objects in the secondary domain to be administered locally (*distributed administration*) rather than from the primary domain. See Chapter 9 for an explanation of centralized and distributed administration.

There are some administrative tasks that must be performed from a secondary domain's own GroupWise Admin program, such as creating post offices for the domain and rebuilding the domain and post office databases. To run GroupWise Admin for a specific domain:

- ▶ run AD.EXE from the directory that contains the WPDOMAIN.DB file; or

- ▶ run AD.EXE with the /PH switch pointing to the directory that contains the WPDOMAIN.DB file.

For example, suppose the primary domain is currently mapped to X:\DOMAIN1 and the secondary domain is located on another file server, which is mapped to Y:\DOMAIN2. You can run AD.EXE from the primary domain's directory for the secondary domain by using the syntax:

AD /PH-Y:\DOMAIN2

When GroupWise Admin is launched with the /PH switch, the domain that is referenced by the switch will be listed as *Current*, as shown in Figure 10.3. Creating post offices is only one of the tasks that need to be performed in the current domain. Some of the other tasks that must be performed from the secondary domain's admininistration program include creating gateways in the secondary domain and rebuilding the secondary domain's post office databases.

FIGURE 10.3

Domain and Post Office
Window in GroupWise
Admin

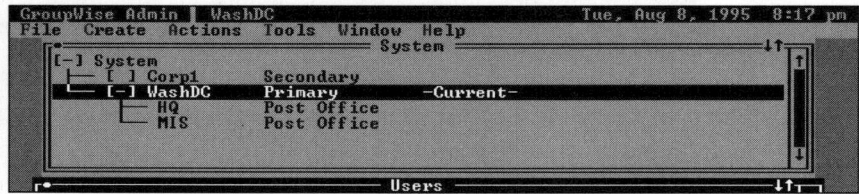

```
GroupWise Admin | WashDC                        Tue, Aug 8, 1995  8:17 pm
 File   Create   Actions   Tools   Window   Help
 ┌─────────────────────────────── System ───────────────────────┤↑┐
 [-] System                                                        ↑
   ├─ [ ] Corp1        Secondary
   └─ [-] WashDC       Primary              -Current-
       ├─ HQ           Post Office
       └─ MIS          Post Office
                                                                   ↓
 ┌──────────────────────────────── Users ────────────────────────┤↑┐
```

Creating Post Offices and Users
in Secondary Domains

The procedure for creating post offices in a secondary domain is identical to the procedure for creating post offices in the primary domain. You just need to remember to run GroupWise Admin in the secondary domain when you want to create a post office there.

Once the post offices have been created in a secondary domain, users and resources can be added to the secondary domain by running GroupWise Admin in that domain or by running GroupWise Admin in the primary domain. (Adding users and resources is an object-level administration task, so it can be done from the primary domain if your system utilizes centralized administration.)

Linking Domains Together

After you have created the first secondary domain in your system, it's time to define links. Links between domains must be defined before the users can send messages from one domain to another.

You must define links in both directions.

IMPORTANT

Because message servers only *push* (or distribute) messages to other domains—as opposed to *pulling* (or picking up) messages—the primary domain must have a link defined to the secondary domain, and the secondary domain must have a corresponding link defined to the primary domain. A link provides a sending domain's message server with the instructions it needs to find the receiving domain's directory.

You will recall that the message server is responsible for transferring messages between domains. You will also recall that every domain in a multiple domain GroupWise system must have its own message server. Link definitions provide message servers with the information they need in order to deliver messages between domains.

Each domain database in a GroupWise system contains a record of every other domain in the system. Each domain's message server has access to that domain's database file (WPDOMAIN.DB). Therefore, each message server is able to tell how to deliver messages to all of the other domains within the system.

There are three types of links that can be used to connect domains:

- ▶ Direct links

- ▶ Indirect links

- ▶ Gateway links

DIRECT LINKS

A direct link can be used if the message server for a domain has direct network access to another domain. Figure 10.4 illustrates two domains connected by a direct link. There are two types of direct links: mapped and TCP/IP. Configuring direct TCP/IP links will be discussed later in this chapter.

FIGURE 10.4

Direct Links Between Domains

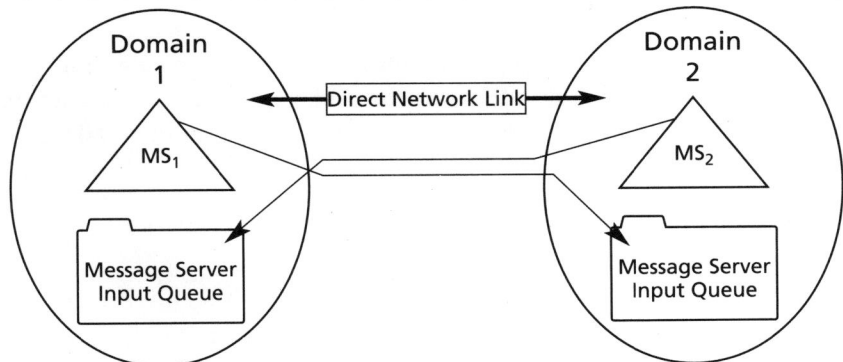

When you create a direct link between two domains, the message server places messages sent between the domains directly into the domains' message server input queues.

Direct links are the most efficient kind of link between domains. When you use a direct link, a message sent between the domains needs to be processed by only two message servers—the message server in the originating domain and the message server in the recipient domain.

A direct link between domains is like a direct, nonstop airplane flight between two cities. When I fly from New York to London, I get on the plane at a New York airport and I get off the plane at a London airport. It's a very quick and painless procedure. I only have to go through the airport "process" twice.

In Chapter 9, I explained three common architectures that can be used in multidomain GroupWise systems. In the simple architecture, every domain is connected to every other domain by direct message server links. That is why the simple architecture is the sturdiest architecture for a GroupWise system. If one domain's message server fails, the problem does not affect communication between other domains in the system.

Follow these steps to create a direct link from a primary domain to a secondary domain:

1 • Run GroupWise Admin from the primary domain.

2 • Highlight the primary domain. (For example, if you need to create a link from the New York domain to the London domain, you would highlight the New York domain.)

NOTE

The primary domain's administrator can also configure the links for secondary domains, but a secondary domain's administrator can configure the link for the secondary domain only.

3 • Select Actions and then select Edit.

4 • If you are using the NLM message server, verify that the UNC path has been entered. (If you are not using the NLM messager server, you can ignore this step.)

5 • Select Message Server Configuration.

6 • Verify that message server platform is correct and that the message-delivery mode is set either to Use Application Threshold or to Server Always.

7 • Select Network Links.

8 • Highlight the secondary domain.

9 • Choose Link Type.

10 • Select Direct.

11 • Enter the path to the secondary domain directory. (If the GroupWise NLM message server is being used and if the UNC path was entered when the secondary domain was created, the UNC path will be entered automatically.)

12 • Choose OK.

The information about the direct link will be stored in the WPDOMAIN.DB file, which can be accessed by the domain's message server. If you are using a DOS message server, the information will be stored in the Connection Server Information (CSI) file.

NOTE

A link must also be created from the secondary domain to the primary domain before two-way message delivery can occur.

INDIRECT LINKS

It is not always practical for every domain in a GroupWise system to have direct links to all other domains. For example, there may be occasions when the number of available network connections is limited by the network operating system. The network configuration may also be a factor in your decision about whether to implement direct links. For example, if you have several domains in your GroupWise system spread across multiple sites, you may decide that you want to limit traffic on the WAN links between the sites by allowing only one domain at each site to have a direct link with the other sites.

When it is not practical to use direct links for all of the domains in a system, you can instead use indirect links to connect some of the domains. Indirect links use one or more *routing domains* between an originating domain and a recipient domain. There must be at least three domains in a system before indirect links can be used. In Figure 10.5, Domain A is directly connected to Domain B and to Domain C, but Domain B and Domain C are not directly connected to each other. There is an indirect link (shown as a broken line in Figure 10.5) between Domain B and Domain C through Domain A, which serves as the routing domain.

FIGURE 10.5

Indirect Link

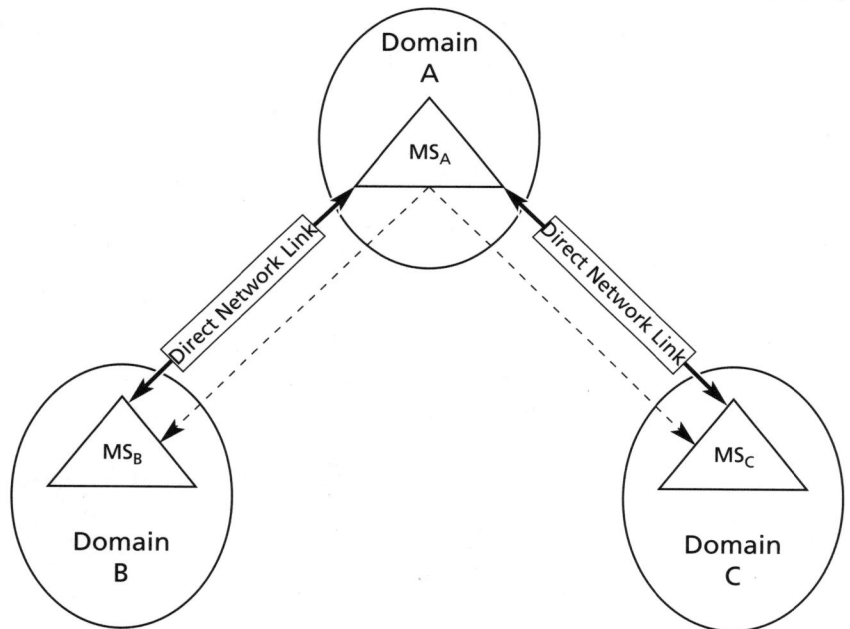

If you use the star configuration explained in Chapter 9, all domains link directly to the hub domain and indirectly to all other domains in the system. When a user sends a message to a recipient in another domain, the message server sends the message to the routing domain. Then the routing domain's message server transfers the message to the recipient's domain. In some configurations, a message may be transferred through several routing domains before it reaches its final destination.

NOTE

A message can be routed through a maximum of 16 domains before a message server terminates the message and generates an error message indicating that the message could not be delivered. This safeguard prevents messages from looping indefinitely between the domains in a GroupWise system.

Again, this is very similar to air travel. If I want to fly from Salt Lake City to London, I usually have to stop over in New York on the way. (If it's a particularly bad travel day, I may have to stop in both Pittsburgh and New York on my way to London.) Just like a message in the star architecture, I have to go through a hub—or several hubs—in order to reach my final destination. Going through a hub is obviously slower and less efficient than traveling directly to my destination. Also, I am bound to be delayed if there is a problem at any one of the hubs I must travel through.

Although indirect links are not as efficient as direct links, they give you more flexibility when you are configuring a GroupWise system. Indirect links are especially useful when it is not practical to establish direct network connections between all domains.

Follow these steps to configure an indirect link:

1 • In GroupWise Admin, highlight the domain from which the link will be made.

2 • Choose Actions, select Edit, and then choose Message Server Configuration.

3 • Choose Network Links.

4 • Highlight the domain to which the indirect link will be made.

5 • Choose Link Type.

6 • Choose Indirect.

7 • Select the domain through which the link will be made (the routing domain).

8 • Choose OK.

> **NOTE**
>
> **The routing domain may have a direct link to the destination domain or it, too, may have an indirect link to the destination domain. The message server will always try to match a message's address to a direct link or to a gateway link, but the message may have to go through one or more routing domains before it finds the destination domain.**

GATEWAY LINKS

Sometimes it is not possible or practical to maintain a full-time, live network connection between domains. This situation often arises when domains are located at two different sites and the cost of a direct network connection between the sites (e.g., a leased line) is very expensive.

In this situation, an asynchronous (*Async*) gateway can be used to link the domains together. The gateway uses a modem to transfer messages through the telephone system. An Async gateway connection is illustrated in Figure 10.6.

F I G U R E 10.6

Domains Connected by a
Gateway Link

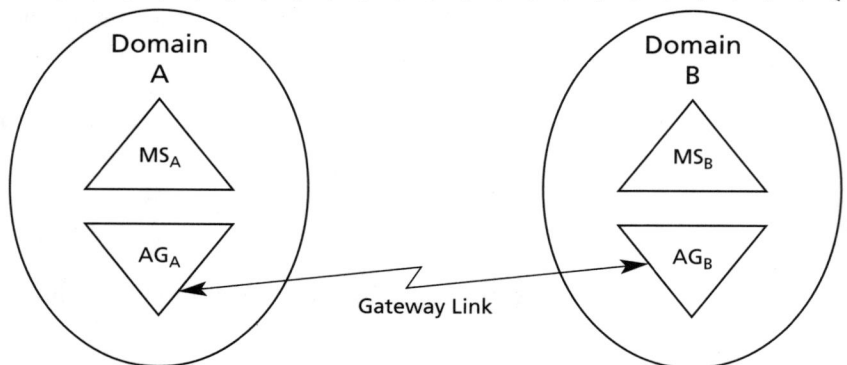

If a message is sent to a domain connected to a GroupWise system by a gateway, the message server will place the message in the gateway's input queue so that the gateway can process the message.

An Async gateway in one domain can be configured to call an Async gateway in another domain whenever a certain number of messages are waiting to be sent, when a specific time interval has elapsed, or when a combination of both factors takes place. I discuss setting up Async gateways in Chapter 13.

Connecting Domains Using TCP/IP Direct Links

If your network uses Transmission Control Protocol/Internet Protocol (TCP/IP), you can configure your GroupWise message servers to communicate with other message servers through direct TCP/IP links, as illustrated in Figure 10.7. GroupWise supports Internet Protocol addressing between domains when you use the GroupWise NetWare NLM message server, the GroupWise OS/2 message server, or a GroupWise UNIX message server. TCP/IP links cannot be used with the DOS message server platform. In the present chapter, I provide instructions for setting up TCP/IP linking for the NetWare NLM message server and the OS/2 message server.

F I G U R E 10.7

TCP/IP Between Message
Servers

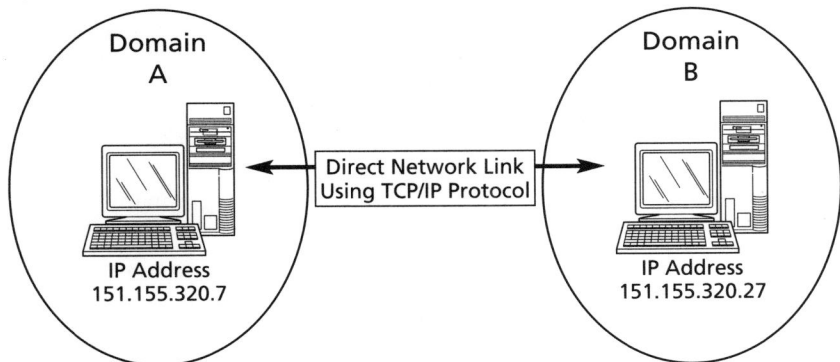

Domain A — IP Address 151.155.320.7 — Direct Network Link Using TCP/IP Protocol — Domain B — IP Address 151.155.320.27

If you are using Novell NetWare and the GroupWise NLM message servers, TCP/IP must be configured at the NetWare level. If you are using GroupWise OS/2 message servers, IBM's TCP/IP version 2.0 must be installed and configured on the network.

IMPORTANT

An Internet Protocol (IP) address is a unique address assigned to a specific computer (referred to as a *host*). The IP address for a computer must be unique within the WAN. An IP address follows a dotted decimal notation—for example, 151.155.320.9. Because an IP address is unique to a specific computer, it is an absolute address within the WAN.

TCP/IP links are often good for large GroupWise implementations in WAN environments. TCP/IP links are particularly useful for connecting domains located on different network operating systems. For example, if a WAN has a NetWare 4.1 file server that houses a GroupWise domain and a UnixWare server that houses another domain, those domains can be configured to use TCP/IP transport for messages sent between the two (assuming TCP/IP has been configured on the network).

TCP/IP links are typically used between domains where different platforms or protocols must communicate with each other. Here are some of the main benefits of using TCP/IP links between domains in an enterprise GroupWise system:

▸ Universal addressing

▸ Connectionless message transfer

▸ Multiple simultaneous connections

▸ Elimination of file incompatibilities

▸ Faster and more reliable message delivery (in many cases)

Universal Addressing   TCP/IP links allow you to use one addressing standard for your links, regardless of the message server platform. For example, in a GroupWise system that consists of a domain running the NLM message server, a domain running the OS/2 message server, and a domain running the UNIX message server, all domains could link directly to each other with TCP/IP links (if the network supports TCP/IP and each message server has its own unique IP address).

If the address of one message server changes, the other message servers are automatically notified of the new address through the GroupWise directory synchronization process. No reconfiguration of the other domains' message servers or network links is necessary. However, the SYS:ETC\HOSTS file must be updated to reflect the change in the IP address if a HOSTS file is used. (A *HOSTS file* is a table containing a list of the computers configured for TCP/IP in the network and their corresponding IP addresses.)

Connectionless Message Transfer   TCP/IP links between domains eliminate the need for message server network access accounts. By using TCP/IP links, you don't have to bother with login restrictions, passwords, and rights.

Multiple Simultaneous Connections   TCP/IP links allow message servers to maintain multiple simultaneous connections with other message servers.

Elimination of File Incompatibilities   When TCP/IP links are used to transport GroupWise messages, the message files are moved in TCP/IP network packets rather than files. In this way, TCP/IP transport eliminates file incompatibilities between platforms.

Faster and More Reliable Message Delivery   If GroupWise domains are located on UNIX servers — or if there is a combination of message server platforms—TCP/IP can provide faster and more reliable message delivery between domains.

TIP

While TCP/IP transport provides many advantages when you have multiple network protocols or multiple message server platforms, TCP/IP links usually do *not* provide significant advantages for networks that run exclusively on Novell NetWare. In a NetWare-only network, direct links with UNC paths are usually more efficient than TCP/IP links.

Setting Up TCP/IP Links Between Domains (NLM or OS/2 Message Servers Only)

Before you can configure GroupWise to use TCP/IP links, you must make sure that the network is configured for TCP/IP. (An explanation of the process for setting up a network and a network operating system for TCP/IP transport would be beyond the scope of this book.) You must also verify that the computers running the message server processes all have unique, valid IP addresses. Once the network has been correctly set up for TCP/IP, you can follow these steps to configure a GroupWise NLM or OS/2 message server to take advantage of TCP/IP transport between message servers:

1   •   Verify that the file server to run the NLM message server has the correct NetWare TCP/IP NLMs loaded (or that the workstation that will run the OS/2 message server has IBM's TCP/IP version 2.0).

2   •   Configure the message server for TCP/IP.

3 • Establish TCP/IP links between domains.

4 • Edit the NLM or OS/2 message server startup file to enable TCP/IP transport.

VERIFYING NETWARE SERVER OR OS/2 WORKSTATION CONFIGURATION

NetWare uses the TCP/IP NLM to enable TCP/IP support on the file server. This NLM should have been installed when NetWare was installed. Each NetWare file server that will run a message server using TCP/IP links must have this NLM loaded.

NOTE

A special problem arises if you need to load multiple message server processes on a single file server and you need TCP/IP to route messages. Each domain's message server configuration must have a unique IP address, but if message servers are on the same machine, that machine cannot have two unique IP addresses. You can get around this problem by installing multiple network-interface cards into the file server, loading TCPIP.NLM for each card, and then binding IP to the cards using different IP addresses.

The file server must have its own unique IP address. The format for an IP address follows a dotted decimal notation. A typical IP address looks like this:

151.155.320.9

The IP address for all file servers should be listed in the HOSTS file, found in the SYS:\ETC directory on a NetWare file server. For details on how to configure a NetWare file server for TCP/IP transport, refer to the documentation that came with your NetWare network operating system. You can also use Domain Name System (DNS) or Network Information Service (NIS) to match IP addresses to a specific host computer. These systems translate symbolic names (e.g., NOVELL.COM, MSMITH, KTHOMAS, and so forth) into valid IP addresses. These systems are third-party products that can be added to your LAN or WAN.

TIP

You can use the NetWare PING utility to verify that NetWare file servers are communicating via TCP/IP.

CONFIGURING THE MESSAGE SERVER IN GROUPWISE ADMIN

The message server configuration must include the correct TCP/IP information before TCP/IP links can be made between domains. Use these steps to configure the message server for TCP/IP communication:

1 • Run GroupWise Admin for the domain that will connect to other domains via TCP/IP.

2 • Highlight the domain.

3 • Choose Actions.

4 • Choose Edit.

5 • Choose Message Server Configuration. The dialog box shown in Figure 10.8 will appear.

F I G U R E 10.8

*Message Server
Configuration Dialog Box*

6 • Choose TCP/IP Settings.

7 • Enter the TCP/IP address of the computer that will be loading the message server process.

IMPORTANT

The TCP/IP address that you enter in the Message Server Configuration dialog box must be the address of the computer that will run the message server for the domain that is being edited. This should not be the address of a computer running a message server in another domain.

8 • Verify that the port number is correct. By default, the GroupWise message server's port is 7100. You usually should not need to change the port number unless other applications are already using it.

Once you have completed these steps, you are ready to create the direct TCP/IP links to other domains.

CREATING DIRECT TCP/IP NETWORK LINKS BETWEEN DOMAINS

Follow these steps to create a TCP/IP direct link to another domain:

1 • Highlight the domain.

2 • Choose Actions.

3 • Choose Edit.

4 • Choose Message Server Configuration.

5 • Choose Network Links.

6 • Select the domain to which the current domain will link via TCP/IP.

7 • Choose Edit Link.

8 • Choose Direct Link.

9 • Choose Protocol.

10 • Choose TCP/IP.

11 • Choose OK to return to the Network Links dialog box.

12 • Choose Close to return to the Domain Information dialog box.

13 • Choose OK to return to the GroupWise Admin screen.

Remember that links must be configured in both directions and that the link types should be the same. In other words, when you define a direct TCP/IP link from Domain A to Domain B, the administrator for Domain B (whether it be you or someone else) needs to configure a direct TCP/IP link from Domain B to Domain A.

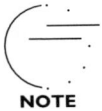

NOTE

Both domains appear as Closed on the message server screen until both file servers have loaded TCP/IP, the message server process restarts, and the message server finds the IP addresses in the link definitions. (The message server process usually restarts automatically when a change in the configuration is detected.)

EDITING AN NLM OR OS/2 MESSAGE SERVER STARTUP FILE

The final step is to configure the message server on the computer that will run the message server. The following instructions are for setting up the GroupWise NLM message server or the OS/2 message server for TCP/IP transport. If you are using the UNIX message server, refer to the documentation for that message server platform.

The GroupWise NLM and OS/2 message server startup files must be edited to enable TCP/IP transport. The necessary commands to enable TCP/IP are included by default in the STARTUP.MS file, but they are marked as comment lines. The lines in the STARTUP.MS file which relate to TCP/IP transport are shown below:

; /TCPAUTOLOAD (NLM message server only)

; /TCPINBOUND

; /TCPPORT-*port number*

; /TCPSYMBIONT (OS/2 message server only)

; /TCPSCREEN (NLM message server only)

; /TCPWAITCONNECT-*seconds*

; /TCPWAITDATA-*seconds*

These options are explained in Table 10.1.

T A B L E 10.1	OPTION	DESCRIPTION
TCP/IP Enabling Commands	/TCPAUTOLOAD (Required for NLM message server)	Automatically loads the TCP/IP support NLM (NGWMSIPL.NLM), which is required to connect to other message servers via TCP/IP. This NLM is also referred to as the TCP/IP *symbiont*.
	/TCPINBOUND-*connections*	Sets the maximum number of inbound TCP/IP connections. The default is 20.
	/TCPSYMBIONT-*path to symbiont* (OS/2 message server only)	Specifies the location of the TCP/IP symbiont (MSOS2IP.EXE). You must include the full path name.
	/TCPSCREEN (NLM message server only)	Loads the message server TCP/IP screen, which displays the TCP/IP logging information. The TCP/IP screen adopts the logging level of the message server.
	/TCPPORT-*port number*	Sets the TCP/IP port number for inbound connections, where *port number* is the number of the port. The default is 7100.
	/TCPWAITCONNECT-*seconds*	Sets the maximum length of time the message server waits for a connection to another message server, where *seconds* is the number of seconds designated. The default is 5 seconds.
	/TCPWAITDATA-*seconds*	Sets the maximum length of time during which the message server attempts to send data over the TCP/IP connection, where *seconds* is the number of seconds designated. The default is 20 seconds.

NOTE

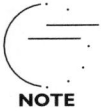

Both the NLM and OS/2 message servers use startup files. However, these switches can be used from the command line with either message server version.

You must edit the message server startup file and remove the comment line from the required switches and any other switches you want to use. Remember to exit and restart the message server after you have edited the startup file in order to implement the changes.

TIP

The startup file for the NLM message server can be edited from the NLM message server screen. The message server must be exited and reloaded to implement the changes. Always use the EXIT command from the GroupWise server screens instead of using the UNLOAD command.

Configuring an NLM or OS/2 Backup Message Server

In certain GroupWise configurations, the failure of the message server process can significantly interfere with an organization's ability to function normally. For example, if the star architecture is used and the message server for the hub domain fails, all e-mail sent between domains will be delayed until the message server process can be restored.

When prompt delivery of e-mail messages is critical, it makes sense to set up a backup message server. A backup message server is a redundant message delivery mechanism that guarantees messages will continue to be delivered even if the main message server process fails.

IMPORTANT

GroupWise messages are not lost when a message server process fails. They are held in the message queues. When the message server process is restored, the messages are delivered in the same order in which they were sent.

A backup message server runs the message server process for the same domain as its primary message server (not to be confused with a *primary domain's* message server), but it only delivers messages if the primary message server fails. The backup message server operates as a standby, monitoring the primary message server. If the primary message server fails, the backup message server recognizes this and begins to handle message delivery. While the backup message server routes messages, it continues monitoring the primary message server. When the primary message server comes back online, the backup message server reverts to standby mode.

WARNING

If the failure of the NLM message server process is due to a failure of the file server itself and the NLM message server is running on the same file server that holds the domain's message queues and database, the backup message server will not be able to continue with message delivery because it will not be able to access the message queues. In that case, the backup message server would only be useful if the message server process fails for some other reason.

To configure a backup message server for the NLM message server or for the OS/2 message server, you need to use the /PRIMARY and /BACKUP *switches.* The /PRIMARY switch should be used on the primary message server and the /BACKUP switch on the backup message server. (The term *primary* in this context does not refer to the primary domain but rather to the main message server for a domain.) These switches can be added to the startup files or they can be used from the command line.

The other required switch is the /HEARTBEAT *switch.*

IMPORTANT

The /HEARTBEAT switch must be used on both the primary and backup message servers.

The /HEARTBEAT switch on the backup server designates how often the backup server checks to see whether the primary message server is working. The /HEARTBEAT switch on the primary message server tells the message server how often to generate a *pulse signal,* which is detected by the backup message server. Both message servers should have the same setting for the heartbeat switch. For example, the command /HEARTBEAT-20 would indicate that the primary message server should pulse every 20 seconds and that the backup message server should check for the pulse every 20 seconds.

HOW IT WORKS

When the primary message server is started with the /PRIMARY and /HEARTBEAT switches, it creates a file in the domain directory called MSMONITR. This file contains the name of the domain and several null characters. Both the primary message server and the backup message server write to and read from this file. For example, if the /HEARTBEAT switch is set to 20 seconds, every 20 seconds the main message server will write to this file indicating that it is functioning, and every 20 seconds the backup message server will check the file to see if the primary message server has recently written to it. If the backup message server detects that the main message server has not written to this file since the last time it checked, it kicks into action. It will continue checking this file until it finds that the primary message server is back online, and then the backup message server reverts back to standby mode.

IMPORTANT

If a domain uses TCP/IP to connect to other domains, the backup message server process must be run on the same machine. To be able to run on a different machine, the backup server would need to take over the primary server's computer IP address, which is impossible because each machine must have a unique IP address.

Setting Up Transfer Pull Directories

In a regular GroupWise message server configuration, the message server *pushes* messages to the recipient domain. For example, suppose a system contains two domains—one called Sales and the other called Accounting. In this particular system, the message servers are configured with direct network links. When a user in the Sales domain sends a message to a recipient in the Accounting domain, the Sales message server *pushes* the message into Accounting's input queue, which is located in the Accounting domain's directory. (Refer to Figure 10.4 earlier in this chapter.)

However, there may be circumstances in which you would not want a message server to push messages to another domain's directory. For example, suppose the Accounting domain was located on a highly secure file server, and the network administrator of the Accounting department's file server refused to grant anyone rights to the directories on that file server. In this case, you could configure a *transfer pull directory*, as shown in

Figure 10.9. When a transfer pull directory is used, a directory structure is created for the originating domain to place messages into. Then the recipient domain's message server *pulls* its incoming messages from the originating domain's transfer pull directory. In the example illustrated in Figure 10.9, a transfer pull directory could be configured on the Sales domain's file server or on a completely separate file server to which both domains' message servers have access.

FIGURE 10.9

Transfer Pull Directory

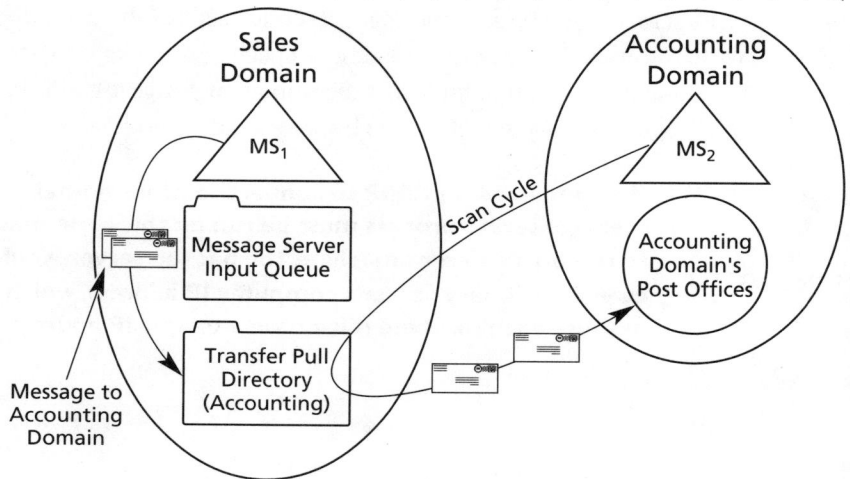

Here are some common situations in which a transfer pull directory may be useful:

▸ When you connect domains that are physically located on file servers that run different file systems. For example, a transfer pull directory could be used if you need to connect a domain located on a NetWare file server with a domain located on a UnixWare server.

▸ When you need to create a very secure environment, as in the example above.

▸ When you want to specify how often a remote domain's message server will connect with another domain. (You can use the poll cycle setting to control the message traffic between sites.)

▶ When there are network connection limitations. When the number of network connections is limited, a transfer pull directory can be set up on a server to which both domains' message servers already have access.

▶ When you need to control use of network lines. For example, if a GroupWise system is set up in the star configuration, instead of making the hub domain's message server push messages across the network to all of the connected domains, transfer pull directories can be configured on the hub domain's file server. The other domains would then pull their messages from the respective transfer pull directories on the hub domain's file server.

Returning to the Sales and Accounting scenario, notice how a transfer pull directory can be used to create a high-security environment for the Accounting domain. Because the Accounting domain's administrator has denied the Sales domain rights to the Accounting domain's file server, the administrator for the Sales domain creates a transfer pull directory on the Sales domain's file server, as shown in Figure 10.10.

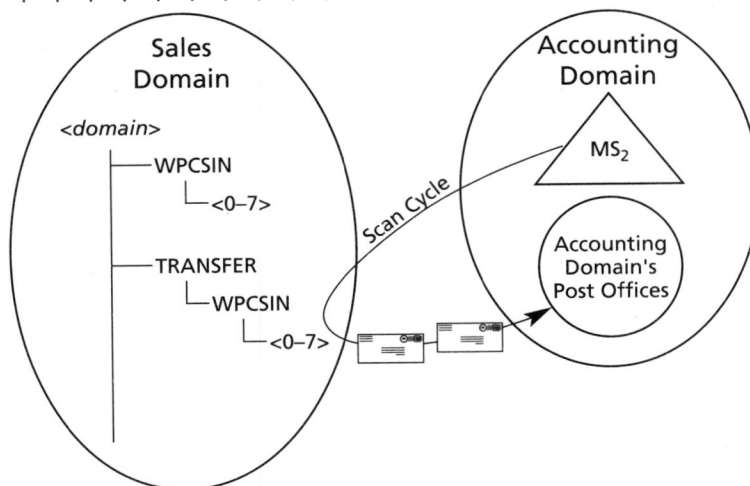

F I G U R E 10.10

Transfer Pull Directory in the Sales Domain

The Sales domain's administrator must manually create the transfer pull directories. Although the transfer pull directory could by created in any directory on the Sales domain's file server, the Sales administrator has decided to create it under the Sales domain directory structure for easy maintenance. You can name the transfer pull directory however you please, but a recommended convention is to name the directory *Transfer.* The WPCSIN directory and the individual subdirectories numbered 0 through 7 under WPCSIN are mandatory.

> **The Sales domain administrator must grant the Accounting message server the rights necessary to access the transfer pull directory structure.**
>
> **NOTE**

To create a transfer pull directory, the administrators for both the Sales and the Accounting domains would need to complete a series of steps.

The administrator for the Sales domain would follow these steps:

1. • Locate a place where both domains' message servers have network rights. (In the example above, the Sales domain's administrator chose the Sales domain as the site for the transfer pull directory structure.)

2. • Create a message server access account on the Sales file server, and grant rights to the transfer pull directory structure.

3. • Run GroupWise Admin for the Sales domain.

4. • Highlight the Sales domain, choose Actions, and then choose Edit.

5. • Choose Message Server Configuration.

6. • Choose Network Links.

7. • Highlight the Accounting domain to define the link.

8. • Choose Edit Link.

9. • Choose Direct as the link type.

10. • Choose the Override Address Option (if using UNC paths) or choose Link Address if using DOS/OS2 paths.

11. • Enter the path to the transfer pull directory, using the appropriate path type.

After the Sales administrator follows these steps, the message server for the Sales domain would know to place all messages destined for the Accounting domain in the transfer pull directory.

IMPORTANT

The administrator for the Sales domain would not enter anything in the transfer pull directory. This is left to the Accounting domain's administrator.

The administrator for the Accounting domain would need to follow these steps to complete the configuration of the transfer pull directory:

1 • Run GroupWise Admin for the Accounting domain.

2 • Highlight the Accounting domain and choose Actions and then Edit.

3 • Choose Message Server Configuration.

4 • Choose Network Links.

5 • Highlight the Sales domain.

6 • Choose Edit Link.

7 • Choose Direct as the link type.

8 • Choose Direct Link to enter the link information.

9 • Choose the Transfer Pull directory option.

10 • Enter the path to the transfer pull directory in the Sales domain using the appropriate path type.

11 • Choose Transfer Pull Cycle.

12 • Specify in seconds how frequently the message server should check the transfer pull directory for messages.

13 • Choose Close and then exit GroupWise Admin.

These steps complete the configuration of the transfer pull directory. The Sales domain's message server would not need direct access to any directories in the Accounting domain. Instead, all messages destined for the Accounting domain would be placed in the transfer pull directory. The Accounting domain's message server would check the transfer pull directory to retrieve all messages from the Sales domain.

Message flow diagrams for transfer pull directory configurations appear in the next section.

Message Transfer Between Domains

The message server input queues located in post office directories have already been discussed. Similar message server input and output queues exist in the domain directory structure. These queues are used for the transfer of messages between domains. The domain-level message server queues are shown in Figure 10.11.

Notice that in the figure the domains have direct access to each other's input queues. As you will recall, these queues are used only for the transfer of messages between domains. They are not used for the transfer of messages between post offices within a domain.

F I G U R E 10.11

Message Delivery Between Two Domains

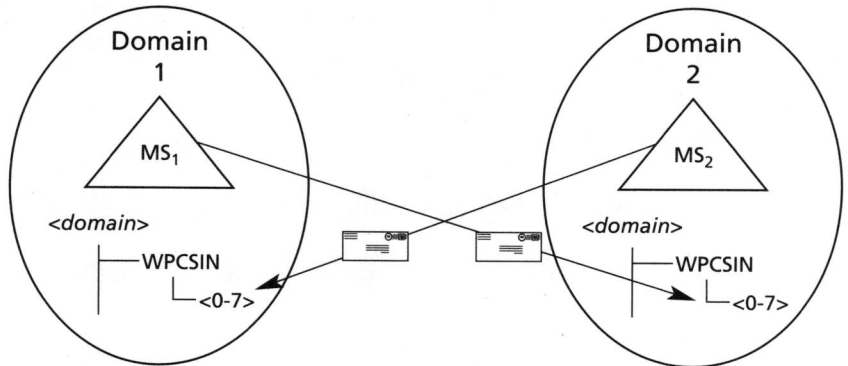

MESSAGE FLOW BETWEEN TWO DOMAINS WITH A DIRECT LINK

Figure 10.12 shows the message flow between domains that are connected by a direct link.

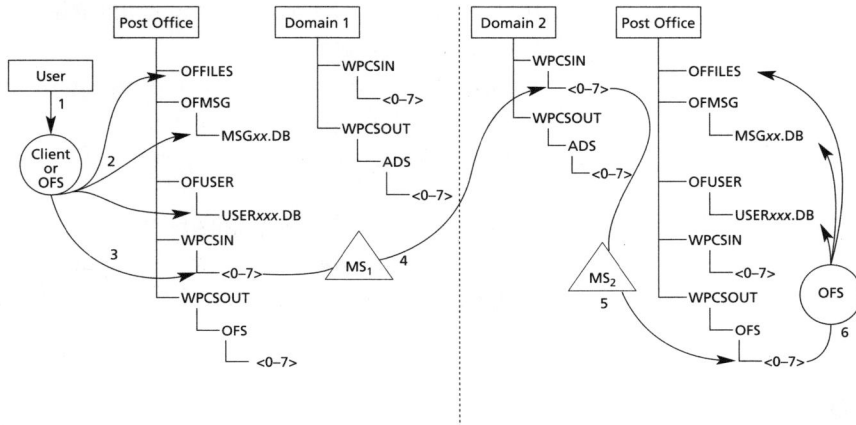

FIGURE 10.12

Message Flow Between
Domains with a Direct
Link

This is the sequence of events depicted in Figure 10.12:

1 • A user in Domain 1 creates and sends a message to a user in Domain 2 using the GroupWise client.

2 • The GroupWise client or the post office server adds the message to the message database, adds a pointer to that message in the user database, and adds information to the OFFILES directory (if necessary).

3 • The GroupWise client or the post office server places the outbound message in the *<post office>*\WPCSIN\<0–7> directory.

4 • The message server for Domain 1 detects the message in the post office message server input queue, *<post office>*\WPCSIN\<0–7>, and places the message in Domain 2's message server input queue, *<domain>*\WPCSIN\<0–7>. (This location was determined by the direct link address that was defined from Domain 1 to Domain 2.)

5 • Domain 2's message server detects the message in its input queue and places it in the post office-level message server output queue, *<post office>*\WPCSOUT\OFS\<0–7>. (This was accomplished because of the direct link address that was defined from Domain 2 to Domain 1.)

6 • The post office server in the recipient's post office detects the message in the post office queue, <*post office*>\WPCSOUT\OFS\<0–7>, and completes delivery to the recipient by placing the message in the appropriate message database, inserting a pointer in the recipient's user database, and placing the file attachments in the OFFILES directory (if necessary).

7 • The post office server in the recipient's post office creates a Delivered status message and places it in the message server input queue, <*post office*>\WPCSIN\<0–7>. See Figure 10.13.

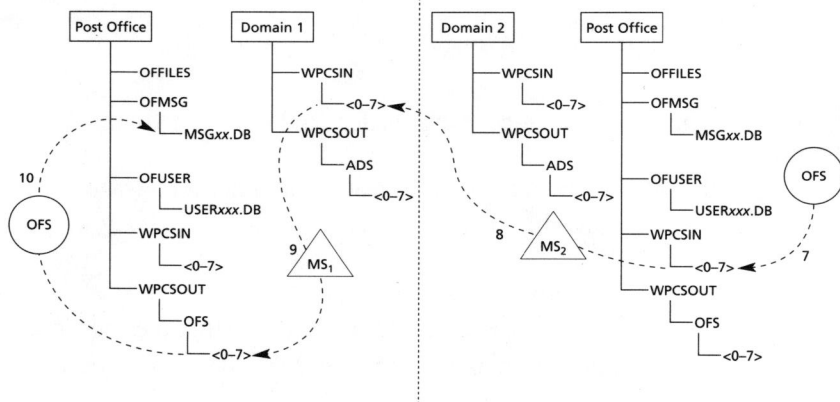

FIGURE 10.13

Status Back Message

8 • Domain 2's message server detects the status message in its input queue and places it in Domain 1's message server input queue, <*domain*>\WPCSIN\<0–7>.

9 • Domain 1's message server detects the status message in its input queue and places it in the output queue of the sender's post office, <*post office*>\WPCSOUT\OFS\<0–7>.

10 • The post office server for the sender's post office updates the message database with the Delivered status message.

MESSAGE FLOW BETWEEN TWO DOMAINS WITH INDIRECT LINKS

Figure 10.14 shows the message delivery between two domains that are indirectly linked. In Figure 10.14, Domain 1 is linked directly to Domain 2, and it is linked indirectly to Domain 3. Domain 2 is the routing domain. Notice the extra message server processes involved in sending a message through an indirect link.

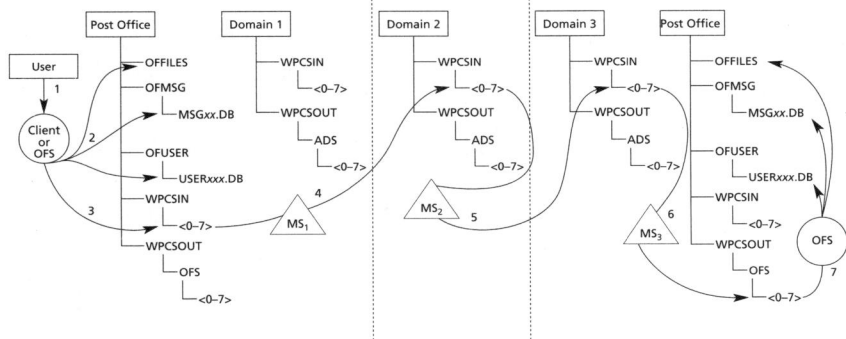

F I G U R E 10.14

Message Flow with an
Indirect Domain Link

Here is the sequence of events depicted in Figure 10.14:

1 • A user in Domain 1 uses the GroupWise client to send a message to a user in Domain 3.

2 • The GroupWise client or the post office server adds the message to the message database, the user database, and the OFFILES directory (if necessary).

3 • The GroupWise client or the post office server places the outbound message in the post office-level message server input queue, *<post office>*\WPCSIN\<0–7>. This occurs because the link record for Domain 1 to Domain 3 is "Indirect through Domain 2." The link address to Domain 2 was read, and then the message was transferred to Domain 2's directory.

4 • The message server for Domain 1 detects the message in the post office-level message server input queue and places the message in Domain 2's message server input queue, *<domain>*\WPCSIN\<0–7>.

5 • The message server for Domain 2 detects the message in its input queue, recognizes that the message is destined for Domain 3, and places the message in Domain 3's message server input queue, *<domain>*\ WPCSIN\<0–7>.

6 • The message server for Domain 3 detects the message in the input queue and sends the message to the post office-level output queue, *<post office>*\ WPCSOUT\OFS\<0–7>.

7 • The recipient's post office server delivers the message by placing the message in the message database, MSG*xx*.DB, placing file attachments in the OFFILES directory (if necessary), and placing pointers to the message and files in the user database, USER*xxx*.DB.

8 • The post office server generates a delivered status message and places it in the *<post office>*\WPCSIN\<0–7> directory. See Figure 10.15.

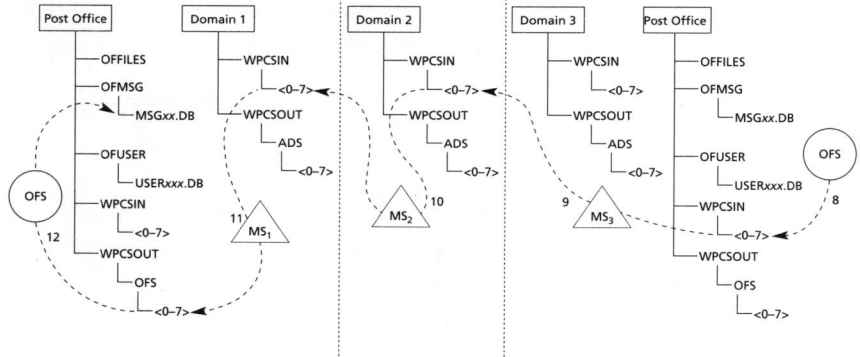

FIGURE 10.15

Status Back

9 • Domain 3's message server detects the message and places it in Domain 2's WPCSIN\<0–7> directory.

10 • Domain 2's message server detects the message and places it in Domain 1's message server input queue, *<domain>*\WPCSIN\<0–7>.

11 • Domain 1's message server places the status message in the post office output queue.

12 • The post office server updates the message database with the delivered status.

> **The message flow for domains connected by a gateway will be discussed in Chapter 12.**
>
> NOTE

MESSAGE FLOW BETWEEN DOMAINS LINKED DIRECTLY WITH TCP/IP

The message flow for domains linked directly using TCP/IP is slightly different from the message flow between domains linked by direct mapped links. See Figure 10.16.

FIGURE 10.16

TCP/IP Message Flow

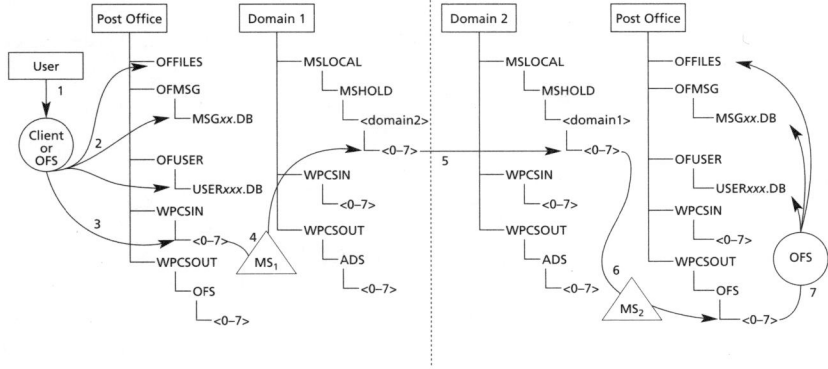

Here is the sequence of events depicted in Figure 10.16:

1 • The user in Domain 1 creates and sends a message to a user in Domain 2 using the GroupWise client.

2 • The GroupWise client or the post office server adds the message to the message database, the user database, and the OFFILES directory (if necessary).

3 • The GroupWise client or the post office server places the outbound message in the *<post office>*\WPCSIN\<0–7> directory.

4 • The message server for Domain 1 detects the message in the post office message server input queue, *<post office>*\WPCSIN\<0–7>, and places the message in the *<domain₁>*\MSLOCAL\MSHOLD*<domain₂>*\ <0–7> directory.

5 • The TCP/IP symbiont running for Domain 1's message server sends the file in TCP/IP packets to the TCP/IP symbiont running for Domain 2's message server, which assembles the packets into a file in the MSHOLD\ *<domain₁>*\<0–7> directory in Domain 2.

6 • Domain 2's message server moves the message to the message server output queue in the post office.

7 • The post office server finishes the processing of the message.

8 • The post office server generates a Delivered status message and places it in the *<post office>*\WPCSIN\<0–7> directory. See Figure 10.17.

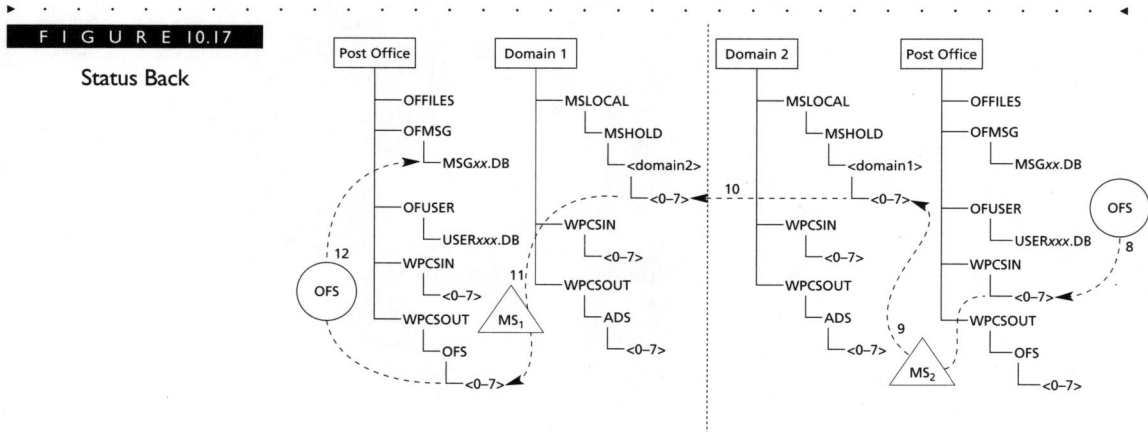

FIGURE 10.17

Status Back

9 • Domain 2's message server detects the message and places it in Domain 2's MSLOCAL\MSHOLD*<domain₁>*\<0–7> directory.

10 • The TCP/IP symbiont running for Domain 2's message server sends the file in TCP/IP packets to the TCP/IP symbiont running for Domain 1's message server, which assembles the packets into a file in the MSHOLD\ <*domain₂*>\<0–7> directory in Domain 1.

11 • Domain 1's message server places the status message in the post office output queue.

12 • The post office server updates the message database with the Delivered status.

MESSAGE FLOW BETWEEN DOMAINS WITH TRANSFER PULL DIRECTORY

Figure 10.18 shows how messages move between two systems when a transfer pull directory is configured. In Figure 10.18, Domain 1 is comparable to the Sales domain in the scenario earlier in this chapter. Domain 2 is similar to the Accounting domain.

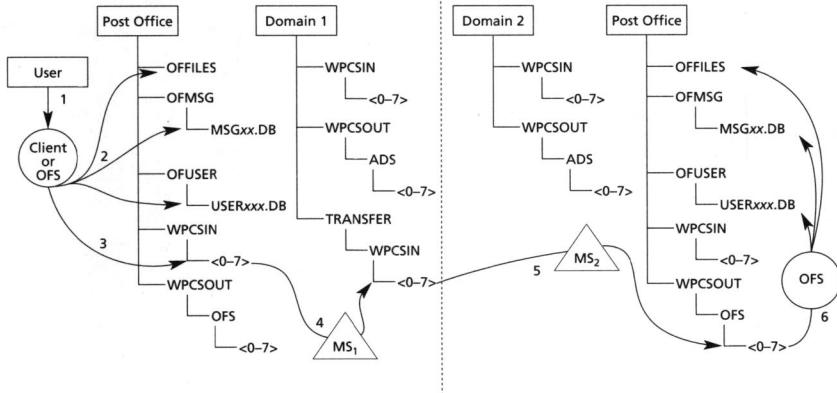

FIGURE 10.18

Message Flow with Transfer Pull Directory

Here is the sequence depicted in Figure 10.18:

1 • A user in Domain 1 creates and sends a message to a user in Domain 2 using the GroupWise client.

2 • The GroupWise client or a post office server adds the message to the message database, the user database, and the OFFILES directory (if necessary).

3 • The GroupWise client or a post office server places the outbound message in the *post office*>\WPCSIN\<0–7> directory.

4 • The message server for Domain 1 detects the message in the post office message server input queue, *post office*>\WPCSIN\<0–7>, and places the message in the TRANSFER\WPCSIN\<0–7> directory on Domain 1's file server.

5 • Domain 2's message server scans the TRANSFER\WPCSIN\ <0–7> directory at the intervals specified in the transfer poll cycle and detects the message. It places the message in the *post office*>\ WPCSOUT\<0–7> directory.

6 • The post office server finishes the message delivery to the recipient.

7 • The post office server generates a Delivered status message and places it in the *post office*>\WPCSIN\<0–7> directory. See Figure 10.19.

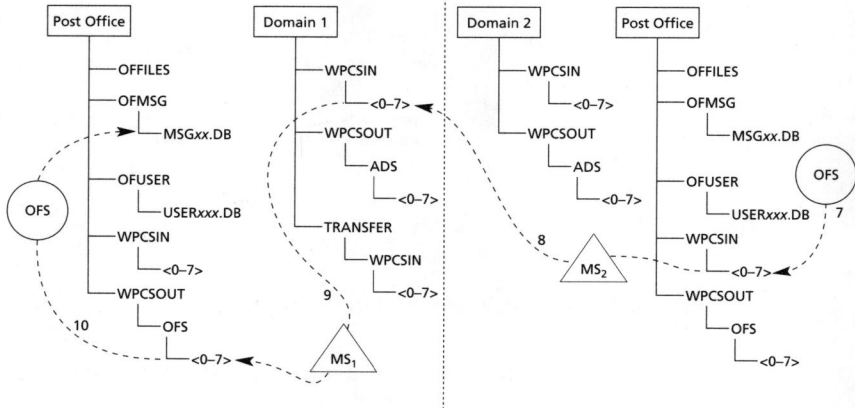

F I G U R E 10.19

Status Back

8 • Domain A's message server detects the message and places it directly in Domain 1's WPCSIN\<0–7> directory.

9 • Domain 1's message server places the status message in the post office output queue.

10 • The post office server updates the message database with the Delivered status.

Notice in Figure 10.19 that messages traveling from Domain 2 to Domain 1 do not go through the transfer pull directory structure. Only messages going from Domain 1 to Domain 2 pass through the transfer pull directories.

Troubleshooting Problems with Message Flow

At this point, you have learned how messages flow through a GroupWise system in several different scenarios:

▶ User-to-user within the same post office

▶ User-to-user in different post offices within the same domain

▶ User-to-user in different domains

Each of the above scenarios involves several processes: the client, the post office server, and one or more message servers. Understanding which processes handle the various parts of message delivery will help you troubleshoot problems that may arise in your GroupWise system.

Here is a procedure for troubleshooting message delivery problems in a GroupWise system:

1 • Identify which step in the message delivery is causing the problem.

2 • Identify which process is responsible for that step.

3 • Determine why that process failed.

4 • Find a solution for that failure.

When a process fails in a GroupWise system, the failure can often be traced to an incorrect configuration or to an underlying support error — such as an operating system failure, a network operating system failure, or hardware failure.

IDENTIFYING WHICH STEP FAILED

Here are some questions to consider as you try to figure out which step in the process failed:

▸ Are messages being delivered within the post office?

▸ Are messages being delivered between post offices?

▸ Are messages being delivered between domains?

Using the detailed message flow diagrams in this book, you should easily be able to identify which step in the process failed.

TIP

You can use explicit addressing to force a message to travel a pre-determined path through the system. By using this technique, you can route a message through the entire system to identify points of failure.

IDENTIFYING THE PROCESS RESPONSIBLE FOR THE STEP

Table 10.2 summarizes the processes involved in each step of message delivery. The processes are listed in the order in which they occur:

TABLE 10.2	SCENARIO	PROCESSES
Message Delivery Processes	User-to-user in the same post office	▸ GroupWise client ▸ Post office server (when the threshold is exceeded)
	User-to-user in different post offices within the same domain	▸ GroupWise client ▸ Post office server in the sender's post office (when the application threshold is exceeded) ▸ Message server (for the message and the status) ▸ Post office server in the recipient's post office
	User-to-user in different domains	▸ GroupWise client ▸ Post office server in the sender's post office (when the application threshold is exceeded) ▸ Message server for the sender's domain ▸ Gateway (if the domains are connected by a gateway) ▸ Message servers for any routing domains if the domains are connected by an indirect link ▸ Message server for the recipient's domain ▸ Post office server for the recipient's post office

DETERMINING WHY THE PROCESS FAILED

When you have determined which process failed, there are several things to check to find out why the failure occurred. It is possible that the machine running the process locked up or failed in some other way. Often just restarting the machine or restarting the process will correct the problem.

If the process previously functioned normally, ask yourself what has changed. Have any drive mappings changed? Has something been modified in GroupWise Admin? Has something in the network failed—such as cabling, routers, or file servers? Has the network changed in some way?

SOLVING THE PROBLEM

Once you have identified the process that failed and why it failed, you should be able to figure out a solution. The solution may be as simple as rebooting a computer or restarting the process—or it may be as complex as finding network patches or reworking network hardware.

OTHER TROUBLESHOOTING RESOURCES

Here are some resources you can use to gather information as you troubleshoot message delivery problems:

▶ Message server log files

▶ Post office server log files

▶ The ERRORS.TXT file

Message Server Log Files   If you determine that the message server is the process causing the problem, the message server log file can help you figure out what went wrong. Until your GroupWise system is fairly stable, you should keep the message server logging level set to Diagnostic. (You can adjust the setting in the Message Server Configuration screen in GroupWise Admin or in the startup file.) The Diagnostic level provides the most detailed information about problems, should they occur. For the

NLM and OS/2 message servers, the log files are stored in the directory specified by the /WORK switch in the startup file. For the DOS message server, the log files are stored in the CSLOCAL directory on the drive where CS.EXE was executed.

Post Office Server Log Files   If you have identified the post office server as the root of the problem, the post office log file can help you to determine why it failed. The logging level options for the post office server are the same as the logging level options for the message server. The post office server log files are stored in the *<post office>*\ WPCSOUT\OFS subdirectory of the post office.

ERRORS.TXT   Many of the errors reported by GroupWise processes have an error code that is associated with them. Sometimes descriptive text accompanies the error code. Detailed information about the probable cause and potential solutions to the error can be found in the ERRORS.TXT file, which is located in the domain directory.

Summary

In this chapter, I explained how to set up secondary domains. You learned a variety of ways to link domains together. You also saw several detailed diagrams that show how messages flow through multidomain systems.

The next chapter will explain how the administration server functions. The administration server's job is to make sure that directory information stays synchronized throughout the GroupWise system.

CHAPTER II

GroupWise Directory Synchronization

One of the main strengths of GroupWise systems is their scalability. As you have seen, GroupWise can be implemented on a very small scale (e.g., a single domain, single post office system) or you can create enormous and complex GroupWise systems with many domains that house numerous post offices.

Another strength of GroupWise is that, from an administrator's standpoint, it is very flexible. You can either administer an entire system from a single location (centralized administration) or you can delegate responsibilities and have administrative tasks performed from different locations within the system (distributed administration).

Another strength of GroupWise, which is equally impressive but which up until this point in the book has received little attention, is the ability of GroupWise systems to keep their directory stores automatically synchronized. When an administrator adds, modifies, or deletes an object anywhere in a system, GroupWise can automatically copy (or *replicate*) that change in all other domains and post offices in the system. This process is known as *automatic directory synchronization*. Automatic directory synchronization is the key to both GroupWise's scalability and to its administrative flexibility.

Directory synchronization is basically the process of keeping databases in a GroupWise system up-to-date with the latest information about each domain, post office, gateway, and object in the system.

Think about the last time you moved into a new home. You undoubtedly recall what a bother it can be to notify people about your new address. You need to update all of your magazine subscriptions. You need to (or at least you should) tell your creditors where to send bills. You have to tell all of your friends where to send your birthday cards. Everyone you want to receive mail from must somehow learn your new address. Wouldn't it be easier if you could simply tell one person where you are moving and then automatically everyone else would know your new address?

That is exactly the way a GroupWise system works. Through directory synchronization, changes made to a domain, to a post office, or even to a single object are automatically broadcast to all other points in the system. Suppose your GroupWise system contains domains in New York, Chicago, and Los Angeles, and you add a user to the New York domain. Automatically, the Chicago and Los Angeles domains would receive information about the new user in New York. Once directory synchronization has occurred, the new user would show up in the address books of all users in the system.

The primary goal of directory synchronization is to ensure that all domain databases and post office databases in a system contain the exact same addressing information for all objects at all times.

Here's a quick review of some key concepts you need to understand as you learn about directory synchronization:

Directory Store   The GroupWise directory store consists of all databases that store object-addressing information. The directory store is comprised of the WPDOMAIN.DB file in each domain directory structure and the WPHOST.DB files in post office directory structures. When you open the GroupWise address book, you see information from the post office's WPHOST.DB file.

Centralized Administration   Centralized administration is one of two ways to perform object-administration tasks in GroupWise. In centralized administration, the administrator performs all object-administration tasks from the primary domain. For example, an administrator for a primary domain would add and delete users in all secondary domains, as well as in the primary domain.

Distributed Administration   Distributed administration is another approach to performing object-administration tasks in a GroupWise system. In distributed administration, object administration is done at the individual domain level. For example, if an object needs to be added to a secondary domain, the secondary domain's administrator runs GroupWise Admin in the secondary domain to accomplish the task.

Store-and-Forward Messaging   GroupWise distributes messages using the store-and-forward messaging architecture. Messages are stored in holding queues and moved from one queue to another (and ultimately to message store databases) by GroupWise server processes (MTAs). Directory synchronization uses store-and-forward messaging to distribute administrative messages throughout the GroupWise system.

The GroupWise Administration Server

The *administration server* is one of the three main components of the GroupWise Message Server Pack. (The other two components are the message server and the post office server, which have already been discussed.) The job of the administration server is to update the domain database (WPDOMAIN.DB) and all of the post office databases (WPHOST.DB files) in a GroupWise domain. There is only one administration server for each domain.

The administration server usually operates on the domain level. However, the NLM and UNIX versions of the administration server can be used at the post office level, as well as the domain level. I will explain how the NLM version works later in the chapter.

The GroupWise administration server process is often called the *ADS process*. (The letters *ADS* typically appear in the administration server's executable filename. For example, the administration server that comes with the NLM Message Server Pack is NGWADS.NLM.) The role of the ADS process is to keep the domain databases and post office databases synchronized (i.e., updated with the latest system information).

Earlier, I described the post office server and explained how it works at the post office level. As I mentioned before, the post office server's job is to update the user and message databases in a post office. The administration server works basically the same way. Instead of facilitating the client program at the post office level, it helps out the GroupWise Admin program at the domain level.

The diagrams you find in this chapter will give you a clearer understanding of how the administration server carries out directory synchronization.

Directory Synchronization Overview

Directory synchronization is the process of keeping all domain and post office databases updated with the latest system and object-addressing information. There are three major players in the directory synchronization process:

- ▸ GroupWise Admin

- ▸ The administration server

- ▸ The message server

GroupWise Admin handles all of the directory synchronization tasks in a single domain GroupWise system. (There is one exception: when a post office in the system is closed. I will discuss that situation later in the chapter).

In a multidomain GroupWise system, GroupWise Admin, the message server, and the administration server all work together to synchronize the directories. The role each plays varies according to the administrative task performed. There are three common situations that arise in multidomain directory synchronization:

- The primary domain's administrator adds, modifies, or deletes an object owned by the primary domain. (This can occur in either centralized or distributed administration.)

- An administrator for a secondary domain adds, modifies, or deletes an object in the secondary domain. (This occurs only in distributed administration.)

- The primary domain's administrator adds or modifies an object in a secondary domain. (This occurs only in centralized administration.)

Each of these situations will be discussed in this chapter.

NOTE

The directory synchronization process usually involves objects, such as users or resources. But system-level changes—such as creating new domains, post offices, or gateways—also need to be replicated throughout a system. In this chapter, I use object-administration tasks to demonstrate how directory synchronization works. Nevertheless, the sequence of events is the same when GroupWise replicates system-level changes.

Directory Synchronization in a Simple System

In a single domain, single post office GroupWise system, there are only two directory store databases that need to be synchronized: the WPDOMAIN.DB file and the WPHOST.DB. In this situation, GroupWise Admin handles all of the directory synchronization. An administration server is unnecessary.

Figure 11.1 illustrates how directory synchronization occurs in a single domain, single post office system. In the diagram, the administrator adds a user (Bob) to the post office.

FIGURE 11.1

Directory Synchronization—Single Domain, Single Post Office System

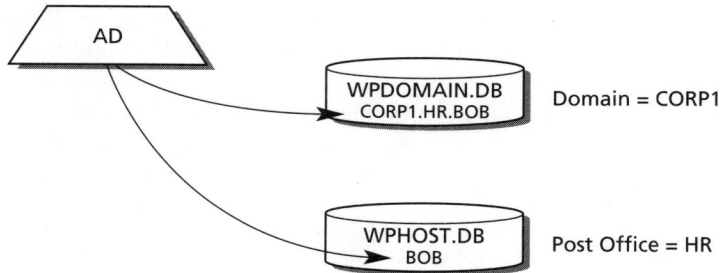

FIGURE 11.1

Directory Synchronization—Single Domain, Single Post Office System

(Notice the geometric shape that represents the GroupWise Admin program here. This same shape will also be used to represent the administration server, which functions as an agent of the GroupWise Admin program. *AD* stands for *GroupWise Admin*, and *ADS* denotes *administration server*.)

As you can see, the procedure is quite simple. The GroupWise administrator runs GroupWise Admin and adds Bob to the post office. GroupWise Admin automatically adds the information about Bob to the domain database and to the post office database.

Keep in mind that the GroupWise Admin program for a domain needs direct network access to all post office databases within the domain. The databases may be on the same file server or on different file servers.

Figure 11.1 illustrates directory synchronization in its simplest form. Neither a message server nor an administration server is required for directory synchronization in a single domain, single post office system.

Directory Synchronization in a Single Domain, Multiple Post Office System

In a single domain, multiple post office system, directory synchronization is virtually the same as in a simple GroupWise system. The only databases to be synchronized are the domain's WPDOMAIN.DB file and the post offices' WPHOST.DB files. Figure 11.2 illustrates the directory synchronization process in a single domain, multiple post office system. Here, the administrator adds a user named Sue to the post office called HR.

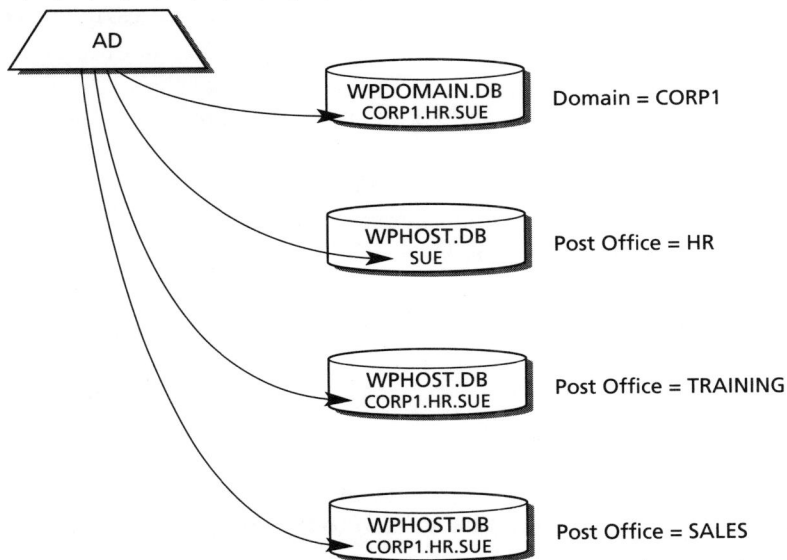

FIGURE II.2

Directory Synchronization—Single Domain, Multiple Post Office System

In Figure 11.2, the administrator adds Sue to the HR post office, and her addressing information is automatically added to the domain database and to the other post offices in the domain. When the directory synchronization is complete, all users in the system will see Sue in their address books (assuming Sue has system-level visibility).

Notice that an administration server is not required in this scenario. Because GroupWise Admin has access to the WPDOMAIN.DB file and to all WPHOST.DB files in the domain, it writes all changes directly to these databases. Even though this GroupWise configuration needs a message server to deliver regular GroupWise messages between the post offices, the message server would not be used for directory synchronization here.

CLOSED POST OFFICES

Normally, an administration server is not necessary for directory synchronization in a single domain GroupWise system. However, there is one case where an administration server is useful in a single domain system. If a post office within the domain is closed when an administrative change is made, both an administration server and a message server are required for successful directory synchronization.

A post office is *closed* if GroupWise Admin cannot access the post office's WPHOST.DB file for some reason. Here are a few situations that can cause a post office to be closed:

▸ The file server that holds the post office directories is not operational.

▸ A drive mapping to the post office directory is incorrect from the standpoint of the computer running GroupWise Admin, or a drive mapping is pointing to a post office directory for the wrong post office.

▸ The post office's WPHOST.DB file has been corrupted or deleted.

When you launch GroupWise Admin, it will call to your attention any closed post offices in the domain.

IMPORTANT

Any administrative changes you make in a domain while a post office is closed cannot be written to the closed post office's database by GroupWise Admin.

GroupWise Admin cannot write changes to a closed post office's database. GroupWise Admin is not a server process. It must be launched by a system administrator, and it does not perform any polling or monitoring. Nevertheless, a closed post office must somehow be notified of any changes as soon as it opens again. Because GroupWise cannot write administrative changes to a closed post office, it must hand that task off to a server process.

GroupWise Admin relies on a domain's message server and administration server to make administrative changes to a closed post office (assuming those server processes are available in the domain). Figure 11.3 illustrates directory synchronization when a post office is closed.

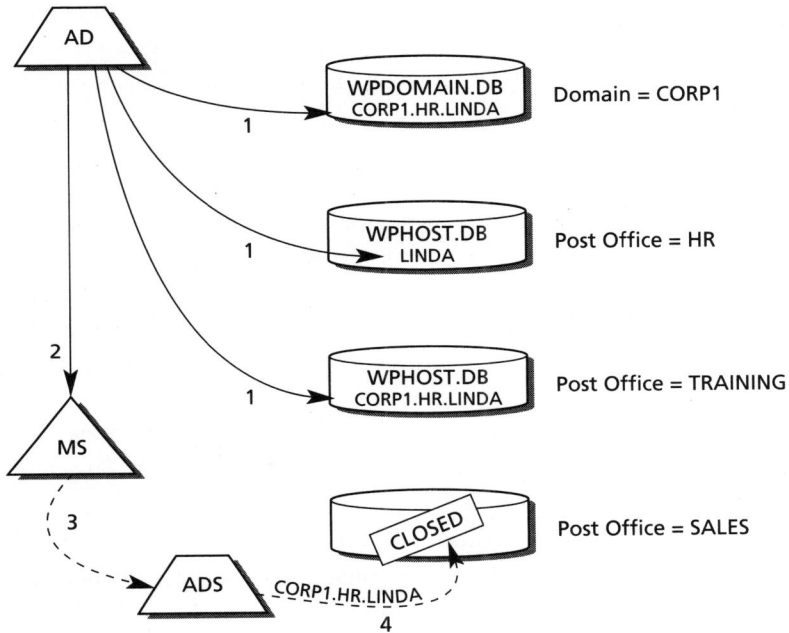

F I G U R E 11.3

Directory Synchronization—
Post Office Closed

In Figure 11.3, the Sales post office is closed. Therefore, GroupWise Admin cannot access that post office's WPHOST.DB file. (Assume that the Sales post office is closed because the file server has been taken down for maintenance.)

When the administrator runs GroupWise Admin for the domain, he gets a message informing him that the Sales post office is closed. However, suppose it is urgent that he add Linda to the HR post office immediately. Instead of waiting until the Sales post office is open again, the administrator proceeds to add Linda to the HR post office. This is what happens:

- GroupWise Admin writes the change to the domain database, adds Linda to the HR post office, and adds Linda's addressing information to all open post offices. GroupWise Admin already knows that it cannot make the change to the Sales post office because it recognized upon startup that the Sales post office is closed.

2 • GroupWise Admin creates an administrative message, which it delivers to the message server. The administrative message contains instructions to add Linda's addressing information to the Sales post office.

3 • The message server notices the message in its input queue and discerns that it is an administrative message for the Sales post office. It holds the message in one of its holding queues until it can access the post office's directories. As soon it can access the directories, it places the message in the post office's administration server queue. (The broken lines in the diagram indicate that the processes occur when the post office subdirectories are accessible—in other words, when the post office is open again.)

4 • The administration server for the domain periodically scans the post office's ADS queue. When it sees the administrative message in the post office's directory, it reads the message and adds Linda's addressing information to the Sales post office's WPHOST.DB file, just as GroupWise Admin would have done if the Sales post office had been open when Linda was added to the HR post office.

In the scenario above, you assumed the post office was closed because GroupWise Admin couldn't access the file server that houses the Sales post office. In that case, the entire post office subdirectory was temporarily inaccessible to the message server.

If the post office were closed because the WPHOST.DB file had been corrupted or deleted (or because that individual file was inaccessible for some other reason) the third and fourth steps would have been different. In that case, the message server would have been able to access the post office directory structure. Instead of keeping the administrative message in its holding queues, the message server would have placed the message in the post office's administration server input queue (*<post office>*\WPCSOUT\ADS\<0–7>). The administration server would then have immediately made regular attempts to access the post office database. As soon as the database could be accessed, the administration server would have completed the directory synchronization.

WARNING

In a single domain, single post office GroupWise system that does not have a message server, you should never make administrative changes when a post office is closed. If a post office is closed, the changes will be put into a message server holding queue that is never scanned. The administrative update will never be processed, and directory synchronization will not occur.

Directory Synchronization in the Primary Domain

A primary domain administrator has administrative authority for objects within the primary domain and for objects in secondary domains. When the primary domain administrator makes a change to an object in the primary domain, two separate events occur:

1 • GroupWise Admin modifies the domain and post office databases in the primary domain.

2 • GroupWise replicates the change in all other domains and post offices in the system.

Figure 11.4 gives an abstract representation of what occurs when the administrator modifies, adds, or deletes an object within the primary domain. In this scenario, a company car is added as a resource to the HR post office in the primary domain. The GroupWise ID for the car is LEMON1.

FIGURE 11.4

*Object Added to the
Primary Domain*

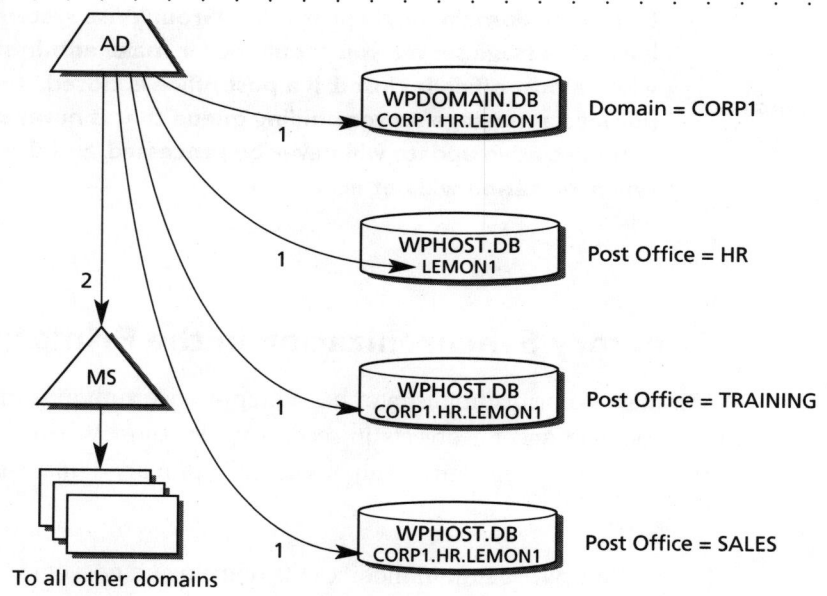

In Step 1, GroupWise Admin adds LEMON1 to the HR post office and adds the addressing information for LEMON1 to the domain database and to all other post offices in the primary domain.

In Step 2, GroupWise replicates LEMON1's addressing information in the rest of the system. When the administrative message reaches the other domains, those domains' message servers pass the message to each domain's administration server, which updates the domain and post office databases, completing the directory synchronization.

Once this process is complete, all domains and post offices in the system should show the company car as a resource in the primary domain.

How It Works

Figure 11.5 is a detailed diagram directory synchronization when a change occurs in a primary domain. Notice how the directory synchronization process follows the store-and-forward model of GroupWise message delivery.

> **In all of the detailed diagrams in this chapter, you should assume that there are direct message server links between the primary and secondary domains.**
>
> NOTE

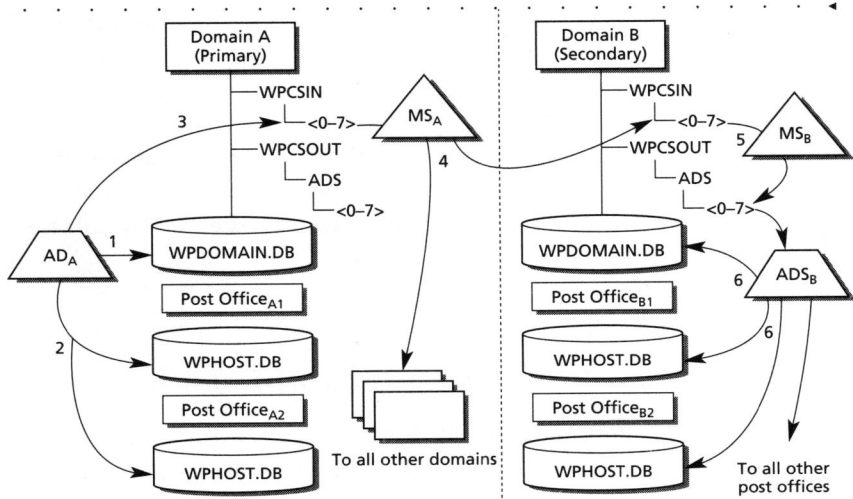

FIGURE 11.5

Directory Synchronization in Detail—Change in Primary Domain

Figure 11.5 illustrates the following steps:

1 • The administrator for Domain A, the primary domain, runs GroupWise Admin and adds an object to a post office in that domain. GroupWise Admin adds the information to the domain database (WPDOMAIN.DB).

2 • GroupWise Admin writes the new object's information to all post office databases within the domain.

3 • GroupWise Admin creates an administrative message addressed to all other domains in the system. This message instructs each domain to add the addressing information about the new object to their directory store databases. GroupWise Admin places this administrative message in the primary domain's message server input queue (<*domain*>\WPCSIN\<0–7>).

4 • Domain A's message server transfers the message to the message server input queues (<*domain*>\WPCSIN\<0–7>) for all secondary domains.

5 • The message server for Domain B (a secondary domain) places the message in that domain's administration server input queue (<*domain*>\WPCSOUT\ADS\<0–7>).

6 • Domain B's administration server adds the new object's addressing information to the domain database and to all post office databases within the domain.

> **NOTE**
>
> **Steps 5 and 6 occur in all secondary domains in the system. If any post offices in a secondary domain are closed, the administrative message is processed in the manner described earlier in this section.**

Directory Synchronization in a Secondary Domain

An administrator for a secondary domain can add, delete, or modify objects within the domain if the system follows the distributed administration model. However, a secondary domain administrator cannot perform those tasks in other domains.

OBJECT ADDED BY SECONDARY DOMAIN ADMINISTRATOR

When a secondary domain administrator adds an object, the process that occurs is very similar to what happens when a primary domain administrator adds an object in a primary domain. The main difference is the replication process that follows.

Figure 11.6 illustrates what happens when a secondary domain administrator adds an object to a post office in the secondary domain.

Here is what happens:

1 • An administrator runs GroupWise Admin for the secondary domain and adds an object to a post office within the domain. GroupWise Admin updates the domain database and all post office databases within the domain.

2 • GroupWise Admin creates an administrative message addressed to the primary domain. The message contains the new object's addressing information. GroupWise Admin delivers the message to the secondary domain's message server.

3 • The secondary domain's message server delivers the message to the primary domain's message server.

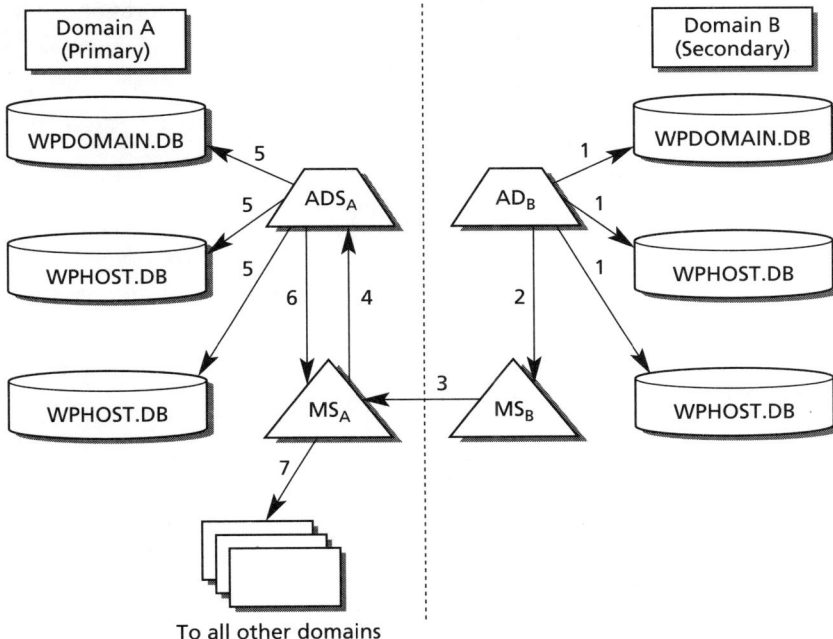

FIGURE 11.6

Directory Synchronization in Detail—Object Added by Secondary Domain Administrator

4 • The primary domain's message server forwards the administrative message to the primary domain's administration server.

5 • The primary domain's administration server adds the object's information to the primary domain database and to all post office databases within the primary domain.

6 • The primary domain's administration server creates an administrative message containing information about the new object and passes on that administrative message to the message server.

7 • The primary domain's message server delivers the message to all other domains in the system. The other domains' message servers pass along the message to their respective administration servers, which update the rest of the domain and post office databases.

Notice that the primary domain serves as central replication point for all administrative messages. In a multiple domain system, it is critical that you make sure every secondary domain maintains a consistent link to the primary domain (through a direct, indirect, or gateway link). If you don't, the directory store databases in the system will quickly become unsynchronized.

How It Works

Figures 11.7 and 11.8 illustrate in detail the directory synchronization process that occurs when a secondary domain administrator adds an object to a post office.

FIGURE 11.7

Secondary Domain

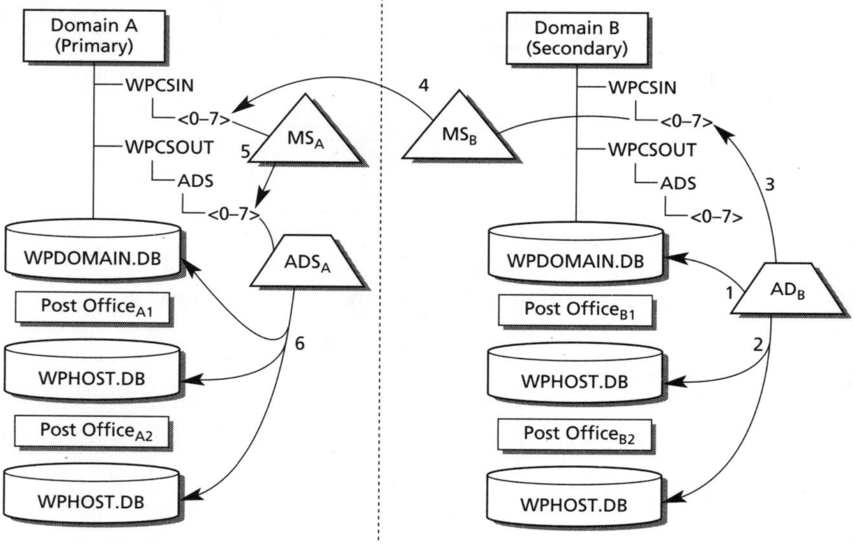

Here is what Figure 11.7 shows:

1 • The administrator for the secondary domain runs GroupWise Admin and adds a user to a post office within the secondary domain. GroupWise Admin adds the new user's information to the domain database, WPDOMAIN.DB.

2 • GroupWise Admin updates all post office databases within the secondary domain with the new user's information.

3 • GroupWise Admin creates an administrative message, *addressed to the primary domain only*, that informs the primary domain of the new user. GroupWise Admin puts the message in the secondary domain's message server input queue (*<domain>*\WPCSIN\<0–7>).

4 • The secondary domain's message server delivers the message to the primary domain's message server input queue (*<domain>*\WPCSIN\<0–7>).

5 • The primary domain's message server delivers the message to the primary domain's administration server input queue (*<domain>*\WPCSOUT\ADS\<0–7>).

6 • The primary domain's administration server receives the message and updates the primary domain database and all post office databases in the primary domain.

At this point, the secondary domain that owns the user object has completed directory synchronization within the secondary domain, and the primary domain has been completely synchronized.

Figure 11.8 illustrates how the information about the new user is replicated in the remaining domains in the system.

7 • The primary domain's administration server creates an administrative message addressed to all other secondary domains in the system. This message instructs those domains to add the new user's information to their directory store databases. This administrative message is placed in the message server input queue (*<domain>*\WPCSIN\<0–7>).

8 • The primary domain's message server delivers the message to all other secondary domains' message server input queues. The domains' message servers pass along the message to the respective domain administration servers, which update the rest of the domain and post office databases with the information about the new user.

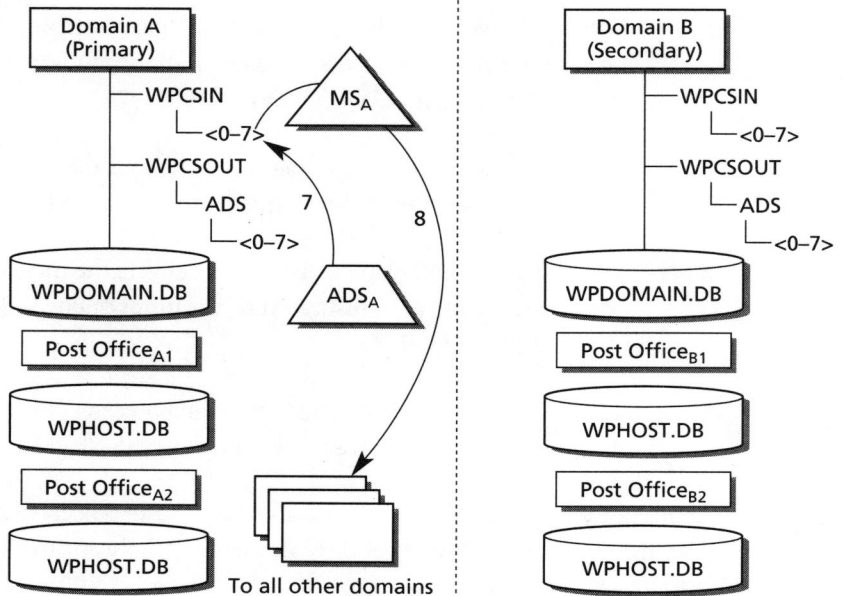

FIGURE II.8

The Replication Process

This completes the directory synchronization process. At this point, all domains and post offices in the system contain information about the new user. All others users in the system can now find that user in the address book (assuming the user has systemwide visibility).

OBJECT ADDED BY PRIMARY DOMAIN ADMINISTRATOR

If your system follows the centralized administration model, the primary domain administrator adds, deletes, or modify objects located in all secondary domains. This is the most complex (and the most network-traffic-intensive) directory synchronization scenario.

Three main phases occur in this process:

▶ Request

▶ Confirm

▶ Replicate

Request   In this phase, the primary domain generates a request for the secondary domain to add the object and sends that request to the secondary domain.

Confirm   In the confirmation phase, the secondary domain makes the change to the object and sends an administrative message to the primary domain confirming that the change has been made.

Replicate   In this phase, the primary domain broadcasts the information about the change to all other secondary domains in the system.

These three steps only occur when a system follows centralized administration and when the primary domain requests a change in one of the secondary domains. If a change occurs in the primary domain, the request and confirm steps do not occur. When a change is made from within the domain that owns the object, there is no need for the request and confirmation process.

Figures 11.9 and 11.10 illustrate directory synchronization when the primary domain administrator adds an object to a secondary domain. Figure 11.9 illustrates the Request phase.

F I G U R E 11.9

Request Phase

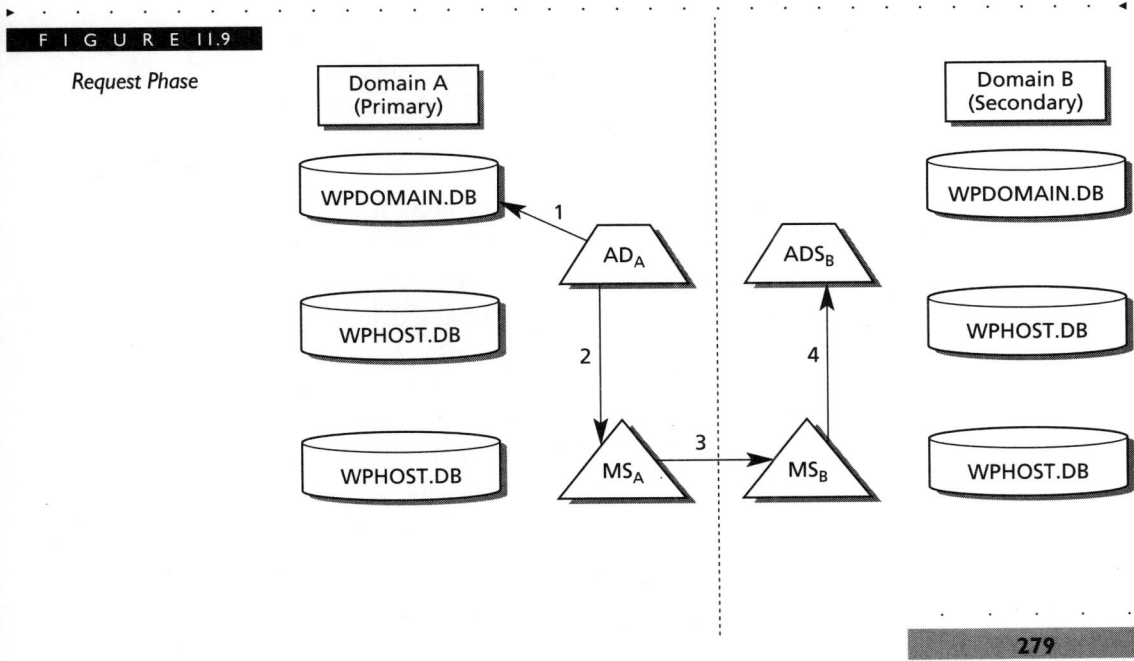

1 • The administrator for the primary domain runs GroupWise Admin and creates a user object in a secondary domain's post office. GroupWise Admin writes the change to the primary domain's database and marks the record as a *Pending Operation*.

2 • GroupWise Admin for the primary domain creates an administrative message addressed to the secondary domain where the new user object will be located. The message asks the secondary domain's administration server to add the user to a post office in the secondary domain. This administrative message is delivered to the primary domain's message server. A message appears in GroupWise Admin that reads "A Remote Management Message has been sent." This message indicates that the primary domain has sent a message requesting that the change be made in the secondary domain.

3 • The primary domain's message server delivers the message to the secondary domain's message server.

4 • The secondary domain's message server passes the message to the secondary domain's administration server.

These steps complete the Request phase. Figure 11.10 is a continuation of this process. This diagram illustrates both the Confirm and the Replicate phase of the directory synchronization process.

5 • The secondary domain's administration server receives the request from the primary domain. The secondary domain's administration server creates the user object and adds the user's addressing information to the secondary domain's domain database and all post office databases in that domain.

6 • Once the object has been added, the secondary domain's administration server generates a confirmation message addressed to the primary domain. The message indicates that the primary domain's request has been successfully completed. This message is delivered to the secondary domain's message server.

7 • The secondary domain's message server delivers the confirmation message to the primary domain's message server.

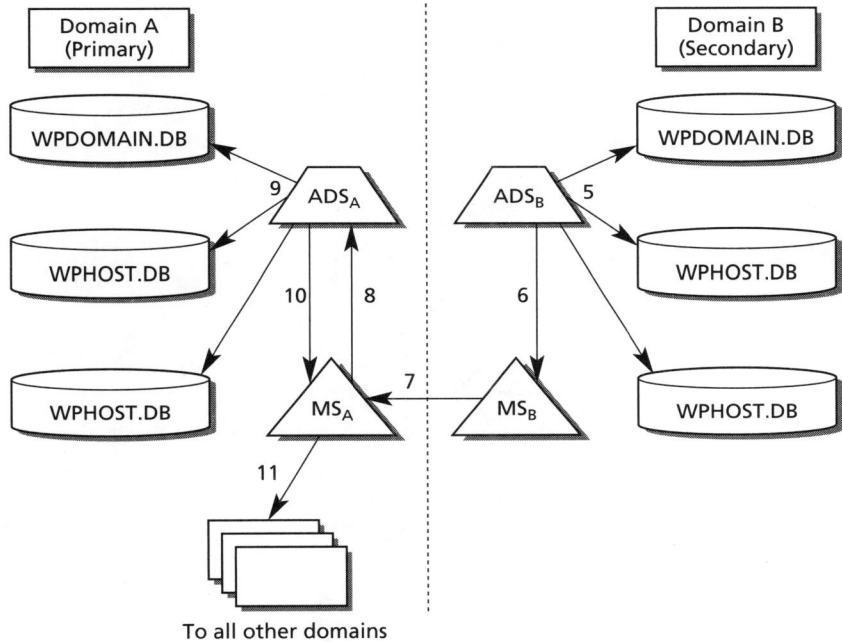

F I G U R E 11.10

Confirm and Replicate Phases

8 • The primary domain's message server sends the message to the primary domain's administration server.

9 • The primary domain's administration server modifies the information in the primary domain database, changing the *Pending Operation* status to *Completed* status. It also adds new user information to all post office databases in the primary domain. This is the end of the Confirm phase.

10 • The administration server for the primary domain generates an administrative message for all other domains in the system informing them of the new user's addressing information. This message is sent to the primary domain's message server.

II • The primary domain's message server delivers the administrative message to all other secondary domains in the system. The administration servers in those domains update their respective domain and post office databases with the new user's information. This is the end of the Replicate phase.

How It Works

Figures 11.11 through 11.13 illustrate in detail the process that occurs when a primary domain administrator adds a user to a post office in a secondary domain.

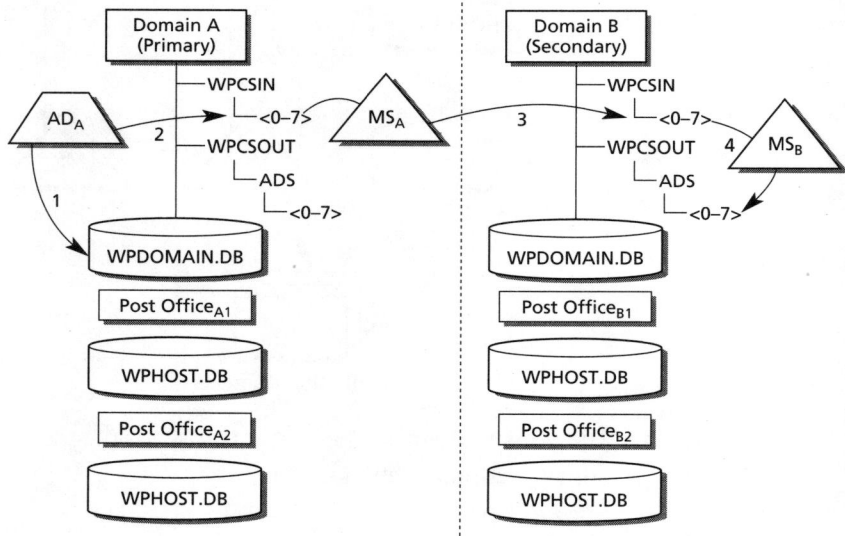

I • The administrator for the primary domain runs GroupWise Admin and creates a user object in a secondary domain post office. GroupWise Admin writes the change to the primary domain's database and marks the record as a *pending operation*.

2 • The primary domain's GroupWise Admin program creates an administrative message addressed to the secondary domain where the new user object will be located. This administrative message is placed in the primary domain's message server input queue (*<domain>*\WPCSIN\<0–7>).

3 • The primary domain's message server delivers the message to the secondary domain's message server input queue (*<domain>*\WPCSIN\<0–7>).

4 • The secondary domain's message server places the message in the administration server's input queue (*<domain>*\WPCSOUT\ADS\<0–7>). This is the end of the Request phase.

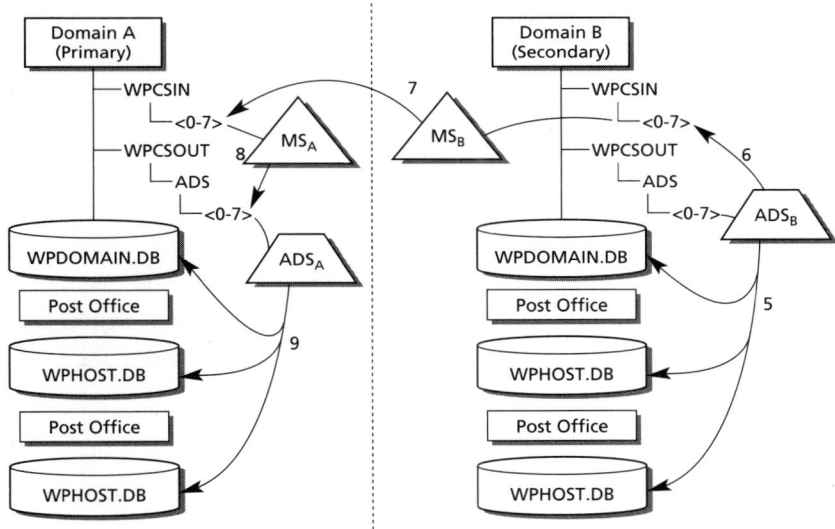

F I G U R E 11.12

Directory Synchronization in Detail—Confirm Phase

5 • The secondary domain's administration server receives the request and creates the user object by adding that user's information to the domain database and to all post office databases within the secondary domain.

6 • Once the user has been successfully added to the secondary domain, the administration server generates a confirmation message addressed to the primary domain and places the message in the secondary domain's message server input queue (*<domain>*\WPCSIN\<0–7>).

7 • The secondary domain's message server delivers the confirmation message to the primary domain's message server input queue (*<domain>*\WPCSIN\<0–7>).

8 • The primary domain's message server delivers the message to the primary domain's administration server input queue (*<domain>*\WPCSOUT\ADS\<0–7>).

9 • The primary domain's administration server modifies the information in the primary domain database, changing the *Pending Operation* status to *Completed* status. The administration server also adds the information to all post office databases in the primary domain. This is the end of the Confirm phase.

10 • The primary domain's administration server generates an administrative message addressed to all other secondary domains in the system informing them of the new user. This message is sent to the primary domain's message server input queue (*<domain>*\WPCSIN\<0–7>).

11 • The primary domain's message server delivers the administrative message to the message server input queue directories (*<domain>*\WPCSIN\<0–7>) for all other secondary domains in the system. The administration servers in those domains update their respective domain and post office databases with the new user's information. This is the end of the Replicate phase.

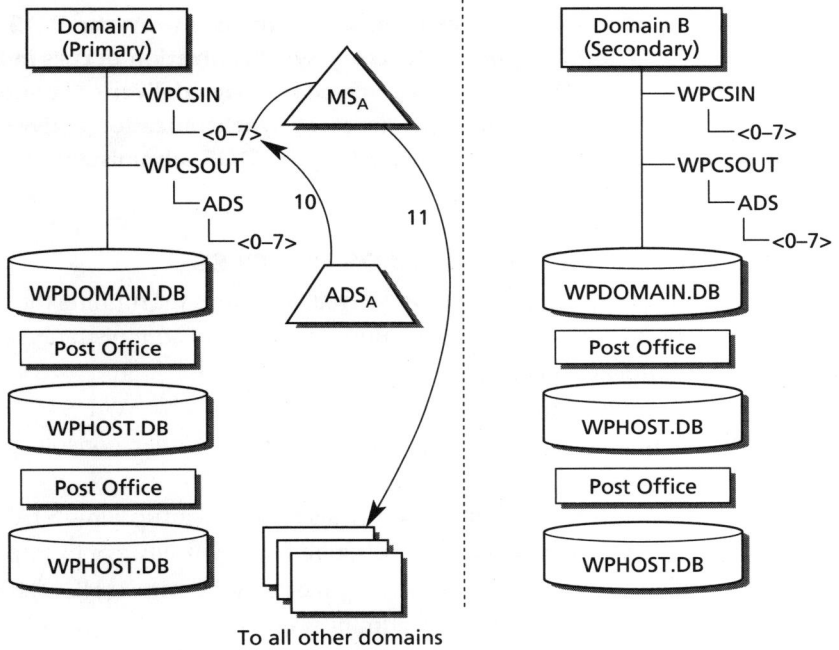

FIGURE 11.13

Directory Synchronization in Detail—Replicate Phase

The GroupWise NLM Administration Server

So far in this chapter you have learned a great deal about the role of the administration server in the directory synchronization process.

In a physical sense, the administration server is like any other GroupWise server. It runs on a dedicated machine or, in the case of the NLM or UNIX versions, on the file server.

The administration server comes with the Message Server Pack. It is not sold as a separate product. It is available for DOS, OS/2, UNIX and NetWare NLM. In this section, I will discuss the NetWare NLM administration server. (Details about running the other administration servers can be found in the message server guides for those platforms.)

NOTE

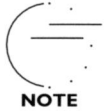

The DOS version of the administration server cannot be run as a stand-alone application. It must be launched from the DOS message server. Therefore, when directory synchronization occurs in a domain running the DOS message server, all message delivery between post offices is suspended until the directory synchronization activities are finished. This is a major drawback of the DOS administration server.

RUNNING THE NLM ADS PROCESS

In previous chapters, I have given instructions for running the NLM message server and the NLM post office server. Running the NLM administration server for a domain is a very similar process.

The name of the NLM administration server is NGWADS.NLM. You can load it on the domain's NetWare file server at the file server console prompt or from the AUTOEXEC.NCF file.

The NLM administration server also uses a startup file—STARTUP.ADS. (This file can be renamed to reflect its function more specifically. For example, if the name of the domain is Headquarters, the startup file could be named HDQTRS.ADS.)

The syntax for loading the administration server is shown below:

```
LOAD NGWADS.NLM @startup filename
```

For example, to load the administration server for the Headquarters domain, you would use this command:

```
LOAD NGWADS.NLM @HDQTRS.ADS
```

The administration server NLM has only one required startup switch, the /HOME switch, which points to the domain directory. When the administration server is loaded, it looks for the domain database file and searches the database for a list of all post offices in the domain.

Each post office record in the domain database contains the UNC path to the post office database. This information is added by GroupWise Admin when the post office is created. The administration server uses the information in the UNC path to find each post office database in the domain.

In most systems, the post office directories are not located on the file server that holds the domain directory structure. Therefore, the administration server usually requires a network access account so that the administration server can log in to the other file servers to access the post office databases.

The login ID and the password for the access account are set by using the /USER-*user ID* and /PASSWORD-*password* switches in the administration server startup file. These switches work the same way they do in the message server startup file.

The /USER-*user ID* switch specifies the user ID for the access account that the administrator must use to log in to each file server that holds a post office directory. This means that identical network access accounts are needed for all of the file servers that house post office directories. The /PASSWORD-*password* switch specifies the password for the network access account on each file server. Again, this password must be identical on all file servers that house post office directories. The access account must have network rights in the directories that contain the post office database and message queue directories.

The administration server scans the domain directory once per minute, and it scans the post office directory once every five minutes. (These are the default settings.) The administration server scans the domain directory more frequently than the post office directory because most administrative messages involve some modification of the WPDOMAIN.DB file.

The post office contains an administration server queue—<*post office*>\WPCSOUT/ ADS\<0–7>. This input queue is used only when the post office is closed (see the "Closed Post Offices" section) or when the NLM administration server is running on the post office level (see below). The administration server scans this queue. If it finds an administration message in this queue, it will attempt to update the WPHOST.DB file.

Using the /DSCAN-*seconds* and /PSCAN-*seconds* switches, you can change how often ADS scans the domain and post office input queues. The variables (*seconds*) represent the number of seconds between scans. For example, /DSCAN-30 would instruct the administration server to scan the domain administration server input queue every 30 seconds. Likewise, /PSCAN-120 would instruct the administration server to scan the administration queues at the post office level every two minutes.

NLM Administration Servers at the Post Office Level

As you saw in the directory synchronization diagrams above, the administration server updates both domain database files and post office database files. To update a post office database file, the ADS process often needs to write to a file located on a different file server. Sometimes the ADS process will have to write to a file through a slow network link (e.g., a 56 Kbps line). Heavy administration traffic between a domain and post office can cause congestion across a slow network link.

If you are running the NLM version of the administration server, you can configure the administration server process to run in *Domain Only* mode on the domain file server. Then you can configure another administration server process to run on the post office file server in *Post Office Only* mode. This strategy eliminates administration server traffic across the network wire. Administrative messages are delivered to the post office by the message server.

NOTE

This strategy does not require the purchase of an additional message server pack. Only a single NLM Message Server Pack (version 4.1a or later) is required. However, the post office file server must have enough RAM to run the NGWADS.NLM.

Running the administration server at the domain and post office levels splits the administration server's tasks into two parts: (1) updating the domain database is handled by the domain-level ADS process and (2) updating the post office database updates is handled by the ADS process at the post office level. Here are the steps you need to follow to configure the NLM administration server to run in this manner:

1 • Set the domain administration server to run in Domain Only mode.

2 • Load the NLM administration server on the post office file server and specify the Post Office Only mode.

DOMAIN ONLY MODE

In Domain Only mode, the administration server only processes those administrative tasks that affect the domain. The effect is similar to what would happen if you were running the administration server in the regular mode but all of the post offices in the domain were closed. In Domain Only mode, administrative messages are sent to the post office via the message server. Those messages must be processed by an administration server running in the Post Office Only mode.

To run the administration server in Domain Only mode, add the following switch to the domain-level administration server startup file:

```
/HOME-domain directory /DOMAIN
```

For example, if the domain name is CORP1 located on the CORPSERV file server, the switch would be:

```
/HOME-CORPSERV\SYS:CORP1 /DOMAIN
```

This switch tells the ADS process to run in Domain Only mode. The domain ADS then only handles updating the domain database, WPDOMAIN.DB. The administration server sends all post office administrative updates to the message server, and the message server places the administrative messages in the post office administration server input queue (*<post office>*\WPCSOUT\ADS\<0–7>) for processing.

POST OFFICE ONLY MODE

To configure the administration server to run at the post office level, you need to install the administration server to the file server that houses the post office, and add this switch to the administration server startup file:

```
/HOME-post office directory /POST
```

If the HDQRTRS post office was running the ADS process, the startup switch would look like this:

```
/HOME-HQSERV\SYS:HDQRTRS /POST
```

In this mode, the administration server processes administrative tasks for the post office only. The administration server for the post office scans the administration server input queue (*<post office>*\WPCSOUT\ADS\<0–7>) for administrative messages. When it finds an administrative message in the input queue, it makes the appropriate changes to the WPHOST.DB file.

NOTE

For ADS to run at the post office level, the post office's UNC path must be entered correctly in GroupWise Admin. Otherwise, ADS will generate an error stating that it cannot open the post office database.

IMPORTANT

To work correctly, both the domain-level administration server must be configured to run in Domain Only mode and the post office administration server must be configured to run in Post Office Only mode.

TROUBLESHOOTING DIRECTORY SYNCHRONIZATION PROBLEMS

Directory synchronization ensures that every domain database and every post office database file in a GroupWise system contains the same information. If a failure occurs in the directory synchronization process, you will notice it in one of two places:

▶ GroupWise Admin

▶ The client address book

You know you have a directory synchronization problem when the user list for one post office or domain in one domain database file is different from the user list in another domain database file. If you think there is a discrepancy, you should check the GroupWise Admin program. Client address books often differ due to varying object visibility settings. If you run GroupWise Admin for one domain and notice that the list is different from the list you see when you run GroupWise Admin for another domain, you know that directory synchronization has failed for some reason.

As I mentioned in an earlier chapter, visibility levels can be set at System, Domain, Post Office, or None. When a user with System visibility does not show up in certain address books, it is clear that there is a directory synchronization problem.

NOTE

When an object is added to a system, that object's addressing information is sent to every domain in the system through the directory synchronization process—regardless of the object's visibility setting. If an object's visibility is set to None, the object's information will be replicated in all domain databases in the system, but it will not be replicated in the post office databases. Thus, the object will not be visible in any address books. The object will also be visible in GroupWise Admin for all domains.

Mail messages and directory synchronization messages are transferred using the same message server and domain links. Usually, if a problem with domain links prevents mail messages from being successfully delivered, the directory synchronization will not take place properly.

The message flow diagrams presented in this chapter should help you identify the exact point at which the directory synchronization process failed. Once you have determined which objects' addressing information has not been successfully synchronized throughout the system, you can manually perform the synchronization using GroupWise Admin. I explain in Chapter 19 how to use GroupWise Admin to perform manual directory synchronization.

Summary

In this chapter, you learned about a key feature of GroupWise systems—directory synchronization. In Part V you will learn about another important component—the Async gateway.

Solution to Part IV Scenario

As you learned in Chapter 3, there are three main steps involved in planning a GroupWise system:

▶ Evaluating the GroupWise substructure

▶ Grouping users into post offices

▶ Grouping post offices into domains

This section presents one possible solution that might result from this approach to GroupWise system planning.

Evaluating the Substructure

The scenario in the Introduction to Part IV gave you numerous details about the substructure of NoCWACs.

The following factors should influence the GroupWise implementation.

CLIENT APPLICATIONS

You should be prepared to support the Windows client for the majority of the employees at NoCWACs. However, because there are still some 386 machines there, you should also be ready to implement the DOS client where necessary. The Publishing Department, of course, should be set up with the Macintosh client.

USE OF PROXY ASSIGNMENTS

Proxy assignments can only be made within post offices, so all managers and their assistants must be placed in the same post office.

MULTIPLE LOGINS ON A SINGLE MACHINE

Because users in the Customer Service Department share PCs, the system administrator should establish program groups within the Windows Program Manager that have the appropriate startup switches. Post office security should be set to High for the entire system so that users can't access other users' mail—either intentionally or unintentionally—especially when using the machines that have multiple logins.

All of the factors above should be analyzed carefully as you decide how to group users into post offices and how to best meet the users' needs.

Grouping Users Into Post Offices

The fact that the employees in the various departments appear to communicate primarily with other employees in their own departments should make it easy for you to group users into post offices.

Here is one way you might group users at the NoCWACs headquarters into post offices:

BUILDING A	BUILDING B	BUILDING C
AcctPay	Claims1	CustServ
Mgmt	Claims2	IS
HR	Claims3	Pub

This arrangement would isolate traffic within each post office, and it would reduce the amount of message-delivery traffic handled by the message servers in each domain. This configuration also takes into account the users' proxy feature requirements.

Grouping Post Offices Into Domains

The layout of the buildings and the current network configuration suggest that each building should have its own domain. The main reason for setting up the system this way is the condition of the network links between the buildings. The IS group should continually assess the capacity of the connections' bandwidth to determine whether the connections are sufficient or whether NoCWACs will need to upgrade. Having a domain at each building would minimize the impact of GroupWise on the existing network system.

Figure IV.2 illustrates a reasonable way of setting up a GroupWise system at the NoCWACs headquarters.

F I G U R E IV.2

*Layout of Domains at
NoCWACs Headquarters*

NoCWACs Headquarters

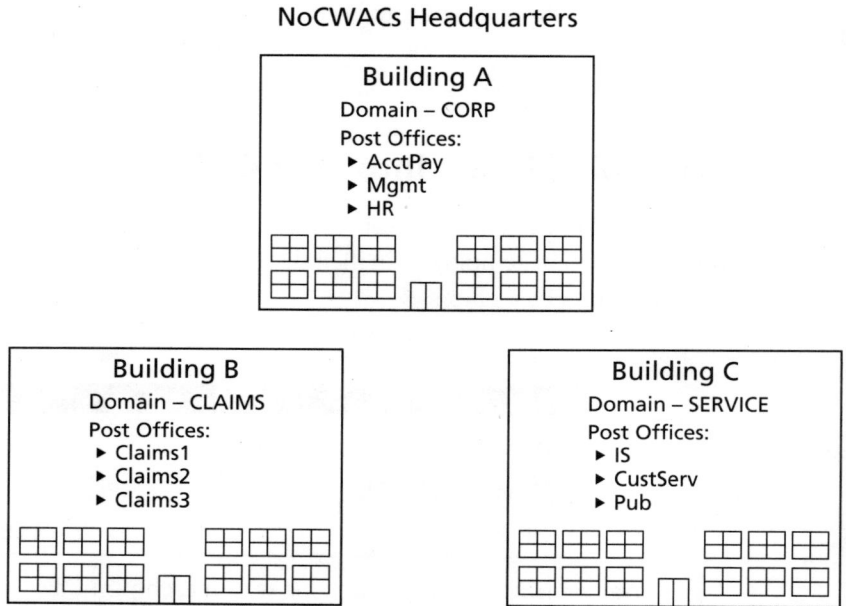

The fact that the IS Department is located in Building C suggests that the SERVICE domain should be the primary domain for the system. The IS team will be able to perform many administrative tasks without leaving the building. Because it can be conveniently accessed by the IS team, the SERVICE domain would also be a good place for future expansion to occur. For example, when gateways and additional domains need to be incorporated into the system, the IS employees will be able to set up and administer those directories from their own offices.

TOPOLOGY

Because of the relatively simple layout of the NoCWACs facility, the domains should be linked to each other with direct network links using the simple architecture. The simple architecture provides the most efficient message-delivery. Also, when you use the simple architecture, there is no Achilles' heel—the whole system is not vulnerable if one domain should go down.

ADMINISTRATION

NoCWACs should use a combination of centralized and distributed administration. It would make sense to have the IS Department personnel in Building C administer the GroupWise system for Building A and Building C. The IS personnel in Building B could handle administration for the Claims domain.

Additional Considerations

NoCWACs might consider sending about five members of the IS department to a local Novell Authorized Training Center to attend courses in the Certified Novell Engineer (CNE) curriculum for GroupWise (course numbers 325, 326, and 328). The trained engineers would then be responsible for system-level maintenance of GroupWise.

In addition, NoCWACs might send about 15 other IS personnel to Course 325, which would qualify them to perform general GroupWise administration tasks. A performance bonus could be offered to any employees who pass the exams for Certified Novell Administrator (CNA) or CNE credentials.

PART V

The GroupWise Async Gateway

In Part IV, I explained how to set up multidomain GroupWise systems in cases where the entire systems could be connected in the same LAN or WAN.

In some situations, however, it is not feasible or cost-effective to connect all of the domains in a system using direct or indirect links. In those cases, a GroupWise Async gateway can be used to connect domains together.

In the Introduction to Part IV scenario, I explained that the first phase of the GroupWise implementation at NoCWACs would be to implement a GroupWise system at the Denver headquarters. In the Part IV Scenario Solution, you saw that the best way to accomplish that task would be to set up three GroupWise domains there. Those three domains could be easily connected because they were located very close to each other.

The second phase of the GroupWise implementation at NoCWACs will be to connect the regional offices located in Salt Lake City and Butte so that all three sites can exchange GroupWise messages.

Scenario

You need to connect the Salt Lake regional office and the Butte regional office to the main GroupWise system. Here are some conditions that will affect the implementation:

▶ Both the Salt Lake City and Butte regional offices currently have a leased line to the main office. However, because the line is almost at full capacity already, use of that line is restricted. NoCWACs can only use the line to upload and download claims reports and access company databases. NoCWACs has anticipated upgrading these leased lines so that it can handle GroupWise traffic; however, that upgrade cannot happen for another three months. NoCWACs management wants the GroupWise rollout to happen immediately.

▶ Both regional offices want to administer their systems locally. Nevertheless, they want directory synchronization to occur between the two systems.

▶ Each regional office is equipped with two file servers—one general purpose file server accessed by all employees and one used solely for local client databases. All four servers are running NetWare 3.12.

▶ It is likely that most of the e-mail traffic between the headquarters and the two
regional sites will be medium- to low-priority messages (such as company
newsletters, memos, etc.) About 60 percent of the e-mail traffic will be local—
that is, among employees at each site. You anticipate that message traffic
between Salt Lake and Butte will be minimal (between 1 and 2 percent of all
messages).

CHAPTER 12

GroupWise Gateway Overview

Gateways have the reputation of being one of the most technical and bewildering parts of GroupWise messaging systems. The mere mention of the term *gateway* often evokes fear and trepidation among rookie GroupWise administrators. If you've ever been dazed and confused by an e-mail guru's discourse on the intricacies of a particular gateway—relax. This chapter will give you a fundamental understanding of GroupWise gateways. When you have finished reading this chapter, you should be able to throw around gateway terminology just like the gurus.

There are a number of reasons why gateways cause so much anxiety. First, there are many different kinds of GroupWise gateways, and each one performs a very specific set of tasks. Second, most gateways are available for several computing platforms. The installation and configuration for the different platforms can vary. Third, in order to use gateways, you often have to be familiar with other messaging systems or networking protocols. Finally, the term *gateway* itself can be a little confusing because different meanings have been attached to it. Certain functionality-enhancing GroupWise add-on modules are sometimes referred to as gateways. However, those add-ons are not gateways in the traditional sense of the word because they don't transfer messages between e-mail systems. Instead, they are used to transmit GroupWise messages to other communications devices, such as pagers and fax machines.

In this chapter, I discuss gateways in a very broad, all-encompassing manner. I do not focus on any specific gateways. Rather, I will explain generally how gateways work and how they can be used. All of the information in this chapter does not apply to each and every gateway.

The Async gateway is a unique gateway in GroupWise because it does not communicate with foreign systems. An Async gateway is a GroupWise-to-GroupWise gateway. It can connect two GroupWise domains to each other, or it can connect a GroupWise Remote user to a GroupWise system. Because of its distinctiveness, not everything you learn in this chapter applies to Async gateways. However, where appropriate, I will point out how Async gateways differ from other, more typical gateways.

NOTE

The X.25 gateway also connects GroupWise sites and allows GroupWise Remote users to access their mailboxes. It is often used to allow GroupWise systems to communicate with other systems that use the X.25 messaging protocol.

On the CD-ROM, you will find documents that provide more detail about specific gateways. In Chapter 13, I will discuss the Async gateway in detail.

Gateways Background

To completely understand how gateways work, you need to understand the terminology. Here are some of the most important terms that relate GroupWise gateways:

▸ Passthrough

▸ Conversion

▸ Directory Synchronization/Directory Exchange

▸ Migration

As I explain each term, I tell you how it relates to the Async gateway, if at all.

PASSTHROUGH

In reference to gateways, the term *passthrough* means that a message retains its original format when it reaches the recipient. In other words, a message that is originally a GroupWise message passes through gateways and is received as a GroupWise message. In the process, a gateway on the sender's side puts the message into a transmittable format and then sends the message to a gateway on the recipient's end. The receiving gateway returns the message to its original form and forwards it to the recipient's GroupWise system for delivery. The important thing to remember is that passthrough message delivery does not cause the original message to be converted into a new format. At the end of the process, the message retains its original format.

A GroupWise gateway that has passthrough capabilities *encapsulates* a GroupWise message and sends it through a non-GroupWise transfer mechanism. Another passthrough gateway at the other end unencapsulates the message. The message is then processed by the receiving GroupWise system as a regular GroupWise message. This process is illustrated in Figure 12.1. The delivery mechanism between the gateways could be the telephone system, the Internet, or some other e-mail provider.

The Async gateway performs passthrough functions by translating GroupWise messages into a format that can be sent over the telephone system by using modems. A receiving Async gateway (or GroupWise Remote) decodes the transmission. The message retains its GroupWise format.

FIGURE 12.1

Passthrough Message Delivery

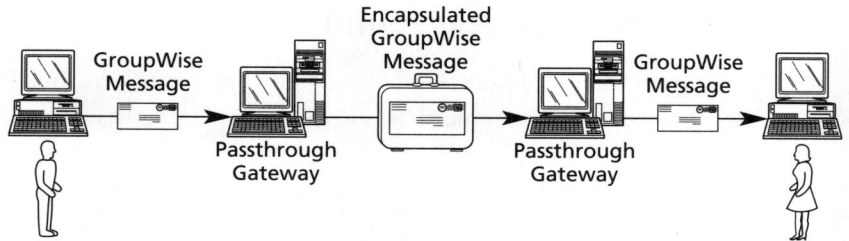

MESSAGE CONVERSION

You may already be familiar with the term *gateway* as it applies to networking. In network terminology, a gateway allows networks running incompatible protocols to communicate with one another. For example, a gateway might convert SPX packets to TCP packets. After a packet has been converted, it is delivered to the appropriate destination. This conversion takes place in both directions. GroupWise conversion gateways basically work the same way. However, instead of converting network packets, a message gateway converts e-mail messages into different electronic messaging formats. This process is illustrated in Figure 12.2.

FIGURE 12.2

Message Conversion

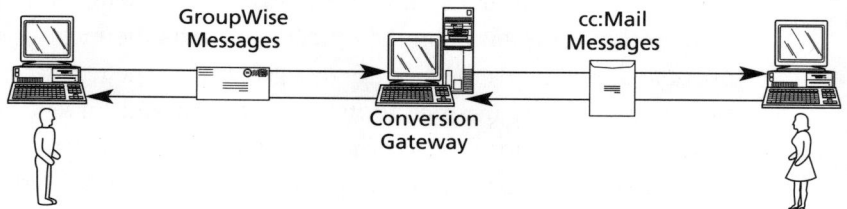

A message conversion gateway is like a foreign language interpreter. If you speak only English and need to communicate with someone who speaks only Japanese, you could consult an interpreter who can translate from English to Japanese and vice versa. This is basically what a conversion gateway does, except that instead of translating spoken languages, the gateway translates electronic messaging formats.

Often GroupWise messages contain elements that cannot be translated into other formats. For example, if I send an *appointment* using GroupWise, it is quite possible that the receiving e-mail system does not recognize appointments as a particular message type. In this case, the gateway has to convert the message into the closest possible format in the receiving system.

The Async gateway does not perform message conversion because it is a GroupWise-to-GroupWise gateway. It either conveys GroupWise messages from one GroupWise domain to another, or it delivers GroupWise messages to and from the GroupWise Remote client. It does, however, compress GroupWise messages in order to speed up message transmission through modems.

DIRECTORY SYNCHRONIZATION AND DIRECTORY EXCHANGE

Some GroupWise gateways perform directory synchronization or directory exchange with foreign mail systems. In Chapter 11 you learned how directory synchronization works in a GroupWise system. When used in reference to gateways, the term *directory exchange* means that a list of users for one system is exported to another system and then placed in the other system's directory. This usually occurs automatically and involves the entire directory store. *Directory synchronization* means that individual changes to a directory are synchronized as they occur. Directory synchronization is an ongoing process.

NOTE

The term *directory exchange* (in the context of GroupWise systems) usually implies that a system adminstrator has taken steps to set the exchange in motion because user information was not exchanged automatically. Special export and import steps must occur before directory exchange can take place.

When a gateway supports directory synchronization or directory exchange, GroupWise users can send messages to users in a foreign system by selecting those users from the GroupWise address book. Likewise, users in a foreign messaging system can use their address lists to send messages to GroupWise users.

A gateway's ability to perform directory synchronization or directory exchange makes sending messages between completely different systems very smooth for the end users. As far as GroupWise users are concerned, everyone appears to be using the same messaging system.

The Async gateway itself does not perform either directory synchronization or directory exchange—it doesn't need to. Remember, the Async gateway connects only GroupWise domains (and the GroupWise Remote client). If domains are part of the same GroupWise system, directory synchronization is handled in the manner described in Chapter 11.

The only difference when an Async gateway is involved is that administrative messages between the domains must pass through the Async gateway. It really doesn't matter how the domains are connected in the GroupWise system.

If the Async gateway is used to connect two GroupWise domains that are not in the same GroupWise system (i.e., external domains), then automatic directory synchronization does not occur. The administrators must use a directory exchange technique (export and import) to keep their systems' address books updated. External domains are explained in Chapter 16.

MIGRATION

Some GroupWise gateways allow users to *migrate* to GroupWise from other messaging systems. For example, the GroupWise cc:Mail gateway allows users from cc:Mail to migrate to GroupWise.

When a user migrates from another system into GroupWise, the user information and all of the user's folders, appointments, and mail are moved into the GroupWise system. When a gateway performs migration, a user object is actually moved to the GroupWise system from another messaging system. Instead of functioning as a message-delivery mechanism, the gateway then acts as a migration and conversion utility.

SUMMARY OF GATEWAY TERMINOLOGY

Sometimes GroupWise aficionados attempt to classify gateways according to the jobs the gateways perform. This is a difficult thing to do because each gateway may play many roles. For example, in some cases the GroupWise SMTP gateway performs passthrough functions, and in other cases it serves as a message conversion utility. I believe that any attempt to label a specific gateway as a "conversion gateway" or a "passthrough gateway" is misguided. When I refer to specific gateways, I will simply tell you which functions those gateways perform.

The above terms apply to what I call *traditional gateways* (i.e., gateways that facilitate message delivery between different electronic messaging systems). I call the add-on modules I mentioned at the beginning of this chapter specialty gateways. The *specialty gateways* include the Fax/Print gateway, the Pager gateway, and the API gateway. The GroupWise telephone access server is also sometimes called a gateway. I will discuss the speciality gateways in more detail in Chapter 21.

When to Use Gateways

Now that you understand the basic terminology, here are some situations in which gateways can be useful:

▶ You need to connect GroupWise to another e-mail system on the same network. In this situation, the gateway will need to perform message conversion between the two systems. Depending on the other messaging system involved, the gateway may also perform directory synchronization, directory exchange, or user migration. The GroupWise cc:Mail gateway is an example of a gateway that performs these functions.

▶ You need to connect GroupWise to an e-mail system running on a different networking protocol or messaging system protocol. In this case, the gateway will need to perform message conversion, message passthrough, or both. The GroupWise SMTP gateway is an example of a gateway that might be used in this situation. When connecting a GroupWise system to the Internet or to a UNIX-based e-mail system, the SMTP gateway performs message conversion. The SMTP gateway can also be used as a passthrough gateway to connect two GroupWise systems.

▶ You need to connect two domains in the same GroupWise system, but a network connection is not possible or practical. The Async gateway is often used in this situation. A gateway that performs passthrough functions could also be used.

▶ You need to connect your GroupWise system to another GroupWise system that is not accessible through a network connection. Again, the Async gateway is normally used in this situation. However, a gateway that has passthrough capabilities could also be used.

▶ Your GroupWise system needs to support GroupWise Remote users. The Async gateway or the X.25 gateway is used to enable support for GroupWise Remote within a GroupWise system.

▶ Users in your GroupWise system need to send messages to different types of communications devices, such as a fax machines, printers, pagers, or voice synthesizers (so the message can be heard instead of read). Specialty gateways are used in these situations.

Installing GroupWise Gateways

Each type of GroupWise gateway has its own installation routine. Some gateways are available for multiple platforms (such as DOS, OS/2, and NLM). Installation routines vary according to the platform. However, almost all gateway installations have some things in common.

A gateway must be located within a domain in a GroupWise system. Gateways are similar to post offices in this regard. Gateways are also similar to post offices insofar as users can be added to gateways in the same manner that they are added to post offices. Adding users to gateways simplifies addressing because users added to a gateway appear in the address book. (Because Async gateways connect only GroupWise systems, users are not usually added to them.) It is wise to place GroupWise gateways in the domains that generate the most gateway traffic. That way, you can reduce the number of domain transfers from gateway to user and vice versa.

In some cases, it makes sense to create a dedicated gateway domain. This strategy is often useful in conjunction with the star architecture discussed in Chapter 9. In the star architecture, a dedicated gateway domain ensures that no more than three domains need to process each message—the gateway domain, the hub domain, and the sender's or recipient's domain.

When you run the installation routine for the first gateway installed in a domain, a WPGATE subdirectory is created under the domain directory. The files for each subsequent gateway will then be installed to a subdirectory of WPGATE. If a domain contains multiple gateways, each gateway will have its own subdirectory under the WPGATE subdirectory. This is illustrated in Figure 12.3.

Message queues are also created for each gateway that is installed. Each gateway's subdirectory contains message server input queues (WPCSIN) and message server output queues (WPCSOUT). The domain's message server interacts with these queues in the same way that it does with post office message server input and output queues. Abstract message-flow diagrams for messages transmitted through gateways are presented later in this chapter.

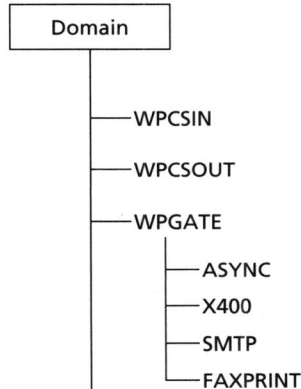

```
┌──────────┐
│  Domain  │
└──────────┘
     │
     ├──── WPCSIN
     │
     ├──── WPCSOUT
     │
     ├──── WPGATE
     │        │
     │        ├──── ASYNC
     │        ├──── X400
     │        ├──── SMTP
     │        └──── FAXPRINT
```

A domain's message server handles messages to and from gateways located in the domain. Therefore, a message server is necessary even in a single domain, single post office system if a gateway is installed.

Gateway Components

GroupWise gateways have special components that enable them to perform their various functions. The main components are:

- ► Message conversion facility

- ► Send/receive facility

- ► Administration facility

The implementation of these components varies from gateway to gateway. For example, some gateways have separate executables for each component. In other gateways, these components are combined into a single executable process.

MESSAGE CONVERSION FACILITY

The message conversion facility is the part of the gateway that actually converts messages from one format to another—from GroupWise to foreign message types and vice versa. This is a gateway's translator.

SEND/RECEIVE FACILITY

A gateway's send/receive component is where message transmission and receipt occurs. This facility sometimes uses a store-and-forward process (in which messages are copied to input queues in foreign systems). Sometimes this facility uses a process-to-process model (where messages are sent as network packets or following other transmission protocols to a receiving process in other systems).

The Async gateway is an example of a gateway that uses the process-to-process model. The Async gateway takes messages and converts them into analog signals that are transferred, using modems, across telephone lines. The recipient Async gateway translates the signal back into a GroupWise message.

ADMINISTRATION FACILITY

Some gateways have an administration facility that handles directory synchronization and directory exchange between GroupWise and foreign systems.

The Async gateway does not need an administration facility to handle directory synchronization. Because the Async gateway is a GroupWise-to-GroupWise gateway, the GroupWise systems handle the directory synchronization between domains connected by an Async gateway. All of an Async gateway's administrative functions are performed by GroupWise Admin.

Gateway Message Flow

Figure 12.4 shows the processes involved when a message is sent from GroupWise to a foreign system.

F I G U R E 12.4

*Message Flow to and from a
Foreign System*

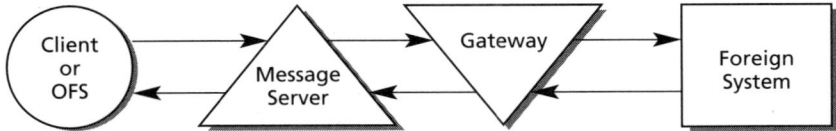

A message originates with the client at the post office level. Assuming that an application threshold has been set, the client passes the message to the message server. (If the Server Always setting is used, this step is handled by the post office server.) The message server then delivers the message to the gateway. Finally, the gateway transfers the message to the foreign system.

When the GroupWise system receives a message from a foreign system, the message arrives at a gateway, it is then passed to a message server, and it is then received by the post office server, which completes the delivery of the message.

Figure 12.5 depicts message transfer when gateways perform passthrough message delivery.

F I G U R E 12.5

*Message Flow with
Passthrough Gateways*

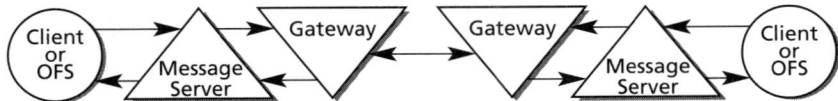

The message is sent from the client, it is forwarded to the message server, and it is then passed to the gateway. The gateway performing the passthrough function packages the message and sends it through some message transport mechanism (e.g., the Internet) to another passthrough gateway in the recipient's GroupWise system. The gateways on both sides must be the exact same gateway type. For example, if an X.400 gateway transmits a message, another X.400 gateway must receive it at the other end.

Because there are so many different kinds of GroupWise gateways, it would not be practical to provide detailed message flow models for each one in this book. However, a detailed message flow diagram for the Async gateway is provided in the next chapter.

Summary

In this chapter you learned about gateways in general. In the next chapter I focus on the most important gateway—the Async gateway.

CHAPTER 13

The GroupWise Async Gateway

In Chapter 12, you were introduced to GroupWise gateways and how they work in general. Now I will explain in much greater detail the role that GroupWise Async gateways play in GroupWise systems.

This chapter will focus primarily on the NLM Async gateway. Because the NLM Async gateway functions in almost exactly the same way as the OS/2 Async gateway, the concepts, terms, and screen shots (graphical computer screen representations) you will find in this chapter coincide very closely with the OS/2 version. The DOS Async gateway uses somewhat different terminology and configuration screens, but the concepts are very similar to those explained in this chapter.

This chapter will show you how to do the following:

▶ Plan for an Async gateway installation

▶ Install the NLM Async gateway software

▶ Create an Async gateway in GroupWise Admin

▶ Configure an Async gateway to connect with another GroupWise domain

▶ Set up gateway links between domains

▶ Load and run the Async gateway

▶ Understand message flow between domains connected by an Async gateway

Purpose of GroupWise Async Gateways

The GroupWise Async gateway has three main functions in GroupWise systems:

▶ It connects domains in the same GroupWise system when the domains cannot be linked by a network connection.

▶ It connects GroupWise systems by providing a gateway link between external domains when a network connection is not feasible.

> ► It allows GroupWise Remote users to access their mailboxes in a GroupWise system.

Often a network connection between domains is too expensive or simply not available. When that is the case, an Async gateway can be very useful. An Async gateway is often used to connect a domain at a remote site to domains within an organization's main GroupWise system. Chapter 13 focuses on this use of Async gateways.

In some cases, organizations need to connect their GroupWise systems to other organizations' GroupWise systems. When that is the case, the administrators of the two systems can define *external domains* and link them with Async gateways installed at both locations. External domains are discussed in Chapter 16.

Many organizations want their GroupWise systems to be accessible to users at remote locations. Chapter 14 deals with setting up an Async gateway to support GroupWise Remote.

Planning an Async Gateway Installation

Planning the installation of Async gateways involves making decisions about several key questions:

> ► How many Async gateways are needed in the GroupWise system, and how many modems should be installed at each gateway?

> ► Where should the Async gateways be located?

> ► Which Async gateway platform should be used?

NUMBER OF ASYNC GATEWAYS

The number of Async gateways needed in a GroupWise system depends on the following factors:

▸ The configuration of the GroupWise system

▸ The volume of gateway traffic that will be generated

▸ How quickly messages need to be delivered through the gateway

If you plan to use an Async gateway to connect a remote domain to a main (local) GroupWise system, you need a minimum of two Async gateways—one in the remote domain and one in a local domain. Other domains in the main system can then be linked indirectly to the remote domain (through the local domain that houses the Async gateway), and the remote domain is likewise linked indirectly to all other local domains in the system.

NOTE

In this chapter, the term *remote* refers to a domain that is not connected to a main GroupWise system through a network link. The term *local* is used to describe a domain or gateway located within a main GroupWise system.

Figure 13.1 illustrates a GroupWise system that is using the star architecture. In this case, the remote site is connected to the hub domain with an Async gateway. This means that the hub domain and the remote domain both need Async gateways. The remote domain is linked to all other domains in the system indirectly through the hub domain.

In a large GroupWise system, a dedicated gateway domain can be established. This type of configuration is shown in Figure 13.2.

When you have a dedicated gateway domain, there are at least two domain transfers for every message sent between the remote location and the main GroupWise system.

A single domain can have multiple Async gateways. Likewise, each Async gateway can have multiple modems. Therefore, you have some flexibility as you decide how many Async gateways you need and where you should locate them.

Star Configuration—Async Gateways in Hub and Remote Domains

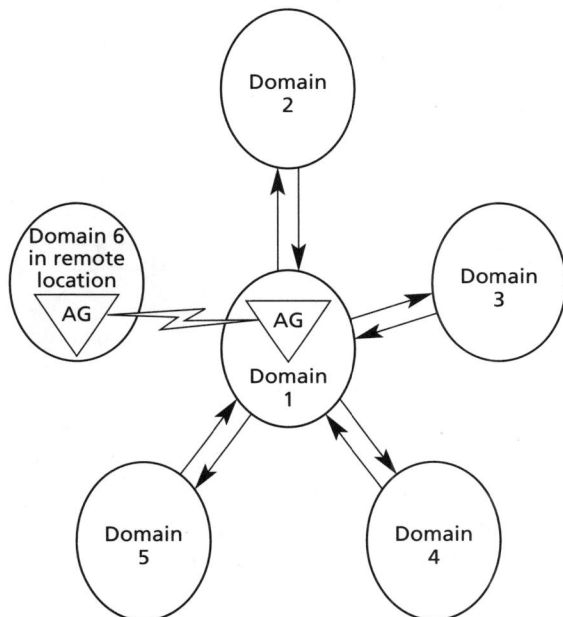

WHERE TO LOCATE THE GATEWAYS

You should have two goals in mind as you determine where to locate Async gateways:

▸ Gateways should be located where they will provide the most efficient message delivery between domains and for GroupWise Remote users.

▸ Gateways should be located where they can be easily administered and maintained.

As a general rule, try to place a gateway close to the users that will generate the most traffic through the gateway. If you can identify a specific domain that will generate a lot of traffic to a remote site—or if you can identify a domain that services a large number of GroupWise Remote users—it makes sense to place an Async gateway in that domain.

Your goal should be to place gateways so that message delivery will be the fastest. Remember—an Async gateway in one domain can also service users who belong to other domains in the system. It simply adds extra domain transfers to their messages.

FIGURE 13.2

Dedicated Gateway Domain

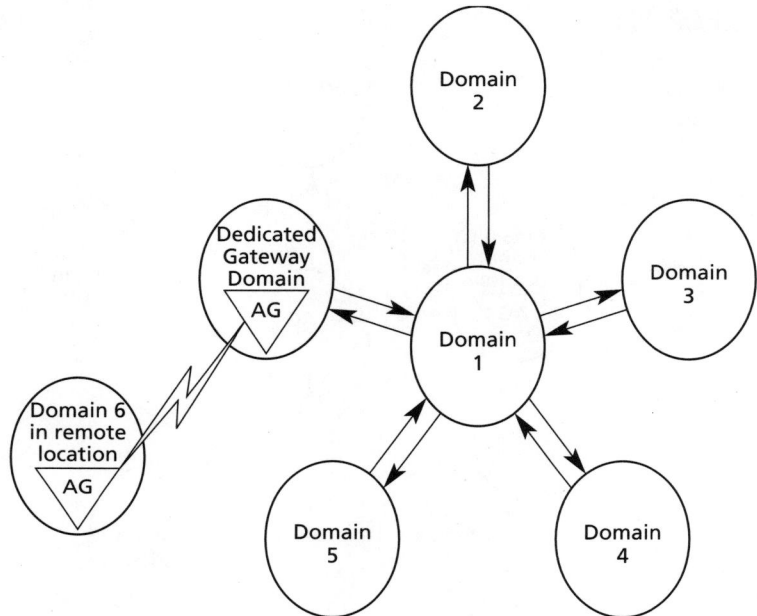

Ease of maintenance is another important consideration. In a large GroupWise system, maintenance considerations often make a dedicated gateway domain a good idea because all gateways are centrally located.

Also, if all domains generate about the same amount of gateway traffic, a centrally located gateway domain usually provides the best overall message delivery speed because all recipients have the same number of domain transfers between their domain and the gateway.

ASYNC GATEWAY PLATFORMS

The GroupWise Async gateway is available in three versions: NLM, OS/2, and DOS. Here is an overview of the advantages and disadvantages of each.

NLM Async Gateway

For NetWare networks, the NLM Async gateway is undoubtedly the best version of the gateway. It provides the following advantages:

▶ The Async gateway can be run on the same file server that holds the domain directory structure. This eliminates the across-the-wire network traffic you encounter with other versions of the Async gateway because the gateway is located on the same machine as the domain message server queues.

▶ There is no need for a dedicated Async gateway workstation because the NLM Async gateway runs on the file server.

▶ It supports up to 32 modems on a single machine.

One possible disadvantage of the NLM Async gateway is that modems must be installed directly on a file server machine. In some organizations, this setup may violate network security policies. However, even though modems are installed on file servers, potential intruders *cannot* use the Async gateway as an entry point into the network file system.

Here are the hardware requirements for running an NLM Async gateway:

▶ 80486 PC or above

▶ Novell NetWare 3.*x* or above

▶ 3MB free disk space for installation files

▶ GroupWise message server

▶ Novell NetWare CLIB.NLM version 3.12g or later

▶ 14.4K or faster AT command-set-compatible modem

▶ 590K memory for a single port (one modem) installation and 57K for each additional port that is configured

▶ NGWLIB.NLM and AIO.NLM modules

Depending upon the configuration, one or more of the following NLMs may also be necessary: AIOCOMX.NLM (when modems are attached to a file server's ports), AIODGMEM.NLM, AIODGXI.NLM, and/or AIODGXEM.NLM (when DigiBoards are connected to a file server).

Specific instructions for installing, configuring, and running NLM Async gateways are given later in this chapter.

OS/2 Async Gateway

The OS/2 Async gateway ranks second in performance behind the NLM Async gateway. The OS/2 Async gateway is recommended by Novell for non-NetWare networks. It is a high-performance gateway that offers the following advantages:

▶ Its multithreading capabilities provide a solid, high-performance operating system for handling Async gateway processes.

▶ All gateway processes are handled by a single executable. Therefore, you only need one dedicated machine for the gateway.

▶ The OS/2 Async gateway supports up to 32 modems on a single gateway machine.

There are two disadvantages to using the OS/2 gateway: (1) It requires a dedicated workstation; and (2) across-the-wire network traffic is generated because the gateway runs on a separate computer from the file server that houses the domain.

The requirements for the OS/2 Async gateway are as follows:

▶ OS/2 2.1 workstation with proper network requestors

▶ 16MB RAM

▶ 120MB hard drive

▶ 14.4K AT command-set-compatible modem

DOS Async Gateway

The DOS Async gateway offers the following advantages:

▸ It is easy to set up and configure.

▸ It is inexpensive.

▸ It runs on low-end machines (although it requires two machines).

▸ It does not require knowledge of other operating systems besides DOS.

▸ It supports up to 160 modems per Async gateway if multiple communication servers are used. However, it is unlikely that this many modems would ever be practical for a single Async gateway.

The disadvantages of the DOS Async gateway are as follows:

▸ The DOS platform is very limited because it does not have multithreading or multitasking capabilities, which results in lower performance levels than the other platforms.

▸ It requires both a dedicated workstation for the DOS Async gateway communication server and a dedicated workstation for the DOS Async gateway server. However, these can be low-end 386 machines.

▸ Novell has discontinued development on the Async gateway for the DOS platform.

NOTE

If the DOS Async gateway is used along with the DOS message server, the message server can be configured to launch the Async gateway server. Only one dedicated machine is needed if you use this configuration. However, running the DOS Async gateway in message-server-launch mode has a substantial negative impact on the performance of the DOS message server.

The requirements for the DOS Async gateway communication server (ASY.EXE) are listed below:

- 80386/25 (or better) workstation

- 450K free RAM on workstation

- DOS 5.0 or higher

- 40MB hard disk

- 14.4K AT command-set-compatible modem

The requirements for the DOS Async gateway server (ASYQ.EXE) workstation are listed below:

- 80386/25 (or better) workstation

- 450K free RAM on workstation

- DOS 5.0 or higher

Setting Up an Async Gateway

Setting up an Async gateway (any version) involves:

- Installing the Async gateway software

- Creating the gateway in GroupWise Admin

- Configuring the gateway's connections

INSTALLING THE ASYNC GATEWAY SOFTWARE

Each Async gateway platform has its own installation routine. The DOS Async gateway must be installed from a workstation running DOS, the OS/2 Async gateway is installed from a workstation running OS/2, and the NLM Async gateway is installed on a NetWare file server.

Refer to the DOS Async gateway manual and the OS/2 Async gateway manual for instructions on how to install gateways for those platforms. The steps for installing the NLM Async gateway are as follows:

1 • Place the gateway installation disk in drive A: on the NetWare file server.

2 • From the system console prompt, load the PINSTALL.NLM, which is the NLM Async gateway installation program, by typing **LOAD A:\PINSTALL.NLM**.

NOTE

The NLM Async gateway installation program is an NLM. It must be run from the file server console.

3 • In the Install To: field, enter the directory where the NLM Async gateway (NGWASYNC.NLM) will be installed. You should install this file in the SYS:SYSTEM directory because that directory is the default location for NLMs.

4 • In the Install Shared NLMs To: field, enter the directory where the shared NLMs will be installed. Again, the SYS:SYSTEM directory is the recommended location for shared NLMs.

5 • In the Domain Path: field, enter the path to the GroupWise domain that will contain the Async gateway. Use the NetWare path syntax. For example, you would type **SYS:HEADQTRS** if you were installing to the SYS volume on the file server and HEADQTRS were the name of the domain directory.

6 • In the Gateway Directory: field, enter the name of the subdirectory that will hold the Async gateway files. This should be the *domain*\WPGATE*async* directory, where *domain* is the name of the domain and *async* is the name of the subdirectory. The default name for the gateway subdirectory is ASYNC, but you can change that name if you wish.

7 • Select Install.

8 • After the installation process is complete, load AIO.NLM from the NetWare console prompt. AIO.NLM should be located in the directory you selected in Step 3 above. Now load AIOCOMX.NLM for each port/modem you intend to use. Make a note of the board number (the number that identifies the modem that is installed) as you load AIOCOMX.NLM. That information will be needed later, and it is only displayed when AIOCOMX.NLM is loaded.

NOTE **There are no required parameters to load these NLMs, but you need to use startup options if you want to override any of the default settings (such as the IRQ or port settings). Refer to the NLM Async gateway documentation for a list of possible startup options.**

CREATING THE GATEWAY IN GROUPWISE ADMIN

At this point, you have installed the files for the NLM Async gateway. Now you need to run GroupWise Admin to create the gateway. Follow these steps:

1 • From a workstation that is logged into the network with appropriate network rights to the domain directory structure, run GroupWise Admin for the domain that will contain the gateway.

NOTE **For a list of necessary rights for GroupWise Admin and for the client programs, see the README.AD file in the domain directory.**

2 • Choose Create and then choose Gateway.

3 • In the GroupWise Name field, enter a unique name that describes the gateway.

> **Keep this name short but descriptive. Naming gateways is similar to naming post offices and domains. The name you choose will be the name that is used when addressing this gateway.**

TIP

4 • (Optional) In the Description field, enter a description of this gateway.

5 • Select the Directory option. A pop-up list of the gateways installed in the domain under the WPGATE subdirectory will appear, as shown in Figure 13.3.

6 • Verify that the Gateway Execution Mode is set to Stand-Alone. This is the required execution mode for the NLM Async gateway.

You have now entered all of the necessary information about the gateway. This information will be added to the WPDOMAIN.DB file when you choose OK or, if you wish to define this gateway further, when you choose Specific. See the following section for an explanation of the options available when you select Specific.

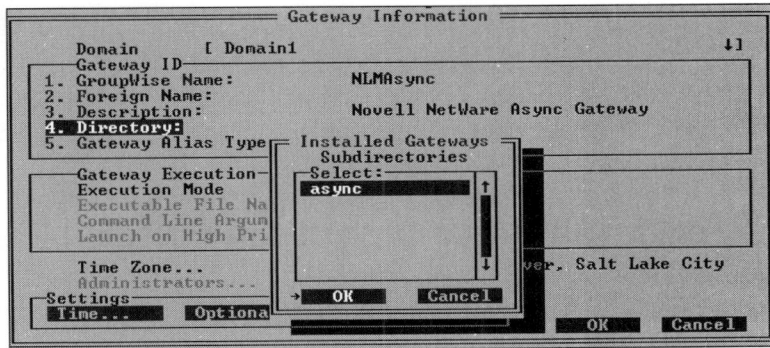

FIGURE 13.3

Gateway Information Screen: Installed Gateways

Specific Async Gateway Setup Options

The information you enter as Specific options is stored in the Async gateway database (ASYNC.DB). It is not contained in the domain database. There are five setup options you can specifically define. These options are shown in Figure 13.4.

Specific Setup Options

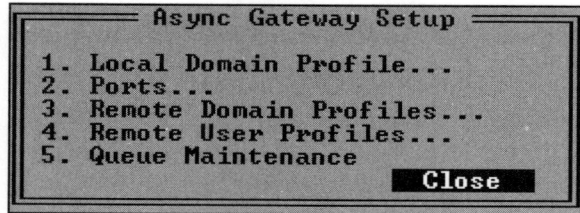

```
════ Async Gateway Setup ════
  1. Local Domain Profile...
  2. Ports...
  3. Remote Domain Profiles...
  4. Remote User Profiles...
  5. Queue Maintenance
                         Close
```

To connect one GroupWise domain to another, you must configure the first option (*Local Domain Profile*), the second option (*Ports*), and the third option (*Remote Domain Profiles*). The fourth option, *Remote User Profiles*, will be discussed in Chapter 14.

The fifth option, *Queue Maintenance*, is used to synchronize the Async gateway queue directory structure with the Async database. When you run the Queue Maintenance option, the gateway deletes the directories for any connections that are no longer listed in the database and creates directories for any connections that have entries in the database but don't have associated queue directories.

Notice that the first option, Local Domain Profile, pertains to a single domain, but the third option, Remote Domain Profiles, pertains to more than one domain. The third option may involve multiple domain profiles because a local gateway can connect to several remote gateways. Each remote gateway needs its own remote domain profile.

CREATING THE LOCAL DOMAIN PROFILE

The local domain profile contains important information about a gateway. Other gateways (i.e., remote gateways) use this information to log into the gateway. The local domain profile contains only two settings—the Default Login ID and the Default Password.

Notice that the local domain profile settings are default settings. This information will automatically be entered into the remote domain profiles for all of the remote gateways. However, you can modify the information in the remote domains' profiles if you want remote gateways to use different login IDs or passwords when they connect to the local gateway. The defaults are often changed for additional security, especially when a local gateway connects to external domains in other GroupWise systems.

CONFIGURING PORTS

After you create the local domain profile, the next step is to configure the ports for the local gateway. Follow these steps to configure the ports:

1 • Choose Ports and then select Create.

2 • Enter the name of the serial port (e.g., COM1, COM2, and so on).

3 • Select the modem type that corresponds to the modem installed in the file server.

4 • Adjust the port parameters if necessary. Port parameters include the baud rate, flow control, parity bit, character length, and stop bits.

5 • Choose OK and then select Close.

NOTE

The above steps only apply when modems are connected to a standard serial port on a file server. If you are using a multiport DigiBoard, refer to the NLM Async gateway documentation and the DigiBoard documentation for instructions on how to configure those ports.

CREATING REMOTE DOMAIN PROFILES

Remote domain profiles contain the information that the local gateway needs in order to connect with the remote gateways. Figure 13.5 shows the information fields you must complete when you create a remote domain profile.

FIGURE 13.5

*Remote Domain Profile
Options*

```
═════════════ Remote Domain Profile Definition ═════════════
1. Remote Gateway ID:

2. Password to Access Remote Gateway:

3. Remote Phone Number:

4. Local Gateway ID:                              NLMASYNC

5. Password to Access Local Gateway:

6. Required Serial Port:                          NONE

7. Calling Schedules and Intervals...
                                            OK       Cancel
```

Here are the steps to follow when you create a remote domain profile:

1 • Choose Remote Domain Profiles and then select Create.

2 • Enter the gateway ID for the remote Async gateway. You may need to obtain this information from the remote gateway's administrator.

3 • Enter the password for the remote gateway. You may need to obtain this information from the remote gateway's administrator.

4 • Enter the phone number of the remote gateway.

5 • (Optional) If you want the remote gateway to use a domain ID and password different from the ID and password you entered in your local domain profile settings, change the Local Gateway ID and Remote Gateway ID fields accordingly. Otherwise, the defaults you entered as local domain profile settings will be used.

6 • (Optional) Select *Required Serial Port*. This selection makes all outgoing messages travel through one port (in other words, through a specific modem). Choose NONE if you do not want to designate a required port. This option can be very useful if you want to designate a high-speed modem for connection to a certain remote gateway. Along the same lines, if a remote gateway has a low-speed modem installed, you may wish to designate a low-speed modem on the local gateway so that high-speed modems are reserved for connections to other domains that have high-speed modems (or for GroupWise Remote users who have fast modems).

7 • *The Calling Schedules and Intervals option* is a complex subject. I explain how to configure calling schedules and intervals in the next subsection.

Configuring Calling Schedules and Intervals

Calling schedules and *intervals* are a vital part of Async-gateway setup. These settings allow you to establish the parameters a local gateway will follow when initiating a connection to a specific remote gateway.

Before you complete this portion of the remote domain profile, you need to answer these questions:

▶ On which days do you want the Async gateway to call the other gateway?

▶ At what time of day should calls be made?

▶ Should the local gateway initiate all calls, should the other gateway initiate all calls, or should both gateways be allowed to initiate calls?

▶ Should calls be initiated whenever a certain period of time has elapsed? Should calls be initiated only when a certain number of messages are waiting? Should both factors be considered when determining when to initiate calls?

▶ If the other gateway cannot receive a call (e.g., the line is busy), how many times should the Async gateway attempt to establish a connection?

Calling schedules and intervals are used to optimize message delivery between domains. You can also use these options to take advantage of discount telephone rates.

The settings you can select under Calling Schedules and Intervals are shown in Figure 13.6.

FIGURE 13.6

*Calling Schedules and
Intervals Dialog Box*

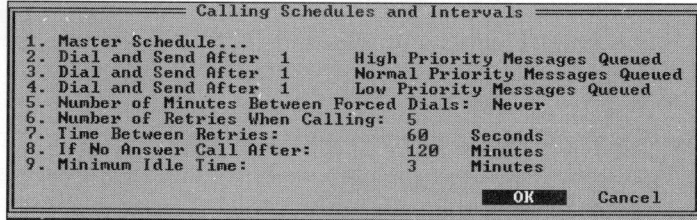

```
╔═════════════════ Calling Schedules and Intervals ═════════════════╗
║ 1. Master Schedule...                                              ║
║ 2. Dial and Send After  1      High Priority Messages Queued       ║
║ 3. Dial and Send After  1      Normal Priority Messages Queued     ║
║ 4. Dial and Send After  1      Low Priority Messages Queued        ║
║ 5. Number of Minutes Between Forced Dials:  Never                  ║
║ 6. Number of Retries When Calling:  5                              ║
║ 7. Time Between Retries:             60    Seconds                 ║
║ 8. If No Answer Call After:          120   Minutes                 ║
║ 9. Minimum Idle Time:                3     Minutes                 ║
║                                                                    ║
║                                          ▐ OK ▌    Cancel          ║
╚════════════════════════════════════════════════════════════════════╝
```

You can set different parameters for the number of high-, normal-, and low-priority messages that must be queued before a call will be initiated. Those parameters, in conjunction with the settings you configure in the master schedule, determine when calls will be made.

Configuring A Master Schedule   A *master schedule* lets you adjust an Async gateway's sending schedule to optimize message delivery and take advantage of discount calling periods. A screen from a master schedule is shown in Figure 13.7.

FIGURE 13.7

Master Calling Schedule

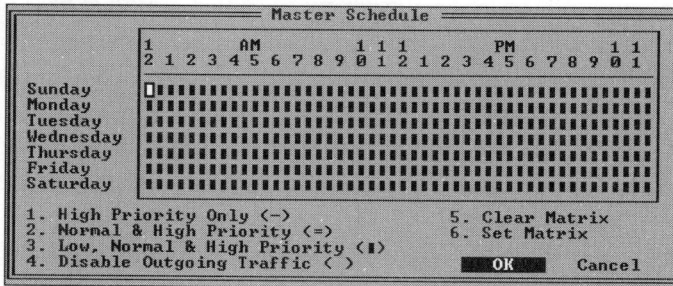

```
╔══════════════════════════ Master Schedule ═══════════════════════════╗
║           1         AM          1 1           PM           1 1        ║
║           2 1 2 3 4 5 6 7 8 9 0 1 2 1 2 3 4 5 6 7 8 9 0 1              ║
║ Sunday    ▯▮▮▮▮▮▮▮▮▮▮▮▮▮▮▮▮▮▮▮▮▮▮▮▮▮▮▮▮▮▮▮▮▮▮▮▮▮▮▮▮▮▮▮▮▮              ║
║ Monday    ▮▮▮▮▮▮▮▮▮▮▮▮▮▮▮▮▮▮▮▮▮▮▮▮▮▮▮▮▮▮▮▮▮▮▮▮▮▮▮▮▮▮▮▮▮▮              ║
║ Tuesday   ▮▮▮▮▮▮▮▮▮▮▮▮▮▮▮▮▮▮▮▮▮▮▮▮▮▮▮▮▮▮▮▮▮▮▮▮▮▮▮▮▮▮▮▮▮▮              ║
║ Wednesday ▮▮▮▮▮▮▮▮▮▮▮▮▮▮▮▮▮▮▮▮▮▮▮▮▮▮▮▮▮▮▮▮▮▮▮▮▮▮▮▮▮▮▮▮▮▮              ║
║ Thursday  ▮▮▮▮▮▮▮▮▮▮▮▮▮▮▮▮▮▮▮▮▮▮▮▮▮▮▮▮▮▮▮▮▮▮▮▮▮▮▮▮▮▮▮▮▮▮              ║
║ Friday    ▮▮▮▮▮▮▮▮▮▮▮▮▮▮▮▮▮▮▮▮▮▮▮▮▮▮▮▮▮▮▮▮▮▮▮▮▮▮▮▮▮▮▮▮▮▮              ║
║ Saturday  ▮▮▮▮▮▮▮▮▮▮▮▮▮▮▮▮▮▮▮▮▮▮▮▮▮▮▮▮▮▮▮▮▮▮▮▮▮▮▮▮▮▮▮▮▮▮              ║
║                                                                      ║
║ 1. High Priority Only <->        5. Clear Matrix                     ║
║ 2. Normal & High Priority <=>    6. Set Matrix                       ║
║ 3. Low, Normal & High Priority <▮>                                   ║
║ 4. Disable Outgoing Traffic < >           ▐ OK ▌    Cancel           ║
╚══════════════════════════════════════════════════════════════════════╝
```

A master schedule lets you specify the time of day and the days of the week during which calls can be made. Notice that you can set specific times when only high-priority messages will trigger calls, when both normal- and high-priority messages trigger calls, or when all messages trigger calls. You can also specify periods when the gateway can never initiate a call.

TIP

Completely clearing the matrix prevents the gateway from initiating calls to the remote gateway. If you want the remote gateway to initiate all calls, you can clear the entire matrix.

Figures 13.8 and 13.9 show an example of how someone might configure a calling schedule and intervals. Suppose that Ernestine sets the calling schedule options as shown in Figure 13.8.

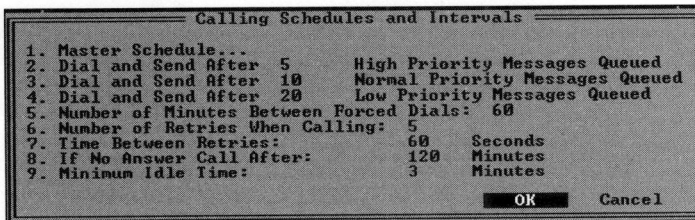

```
============= Calling Schedules and Intervals =============
1. Master Schedule...
2. Dial and Send After   5       High Priority Messages Queued
3. Dial and Send After  10       Normal Priority Messages Queued
4. Dial and Send After  20       Low Priority Messages Queued
5. Number of Minutes Between Forced Dials:  60
6. Number of Retries When Calling:  5
7. Time Between Retries:             60      Seconds
8. If No Answer Call After:         120      Minutes
9. Minimum Idle Time:                 3      Minutes

                                     OK      Cancel
```

In this example, Ernestine's Async gateway will initiate a call to the remote Async gateway (let's call it the 1RINGYDINGY remote gateway) if the following conditions are met:

▶ Five high-priority messages are queued, OR

▶ Ten normal-priority messages are queued, OR

▶ Twenty low-priority messages or queued, OR

▶ Sixty minutes have passed since the last call, AND

▶ If the master schedule permits the gateway to make a call to 1RINGYDINGY when any of the four conditions above has been met.

A master schedule always has the last word. No calls can be initiated if the master schedule does not permit calls at a certain time.

IMPORTANT

Now suppose that Ernestine has configured the master schedule as shown in Figure 13.9.

FIGURE 13.9

Master Calling Schedule

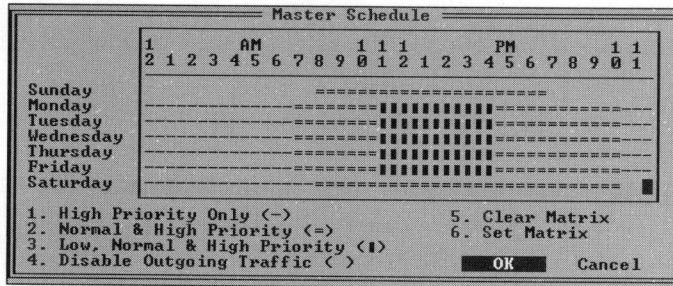

```
═══════════════════════ Master Schedule ═══════════════════════
1            AM          1 1 1          PM          1 1
2 1 2 3 4 5 6 7 8 9 0 1 2 1 2 3 4 5 6 7 8 9 0 1
Sunday      ─────────────════════════════════─────────────
Monday      ─────────────════════║║║║║║║║║║║════════─────────────
Tuesday     ─────────────════════║║║║║║║║║║║════════─────────────
Wednesday   ─────────────════════║║║║║║║║║║║════════─────────────
Thursday    ─────────────════════║║║║║║║║║║║════════─────────────
Friday      ─────────────════════║║║║║║║║║║║════════─────────────
Saturday    ─────────────══════════════════════════     ■

1. High Priority Only (-)              5. Clear Matrix
2. Normal & High Priority (=)          6. Set Matrix
3. Low, Normal & High Priority (║)
4. Disable Outgoing Traffic ( )             OK      Cancel
```

At certain times, Ernestine's Async gateway cannot call 1RINGYDINGY at all. For example, from 10:00 p.m. on Saturday until 8:00 a.m. on Sunday, the Async gateway cannot make any calls to the remote gateway. During this period, it does not matter how many high-, normal-, or low-priority messages are in the queue. The master schedule also overrides the Number of Minutes Between Forced Dials setting.

At other times, Ernestine's Async gateway can only call when the high-priority message count is met (that is, when there are five or more high-priority messages queued). For example, on weekdays between 12:00 a.m. and 7:00 a.m., only high-priority messages can trigger a call. However, because the Number of Minutes Between Forced Dial options is set to 60, Ernestine's gateway *will* call the 1RINGYDINGY gateway every 60 minutes during this time—regardless of how many messages are queued.

All queued messages are sent when a connection is established, not just messages with the priority level that triggered the call.

IMPORTANT

When a call is inititated and received, all messages are sent. For example, suppose that on Monday at 4:00 a.m. there are 30 normal-priority messages in the queue waiting to be sent from Ernestine's gateway. Even though the message count for normal-priority messages has been exceeded, the master schedule is set so that only high-priority messages can trigger a call at that time. (See Figure 13.9.) Now suppose that at 4:15 a.m., five high-priority messages arrive in the queue—enough to trigger a call. When the connection is established, all messages will be sent to the 1RINGYDINGY remote gateway, including the 30 normal-priority messages that were waiting in the queue. Furthermore, when the connection is established, all messages in the queues of *both* domains are sent.

Refer to Figures 13.8 and 13.9 again. Between the hours of 7:00 a.m. and 11:00 a.m. on weekdays, both normal and high-priority message counts can trigger calls. Weekdays between 11:00 a.m. and 4:00 p.m., the message counts for all three priority levels can trigger calls.

As you establish master schedules, you should keep in mind how message priority levels are established. The default priority level for messages sent using the GroupWise client is normal. However, users can specify a different priority level by using the Send Options feature in the client. Administrative messages (for example, directory synchronization messages), GroupWise Remote user requests, and busy searches are all high-priority messages (that is, they are sent through the <0–3> message queue directories). Status messages have the same priority level as the messages that initiate them. In other words, a status message for a high-priority message comes back as a high-priority status message. Normal-priority messages use the number 4 or 5 queue directories, and low-priority messages use the number 6 and 7 queue directories.

The Minimum Idle Time option in the Calling Schedules and Intervals dialog box determines how long a connection remains open when there is no activity through the connection. If this setting is set high, Delivered status messages can make it back to the gateway before the connection is broken. However, you don't want this setting too high because that causes wasted connection time, which is often expensive. The timer that keeps track of idle time is reset every time a message reaches either gateway through the connection.

Linking the Domains

After you have created an Async gateway, established the local domain profile, configured the ports, and completed a remote domain profile, the local gateway is ready to communicate with the remote gateway. However, the two domains are not yet ready to communicate. You still need to create gateway links between the domains. As you learned in Chapter 10, there are three different kinds of message server links: direct, indirect, and gateway. When you use Async gateways to connect domains, you must configure a gateway link between the domains.

In GroupWise Admin, follow these steps to create a gateway link between domains:

1 • Highlight the domain that contains the Async gateway.

2 • Select Actions.

3 • Select Edit.

4 • Choose Message Server Configuration.

5 • Choose Edit Link.

6 • Select Link Type.

7 • Select Gateway as the link type. You will see the dialog box shown in Figure 13.10.

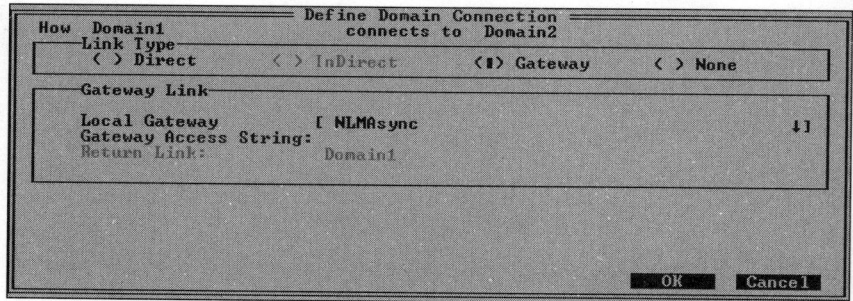

FIGURE 13.10

Define Domain Connection Dialog Box

8 • Choose Gateway Link.

9 • Select Local Gateway.

10 • You should see a list of all gateways installed in the domain. Choose the local gateway from the drop-down list.

11 • Fill in the Gateway Access String field. The *gateway access string* is the remote gateway's login ID.

NOTE

The return link option will not be available if the domain to which you are linking is in the same GroupWise system.

12 • Choose OK.

IMPORTANT

The administrator of the remote domain must also establish the gateway link to your domain.

Running the NLM Async Gateway

At this point, the domains should be ready to communicate via the Async gateway.

IMPORTANT

Before you launch the Async gateway, you must run the domain's message server (if it is not already running). The message server will create the required message server input and output queues in the gateway subdirectory.

Loading the NLM Async gateway is very similar to loading other GroupWise NLMs. The default name of the NLM Async gateway startup file is STARTUP.ASY. You need to modify the /HOME switch in the startup file to point to the gateway directory. For example, if the name of the local domain's directory is DOMAIN1 and it is located in the file server's SYS volume, the switch should look like this:

```
/HOME-SYS:DOMAIN1\WPGATE\ASYNC
```

Table 13.1 shows optional gateway switches and a brief explanation of each switch. (Italics indicate variable information.)

SWITCH	DESCRIPTION
/USER-*user ID*	Provides the NLM with the remote file server's NetWare user ID. Include this switch only if the NLM Async gateway is running on a file server separate from the domain's file server.
/PASSWORD-*NetWare password*	Provides the NLM with the remote file server's NetWare password. Include this switch only if the NLM Async gateway is running on a file server separate from the domain's file server.
/HELP	Displays the startup switch help screen.
/LOGLEVEL-*log level*	Overrides the log level for the log files. The levels—from the most logging detail to the least amount—are diagnostic, verbose, and normal. The default value is set in Admin.
/LOG-*pathname*	Points the NLM to the path where the logfiles are written. This path must point to a directory on the local server or to the server where the GroupWise domain directory resides.
/LOGDAYS-*number of days*	Sets the number of days that a logfile resides on the disk before it is automatically deleted. The default is set in Admin.
/LOGMAX-*kilobytes*	Determines the maximum disk space used for all logfiles. The default is set in Admin.

IMPORTANT

The /USER and /PASSWORD switches are only used if the NLM Async gateway is running on a file server separate from the file server that holds the domain subdirectory. In most cases, these switches should not be used because the Async gateway is running on the same file server that houses the domain.

Follow these steps to start an Async gateway from the file server's console prompt or from a workstation running RCONSOLE:

1 • Load AIO.NLM.

2 • Load AIOCOMX.NLM for each port that has a modem connected to it.

3 • Load NGWASYNC.NLM with the *@startup filename* option. For example, type: **LOAD NGWASYNC.NLM @STARTUP.ASY**.

The NLM Async gateway screen will appear.

> **TIP**
>
> **You can automate the loading of these NLMs by adding the load commands to the file server's AUTOEXEC.NCF file.**

Domain Administration and Async Gateways

When two domains within the same system are connected by an Async gateway, directory synchronization occurs as if the domains were connected by a direct link. The only difference is that the administration messages have to be sent through the Async gateway. Therefore, when a primary domain is connected to a secondary domain through an Async gateway, centralized administration of objects in the secondary domain is still possible.

However, you cannot create a secondary domain from the primary domain through an Async gateway link. In order to create a secondary domain, GroupWise Admin for the primary domain must have direct access to the directory where the secondary domain will reside. In Chapter 17, I discuss a technique for creating secondary domains when the primary domain does not have a direct network connection.

Here's a general rule for administering secondary domains connected to the primary domain through an Async gateway: If an administration task requires a direct network connection and network access rights to the secondary domain database from the primary domain's Admin program, the task cannot be performed through the Async gateway connection. If a task can be acccomplished using an administrative message sent to the administration server, the task can be done through the Async gateway.

The following tasks can be performed for a secondary domain from the primary domain through an Async gateway link:

▸ Adding objects

▸ Deleting objects

▶ Modifying objects

▶ Synchronizing object records

▶ Modifying message server configuration settings

▶ Modifying domain links

The following tasks cannot be performed for a secondary domain from the primary domain through an Async gateway link:

▶ Creating a domain

▶ Copying software to a domain

▶ Rebuilding a domain database

▶ Rebuilding indexes for name lists

▶ Reclaiming unused domain database space

▶ Synchronizing primary and secondary domain databases

▶ Validating a domain database

Message Flow through an Async Gateway

Figure 13.11 shows how a message travels between a sender and a recipient when their domains are connected by an Async gateway.

FIGURE 13.11

Message Flow
through an Async
Gateway

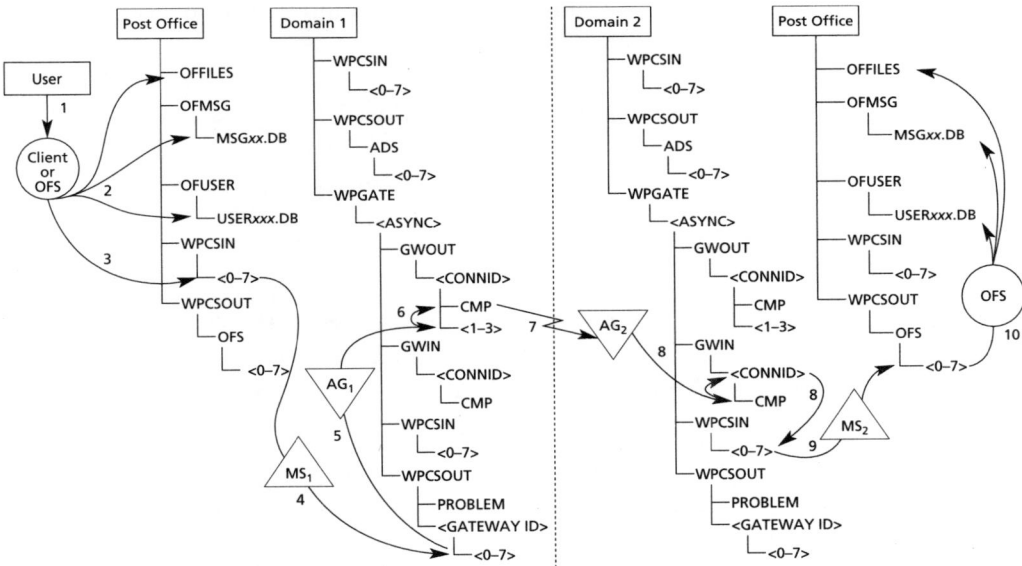

Here are the steps depicted in Figure 13.11:

1 • Using the GroupWise client, a user in Domain 1 creates and sends a message to a user in Domain 2.

2 • The GroupWise client or the post office server adds the message to the sender's message database, user database, and OFFILES directory (if necessary).

3 • The GroupWise client or the post office server places the outbound message in Domain 1's message server input queue directory (*<post office>*\WPCSIN\<0–7>).

4 • The message server for Domain 1 detects the message in the post office message server input queue (*<post office>*\WPCSIN\<0–7>) and places the message in Domain 1's Async gateway's input queue subdirectory (*<domain>*\WPGATE*<async>*\WPCSOUT*<gateway ID>*\<0–7>).

NOTE A *gateway ID* subdirectory is created under the **WPCSOUT** subdirectory for every gateway that has a remote domain profile defined. This is the message server output queue for that specific gateway.

5 • NGWASYNC.NLM reads the message to determine which connection directory to place the message in. Then, it places the message in the *<domain>*\WPGATE*<async>*\GWOUT*<connection ID>*\<1–3> directory.

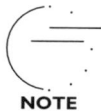

NOTE The *connection ID* directory corresponds to the port through which the connection is to be established. The message is placed in the 1, 2, or 3 directory depending upon its priority. The master schedule and calling intervals will use the different priority-level message counts in these directories to determine when the gateway initiates a call.

6 • When a connection is triggered, NGWASYNC.NLM reads the messages in the *<connection ID>**<1–3>* directory, compresses it, and moves it to the *<domain>*\WPGATE*<async>*\GWOUT*<connection ID>*\CMP directory. This is the directory where compression (hence, CMP) is performed prior to the message being transmitted to the other Async gateway.

7 • NGWASYNC.NLM transmits the message through the modem to the receiving Async gateway in Domain 2.

8 • Domain 2's NGWASYNC.NLM receives the message in the *<domain>*\WPGATE*<async>*\GWIN*<connection ID>*\CMP directory. Domain 2's Async gateway then decompresses the file and places it in the *<domain>*\WPGATE*<async>*\GWIN*<connection ID>* directory and moves it to the Async gateway's message server input queue directory (*<domain>*\WPGATE*<async>*\WPCSIN*<0–7>*).

9 • Domain 2's message server transfers the message from the *<domain>*\WPGATE*<async>*\WPCSIN*<0–7>* directory to the receiving post office's message server output queue (*<post office>*\WPCSOUT\OFS*<0–7>*).

10 • The post office server delivers the message to the recipient by placing the message in the message database, adding file attachments to the OFFILES directory, and placing a pointer in the user database.

Summary

The Async gateway plays an integral role in remote computing—the subject of Part VI.

Solution to Part V Scenario

On your recommendation, NoCWACs has decided to implement GroupWise in Salt Lake City and Butte as follows:

▶ Secondary domains will be created in both locations—each with one post office.

▶ The regional offices will purchase the NLM Message Server Pack. The message server, the post office server, and the administration server will run on the general purpose file servers at each location.

▶ An Async gateway will be installed in the Service domain in Denver. An NLM Async gateway will be used. To start out, two modems will be installed and configured in the Service domain, with the possibility of later adding a DigiBoard and additional modems.

▶ NLM Async gateways will be installed in Salt Lake City and Butte.

▶ Salt Lake City and Butte will link directly to the Service domain with a gateway link. They will be linked indirectly to all other domains in the system. The Service domain will serve as the routing domain.

▶ Calling schedules and intervals will be monitored and adjusted as needed to provide optimal message delivery time while at the same time minimizing telephone system costs.

The system is shown in the following illustration:

Connection to NoCWACs
Regional Offices

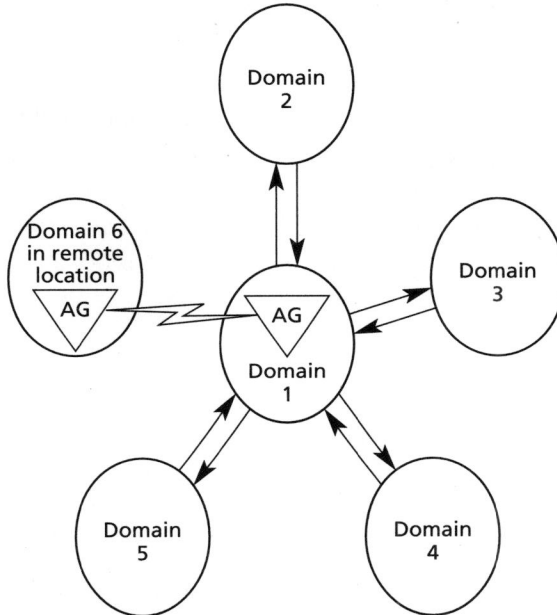

ADVANTAGES

By installing a domain at each location, message traffic will be isolated. Furthermore, there will be no impact on the existing leased line once the domains are configured. All GroupWise traffic will pass through the Async gateways.

The NLM post office and message servers should adequately support a single post office at each regional site with room for more users and, possibly, more post offices later on.

Directory synchronization will occur automatically between the sites through the Async gateway. (The administration server will need to be used for every domain in the system—including the regional offices' domains.)

By installing the NLM Async gateway in Denver, you have planned ahead so that the gateway will be able to support GroupWise Remote users in the future. The NLM Async gateway in the regional offices allows all GroupWise processes to run on individual file servers, without the need for additional hardware (except possibly a RAM upgrade to handle the GroupWise NLMs).

ADDITIONAL CONSIDERATIONS

After the leased line has been upgraded to handle greater capacity, NoCWACs should evaluate the costs and benefits of direct network links between the sites. Because each site will initially be set up as its own domain, the transition to direct links in the future should be fairly easy. The only traffic that would be generated across the leased line once it is upgraded is message-delivery traffic.

Because each site will be administered locally (distributed administration), the e-mail administrators in Salt Lake City and Butte should consider attending the GroupWise Administration Course 325 and the Async Gateways Course 326 at a local Novell Authorized Training Center.

PART VI

Remote Computing with GroupWise

Part V explained one of the two main functions of GroupWise Async gateways—connecting domains together. The other main function of Async gateways is to allow GroupWise Remote users to dial in to a GroupWise system so they can access information in their master mailboxes.

GroupWise Remote allows users to retrieve information using a modem and the telephone system. This feature is particularly useful for employees who travel on business and need to stay in touch with their main office. GroupWise Remote is also useful for employees who work away from their main corporate office and who are unable to access the company network.

Part VI explains how to set up an Async gateway for GroupWise Remote and how to roll out GroupWise Remote successfully. Before you implement GroupWise Remote, you need to consider the impact it will have on your GroupWise system. If you approach GroupWise Remote implementation in an organized manner, you can minimize the impact it will have on your system's efficiency.

There are two stages involved in organizing the implementation of GroupWise Remote:

▸ Planning the location and number of Async gateways

▸ Preparing for the GroupWise Remote client implementation

Chapter 14 deals with the first stage (planning the Async gateways), and Chapter 15 covers the second (client implementation).

In order help you understand the GroupWise Remote implementation process better, I will once again use a demonstrational scenario. In the introductions to Parts IV and V, I used scenarios involving NoCWACs, a major health insurance provider. Phase 1 of NoCWACs' GroupWise rollout involved implementing GroupWise at the corporate headquarters. In Phase 2, the regional offices of NoCWACs were set up as secondary domains and then linked to the main system through Async gateways. The third stage of the implementation involves equipping NoCWACs' employees and agents with GroupWise Remote.

Scenario

NoCWACs employs 400 independent insurance agents throughout the intermountain western region of the United States. All of these employees work out of their homes or out of small offices. They have no way to connect with the corporate network.

The independent agents need to communicate with all NoCWACs departments and with other independent agents.

There are also many employees at NoCWACs' company headquarters who need to use GroupWise Remote when they travel on business.

Configuring Async Gateways for GroupWise Remote

Most organizations that implement a GroupWise system eventually decide to equip their users with GroupWise Remote. GroupWise Remote allows users to access their GroupWise master mailboxes without a network connection to a post office.

The first step in implementing GroupWise Remote involves deciding how many Async gateways you need and where they should be located.

Planning the Async Gateways

At a minimum, a system that supports GroupWise Remote will have to have one Async gateway that the remote users can use when they connect to the system through a modem. If you already have an Async gateway in your system, you will need to decide whether the existing Async gateway can handle GroupWise Remote users or whether you should install additional Async gateways.

If an Async gateway currently connects two GroupWise domains, you do not want GroupWise Remote traffic to bog down the gateway and interfere with domain-to-domain message traffic. Before you allow that gateway to handle GroupWise Remote messages, you need to determine whether the gateway has the capacity to handle the extra work created by GroupWise Remote requests. You may also need to add modems to the existing gateway. See Chapter 13 for more information about the hardware and software Async gateways need in order to function properly.

Often, dedicated Async gateways should be installed to support GroupWise Remote users. If you do not already have an Async gateway—or if you need additional gateways—you must first determine the best locations for the Async gateways to be used for GroupWise Remote.

There are three questions you should ask yourself as you decide where to locate gateways:

▸ Where are the GroupWise Remote users located in the system?

▸ What will GroupWise Remote usage patterns be like?

▸ Will there be users who always use GroupWise Remote, users who only occasionally use GroupWise Remote, or both?

LOCATION OF REMOTE USERS IN THE SYSTEM

As a general rule, you should locate the Async gateway as close as possible to GroupWise Remote users' post offices. This strategy has two advantages: (1) It avoids causing a lot of extra domain-to-domain message traffic and therefore does not put a strain on domain message servers; and (2) it provides the fastest message-processing for GroupWise Remote users.

If you can predict which domains will service a large number of GroupWise Remote users, you should consider placing an Async gateway in those domains. For example, if your system supports a company with a large number of sales reps located throughout the country, it would make sense to place an Async gateway in a domain that is used by the Sales Department. This can isolate a good portion of the GroupWise Remote traffic to a single domain. No additional burden will be placed on message servers in other domains. You might design that gateway to take into account the sales force's peak calling periods by increasing the number of modems installed on the Async gateway.

USAGE PATTERNS

You should also try to predict the usage patterns of the GroupWise Remote users. This will help you determine where to locate Async gateways and how to configure them. A pilot test of GroupWise Remote can be used to help you answer the following questions:

▶ When will the majority of GroupWise Remote users call in for their messages?

▶ Will users be uploading and downloading large messages and file attachments? How large will the file attachments be?

▶ Will users expect their requests to be received immediately? Are they willing to upload their requests, disconnect, and then reconnect later to receive the information requested?

▶ How fast are the users' modems?

Call-In Times

If you know that many GroupWise Remote users will call in for their messages at certain times (for example, around 5:00 p.m.), you can adjust your Async gateways to accommodate the increased traffic generated at that time.

File Attachments

The size of users' messages and file attachments can affect connection time and thereby reduce the amount of traffic an Async gateway can handle. Large file attachments significantly increase connection time. You can mitigate this problem by instructing GroupWise Remote users on how to use the download options in the GroupWise Remote client. (See Chapter 15.)

TIP

View Designer, which ships with GroupWise, is a utility that allows users to define custom *views* for the Macintosh or Windows client. (For an explanation of views and the View Designer utility, see Appendix A.) Custom views, like file attachments, can significantly increase the time it takes to download messages.

Performance Goals

Remote users' needs and expectations with regard to GroupWise Remote's performance should influence your decision about where to locate Async gateways and how to configure them. If users expect messages to be immediately downloaded from their mailboxes when they connect to the gateway, you should place the Async gateways close to the users' mailboxes. Also, to meet the users' expectations, you should use high-performance gateways, message servers, and post office servers. On the other hand, if users are willing to call in and upload message requests and then disconnect and wait for some time before reconnecting, you will have more flexibility as you plan your gateways.

Modem Speed

If both the users and the Async gateway have high-speed modems, download time can be reduced significantly.

TIP

If possible, use the same type of modem in the Async gateway and in the remote users' machines—or at least test different modems to make sure they work well together. Modem incompatibilities can cause connections to fail or to be unreliable. Also, you should disable any compression that may be performed by the modems. GroupWise takes care of all necessary file compression and decompression.

PILOT ROLLOUTS

Before you give all of the users in your system access to the GroupWise Remote client, it is a good idea to implement a pilot rollout. By first giving a small group of users access to GroupWise Remote, you will be able to make more accurate projections about the volume of traffic that remote users will generate.

A pilot program will also help you determine peak times during the day when remote users dial in to their mailboxes. If your GroupWise system is going to support a large number of users who can only access the system through GroupWise Remote (for example, a national sales force) you may notice peak dial-in periods during lunch hours and after work. Employees who are away on business trips also tend to call in to the system during the mid- to late-evening hours (when they return to their hotel rooms).

Once you determine peak calling hours, you can decide whether you will need to add modems to your gateway. You may even decide you need to add gateways to domains that service a large number of GroupWise Remote users.

TIP

As a rule, you should be conservative when you estimate the number of modems you need. You can always add more later.

TYPES OF REMOTE USERS

There is one more factor you should consider when when you plan a GroupWise Remote implementation—the different kinds of remote users in your system. There are basically two distinct types of GroupWise Remote users:

► Users who only use GroupWise Remote when traveling (and occasionally from home). I'll refer to these users as *occasional* GroupWise Remote users.

> ▸ Users who work away from the main offices and who can only contact the GroupWise system using GroupWise remote. I'll refer to these as *routine* GroupWise Remote users.

Occasional Remote Users

Occasional remote users typically access their master mailboxes during business trips (often from hotels or trade shows). Sometimes these users work at home in the evenings and want to connect to the main GroupWise system. These GroupWise Remote users almost always access their mailboxes using the regular network GroupWise client.

In most systems, you will not be able to group all of the occasional remote users into a single domain. Therefore, you probably won't be able to place an Async gateway in every domain that has occasional GroupWise Remote users. When you are faced with this situation, the best solution is to place an Async gateway in a centrally located domain that can be easily accessed by all domains.

Routine Remote Users

Routine GroupWise Remote users never (or very seldom) use the network GroupWise client to access their mailboxes. Instead, they routinely use the GroupWise Remote client to communicate with other employees.

If your organization has a substantial number of routine remote users, you should strongly consider grouping them into a domain that can contain one or more dedicated Async gateways. There are two advantages to this strategy. First, the remote users get a better response time. Because they rely so heavily on remote access, they are bound to be concerned about message delivery speed. Second, grouping these users into one domain reduces the impact that processing their messages will have on the rest of the system. Off-site employees often work in the same department. For example, a sales department may have a large number of off-site sales reps. These employees often send a lot of messages between themselves. By placing them in their own domain, a large percentage of their messages are isolated within that domain.

The demands that routine remote users place on a GroupWise system are very different from the demands of occasional remote users. You need to consider the needs of each type of remote user as you plan your implementation of GroupWise Remote.

GroupWise Remote and System Security

The potential for security breaches is frequently a major concern of system administrators, especially when a network or messaging system can be accessed through the telephone system.

GroupWise Remote operates on a request-and-response basis. (The request-and-response model is explained in detail later in this chapter.)

GroupWise Remote users who use modem connections to an Async gateway never log in to the network and never have live access to the network file servers, volumes, and directories.

IMPORTANT

The GroupWise Remote client uploads all requests to the Async gateway. The Async gateway then routes requests to the other GroupWise server processes. These server processes access the GroupWise message stores and route information back to the Async gateway. This store-and-forward-mechanism makes it impossible for GroupWise Remote users to gain unauthorized access to network directories and files.

How GroupWise Remote Works

GroupWise Remote operates on two basic principles:

- Database synchronization

- Request-and-response

These two principles are the major difference between how the regular GroupWise client functions and how GroupWise Remote works. Unlike GroupWise Remote, the regular GroupWise client uses live network connections to post offices.

DATABASE SYNCHRONIZATION

Each user in a post office has a user database—commonly referred to as the user's *master mailbox*. The master mailbox contains pointers to messages in a message database. If a particular message contains a file attachment, the message in the message database contains a pointer to a file in the file attachments directory.

When you access your master mailbox with the regular GroupWise client, you have a live connection between the client program and the master maibox. The client directly reads from and (in most cases) directly writes to the user database. This is the major difference between the regular GroupWise client and the GroupWise Remote client.

The regular GroupWise client maintains a constant connection to the message store, and regularly polls it for new messages. The GroupWise Remote client, on the other hand, never connects directly to the message store, and it never polls the user database. Instead, the GroupWise Remote user initiates a connection to the GroupWise system and relies on the Async gateway, the message server, and the post office server to transfer information between the message store and the Remote client.

GroupWise Remote allows GroupWise users to access their master mailbox without a live network connection to the post office message store. Because the GroupWise Remote client does not have a live network connection to the message store, it cannot read directly from the user database, the message database, or the file attachments directory.

IMPORTANT

Even a remote user who *never* uses the regular GroupWise client must have a master mailbox within a GroupWise post office. Consequently, a single-user license is still required for that user. However, a user who accesses the message store with both the regular GroupWise client and the GroupWise Remote client only needs one license because the same master mailbox is used.

To give GroupWise Remote users access to the information in their master mailboxes, the GroupWise Remote client maintains a *replica* (a copy) of the user database on the remote user's hard drive. Just like a user database in a post office, the remote client's user database does not contain actual messages or file attachments. GroupWise Remote maintains a miniature message store on the hard drive in a directory known as *ROFDATA*. (ROFDATA is another term carried over from WordPerfect Office. It stands for "Remote Office Data").

The ROFDATA directory also serves as a file attachments directory. Files stored in the ROFDATA as attachments are encrypted with the same GroupWise encryption technology used for all GroupWise messages. Therefore, these files are very secure.

Figure 14.1 illustrates the similarities between the post office message store and the GroupWise Remote message store on the remote user's hard drive.

Post Office

GroupWise Remote

<Post Office>

ROFDATA

OFFILES
(File Attachments)

MSG.DB

OFMSG

USER.DB

MSG*xx*.DB

(File Attachments)

OFUSER

USER*xxx*.DB

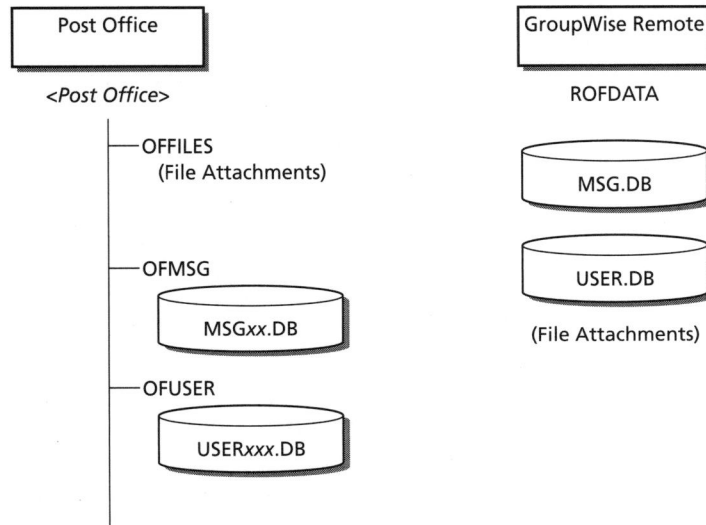

The difference between the databases in the post office message store and the databases in the ROFDATA directory is that the GroupWise Remote databases *only store information for a single user*. The ROFDATA databases are not exact replicas of a post office's databases; they are a very abridged version. Furthermore, often a GroupWise Remote user database does not even contain all of the information stored in the remote user's master mailbox because the remote user can control how much information is downloaded from the master mailbox.

For example, a GroupWise Remote user might choose to download only unopened mail messages and appointments from the prior two days. In this situation, the master mailbox could contain tasks, notes, and opened mail that would not be downloaded to the remote mailbox.

A GroupWise Remote user can only work offline. In other words, all tasks that a user performs with GroupWise Remote occur in the GroupWise Remote message store and message queues. These tasks include reading messages, sending new messages, maintaining a personal calendar, and so forth. When a connection is initiated, the databases in the GroupWise Remote message store and in the user's post office directory store are synchronized. In other words, all work done offline is then sent to the master mailbox in the user's post office. This process should become clearer to you as you read this chapter.

REQUEST-AND-RESPONSE

GroupWise Remote communicates with a main GroupWise system by using a request-and-response model.

When a GroupWise Remote user works offline in the Remote client, the Remote client generates requests. A request is: (1) any type of update that must occur in the master mailbox, or (2) a solicitation for information from the master mailbox. A request is generated when a remote user performs any of these actions:

► Sends, replies to, forwards, or delegates an item (for example, a message)

► Creates or deletes a personal item, a folder, a group, or a rule

► Opens, deletes, undeletes, or retracts an item, or empties items from the Trash

► Makes a specific request that message items, folders, groups, etc. be sent from the master maibox.

► Requests the address book

► Moves or links items to folders

NOTE

This is not a comprehensive list. These are the most common actions that generate requests.

All of the above actions generate requests, which are stored in the pending requests queue until the user initiates a connection to the main GroupWise system. A request should be thought of as a request for the master system to take some kind of action. A request is not necessarily a request for information to be downloaded.

Master mailboxes in a GroupWise system serve as central repositories for all of the users' messages—both incoming and outgoing. GroupWise Remote users dial in and upload requests and messages. The system processes these requests and prepares responses for the users, which are downloaded either during the same connection or at a later time.

GroupWise Remote users have two ways to connect to the main GroupWise system—through modem connections or through a network connection. Modem connections are used most of the time. I will discuss using network connections with GroupWise Remote later in this chapter.

The GroupWise Remote client is simply another way for GroupWise users to access their master mailboxes. The post office message store does not distinguish between the GroupWise Remote client and the regular GroupWise client. As I mentioned earlier, the only difference is that the regular GroupWise Remote client does not have a live network connection to the master mailbox, and it cannot read the actual user database. Because the GroupWise Remote client cannot directly access the master mailbox, it must generate requests for information, and those requests must be processed by the GroupWise servers—Async gateway servers, message servers, and post office servers.

The request-and-response process is illustrated in Figure 14.2:

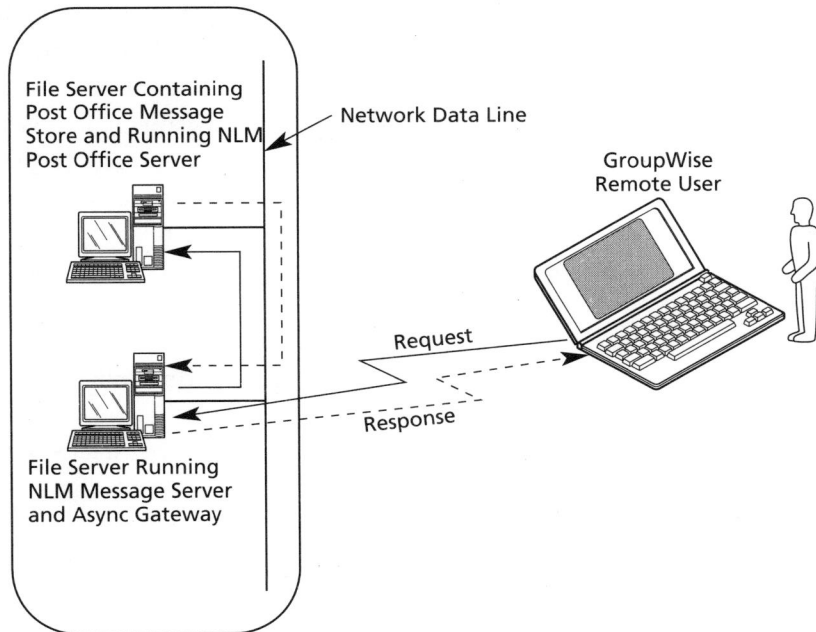

FIGURE 14.2

Request-and-Response

As shown in the diagram, a GroupWise Remote user creates a request in the GroupWise Remote client program. The request is stored in the pending requests queue on the user's hard drive until a connection is made to the GroupWise system.

When the user initiates a connection, GroupWise Remote activates the modem and dials the Async gateway. The Async gateway receives the request and sends the request to the message server. (In Figure 14.2, the Async gateway and the message server are running on the same file server. The Async gateway needs to run on a dedicated workstation if the DOS Async gateway or the OS/2 Async gateway is used.)

The message server then routes the request to the post office that contains the GroupWise Remote user's master mailbox. The message server may have to route the request to one or more messages servers to reach the user's master mailbox. (In Figure 14.2, you should assume that the Async gateway is in the same domain as the user.) GroupWise Remote achieves the best performance when the Async gateway is in the same domain as the remote user's master mailbox because only one message server is involved.

The post office server in the remote user's post office gathers the requested information, generates a response to the request, and updates the user's mailbox. The post office server sends the response to the message server, which then routes the response back to the Async gateway. (In Figure 14.2, the broken lines indicate the response process.) If the GroupWise Remote user still has a live connection to the Async gateway, the user receives the response during that connection. If the user has disconnected, the response is stored in a holding queue in the Async gateway subdirectory and is delivered to the GroupWise Remote user during the next connection.

You can see from Figure 14.2 that a number of processes—the Remote client, Async gateways, message servers, and post office servers—are all involved in handling requests from GroupWise Remote users.

Suppose a system is designed according to the star configuration, as shown in Figure 14.3.

In Figure 14.3, the GroupWise Remote user's master mailbox is located in the Sales post office in Domain 2, and the Async gateway is located in a dedicated GroupWise domain (Domain 6).

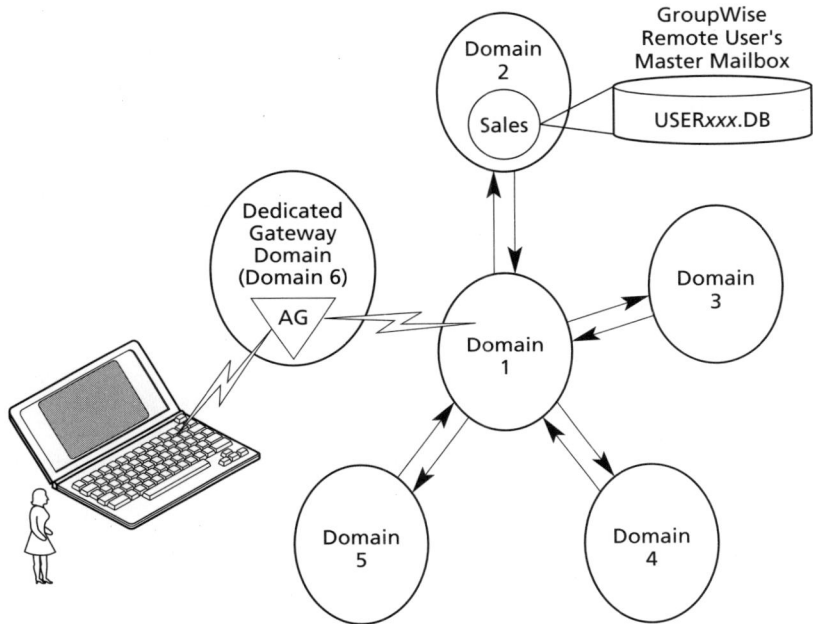

FIGURE 14.3

*Star Configuration with
Dedicated Gateway Domain*

In this configuration, when the GroupWise Remote user dials in for new messages the following processes must handle the request and response:

1 • The Async gateway in Domain 6 receives the request.

2 • The Async gateway passes the request to Domain 6's message server.

3 • Domain 6's message server passes the request to Domain 1's message server.

4 • Domain 1's message server passes the request to Domain 2's message server.

5 • Domain 2's message server passes the request to the Sales post office server.

6 • The Sales post office server receives the request, gathers the requested data from the user's master mailbox and the post office message store, and generates a response that contains the requested data.

7 • The Sales post office server sends the response to Domain 2's message server.

8 • Domain 2's message server passes the response to Domain 1's message server.

9 • Domain 1's message server passes the response to Domain 6's message server.

10 • Domain 6's message server passes the response to the Async gateway.

11 • The Async gateway sends the response back to the GroupWise Remote user.

> **All of the steps listed above are not specifically represented in the diagram.**
>
> **NOTE**

Obviously this entire process takes some time, even in a GroupWise system equipped with very fast servers. To help expedite this process, GroupWise systems treat all GroupWise Remote requests as high-priority messages. In other words, the messages are routed through the high-priority message queues (WPCSIN\<0–3>), which are scanned more frequently by the GroupWise server processes.

The examples illustrated in Figures 14.2 and 14.3 demonstrate three important points. First, GroupWise Remote users' requests will be processed much faster if the Async gateway is located in the same domain as the remote users' master mailboxes. Second, if messages have to go through more than one domain, the response time will be longer, which often results in a remote user having to reconnect to the system in order to receive the response. Third, if a lot of GroupWise Remote requests need to be processed, it can adversely affect the delivery of normal messages within the system because GroupWise Remote requests are always treated as higher-priority messages.

You should keep all three of these considerations in mind as you decide where to locate the GroupWise Remote users and where to locate the Async gateways in your system.

Setting Up Async Gateways for GroupWise Remote

There are two basic requirements that must be met if a GroupWise system is going to support remote users:

▶ An Async gateway must be installed somewhere in the system.

▶ The domain that houses the Async gateway must have a message server.

Even if a small GroupWise system only contains a single domain and a single post office, a message server will be needed to support GroupWise Remote users. It does not matter which message server platform (i.e., DOS, OS/2, NLM, or UNIX) you are using — or which Async gateway platform you have — when you implement GroupWise Remote. All message server platforms and Async gateway platforms can support GroupWise Remote users.

The steps for installing the Async gateway software and for creating the Async gateway in GroupWise Admin are identical to the steps explained in Chapter 13. A single Async gateway can support both domain-to-domain and GroupWise Remote communication. You do not need to install separate Async gateways for different uses (although in many cases it is best to have separate Async gateways so that remote communications do not slow down domain-to-domain traffic).

When you choose the Specific option in the Async gateway setup screen, you will see the options shown in Figure 14.4:

Async Gateway Setup Screen

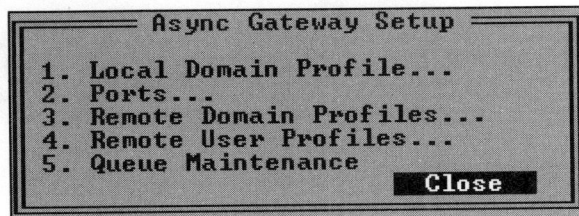

```
════════ Async Gateway Setup ════════
  1.  Local Domain Profile...
  2.  Ports...
  3.  Remote Domain Profiles...
  4.  Remote User Profiles...
  5.  Queue Maintenance
                          Close
```

To support GroupWise Remote users, you must configure the local domain profile, the ports, and one or more *remote user profiles*. If the Async gateway will not be used to connect to another domain and will only be used to support GroupWise Remote users, you do not need to configure a remote domain profile. Refer to Chapter 13 for an explanation of how to configure local domain profiles and ports.

A remote user profile establishes the parameters that GroupWise Remote users must follow when connecting to an Async gateway.

Follow these steps to create a remote user profile (assuming that the gateway software has already be installed and the gateway has been created in GroupWise Admin):

I • Run GroupWise Admin for the domain that houses the Async gateway.

2 • Highlight the Async gateway.

3 • Choose Actions and then choose Edit.

4 • Choose Specific.

5 • Choose Remote User Profile.

6 • Choose Create.

The dialog box shown in Figure 14.5 will appear.

Remote User Profile Dialog
Box

```
═══ Remote User Profile Definition ═══
  Login ID:        [                  ]
  Password:
  Days Before Auto Purge of Messages:  7
  Minimum Idle Time:  4
  Description:

                            OK      Cancel
```

The options you must select as you create a remote domain profile are explained in Table 14.1.

TABLE 14.1

*Remote Domain Profile
Options*

OPTION	DESCRIPTION
Login ID	Remote users must use this ID to access the Async gateway.
Password	Remote users must use this password to access the Async gateway. *This password is case-sensitive.*
Days Before Auto Purge of Messages	The first time a remote user connects to the system, an account is created for that user. This account is a subdirectory under the Async gateway directory structure, and it is used to store responses that arrive at the gateway after the user has disconnected. This option lets you specify the number of days before the responses are deleted if the user does not reconnect.
Minimum Idle Time	Minimum Idle Time is the amount of time in minutes that the Async gateway will remain connected while waiting for responses to be received from the GroupWise system.

NOTE

If a remote user's account in the Async gateway directory structure is deleted, the user does not lose messages. The messages are still available in the user's master mailbox. Only the responses that were not downloaded during the previous connection are deleted. The remote user would need to request that information again.

WARNING

If you set Minimum Idle Time to 0, the Async gateway will disconnect immediately after a user uploads requests. Users will have to initiate another connection to receive responses to requests. If you want to keep the connection open for awhile to give users an opportunity to receive responses, you can specify a period of time (in minutes).

Users will need both the gateway login ID and the gateway password when they set the preferences in the GroupWise Remote client program.

As you create remote user profiles, there are couple different strategies you can use. One strategy is to create a single remote user profile that all GroupWise Remote users share when accessing the main GroupWise system. Another strategy is to create remote user profiles for individual users or for groups of users. The second strategy is particularly useful when you have certain users who need unique remote profile settings (for example, if they need longer Minimum Idle Time settings because they prefer not to connect more than once to receive responses).

Master Mailbox Passwords

There is one last matter to take care of before GroupWise Remote users can establish a connection to their mailboxes. All GroupWise Remote users must have a password set on their master mailbox (assuming post office has been set to high security). Setting a password is easy for occasional GroupWise Remote users because they can set the password from within the regular network GroupWise client.

However, for routine GroupWise Remote users, you usually need to set a password on their master mailboxes using GroupWise Admin. You cannot select multiple users and set a global password. The passwords must be set on an individual-user basis.

Assuming a user object has already been created and a master mailbox exists in the post office message store, here are the steps for setting a master mailbox password using GroupWise Admin:

1 • Run GroupWise Admin from the primary domain or from the secondary domain that owns the user.

2 • Open the Users window if it is not already open.

3 • Highlight the user for whom you wish to set password.

4 • Choose Actions.

5 • Choose GroupWise 4.x Options.

6 • Choose Security Access.

7 • Choose Set Password.

8 • Enter the user's password.

IMPORTANT

This password is case-sensitive. You will need to provide the routine GroupWise Remote user with the password that you set in GroupWise Admin.

9 • Choose OK and then choose Close.

10 • With the user still highlighted, select the Tools option.

11 • Choose Check GroupWise Files.

12 • Select Action.

13 • Select Reset Preferences.

14 • Choose Run.

NOTE

Steps 10 through 14 cause the user's preferences to be reset and add the password information to the user's USERxxx.DB file.

In the above steps, I am assuming that the user object has already been created in GroupWise Admin and that the user's master mailbox already exists in the post office message store. If that is not the case when you create an account for the GroupWise Remote user, there is a preliminary step you must take before you can set the password for the user — you must cause the user's USERxxx.DB file to be created in the post office message store.

The easiest way to force the creation of a USERxxx.DB file is to send a message to that user from the GroupWise client. You may want to send users a message welcoming them to GroupWise Remote. This has two benefits: (1) It creates users' USERxxx.DB files, and (2) it provides users with something to download the first time they connect to the GroupWise system.

Using Network Connections

I mentioned earlier that GroupWise Remote users can select from two connection options: modem or network. As you know, GroupWise Remote does not maintain a constant connection to a GroupWise post office as does the normal GroupWise client. When GroupWise Remote users use a network connection, they do not establish a live connection to their master mailboxes. Rather, they merely upload their requests through a network to a post office-level queue (instead of sending their requests through a modem to the Async gateway). GroupWise Remote still operates according to the request-and-response model when a remote user utilizes a network connection.

GroupWise Remote users can use a network connection if their computer has a drive mapping to *any* post office within the GroupWise system. It does *not* have to be their home post office. When GroupWise Remote requests are uploaded through the network to post office directories, the message servers and the post office servers work together to process the requests and responses.

There are several tasks for which a network connection can be very useful:

▶ Updating a GroupWise Remote mailbox before leaving on a trip

▶ Downloading the address book

▶ Connecting to another post office within a GroupWise system

▶ Providing GroupWise access to users at sites that are too small for a GroupWise domain

UPDATING REMOTE MAILBOXES

Before leaving for a business trip, GroupWise Remote users can connect their computers to the network and request all necessary items from their master mailboxes. By doing this, users obviate lengthy long-distance phone calls later because the GroupWise Remote message store databases will already be synchronized.

DOWNLOADING THE ADDRESS BOOK

A network connection is a very convenient way to download the address book from a post office to a GroupWise Remote directory. The address book is often very large and takes a long time to download. Again, this avoids the need for lengthy modem connections later.

CONNECTING TO ANOTHER POST OFFICE

GroupWise Remote users who travel to sites within the same company can use a GroupWise Remote network connection to access their home post offices.

For example, suppose that a company has GroupWise domains in Los Angeles and New York. Suppose an employee who works in Los Angeles needs to spend a week at the New York office. While in New York, that employee can use GroupWise Remote with a network connection to a post office in New York. When the employee initiates a connection, the GroupWise system will route the requests and responses to and from the employee's home post office in the Los Angeles domain.

PROVIDING GROUPWISE ACCESS TO SATELLITE OFFICES

GroupWise Remote can also be used as a solution for users who work in a satellite office that is not large enough to warrant its own post office or domain.

For example, suppose that a company has 30 employees who work in a branch office away from the main site. That branch office only has a small file server, and the users are linked to the corporate network through a slow WAN link. The file server is not large enough to support a GroupWise domain or a post office at the branch. Nevertheless, these employees need to be able to communicate with the rest of the company.

If the employees in the branch office use the regular GroupWise client to access master mailbox in a post office at the main company site, the GroupWise client will not perform well because it must access the databases across a slow WAN link.

In this situation, the users in the branch office could use GroupWise Remote to access their master mailbox across the WAN link. The users would generate requests and then initiate the connection to the post office only when they wanted their mailboxes updated. The polling traffic across the WAN link would be eliminated because the GroupWise Remote client would only generate traffic when a connection to a master mailbox was established. The downside of this approach is that there are a few GroupWise features that are not available to GroupWise Remote users. I discuss those features in Chapter 15 and explain why GroupWise Remote does not include them.

GroupWise Remote Message Flow

Before I explain the details of message flow between GroupWise Remote and a main GroupWise system, I need to give you some more background on GroupWise Remote's directories. Figure 14.6 shows the GroupWise Remote directory structure.

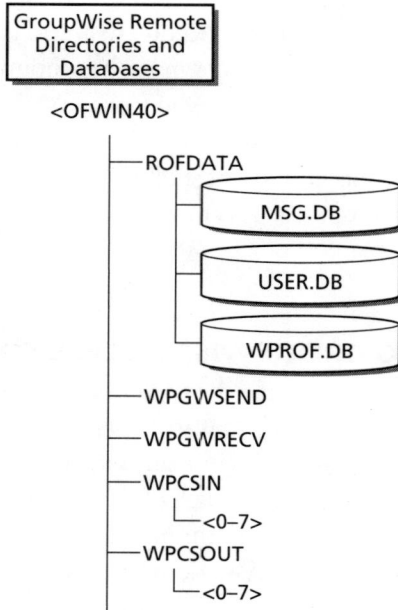

*GroupWise Remote
Directory Structure*

GroupWise Remote
Directories and
Databases

<OFWIN40>

```
├── ROFDATA
│         ┌──────────────┐
│         │   MSG.DB      │
│         └──────────────┘
│         ┌──────────────┐
│         │   USER.DB     │
│         └──────────────┘
│         ┌──────────────┐
│         │   WPROF.DB    │
│         └──────────────┘
├── WPGWSEND
├── WPGWRECV
├── WPCSIN
│      └── <0–7>
├── WPCSOUT
       └── <0–7>
```

I have already explained how the ROFDATA directory functions as the GroupWise Remote message store. However, there is one database file in ROFDATA that I have not yet mentioned—WPROF.DB. This file contains the GroupWise Remote user's address book (directory store), and it is similar to the WPHOST.DB file found in the post office subdirectory. I'll say more about this file in Chapter 15.

Notice that the GroupWise Remote directory structure contains WPCSIN and WPCSOUT directories. These directories function as input and output queues for the GroupWise Remote client. When a GroupWise Remote user creates a request, the request is placed in these queues to await the connection to the Async gateway. In addition, there are two other directories used by GroupWise Remote—WPGWSEND and WPGWRECV. (These directory names are carryovers from WordPerfect Office, where the directories were called "WordPerfect Gateway Send" and "WordPerfect Gateway Receive.") These directories are used during the connection to a gateway when information is sent by or received from the gateway.

MESSAGE FLOW WITH A MODEM CONNECTION

Because each GroupWise Remote user works offline, when a user creates a message and chooses the Send option, the message is not sent at that time. It goes to the pending requests queue until the user connects. Figure 14.7 shows what happens when a user sends a message from GroupWise Remote to the main system via a modem connection to an Async gateway.

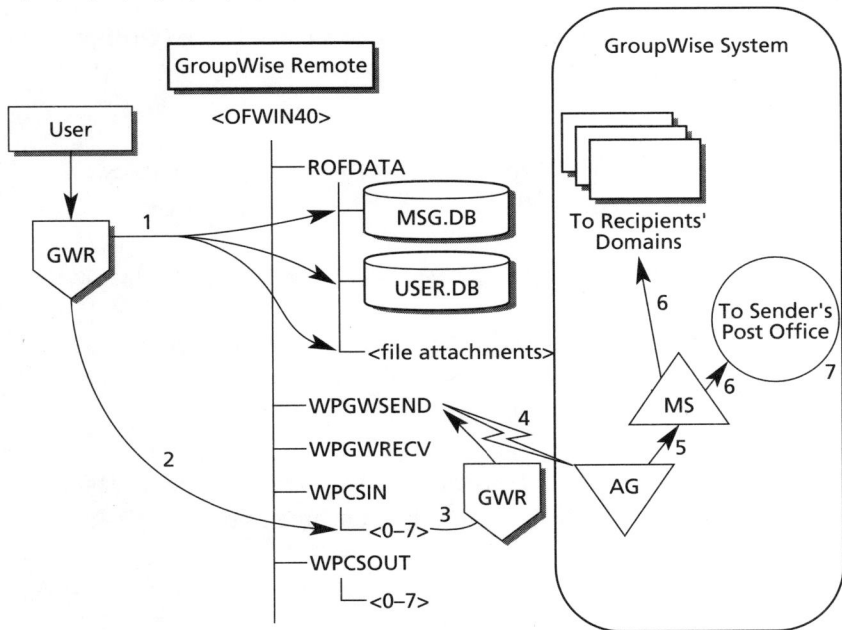

F I G U R E 14.7

Message Flow with a Modem Connection

1 • A GroupWise user creates a message and chooses Send. GroupWise Remote updates the message database and the user database and adds any file attachments to the ROFDATA directory in the GroupWise Remote message store.

2 • GroupWise Remote places the message in the WPCSIN\<1–7> directory in the GroupWise Remote subdirectory structure. All remote requests are priority 0 or 1, where 0 is the highest priority.

3 • When the user initiates a connection, GroupWise Remote checks the WPCSIN directory for messages that are waiting to be uploaded to the main GroupWise system. GroupWise Remote reads the information in the WPCSIN directory, compresses the information into one or more files (to reduce connection time), and then moves the file to the WPGWSEND directory.

NOTE

The file compression takes place before GroupWise Remote calls the gateway.

4 • GroupWise Remote then dials the Async gateway, establishes a connection, and sends the file to the Async gateway.

5 • The Async gateway passes the message to the message server.

6 • The message server delivers the message to the recipients' domains and to the sender's post office server (assuming the gateway is located in the sender's domain).

7 • The sender's post office server updates the sender's user database, the message database, and the file attachments directory.

When information is downloaded from the main GroupWise system, the events shown in Figure 14.8 occur.

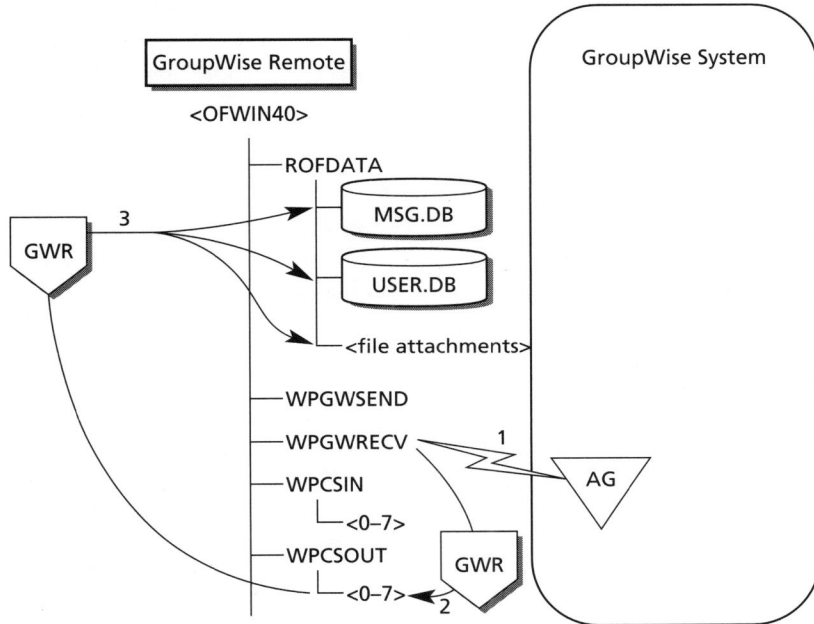

FIGURE 14.8

Message Flow of Information Downloaded from Main System

Here are the steps illustrated in Figure 14.8:

1. • When a message is received from the Async gateway, GroupWise Remote receives the information and builds a response file in the WPGWRECV directory.

2. • When the download is complete, GroupWise Remote disconnects and then decompresses the downloaded response file. The response file may contain more than one message. As the information is decompressed, the individual messages are moved to the WPCSOUT directory.

3. • GroupWise Remote then reads the information in the WPCSOUT directory and updates the information in the USER.DB, MSG.DB, and ROFDATA directory.

MESSAGE FLOW WITH A NETWORK CONNECTION

When a GroupWise user sends messages from GroupWise Remote to the main GroupWise system using a network connection, the steps illustrated in Figure 14.9 occur:

Message Flow with a Network Connection

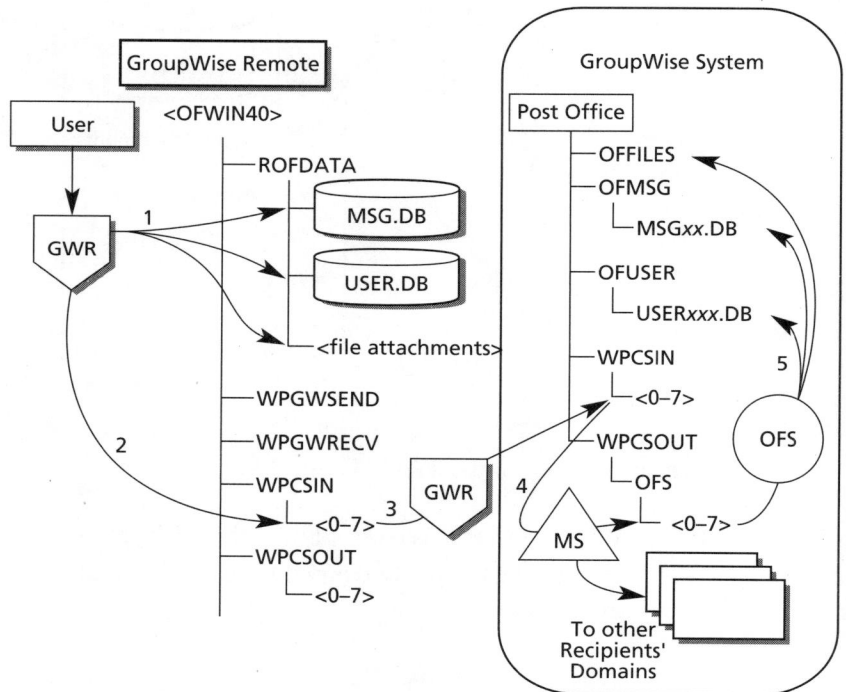

The steps are as follows:

1 • A GroupWise Remote user creates a request. GroupWise Remote places a copy of the message in the MSG.DB, updates the USER.DB, places any file attachments in the ROFDATA directory.

2 • GroupWise Remote then inserts the request in the WPCSIN\1 directory.

3 • When a connection is initiated by the user, GroupWise Remote places the message or the request in the post office WPCSIN\1 directory.

(Note: GroupWise Remote users will need Write, Create, Modify, and File scan rights to this directory.)

4 • The message server delivers the request to the WPCSOUT\OFS\1 directory. (In the diagram, I assume that the user connects to the home post office. If the user accesses a post office other than the home post office, the message server will route the request to appropriate message server for processing.)

5 • The post office server processes the request by updating the message store databases or retrieving the requested information.

Figure 14.10 shows the *status back*—the response being delivered back to the GroupWise Remote user through the network connection.

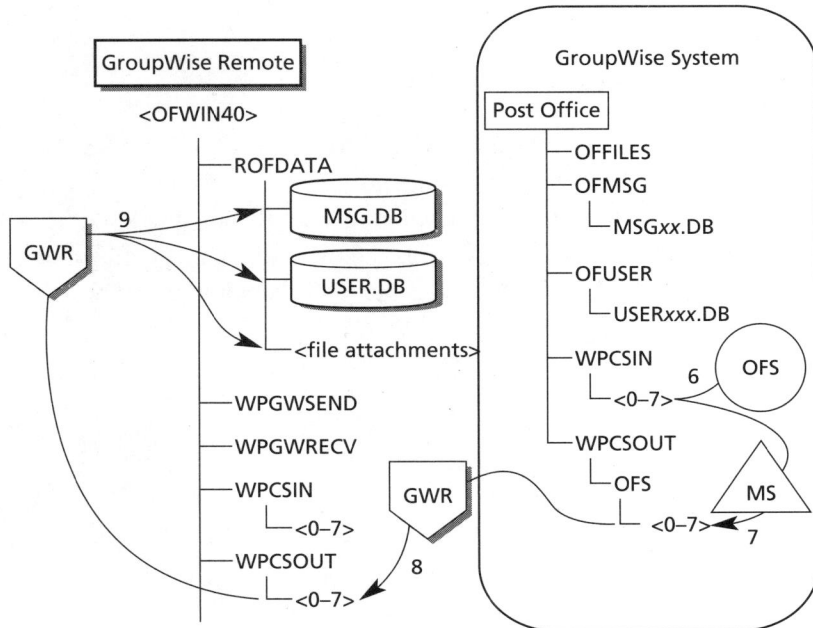

FIGURE 14.10

Response Delivered to the GroupWise Remote Client

The steps are as follows:

1 • The post office server places the status message or the response in the post office WPCSIN\1 directory.

2 • The message server picks up the message and places it in the OFWORK\DIRECT\<*connection ID*> directory that is specific to the GroupWise Remote user.

3 • If the GroupWise Remote connection is still valid, GroupWise Remote picks up the message from the <*connection ID*> directory and inserts the message into the GroupWise Remote WPCSOUT\OFS\1 directory.

4 • GroupWise Remote then updates the remote databases.

Summary

In this chapter, I explained how to plan a GroupWise Remote implementation, how to configure Async gateways, and how to set a password on a user's mailbox. I also explained in some detail how GroupWise Remote works.

In the next chapter, I'll explain how to set up and configure a workstation or laptop computer with the GroupWise Remote client and how to troubleshoot problems with GroupWise Remote.

Implementing the GroupWise Remote Client

In Chapter 14 you learned how to plan a system in preparation for GroupWise Remote implementation, how to set up Async gateways to support remote users, and basically how GroupWise Remote works.

Chapter 15 explains how to set up the GroupWise Remote client application. I devote an entire chapter to the GroupWise Remote client for several reasons:

▶ As a GroupWise administrator, you will frequently be asked to troubleshoot problems with GroupWise Remote. Often, users' problems relate to proper use of the client application, as opposed to the actual configuration of the system.

▶ The initial setup of the GroupWise Remote client is somewhat complicated— more so than the setup of the network GroupWise client.

▶ By choosing certain options, you can configure the GroupWise Remote client so that connection times will be kept to a minimum. If you thoroughly understand these options, you can train remote users how to maximize system efficiency and reduce connection times.

After reading this chapter, you should be able to answer most of the questions that remote users commonly ask.

GroupWise Remote Client Platforms

GroupWise Remote clients are available for DOS, Windows, and Macintosh platforms. The Windows client is the most commonly used, and the screen shots (graphical representations of computer screens) in this chapter have been taken from that client platform. Figure 15.1 shows the GroupWise Remote client for Windows. The only difference between the GroupWise Remote client screen and the network GroupWise client screen is the Remote menu. Otherwise, the interface is identical.

FIGURE 15.1

GroupWise Remote Windows Client

For occasional GroupWise Remote users, it makes sense to use the version of the GroupWise Remote client that corresponds to the network GroupWise client they use. For routine GroupWise Remote users, however, you should use the version that corresponds to the operating systems on their PCs. From the GroupWise system's perspective, it makes no difference which GroupWise Remote client version is used.

GroupWise Remote Installation Strategies

The strategy you use for installing and configuring GroupWise Remote will depend on how many remote users in your system will use each platform. It is a good idea to sponsor special training classes for occasional remote users in a system because it is often difficult to predict when and where these users will use the GroupWise Remote client. For routine GroupWise Remote users, it may be possible to configure the users' PCs onsite. If offsite routine remote users convene regularly (for example, at an annual conference at company headquarters), you could install GroupWise Remote on their laptops at that time.

ADVANTAGES OF ONSITE CONFIGURATION

It is preferable to set up remote users' computers onsite if you can. There are several advantages to configuring a computer onsite:

▶ You can troubleshoot problems with the computer right in front of you instead trying to handle them over the phone.

▸ You can manually add a copy of the address book (WPROF.DB) to the GroupWise Remote directory structure. This will save a lot of phone connect time at the outset because the address book is usually very large and it takes a long time to download.

▸ You can add Check GroupWise (OFCHECK) and other utilities (such as the GSC.EXE shared code utility I mentioned in Chapter 5) to the remote user's computer. Additional utilities can be very useful—especially for routine GroupWise Remote users. The utilities also come in handy when you have to troubleshoot problems over the phone.

▸ You can confirm that the right user settings are in place. For example, you can enter the name of the domain, the name of the post office, the gateway login ID, and the gateway password instead of having the remote user perform these tasks.

▸ You can test the GroupWise Remote configuration and the modems to make sure they work properly.

If it is impossible for you to set up GroupWise Remote for the users, a good alternative is to provide a worksheet with the instructions and information that the users will need. Appendix E contains a sample worksheet for you to use.

It may also be helpful for you to create supplemental disks that contain copies of the address book file and the Check GroupWise utility files. You can send remote users supplemental disks and instructional worksheets along with the GroupWise Remote disks to assist them with the installation and configuration of GroupWise Remote.

Installing and Configuring GroupWise Remote

Thorough instructions for installing and configuring the GroupWise Remote client are provided in the software documentation and in the Instant Expert guides on the CD-ROM that comes with this book. (See the files DOSREM.TT, MACREM.TT, and WINREM.TT.) The actual installation process is simply a matter of running the Install program and inserting disks when prompted. The tricky part is the configuration the GroupWise Remote client for the users.

REQUIRED SETTINGS

The first time users run the GroupWise Remote client, they are required to enter certain information, as shown in Figure 15.2:

FIGURE 15.2

GroupWise Remote Required Settings

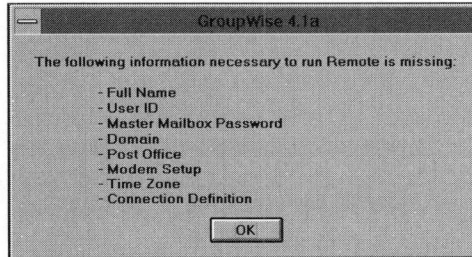

This is where a worksheet can be handy for remote users if they install the program themselves. Here is a brief explanation of the required information:

Full Name   This is the name that will appear in the From: field when someone receives a message from the GroupWise Remote user. It does not have to be the GroupWise user ID or the user's name as it appears in the address book. For example, I have set my full name in the GroupWise Remote client as "Shawn Rogers (Remote)" so that when my boss reads the e-mail I send him, he knows that I have been working at home late at night.

User ID   This is the GroupWise user ID that is entered when a user's GroupWise account is created

Master Mailbox Password   This is the password that has already been set on the user's master mailbox.

This password is case-sensitive. (In other words, uppercase and lowercase letters must be matched exactly.)

IMPORTANT

The master mailbox password cannot be set using the GroupWise Remote client. Therefore, either the user will have to set the password from the network GroupWise client, or you will have to set it for the user through GroupWise Admin. (Instructions for setting this password can be found in Chapter 14.) When post office security is set to High, the GroupWise Remote client cannot access the mailbox without a password.

If post office security is set to low, the GroupWise Remote user can simply enter a fake password.

TIP

Domain Name   This is the name of the user's domain. It is not the name of the domain that houses the Async gateway (unless, of course, the gateway happens to be in the user's domain).

Post Office Name   This is the name of the user's post office.

Modem Setup   The user must select a modem definition in the GroupWise Remote client, even if a network connection will be used exclusively (which is rarely the case). In most cases, a user's modem definition will be available from the list of supported modems and you should not need to edit or create the definition. The WPMODEM.DB file, which is accessed automatically when you select a modem definition, contains the listing of supported modems. If you create a new modem definition, that definition is stored in the WPMODEM.DB file.

FIGURE 15.3

Modem Definition Screen

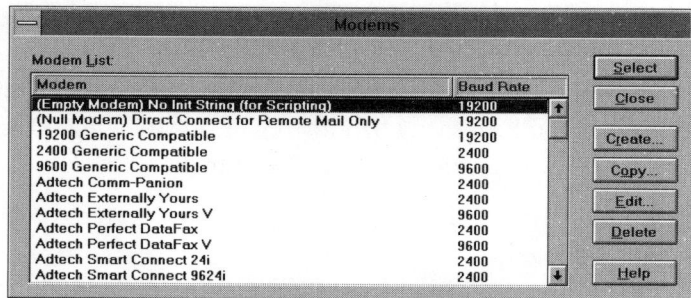

Novell updates the modem definition file regularly. If you have a new modem and cannot find it listed, check NetWire, Novell's World Wide Web site or Novell's FTP site the for the latest version of the WPMODEM.DB file. The WWW home page URL is HTTP:// WWW.NOVELL.COM, and the FTP site is FTP.NOVELL.COM.

TIP

Time Zone   This is the user's time zone, *not* the time zone of the GroupWise system. This setting ensures that appointment times and message time-stamps are correctly adjusted for GroupWise Remote users in different time zones. If a user in Los Angeles schedules a 3:00 p.m. conference call with a sales rep in New York, the conference call will be scheduled at 6:00 p.m. in the New York user's calendar—not 3:00 p.m. A good rule of thumb to remember is that the time zone setting should always correspond to time set for the computer's internal clock. If a user travels to New York and sets the computer clock to correspond with New York time, the GroupWise Remote time zone setting should be set for Eastern Standard Time.

Connections   The GroupWise Remote user must set up at least one connection definition. There are two types of connections available: *modem* and *network*. A remote user can have multiple connection definitions of each type. Connection definitions are discussed at length in the next subsection.

MODEM CONNECTION DEFINITIONS

Most of the time, GroupWise Remote users connect to the main GroupWise system with a modem connection. I explain modem connections in Chapter 14. Figure 15.4 shows the modem connection definition screen.

FIGURE 15.4

Modem Connection Dialog Box

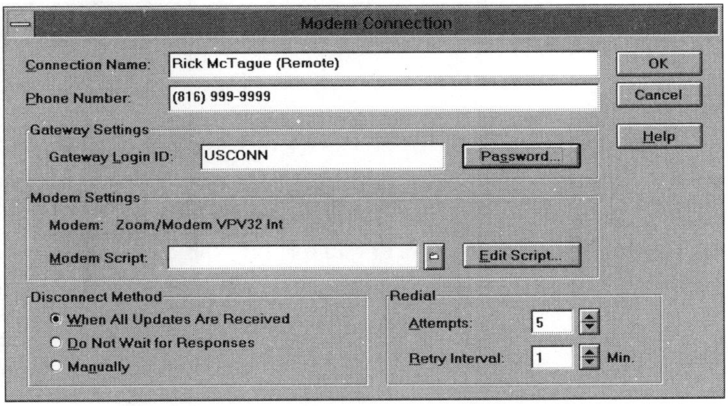

A modem connection definition consists of the following information:

Connection Name   This name is determined by the user. For example, a user might have a connection named "Local phone number" and another named "Toll-free phone number."

Phone Number   This is the phone number to the Async gateway. Users can add other strings of numbers before the gateway's phone number to charge calls to a credit card or a calling card.

Gateway Login ID   This is the Async gateway login ID set in the Async Gateway Remote User Profile screen.

Gateway Password   This is the Async gateway password set in the Async Gateway Remote User Profile screen. This password is case-sensitive.

Disconnect Method   This setting can be used to minimize the time spent on live connections to the Async gateway. The options are explained in Table 15.1.

	OPTION	FUNCTION
T A B L E 15.1 *Disconnect Method Options*	When All Updates Are Received	This option keeps the GroupWise Remote connection open until all responses have been received. However, even when a remote user chooses this disconnect method, the setting may be overridden by the Minimum Idle Time option in the remote user profile. In most cases, this option should only be used when the length of the connection time is not an issue (for example, when users dial in from a local phone number and when demand for Async gateway connections is low). If a user's requests cannot be processed quickly, the user should choose a different disconnect method.
	Do Not Wait for Responses	This option forces disconnection as soon as requests are uploaded. When this method is used, the user must reconnect later in order to receive responses. This method should be used when it takes several minutes (or longer) for responses to be processed by the GroupWise system. As you decide whether users should select this method, you need to balance the telephone toll savings against the users' willingness to connect twice.
	Manually	This allows the user to disconnect manually. The user will remain connected indefinitely (unless the connection is terminated by the gateway or manually by the user).

NETWORK CONNECTIONS

Network connections are very useful for synchronizing a remote mailbox with a master mailbox and for downloading the address book. Travelers often use network connections to update their In Box, Out Box, and Calendar prior to leaving for a business trip. This eliminates the need for a lengthy long-distance telephone connection when they arrive at the hotel. Network connections process requests much faster than modem connections.

Another common use of network connections is when a traveling GroupWise Remote user visits another company site that is also part of the same GroupWise system. He or she can use a network connection to connect to any post office at the other site. When she uploads requests to the local post office, the post office server and message server will route her request to her home post office and deliver requests back to her.

The Network Connection dialog box is shown in Figure 15.5.

F I G U R E 15.5

Network Connection Dialog Box

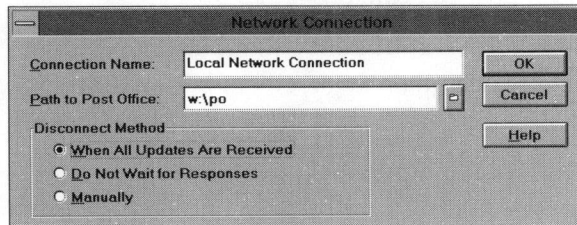

Network Connection

Connection Name: Local Network Connection

Path to Post Office: w:\po

Disconnect Method
- ◉ When All Updates Are Received
- ○ Do Not Wait for Responses
- ○ Manually

OK   Cancel   Help

A network connection definition consists of the following:

Connection Name   This is the name of the connection. It is determined by the user.

Path to Post Office   This is the path to the user's home post office or to any other post office in the GroupWise system. Typically, users enter the path their home post offices when they update their remote mailboxes and download the address book.

TIP

If an organization has a standard drive mapping to the GroupWise post office directory (for example, Y:\PO), using that drive mapping would make a network connection valid anywhere in the GroupWise system.

User Training

One of the keys to a successful rollout of GroupWise Remote is an effective training program. This section contains the important topics for a good training session when you roll out GroupWise Remote to your users. Of course, users should first learn how to use the regular GroupWise client. The following discussion deals with issues that are specific to the use and operation of the GroupWise Remote client.

UNSUPPORTED FEATURES IN GROUPWISE REMOTE

There are only a few GroupWise features that are unavailable to remote users:

Proxy   The proxy feature lets users read from other users' master mailboxes. A live network connection to a post office is needed so users can view the portions of others' mailboxes to which they have been granted access rights. The proxy feature cannot be used with GroupWise Remote.

Busy Searches   For the same reasons that proxy is not supported, busy searching other users' calendar information cannot be performed using the GroupWise Remote client.

Archiving   The GroupWise archive feature allows users to keep their messages in an archive message store on a local drive or on an assigned network drive instead of in the post office message store. This cannot be done using GroupWise Remote.

CREATING A MESSAGE

GroupWise Remote users perform exactly the same steps for creating a message with the Remote client as they would use in the network GroupWise client. However, when a user chooses Send, the message is not immediately sent. Instead, it is stored in a pending requests queue a connection to the system is initiated by the user. When a connection is made, all messages and requests held in the pending requests queue are sent to the GroupWise system for processing.

Pending requests can be viewed in the GroupWise Remote client by choosing the Pending Requests option from the Remote drop-down menu.

TIP

REQUESTING ITEMS FROM THE MASTER MAILBOX

The Send/Receive option is used to request items from a master mailbox. Users can request items from the In Box, Out Box, and Trash. Users can select the types of items that they want downloaded to their Remote mailbox, such as message items, folders, the address book, and rules.

The Send/Receive dialog box is shown in Figure 15.6.

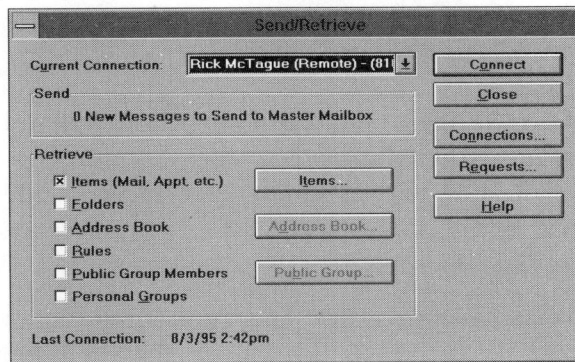

MINIMIZING CONNECTION TIME

In terms of minimizing the expense of connection time, a little user-training can go a long way. There are several options in the Send/Receive dialog box that can help reduce download time. When users select the check box next to Items in the Send Receive dialog box and then click on the Items button, they are given several more options to narrow down the types of items they want to retrieve. The Select Items to Retrieve dialog box is shown in Figure 15.7.

File attachments can make downloading items from the master mailbox extremely time-consuming. (Custom views can also be very large and can increase the download time.) The Item Size Limits field lets users specify how much information they want to receive. To give you an idea of how much time it takes to download items, if I connect to my GroupWise system and download 500K of information, it takes about 7 to 8 minutes with a 14.4 Kbps modem. If I'm downloading messages without large file attachments, I can download 30–40K of information in only a minute or two—once the gateway receives the response and the download begins.

F I G U R E 15.7

*Select Items to Retrieve
Dialog Box*

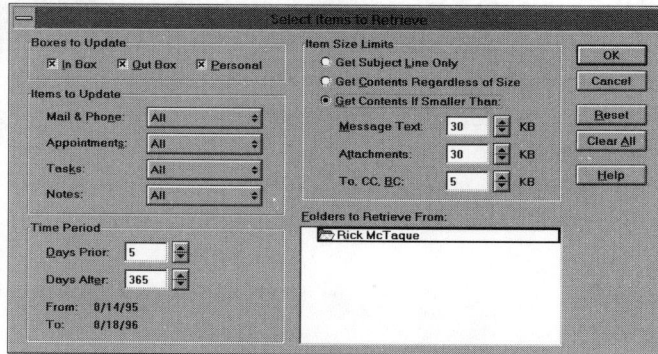

Get Subject Line Only   This option allows users to download only the subject lines of the mail in their master mailboxes. Once they have downloaded the subject lines, they can determine which items warrant further attention and then make specific requests for only those items. This technique minimizes download time, but it involves multiple connections to the Async gateway.

Get Contents Regardless of Size   This option causes entire messages to be downloaded, along with all file attachments. Selecting this option results in the longest connection times. File attachments can be huge. If every GroupWise Remote user at a large company were to download a lengthy company newsletter and *all* of its file attachments, you can only imagine the burden this would place on an Async gateway (not to mention the phone bill the company would incur). You should instruct remote users to use discretion when they download file attachments.

Get Contents if Smaller Than   This option lets users find a happy medium between the previous two options. For example, users might set this option to cause all messages and file attachments under 100K to be downloaded. They would then probably get most file attachments, but the largest ones would not be downloaded. If they then decide that they need to get one of the larger file attachments, they can initiate a request for that attachment only. Users can tell when an attachment has not been downloaded because the icon is dim, as illustrated in Figure 15.8.

FIGURE 15.8

*File Attachments —
Downloaded versus Not
Downloaded*

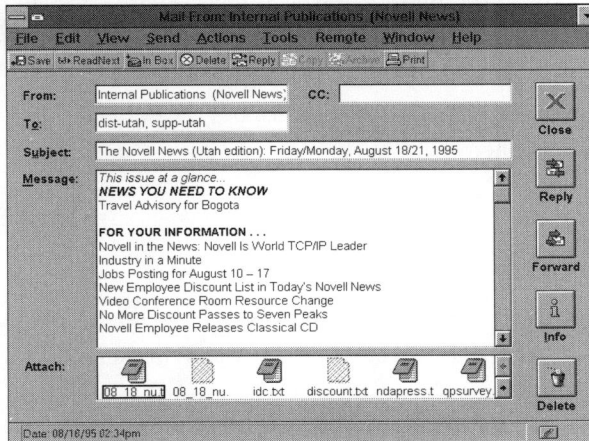

GroupWise Remote Troubleshooting

This section explains some of the most common things to look for when users experience problems with GroupWise Remote.

MODEM PROBLEMS

Many of the problems users encounter with GroupWise Remote are caused by modems not correctly configured or that fail to maintain connections. Here are some things to try when users have difficulty connecting to the system:

▶ Lower the selected baud rate to see if the modems will synchronize.

▶ Change Auto Baud Detect mode to off.

▶ Make sure flow control is set to CTS/RTS.

▶ Disable data compression on the modem.

▶ Create a new modem initialization string (refer to your modem's documentation).

For details on these troubleshooting techniques, refer to "Creating or Editing a Modem Definition" and "Troubleshooting Modems" in the *GroupWise 4.1 Async Gateway Guide*, which comes with the software.

If the modems connect and synchronize but the connection is abruptly terminated, check the following items:

▶ Make sure the Gateway Login ID and Gateway password are set correctly in GroupWise Remote preferences.

▶ Make sure that a password has been set on the master mailbox and that the password is entered correctly in the GroupWise Remote preferences.

▶ Make sure the right domain and post office names have been entered for the user.

GroupWise Remote creates a log file named REMOTE*x*.LOG (where *x* equals 1, 2, or 3). This file keeps track of the Remote connections, and it may provide clues as to why a connection or a specific request is failing. This ASCII file can be found in the default GroupWise Remote directory.

DATABASE PROBLEMS

If remote users report that they cannot access their In Box or specific messages, they may be experiencing problems with the Remote message store databases (USER.DB and MSG.DB). You can run Check GroupWise (OFCHECK.EXE) to examine the Remote databases. You can fix problems with the databases, rebuild the databases, check for orphaned file attachments, and reclaim disk space by using Check GroupWise.

To rebuild a database, the user must have at least as much free disk space as the MSG.DB file currently occupies.

TIP

These types of problems usually need to be addressed quickly because they involve loss data and because users may not be able to access critical information in the Remote mailbox. It is especially important for routine GroupWise Remote users to have access to the Check GroupWise program.

If a database cannot be recovered, the GroupWise Remote user can request all items from the master mailbox and get a replica of the data that exists in the master mailbox at the time. Items that have been deleted from the master mailbox (for example, if you have set an automatic deletion period) would be lost.

DUPLICATE USERS IN THE REMOTE ADDRESS BOOK

One of the most common problems encountered with GroupWise Remote is duplicate user information appearing in the remote address book. Here's an explanation of why this sometimes occurs and how you can fix the problem.

When a remote user initially downloads the address book, duplicate users are not listed in the remote address book. Suppose that after the address book has been download by the remote user, the system administrator goes into GroupWise Admin and changes some of the information for a user named David. David then sends a message to Keith, who is a routine GroupWise Remote user. When Keith downloads David's message, GroupWise Remote checks the message header and—because some of David's information has changed—GroupWise Remote thinks that the message came from a user not already listed in the address book. Therefore, GroupWise Remote adds David's information to the remote address book again. The next time Keith uses the address book to send a message to David, David will be listed twice.

If you encounter this problem with your GroupWise Remote users, ask them to delete the WPROF.DB file and then download the address book again. This process creates a new WPROF.DB file with the information contained in the remote user's post office database.

Summary

In this section, you learned how to install GroupWise Remote, how to configure it for a remote workstation, and how to troubleshoot problems that may occur.

The CD-ROM that comes with this book contains these additional documents that relate to GroupWise Remote:

- DOSREM.TT — GroupWise 4.1 DOS Remote Client

- WINREM.TT — GroupWise 4.1 Windows Remote Client

- MACREM.TT — GroupWise 4.1 Macintosh Remote Client

- REMNET.TT — Troubleshooting Remote Network Connections

- MULTREM.TT — GroupWise 4.1 Remote Clients: Multiple Remote Clients Accessing Mail

Solution to Part VI Scenario

NoCWACs has decided to take the following steps to implement GroupWise Remote for its employees and agents.

Another file server will be obtained for Building C to house an additional post office for the agents. A GroupWise post office called AGENTS will be created in the SERVICES domain. This post office will house the 250 independent agents' mailboxes.

For now, NoCWACs will use the existing Async gateway in the SERVICES domain to support the GroupWise Remote users. Because that gateway is currently servicing the domain-to-domain communication between Salt Lake City and Butte, a Digiboard with eight additional modems will be added to accommodate the GroupWise Remote employees. Of these eight phone lines, six will be dedicated to supporting the independent agents who exclusively use GroupWise Remote for electronic messaging. The other two will be set up to support users who travel on business. IS should monitor the message traffic and keep track of the calls that are rejected due to busy signals. This will help IS make plans for adding more modems — or possibly another Async gateway — if necessary (for example, if the GroupWise Remote traffic becomes disruptive to the domain-to-domain Async gateway traffic).

The new configuration is shown in Figure VI.1.

ADVANTAGES

▶ Because the agents who use GroupWise Remote are all in the same post office, any messages that they send among themselves will be handled by a single message server and a single post office server. This configuration will allow for very fast processing of their requests and responses.

▶ NoCWACs users who travel on business will have a maximum of two domain hops between the receiving Async gateway and their post office. This should provide adequate request-and-response performance.

FIGURE VI.I

Configuration of NoCWACs System to Support GroupWise Remote

NoCWACs Headquarters

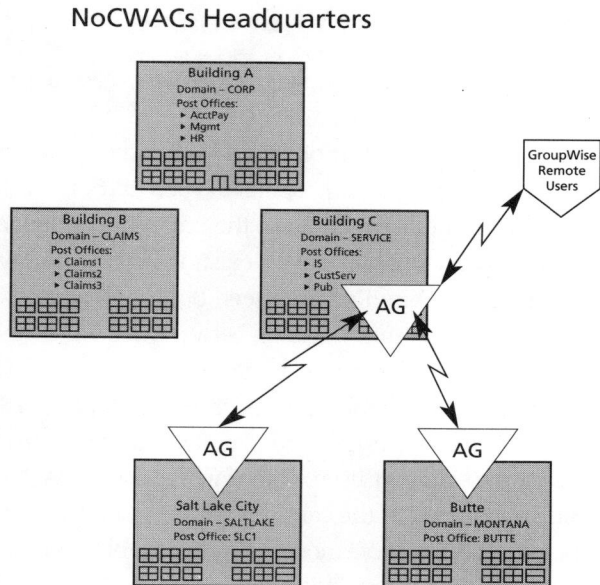

Building A
Domain – CORP
Post Offices:
▸ AcctPay
▸ Mgmt
▸ HR

Building B
Domain – CLAIMS
Post Offices:
▸ Claims1
▸ Claims2
▸ Claims3

Building C
Domain – SERVICE
Post Offices:
▸ IS
▸ CustServ
▸ Pub

GroupWise Remote Users

AG

AG

AG

Salt Lake City
Domain – SALTLAKE
Post Office: SLC1

Butte
Domain – MONTANA
Post Office: BUTTE

ADDITIONAL CONSIDERATIONS

▸ At this point, the SERVICES domain is acting as a hub domain for messages to and from the Salt Lake City and Butte regional offices. It is also handling the routing of all GroupWise Remote traffic. IS should consider establishing a backup message server for the SERVICES domain so that a message server failure will not disrupt communications.

▸ Another option would be to add the agents to either the IS post office or to the PUB post office, since these two post offices currently support a fairly small number of users.

PART VII

Using External Domains and Combining GroupWise Systems

In Parts IV through VI, you learned how to configure a multidomain GroupWise system, how to connect domains through an Async gateway connection, and how to enable support for GroupWise Remote.

There are two more important topics that relate to configuring multiple domain GroupWise systems. The first is setup and use of external domains. External domains are used to connect separate GroupWise systems together and to make the connection invisible to the users in the different systems. I discuss external domains in Chapter 17. The second is how to consolidate two GroupWise systems into a single system. The process of consolidating GroupWise systems involves first connecting the systems with external domain definitions and then merging the domains from one system into the other. I explain consolidating systems in Chapter 18.

Scenario for Part VII

NoCWACs was so pleased with the way you handled the GroupWise implementation that you were given several months of paid vacation. You have just returned to work, and in the interim two major events occurred that will have a significant impact on NoCWACs' GroupWise system.

First, NoCWACs has established a physicians council that consists of 50 physicians located in two major medical centers in the intermountain western region of the United States. This council will consult with NoCWACs to help determine how to structure health insurance policies and policy coverages. Thirty of the physicians are affiliated with the University of Northern Utah Medical Center (UNUMED), located in Ogden, Utah. The other 20 physicians are based in the Denver Regional Medical Center (DRMC). UNUMED runs a GroupWise system within the medical center. The DRMC does not have an established e-mail system.

Second, NoCWACs entered the dental insurance business by acquiring Denver Dental Insurance, Incorporated (DDI). DDI is currently set up as a two-domain GroupWise system. The company is based in Denver.

As you read the chapters in Part VII, consider how you would modify the existing GroupWise system to adapt to these organizational changes.

External GroupWise Domains

You have already learned how to create a multidomain GroupWise system that consists of a primary domain and one or more secondary domains. You should also now understand how to link domains together.

In a GroupWise system with only a primary domain and secondary domains, you can use centralized or distributed administration (or both) to perform administration tasks. When a change is made in one domain, information about the change is distributed to the primary and all secondary domains in the system through automatic directory synchronization.

There may be circumstances where GroupWise users in two separate GroupWise systems need to communicate with each other. When that is the case, you can use *external* GroupWise domains for communication between the two distinct GroupWise systems. Here are some of the common situations where external GroupWise domains are useful:

▸ Two separate companies (or other organizations), both running GroupWise systems, need to communicate with each other.

▸ Two divisions in the same organization maintain separate GroupWise systems, and users in the two systems need to communicate with GroupWise.

▸ Separate government agencies that run GroupWise need to communicate with each other.

▸ Separate electronic messaging administration is mandated. For example, some departments within the same organization may need their e-mail systems to be isolated and administered separately for security reasons.

▸ Visibility of certain users must be controlled.

This chapter will explain how to define external domains, how to link to them, how to exchange user lists between systems, and how to keep the user lists current.

Using External Domains

External domains allow you to connect your GroupWise system to another GroupWise system. When you define an external system's domains, post offices, and users in your GroupWise system, your users can send messages to users in the other system without any additional steps. They can simply select users in the external system from your system's address book.

Figure 16.1 illustrates two GroupWise systems for two different companies. External domain definitions can be used to establish communication between these two systems.

F I G U R E 16.1

*Separate GroupWise
Systems*

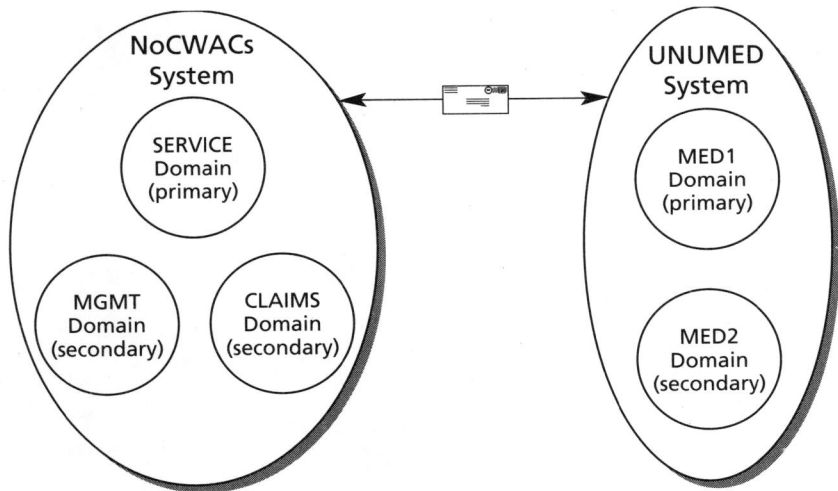

When you connect your system to another GroupWise system, you *define* the other system's domains, post offices, and users in your system.

Notice that I did not use the word *create*. The information for the external system is entered into your system's databases for the sole purpose of addressing messages to users in the other system. No directories or databases are created on the file servers in your system when you define an external domain.

External domains differ from primary and secondary domains in many ways. Within your system, primary and secondary domains are *created*. They have directory structures and databases on your file servers. They are administered by someone in your system, and automatic directory synchronization occurs whenever you make changes in the domains. External domains, on the other hand, are not created but rather *defined.* No directory structures or databases are added to your file servers. You have no administrative rights to external domains, and automatic directory synchronization does not occur for external domains. When a change is made to an external domain by the external system's administrator, you must manually make that change in your external system definition. Conversely, when you make a change in one of your domains, that change must be made manually in the external system by that system's administrator.

There are several steps involved in connecting to (and maintaining communication with) an external GroupWise system. These steps include:

▶ Defining the external system's domains in your system

▶ Defining the external system's post offices in your system

▶ Establishing a physical connection to the external system and defining links to the external domains

▶ Defining the users in the external domain

▶ Developing a strategy for keeping the external domain's addressing information up-to-date

(The external domain's system administrator must also perform these same steps in the external system to enable and maintain communication with your system.) I explain all of these procedures in this chapter.

NOTE

In this chapter, I assume that you want to make all users in the external system visible to all users in your system. If you merely want to connect the two systems, you would only need to define the external domains and establish a link between the systems. If those are the only steps you take, users will need to use explicit addressing when they send messages between the two systems.

Defining the External System's Domains

You need to decide how the external system will connect to your system. You may decide to have one domain in your system connect to the external system, or you may connect more than one domain in your system to the external system. If you decide to have more than one domain connect to the other system, you need to determine which domains in the external system your domains will connect to.

In Figure 16.2, NoCWACs' primary domain, SERVICE, serves as the connecting point to UNUMED's GroupWise system (an external system). All messages sent from NoCWACs' secondary domains will be routed through the SERVICE domain. The secondary domains all have indirect links to UNUMED's domains.

FIGURE 16.2

Connecting Two Systems

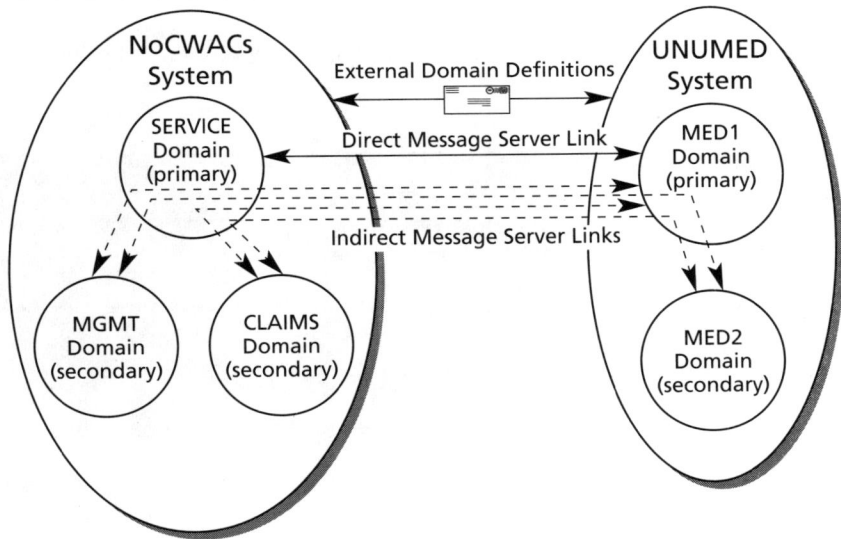

NoCWACs
System

External Domain Definitions

UNUMED
System

SERVICE
Domain
(primary)

Direct Message Server Link

MED1
Domain
(primary)

Indirect Message Server Links

MGMT
Domain
(secondary)

CLAIMS
Domain
(secondary)

MED2
Domain
(secondary)

This is just one possible configuration. There is no reason why a secondary domain in NoCWACs' system could not link directly to a domain in UNUMED's system.

NOTE

External domains can be linked to your system with the same types of links available for connecting primary and secondary domains — direct, indirect, or gateway.

In this chapter, I assume that you will use a gateway link to the external system if you don't already have some type of physical network connection to that system.

Defining an external domain is very similar to defining a secondary domain. The steps are as follows:

1 • Run GroupWise Admin from the primary domain.

2 • Choose Create.

3 • Choose Domain.

4 • Enter the name of the external domain.

5 • Choose Domain Type. The dialog box shown in Figure 16.3 will appear.

FIGURE 16.3

Domain Information Dialog Box

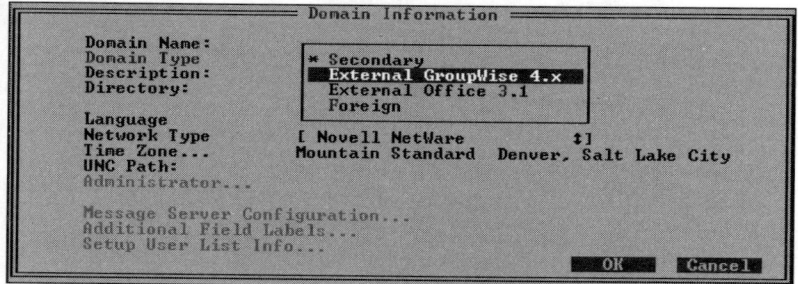

```
                              Domain Information
        Domain Name:
        Domain Type        * Secondary
        Description:         External GroupWise 4.x
        Directory:          External Office 3.1
                            Foreign
        Language
        Network Type       [ Novell NetWare        ↕]
        Time Zone...       Mountain Standard  Denver, Salt Lake City
        UNC Path:
        Administrator...

        Message Server Configuration...
        Additional Field Labels...
        Setup User List Info...
                                                    OK      Cancel
```

6 • Select External GroupWise 4.*x*.

7 • Select the time zone where the external domain is located.

8 • Fill in the UNC path if you will be using a direct message server link to the external system and if you are using the NLM message server. Otherwise, leave this field blank.

9 • Choose OK.

The new domain will appear in GroupWise Admin as an External 4.*x* domain. You should repeat the above steps for each domain in the external system that contains users whom you want to appear in your system's address book. Figure 16.4 shows how NoCWACs' system looks after the external domains have been defined. The broken lines indicate that the domains are *defined* in the WPDOMAIN.DB files, but no domains have actually been *created* within the NoCWACs GroupWise system.

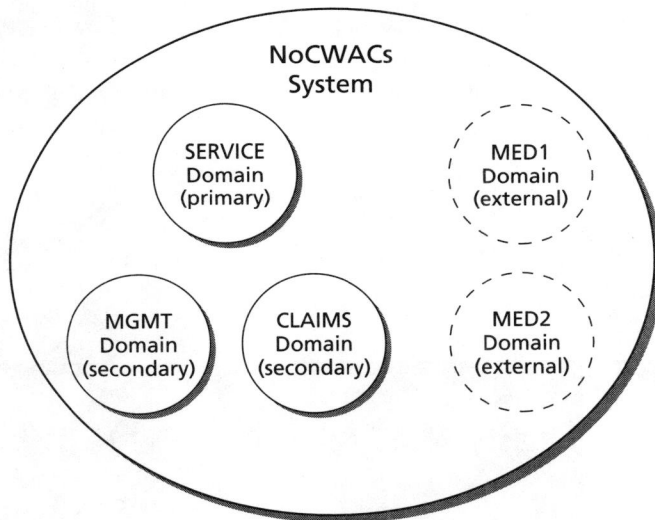

Notice that you are not prompted to copy software to the new domain, as you would have had to do if you were creating a secondary domain. It is important to remember that you are only *defining* the other system's information, not actually creating it.

Once an external domain has been defined, you should define the links between your domain and the external domain. After the links are defined, users will be able to send messages to the other system using explicit GroupWise addressing. (See Chapter 2 for an explanation of explicit addressing.) However, if you want users in your system to be able to use the address book to send messages to the other system, you need to define the post offices and users that belong to each external domain.

Defining an External System's Post Offices

After an external domain has been defined, you can define the post offices that are located in that domain. The steps for defining a post office in an external domain are identical to the steps for creating a post office in a primary or secondary domain, except you do not enter any path to the external post office. Just as no new databases are created when you define external domains, no post office directory structures or databases are created.

The steps for defining an external post office are as follows:

1 • Running GroupWise Admin in the primary domain, highlight the external domain.

2 • Select Create.

3 • Select Post Office. The dialog box shown in Figure 16.5 will appear.

F I G U R E 16.5

*Post Office Information
Dialog Box*

```
═════════════════════ Post Office Information ═════════════════════
   Domain           [ MED1                                       ↓]
   Post Office Name:
   Description
   Directory:

   Language              [ English - US              ↓]
   Network Type          [ Novell NetWare            ↓]
   Time Zone...          Mountain Standard  Denver, Salt Lake City
   UNC Path:

   Default Security Level       [ LOW  ↓]
   [ ] Disable Post Office
   Build USERID.FIL    Alias...                    OK    Cancel
```

4 • Enter the name of the post office.

5 • Enter the time zone in which the post office is located.

6 • Select OK.

Notice in Figure 16.5 that the Directory option is not available. A directory to the external system's post office is unnecessary because all messages addressed to users in that post office will be routed by the external domain.

The post office name you enter in Step 4 must match the name of the post office in the external system. Keep in mind that you are defining the post office names for message-addressing purposes. If the name does not match exactly, the address is incorrect.

Once you have defined the post offices for each external domain, you need to define the users in each post office.

Defining an External System's Users

You need to define the users in the external system if they are to appear in your system's address book. If you are only defining a few users in the external system, you can enter them manually. However, if you are defining a large number of users in the external system, you should import them from a file created by the external system's administrator. The users in the external system will probably want use their own address book to send messages to users in your system, so you will need to export your users' information to the external system's administrator, as well. In Figure 16.6, NoCWACs has created three export files that will be imported into the UNUMED system. UNUMED will also create export files for NoCWACs to import.

TIP

If you have domains or post offices in your system that you do not want to export, you should export your files at the domain or post office level rather than the system level. Use descriptive filenames for any domains or post offices you import and export.

GroupWise can export files into two different formats: ASCII and WordPerfect Office Notebook. ASCII files are used more frequently. WordPerfect Office Notebook files are commonly used when connecting to WordPerfect Office 3.1 systems.

IMPORTANT

ASCII files should not be modified with a text editor after exporting, because the text editor could cause the lines to wrap incorrectly, causing the import to fail.

FIGURE   16.6

Exchanging Directory
Information

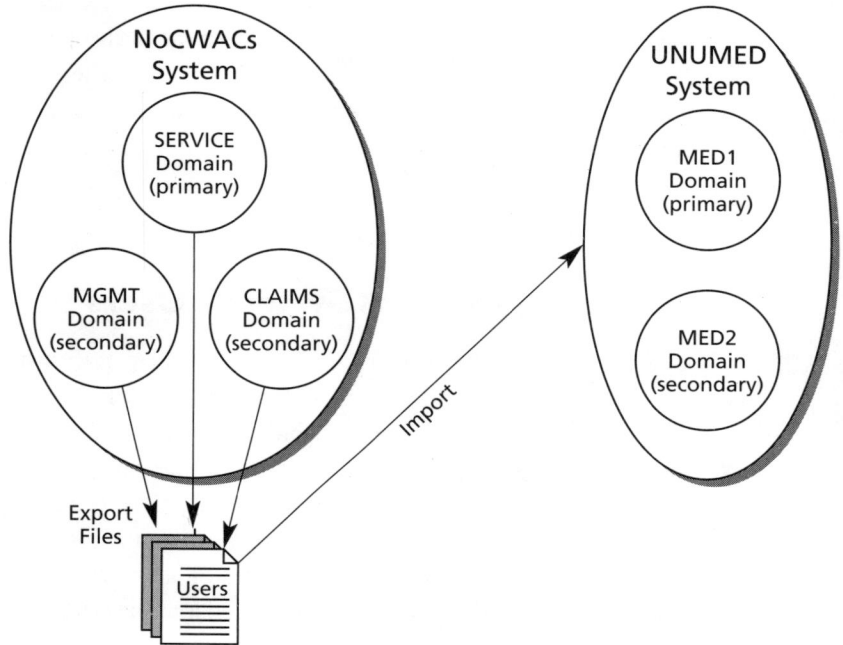

EXPORTING USER INFORMATION

You can export users' information at the system level, the domain level, or the post office level. If you export at the system level, information on all users in the entire system will be exported. If you export at the domain or post office level, you should use descriptive filenames so it will be clear exactly which users' information is contained in the files. The steps to export a user list are as follows:

1 • From the main GroupWise Admin screen, highlight the system, a specific domain, or a post office.

2 • Choose File.

3 • Choose Export.

4 • Select the appropriate format (WordPerfect Office Notebook or ASCII Text File).

5 • Select Users. The dialog box shown in Figure 16.7 will appear.

```
═══════════ Export Users to ASCII Text File ═══════════
Domain.PO [ Domain1                                      ↓]
┌──────────────────────────────────────────────────────────┐
│ 1. File Name:  C:\DOM1.TXT                                │
└──────────────────────────────────────────────────────────┘
┌Fields────────────────────────────────────────────────────┐
│ 2. [X] Domain Name      7. [ ] Phone       N. [ ] Fax Number │
│ 3. [X] Post Office Name 8. [ ] Department  U. [ ] Visibility │
│ 4. [X] User ID          9. [ ] Title       X. [ ] Expire Date │
│ 5. [X] First Name       K. [X] Network ID I. [ ] FID        │
│ 6. [X] Last Name        A. [ ] Acct ID                      │
└──────────────────────────────────────────────────────────┘
┌Additional Fields─────────────────────────────────────────┐
│      [ ] User Defined  1        [ ] User Defined  6        │
│      [ ] User Defined  2        [ ] User Defined  7        │
│      [ ] User Defined  3        [ ] User Defined  8        │
│      [ ] User Defined  4        [ ] User Defined  9        │
│      [ ] User Defined  5        [ ] User Defined 10        │
└──────────────────────────────────────────────────────────┘
 List Files = F5                           OK      Cancel
```

6 • The recommended fields should already be selected for you. Select any additional user fields that you want to export.

At a minimum, you should export the required user fields—Domain Name, Post Office Name, and User ID. I recommend that you also export First Name, Last Name, and Network ID. The Additional Fields are custom fields that can be defined by the administrator and would not normally be used when exporting files to external domains.

7 • Choose File Name.

8 • Enter the path and filename of the export file.

9 • Choose OK.

> **You can also export resource objects if you want the external system to be able to see your system's resources.**
>
> **NOTE**

IMPORTING USER INFORMATION

When you have obtained an export file from the other GroupWise system's administrator, go through the following steps to import that file into your system:

1 • From the main GroupWise Admin screen, choose File.

2 • Choose Import.

3 • Choose the appropriate file format. An Import dialog box similar to the one shown in Figure 16.8 should appear.

*Import ASCII Text File
Dialog Box*

```
================= Import ASCII Text File =================
1. FileName:
 ┌Method──────────────────────┐  ┌Object──────────────────┐
 │ 2. < > Automatic            │  │ 4. <I> Users            │
 │ 3. <I> Interactive          │  │ 5. < > Resources        │
 └─────────────────────────────┘  └─────────────────────────┘
 ┌6. [ ] Override Domain.PO Specified in Import File ──────────
 │ Import to Domain.PO [ Domain]                          ↓↑
 └──────────────────────────────────────────────────────────
   List Files = F5                      Import        Close
```

4 • Choose File Name.

5 • Enter the complete path and filename.

6 • Choose Automatic or Interactive.

An *automatic import* will import all information without requiring any input from you. An *interactive import* will let you select exactly which users you want to import. If you know that you want all of the information from the export file, you should select Automatic.

NOTE

If an import file contains records that are identical to records already in the system, the record in the import file will be ignored. If you are importing resources, you should make sure that the users who own the resources have already been imported.

7 • Verify that Users has been selected.

8 • Choose Import.

9 • Choose Continue when you see the screen showing the results.

10 • Repeat the above steps for each file you wish to import.

All objects will be automatically imported into the external domain and post office that you defined previously.

IMPORTANT

You should not select the Override Domain.PO option when defining information imported from an external system. This feature would cause all objects to be placed into whichever domain or post office happened to be highlighted when you started the import process. Remember—you are defining the external system's information for addressing purposes. If users are imported into the wrong post office, their addresses will be incorrect. The addresses for external users must match their domains and post offices in the external system exactly.

Establishing a Connection and Defining Links

Once you have defined an external domain, you must define the link between your system and the external domain. The link must be created from both directions. In other words, you need to define the link from your system to the external domain, and the external domain's administrator must define the link to your system.

The process for defining a link to an external domain is exactly the same as defining a link to a secondary domain.

1 • Highlight the domain that will link to the external domain.

2 • Choose Actions.

3 • Choose Edit.

4 • Choose Message Server Configuration.

5 • Choose Network Links.

6 • Highlight the external domain.

7 • Choose Edit Link.

8 • Select the correct link type—direct, indirect, or gateway.

9 • Choose OK.

10 • Choose Build CSI File to alert the message server of the change.

11 • Choose OK.

Repeat the above steps for each domain in your system that contains users who will need to send messages to external systems.

Maintaining the Directories

At the time you import users and resources from an external system, the addressing information should all be up-to-date.

However, as I mentioned earlier, automatic directory synchronization does not take place in external domains. Because changes occur frequently in GroupWise systems, addressing information for objects in the external system will eventually become obsolete. For example, if the administrator for the external system adds, deletes, or moves a user, your information about that user will not be accurate.

You need to work with external systems' administrators to establish procedures for keeping the address book current. It is very likely that you will have to exchange export files on a regular basis.

Message Flow Between External Domains

The message flow between external domains and other domains is exactly the same as the message flow between primary and secondary domains in a GroupWise system. Refer to Chapter 10 for information about message flow between domains linked by direct and indirect links. Refer to Chapter 13 for information about message flow between domains connected by gateway links.

Summary

In this chapter you learned how external domains work. Understanding external domains is crucial when you are consolidating GroupWise systems. Consolidation of GroupWise systems is the subject of Chapter 17.

Combining GroupWise Systems

In Chapter 16, you learned how to connect separate GroupWise systems by using external domains. Sometimes, however, a connection with external domains is not enough. In those cases, you may determine that it would be best to consolidate the different systems. Before you can consolidate two separate GroupWise systems into a single GroupWise system, you first need to define external domains. Then you can merge those external domains into your system. In Chapter 17, I explain the steps involved in consolidating GroupWise systems.

When two systems are consolidated into a single system, one system takes over the other. Before you begin the process, there are two separate GroupWise systems—each with its own primary domain and, possibly, its own secondary domains. When the process is finished, the combined system has only one primary domain. All domains from the acquired system become secondary domains in the consolidated system.

NOTE

The merge-and-release processes explained in this section can also be used to move individual domains from one system to another. For example, if a company sells a division to another company, that division's domain could be released and then merged into the acquiring company's system. The two systems would, however, remain separate.

There are a two main advantages to having a combined system (as opposed to having two separate systems connected with external domains). Those advantages are:

▶ Before systems are consolidated, they must be maintained separately. After consolidation, centralized administration is possible.

▶ Before consolidation, external domains must be updated manually. After consolidation, directory synchronization occurs between the domains.

WARNING

When you consolidate GroupWise systems, you restructure system configurations significantly. Therefore, consolidation should only happen when it is absolutely necessary. You should back up everything completely before you begin the process. Be sure you have backups of the domain and post office databases so you can restore the systems to their original form if any problems should occur during consolidation.

Preparing to Consolidate

In the scenario for Part VII, NoCWACs has decided to diversify and enter the dental insurance business by acquiring Denver Dental Insurance, Incorporated (DDI). DDI has two existing domains: DDI1 and DDI2. DDI1 is the primary domain, and DDI2 is a secondary domain. Each domain has four post offices. NoCWACs' and DDI's configurations are shown in the illustrations throughout this chapter.

NoCWACs consists of three domains before the consolidation. Because NoCWACs has acquired DDI, the management of NoCWACs has decided to combine their GroupWise systems. The first step in combining systems is to define external domains. The acquired system's domains must be defined as external domains of the system that will endure (and vice versa). In the present case, NoCWACs should define the two DDI domains as external domains, and DDI should define the three domains in NoCWACs' system as external domains. Links should also be established for all domains. The procedure for defining external domains is explained in Chapter 16.

Figure 17.1 illustrates how the domains in both systems see the other domains in the systems after all external domains have been defined. The diagram shows how all other domains would be listed in the System window if you were to run GroupWise Admin for any one of the domains.

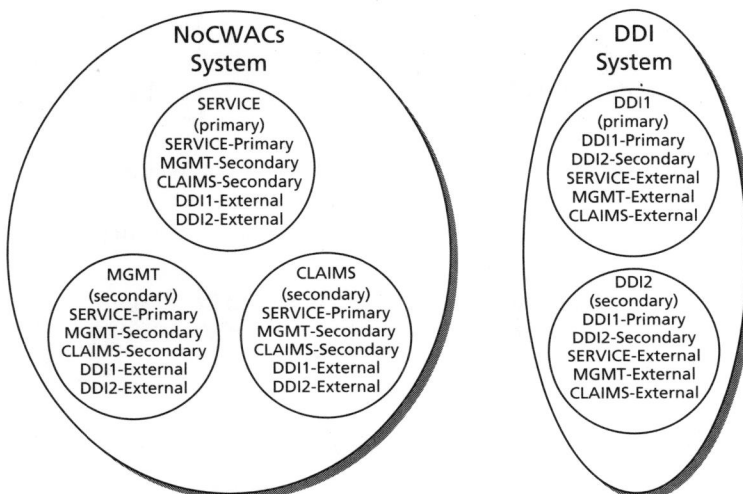

FIGURE 17.1

External Domain Definitions

NoCWACs System

SERVICE
(primary)
SERVICE-Primary
MGMT-Secondary
CLAIMS-Secondary
DDI1-External
DDI2-External

MGMT
(secondary)
SERVICE-Primary
MGMT-Secondary
CLAIMS-Secondary
DDI1-External
DDI2-External

CLAIMS
(secondary)
SERVICE-Primary
MGMT-Secondary
CLAIMS-Secondary
DDI1-External
DDI2-External

DDI System

DDI1
(primary)
DDI1-Primary
DDI2-Secondary
SERVICE-External
MGMT-External
CLAIMS-External

DDI2
(secondary)
DDI1-Primary
DDI2-Secondary
SERVICE-External
MGMT-External
CLAIMS-External

After all external domains have been defined and linked properly, there are several more steps you must take to consolidate the systems:

▶ If the acquired system is a multidomain system, it must first be broken up into several single-domain systems. You can accomplish this by *releasing* the secondary domains. In the previous example, DDI's primary domain (DDI1) would release the secondary domain (DDI2).

▶ The enduring system must *merge* each of the acquired domains into its system. In the example, NoCWACs would merge DDI1 and DDI2 into its system.

▶ All domain and post office databases in the consolidated system need to be rebuilt after the consolidation to ensure that all domains and post offices are properly connected and synchronized.

These steps will be explained in depth in this chapter.

Releasing Domains

Once you have determined that two systems are to be combined, you must break the system to be acquired system into independent, single-domain systems. In this chapter's scenario, DDI would be divided into two separate systems—each system consisting of only one domain. The act of separating a secondary domain from its primary domain is called *releasing*.

The steps for releasing a domain from a system are as follows:

1 • Run GroupWise Admin for the primary domain (e.g., DDI1).

2 • Highlight the secondary domain to be released (e.g., DDI2).

3 • Choose Actions.

4 • Choose Edit.

5 • Change domain-type from Secondary to External GroupWise 4.*x*. The dialog box shown in Figure 17.2 will appear.

F I G U R E 17.2

Release Domain Dialog Box

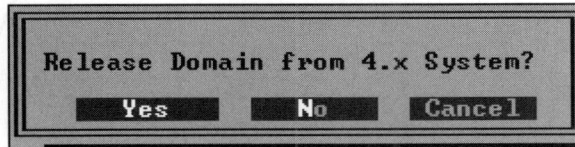

Release Domain from 4.x System?

Yes   No   Cancel

6 • Answer Yes when prompted to release the domain from the system.

7 • Verify that the path to the domain database is correct.

8 • If a password has been set for the domain, enter the password.

9 • Choose OK to release the domain.

10 • Choose Continue when the Domain Release is Complete dialog box appears.

The released domain will then appear as an external domain.

The released domain is now an independent GroupWise system. If you run GroupWise Admin for the released domain, you will see that it is a primary domain. All other domains are defined as externals. Figure 17.3 illustrates how each domain's WPDOMAIN.DB file lists all other domains in the systems. Notice that nothing has changed in the system that will endure (e.g., NoCWACs).

NOTE

In the steps above, I assume you have direct access through the network to the domain database (**WPDOMAIN.DB**) of the domain to be released. If you do not have direct network access to the **WPDOMAIN.DB** file—for example, if the primary and secondary domains communicate through a gateway—you can obtain a copy of the **WPDOMAIN.DB** file and place it in a local directory. In Step 7, you would then specify the path to the local directory. Once you have released the domain, you can copy the **WPDOMAIN.DB** file back to its original location.

NoCWACs System

SERVICE
(primary)
SERVICE-Primary
MGMT-Secondary
CLAIMS-Secondary
DDI1-External
DDI2-External

MGMT
(secondary)
SERVICE-Primary
MGMT-Secondary
CLAIMS-Secondary
DDI1-External
DDI2-External

CLAIMS
(secondary)
SERVICE-Primary
MGMT-Secondary
CLAIMS-Secondary
DDI1-External
DDI2-External

System

DDI1
(primary)
DDI1-Primary
DDI2-External
SERVICE-External
MGMT-External
CLAIMS-External

System

DDI2
(primary)
DDI1-External
DDI2-Primary
SERVICE-External
MGMT-External
CLAIMS-External

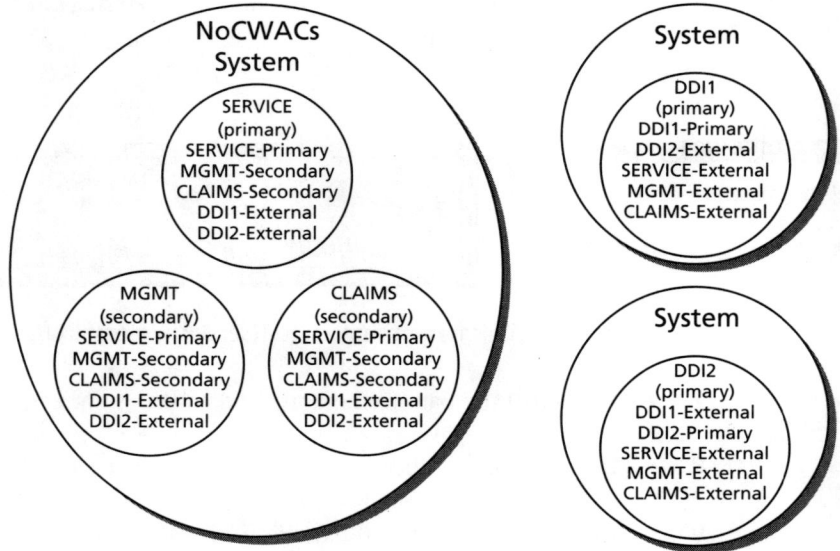

You need to repeat the release process until all domains to be merged into the new system are independent GroupWise systems. You must merge one domain at a time. You cannot merge a primary domain into your system if that primary domain still owns a secondary domain.

HOW IT WORKS

When a domain is released, the following processes occur:

1 • GroupWise Admin for the primary domain changes the primary domain's WPDOMAIN.DB to indicate that the secondary domain has become an external domain.

2 • GroupWise Admin changes the secondary domain's WPDOMAIN.DB, so that the secondary domain becomes a primary domain and the former primary becomes an external domain.

3 • GroupWise Admin updates the post office(s) in the original primary domain (i.e., the primary domain that released the secondary domain).

4 • GroupWise Admin replicates the change throughout the system.

The two primary domains recognize each other as external domains. Directory synchronization no longer occurs between those domains. However, the links between the domains do not change. If a direct network link connected the domains before they were separated, the direct network link definition still exists.

Merging the Domains

The merge process is basically the same as the release process in reverse. Follow these steps to merge a domain into a GroupWise system:

1 • Run GroupWise Admin for the primary domain acquiring a new domain.

2 • Highlight the domain to be incorporated into the system. It should currently be defined as an external domain.

3 • Choose Actions.

4 • Choose Edit.

5 • Select Domain Type.

6 • Change the domain-type from External 4.x to Secondary. The dialog box shown in Figure 17.4 will appear.

Merge Domain Dialog Box

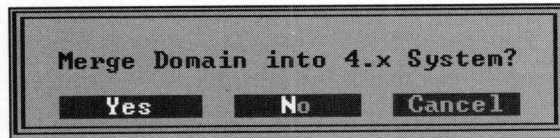

Merge Domain into 4.x System?

Yes   No   Cancel

7 • Answer Yes when prompted to merge the domain.

8 • Verify that the path to the WPDOMAIN.DB file is correct.

9 • If a password has been set on the domain you are merging, enter that password.

10 • Choose OK to merge the domain into your system.

In the steps above I assume that the machine running GroupWise Admin has direct network access to the WPDOMAIN.DB file of the domain to be acquired. If you do not have direct network access, you can obtain a copy of the WPDOMAIN.DB file, place it in a local directory, and perform the merge using that file. In Step 7, you would specify the path to the local directory. After the merge is complete, you can copy the acquired domain's WPDOMAIN.DB file back to its original location. Later in this chapter I explain how to *create* a domain when you don't have direct network access. This is a common situation that involves merging a domain into your system without a direct network connection.

IMPORTANT

If you are using a copy of a WPDOMAIN.DB file, you should make sure that no changes are made to the original WPDOMAIN.DB file in the meantime. You can ensure that no changes are made to the original WPDOMAIN.DB file by preventing GroupWise Admin from being used in that domain and by disabling the administration server process (ADS).

HOW IT WORKS

When a domain is merged into a system, these processes occur:

▸ GroupWise Admin changes the primary domain's WPDOMAIN.DB file to indicate that the merged domain has become a secondary domain instead of an external domain.

▸ GroupWise Admin modifies the merged domain to reflect its new status as a secondary domain.

▶ GroupWise Admin updates the post offices in the primary domain and sends an administrative message to all other secondary domains notifying them of the new domain in the system.

▶ GroupWise Admin synchronizes the WPDOMAIN.DB records of the two domains. The primary domain database receives post office and user information from the domain database of the domain to be acquired, and that domain receives information about the rest of the system from the primary domain database. When this process is complete, both databases contain identical information about the consolidated GroupWise system.

Rebuilding Databases

Once you have merged domains into your consolidated GroupWise system, you need to rebuild the domain and post office databases for the entire system. This is necessary because the administration server (ADS) process does not synchronize objects in the system during the merge-and-release processes. When you rebuild domains and post offices, you ensure that all objects in the system are synchronized throughout the system.

When you merge a domain into a system, only two domains immediately reflect updated information about the objects in the system—the primary domain and the domain that has been merged. Even though the other secondary domains are notified of the merged domain and its post offices through directory synchronization, they don't receive updated information about the objects that reside in the merged domain. Therefore, right after the merge process, only two domains contain completely accurate information about the objects in the system.

For example, suppose that NoCWACs merges DDI1 first. During that merge, DDI1 receives information about all of the objects in the system from the primary domain, and the primary domain receives information about all of DDI1's objects. The primary domain replicates the information about the new domain and its post offices to all of its secondary domains, but it does not replicate information about DDI1's *objects* to all of the existing secondary domains. The database-rebuilding process ensures that all domains are updated with information about all of the other domains' objects.

NOTE

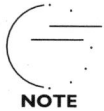

You cannot rebuild a domain database unless you have direct network write access to the **WPDOMAIN.DB** file. If you are merging domains into a system by using copies of the **WPDOMAIN.DB** files on local directories, you should rebuild the domain databases in the local directories before you place the **WPDOMAIN.DB** files back in their original locations.

REBUILDING DOMAIN DATABASES

The steps for rebuilding a domain database are as follows:

1 • Run GroupWise Admin for the primary domain.

2 • Highlight the domain whose database needs to be rebuilt.

3 • Choose Tools.

4 • Choose Database Maintenance.

5 • Choose Rebuild Database.

6 • Choose Yes to rebuild the database.

7 • Verify the path to the database.

8 • Choose OK.

The database will be rebuilt from the information contained in the primary domain database. In Chapter 19, I explain in more detail exactly what occurs when a database is rebuilt.

NOTE

While a database is being rebuilt, no other processes should be allowed to open the **WPDOMAIN.DB** file for the domain. You should disable any gateway processes running in that domain and you should also make sure that GroupWise Admin cannot be run for that domain.

REBUILDING THE POST OFFICE DATABASES

After each domain database has been rebuilt, you should rebuild the databases for all of the post offices in the system. This ensures that address books are correct throughout the system.

NOTE

If you performed the domain merge on copies of the WPDOMAIN.DB files, you should move those files back to their original locations in their domain directory structures before rebuilding the post office databases in those domains.

Follow these steps to rebuild a post office database:

1 • Run GroupWise Admin for the domain that owns the post office. (You cannot rebuild a secondary domain's post offices from the primary domain.)

2 • Highlight the post office whose database needs to be rebuilt.

3 • Select Tools.

4 • Select Database Maintenance.

5 • Choose Rebuild Database.

6 • Choose Yes to continue with the rebuild.

7 • Verify the path to the database.

8 • Choose OK.

NOTE

No processes should be allowed to access the WPHOST.DB file while it is being rebuilt. You should make sure that the administration server, the post office server, and the clients for the post office are disabled. You may wish to copy the WPHOST.DB file, rebuild it in a local directory, and then replace the original WPHOST.DB file with the rebuilt file. This helps to minimize downtime for the post office users.

Establishing a Secondary Domain in a Remote Site

Sometimes it is necessary to create a secondary domain in a remote site. For example, suppose that NoCWACs establishes a branch office in Cameron, Missouri but a direct network connection is not possible. NoCWACs wants to be able to communicate with this secondary domain through an Async gateway.

In that case, you would have a dilemma: You cannot create a secondary domain through an Async gateway link. Nor can you copy software from the primary domain to a secondary domain through an Async gateway link.

However, the merge-and-release process can be used to set up the secondary domain in the remote location.

There are three main steps involved in creating a secondary domain in a remote location:

▸ An independent GroupWise system needs to be set up in the remote location.

▸ The two systems need to be connected together using external GroupWise domain definitions and a gateway link.

▸ The system at the remote site needs to be merged into the main GroupWise system.

STEP 1:
SETTING UP AN INDEPENDENT GROUPWISE SYSTEM

The first step is to set up a fully functional GroupWise system in the remote location. The e-mail administrator in the remote location needs to complete these tasks:

1 • Install GroupWise Admin from diskettes.

2 • Install the message server software from diskettes.

3 • Install the client software to the domain from diskettes.

4 • Run GroupWise Admin and create a primary domain.

5 • Create all post offices for the domain and copy the client software to the post offices.

6 • (Optional) Add users to the system. (This could be done from the main GroupWise system through the Async gateway after the systems have been consolidated.)

7 • Enable the message server for the system.

8 • Install the Async gateway software from diskettes.

9 • Create the Async gateway in GroupWise Admin.

10 • Configure the Async gateway, including the general gateway information, the local domain profile, and the remote domain profile for the Async gateway at the main GroupWise site.

At this point, a fully functional GroupWise system consisting of a single primary domain exists in the remote site.

STEP 2:
CONNECTING THE SYSTEMS WITH EXTERNAL DOMAIN DEFINITIONS

The next step is to connect the GroupWise system at the main GroupWise site with the GroupWise system at the remote site.

1 • The e-mail administrator at the main site (e.g., NoCWACs) needs to configure a remote domain profile for the Async gateway in the remote site.

2 • The e-mail administrator at each site needs to configure an external domain in the other system. In the example, the NoCWACs administrator would define the Cameron site as an external GroupWise 4.*x* domain, and the administrator in Cameron would configure NoCWACs' domain as an external GroupWise domain.

3 • Both administrators need to define Async gateway message server links to the external domains.

NOTE

An administrator in a remote location could create all of a main system's domains as externals, but this is not necessary if the consolidation process is going to occur relatively soon. The remote domain will receive the information about all of the main system's secondary domains through the merge process that occurs later.

At this point, the two systems can communicate through the Async gateway link. The next step is to merge the systems into a single system so that the remote site becomes a secondary domain.

STEP 3:
MERGING THE SYSTEMS TOGETHER

Once a system in a remote site has been created and the two sites can communicate through external domain definitions and an Async gateway link, the two systems are ready to be consolidated. However, because the two systems cannot communicate through a live network link, the consolidation process involves a few extra steps. An administrator for the main system needs to obtain a copy of the domain database of the system at the remote location, and the merge needs to be performed on the copy. Afterwards, the merged domain database must be sent back to the remote site to replace the existing domain database. Here are the steps in detail:

1 • The administrator in the remote site sends a copy of the WPDOMAIN.DB file to the administrator at the main GroupWise site. If the two systems can communicate, the file could be sent as an attachment to an e-mail message.

2 • The administrator at the remote site should make sure that no changes occur to the WPDOMAIN.DB in the remote location until the new database has been returned. This means that GroupWise Admin should not be run at the remote site. The administration server should be disabled there.

3 • The main GroupWise system's administrator places the copy of the remote domain's WPDOMAIN.DB file in a location accessible to the primary domain's GroupWise Admin program.

4 • The main GroupWise system's administrator then performs the merge operation on the WPDOMAIN.DB file in the local directory. This is accomplished by specifying the local directory as the path to the WPDOMAIN.DB file.

5 • The main GroupWise system's administrator rebuilds the domain and post office databases for all other secondary domains in the main GroupWise system.

6 • The copy of the merged WPDOMAIN.DB file is then sent back to the system administrator at the remote site.

7 • The remote site's administrator replaces the original WPDOMAIN.DB file with the copy that was merged. At this point, the remote domain is a secondary domain.

8 • The remote site's administrator rebuilds all post office databases. This gives all local post offices complete and up-to-date information about the entire GroupWise system.

When this process is complete, the domain in the remote site is a secondary GroupWise domain. Automatic directory synchronization will occur through the Async gateway connection.

ALTERNATE METHOD FOR CREATING DOMAINS IN REMOTE LOCATIONS

There is another way to create secondary domains in remote locations. This method does not require merging domains; instead, part of the consolidation process is performed at the main site and then transported to the remote site. Here are the steps:

1 • At the main site, set up a file server that can be accessed through the network.

2 • Create a new secondary domain in the usual manner and copy the necessary software (GroupWise Admin, GroupWise clients, etc.) to that domain.

3 • Transport the server directory structure or the complete domain directory structure to the remote site.

4 • Install and configure the gateways at both sites.

5 • Define the gateway links from both sites.

6 • Run the gateways.

7 • Create the post offices and users at the remote site. These changes will be replicated to the main system through the functioning gateway.

The first method that I explained requires a qualified GroupWise administrator at the remote site who can install and configure a GroupWise system. The second method is often used when a qualified GroupWise administrator is not available at the remote location.

Summary

In this chapter you learned how to consolidate separate GroupWise systems. The next part of the book shifts focus. Rather than discussing setup methods and strategies, I introduce you to the day-to-day issues faced by an administrator once a system has been implemented.

Solution to Part VII Scenario

NoCWACs has decided to modify their GroupWise system as follows:

CONNECTION TO PHYSICIANS' COUNCIL

The IS department has decided to connect to UNUMED by defining an external domain and connecting to that domain through an Async gateway. Because the physicians' council will communicate exclusively with NoCWACs management, an OS/2 Async gateway will be established in the CORP domain, running on a dedicated OS/2 machine. This provides for the most efficient message-delivery (no extra domain transfers) and does not place an additional burden on the primary domain's message server or on the Async gateways in the primary domain.

User administration must be done manually because only some users in both systems can be defined. NoCWACs will need to define only the users in the physicians' council, and UNUMED will need to define only the key members of the Insurance Policy Committee and NoCWACs' management. A *public group* will be created for the physicians' council members, which should make for easy addressing by NoCWACs employees.

The 20 physicians who are affiliated with DRMC will use GroupWise Remote to communicate with NoCWACs' management. They will be set up with user accounts in the MGMT post office and will only be given post office visibility. A remote user profile will be established for the Async gateway in the CORP domain that will allow them to connect directly to the domain that houses the users with whom they need to communicate.

> **Additional GroupWise licenses will need to be purchased for the 20 physicians affiliated with DRMC.**

NOTE

NoCWACs anticipates establishing e-mail connectivity to the Internet. In the future, the 20 physicians with DRMC should be able to use the Internet to communicate with NoCWACs, and the 20 GroupWise licenses could then be used for NoCWACs employees. (Connecting to the Internet is covered in Chapter 22.)

DDI ACQUISITION

NoCWACs' management has decided that the two GroupWise domains currently at DDI should be merged into the NoCWACs GroupWise system as secondary domains. NoCWACs has already established direct network connections with DDI. Therefore, these two domains can readily be merged into the NoCWACs system. You will make them into secondary domains using the consolidation procedures explained in Chapter 17. Direct network links will be established between these two domains and the three domains at NoCWACs headquarters. Indirect links will be established through the SERVICES domain to the two regional offices in Salt Lake City and Butte.

The following diagram shows NoCWACs' system after these changes have been implemented:

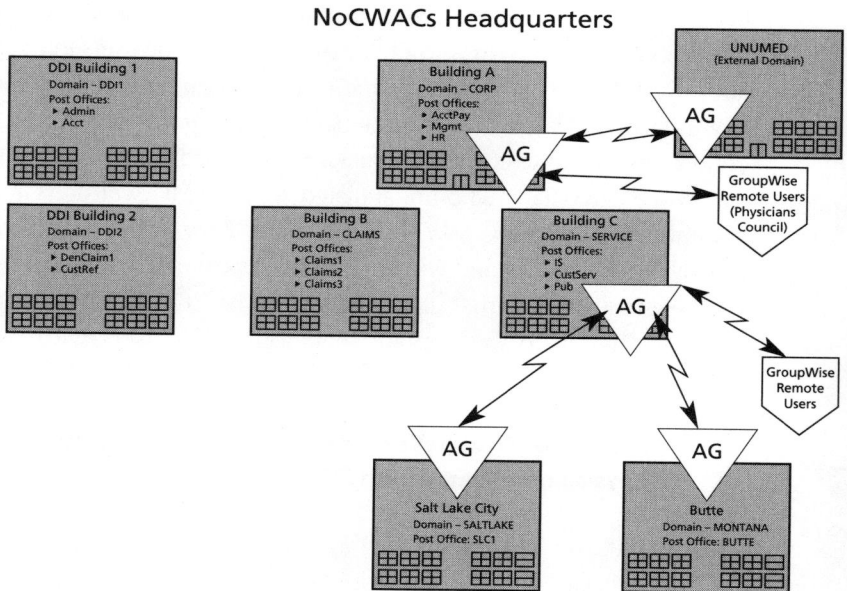

FIGURE VII.1

NoCWACs' New System Configuration

NoCWACs Headquarters

PART VIII

GroupWise User and Database Administration

Up to this point, I have focused on administration tasks related to system-level setup and configuration—such as setting up post offices, domains, and gateways, and making them all capable of communicating with each other.

In Part VIII, I will change the focus to tasks that you will perform as an administrator after the system is set up and running.

Chapter 18 explains how to perform user-related GroupWise administration tasks—such as renaming users and moving users from one location in the GroupWise system to another. Once you know how to move users, I will explain how this technique can be used to change the names of post offices or domains.

Another major duty of GroupWise administrators is to maintain databases. You will need to develop a strategy for maintaining the message store and directory store databases in your system. In Chapter 19, I explain how to use the Check GroupWise utility (known as OFCHECK) to maintain and repair GroupWise message store databases and how to use the options in the GroupWise Admin Tools menu to maintain directory store databases. I also explain strategies for backing up your GroupWise databases.

User-Related Administration Tasks

In previous chapters, I have focused on system-level administration tasks. In this chapter I change the focus to user-related administration tasks that you will be called on to perform once your GroupWise system is up and running.

Once your GroupWise system is functioning, there are myriad day-to-day administration tasks. In this chapter I explain how to perform the following user-related administration tasks:

► Setting user-environment options

► Terminating a GroupWise user's account

► Removing users from a GroupWise system

► Renaming users

► Moving users

In addition to outlining the steps for these tasks, I will discuss several preparatory measures, general principles, and guidelines that will make these tasks go smoothly.

GroupWise 4.x Setup Options

As a GroupWise system administrator, you will most likely need to establish certain user defaults at the system level. You will want to prevent users from modifying some of these defaults and allow them to change others.

You can use GroupWise Admin to set default user-options for all of the client programs in the system. For example, you may want to specify certain default locations for users' files or you may want to set a default message priority level for some or all of the users.

USING GROUPWISE ADMIN TO SET OPTIONS

By using the GroupWise 4.x Setup options in GroupWise Admin, you can set global defaults for the GroupWise client program. You can lock the options, or you can establish certain options as defaults and then allow users to reset the options at will from the Preferences menu in the GroupWise client.

Each option under the GroupWise 4.x Setup options menu is explained in the *Novell GroupWise Administration Guide* under the heading "GroupWise 4.x Options: Setting and Locking." In this book, I will explain only those options that an administrator would be likely to modify (and I will explain the reasons why an administrator might want to change the options).

You can set the GroupWise 4.x Setup options at the domain, post office, or user level. To access the environment options, highlight the domain, post office or user in the main GroupWise Admin screen, and then:

1 • Choose the Actions menu.

2 • Choose GroupWise 4.x options. The dialog box shown in Figure 18.1 will appear.

F I G U R E 18.1

*GroupWise 4.x Options
Screen*

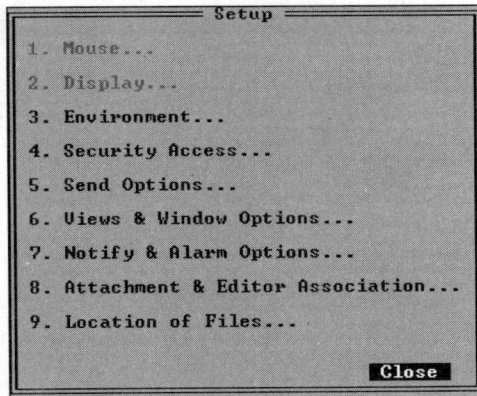

```
═══════════════ Setup ═══════════════
1. Mouse...
2. Display...
3. Environment...
4. Security Access...
5. Send Options...
6. Views & Window Options...
7. Notify & Alarm Options...
8. Attachment & Editor Association...
9. Location of Files...

                              Close
```

TIP

When you select GroupWise 4.x Setup options at the user level, you can select multiple users and change their options at the same time by pressing the space bar or typing an asterisk when a particular user object is highlighted. You can select all users at the same time by pressing Alt-F5.

ENVIRONMENT OPTIONS

When you choose Environment options from the GroupWise 4.x Setup dialog box, you see the dialog box shown in Figure 18.2.

F I G U R E 18.2

Environment Options
Dialog Box

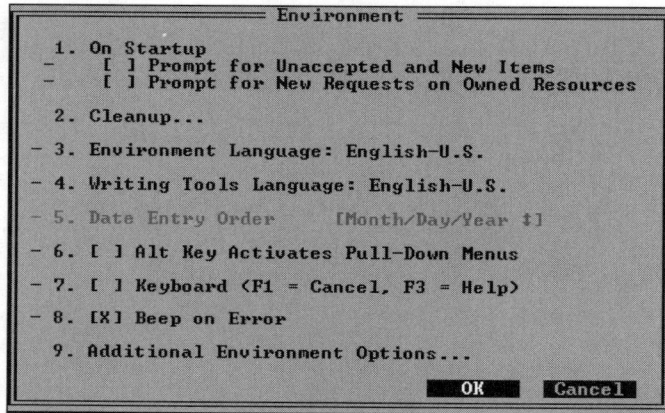

```
╔══════════════════════ Environment ══════════════════════╗
║   1. On Startup                                          ║
║   -    [ ] Prompt for Unaccepted and New Items           ║
║   -    [ ] Prompt for New Requests on Owned Resources    ║
║                                                          ║
║   2. Cleanup...                                          ║
║                                                          ║
║ - 3. Environment Language: English-U.S.                  ║
║                                                          ║
║ - 4. Writing Tools Language: English-U.S.                ║
║                                                          ║
║ - 5. Date Entry Order      [Month/Day/Year ↕]            ║
║                                                          ║
║ - 6. [ ] Alt Key Activates Pull-Down Menus               ║
║                                                          ║
║ - 7. [ ] Keyboard <F1 = Cancel, F3 = Help>               ║
║                                                          ║
║ - 8. [X] Beep on Error                                   ║
║                                                          ║
║   9. Additional Environment Options...                   ║
║                                                          ║
║                                     ▐ OK ▌   Cancel      ║
╚══════════════════════════════════════════════════════════╝
```

Notice that there is a dash next to each of the options. This indicates that the option is not locked, and can therefore be changed by the user. To lock an option, click with the mouse on the dash, or use the Tab key to highlight the dash and then press the space bar. The letter *D, P,* or *U* will appear, depending upon whether you are locking the option at the domain, post office, or user level. For a more detailed explanation, see "Locking the Options" below.

There are two main options under the Environment menu that you may want to modify for administrative purposes—Cleanup and Threshold. (Threshold is located under Option 9, Additional Environment Options.)

Cleanup

There are two reasons why an administrator might want to modify Cleanup options:

▶ Many organizations have policies regarding how long electronic correspondence must remain in their systems. These policies often result from legal considerations. You may need to set Cleanup options that conform to your organization's requirements.

▶ The Cleanup options can be used to maintain the size of a system's message stores by regulating how long data remains in the system before it is automatically deleted.

When you choose Cleanup options, you see the dialog box shown in Figure 18.3.

```
═══════════════════════ Cleanup Options ═══════════════════════
┌─ Mail and Phone ──────────────────────────────────────────┐
│    1. <●> Manual Delete and Archive                        │
│    2. < > Auto-Archive After  0      ▲▼   Days             │
│    3. < > Auto-Delete After   0      ▲▼   Days             │
├─ Appointments, Tasks and Notes ───────────────────────────┤
│    4. <●> Manual Delete and Archive                        │
│    5. < > Auto-Archive After  1      ▲▼   Days             │
│    6. < > Auto-Delete After   1      ▲▼   Days             │
├─ Trash ───────────────────────────────────────────────────┤
│    7. < > Manual Empty                                     │
│    8. <●> Auto-Empty After    7      ▲▼   Days             │
└───────────────────────────────────────────────────────────┘
                              [  OK  ]    [ Cancel ]
```

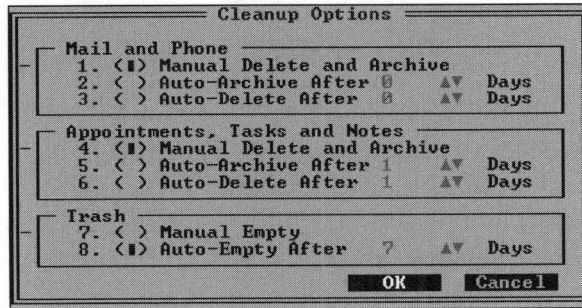

You can set the Cleanup options for manual deletion and archival, automatic archival after a specific number of days, or automatic deletion after a certain number of days. If you lock a Cleanup option, users cannot change it. If you set the option but do not lock it, it will be a modifiable default that users can change at will.

NOTE

When an item is automatically deleted because it has been stored for a certain number of days, the item is moved to the owner's Trash. It will then stay in the Trash until the user empties the Trash or until the Auto-Empty After X Days option causes the Trash to be emptied. A user can undelete an item from the Trash and archive it before the Trash is emptied. If you set the Auto-Empty Trash option to 0 days, the Trash will automatically be emptied every time the user exits GroupWise.

Threshold

In Chapter 7, you learned how Application Threshold settings help you balance the message-delivery load between the client and the post office server. The order of preference for the Threshold setting is: user, post office, and then domain. A user's setting overrides the post office setting, and the post office setting overrides the domain setting. The Additional Environment Options dialog box, where the Threshold option appears, is shown in Figure 18.4.

*Additional Environment
Options Dialog Box*

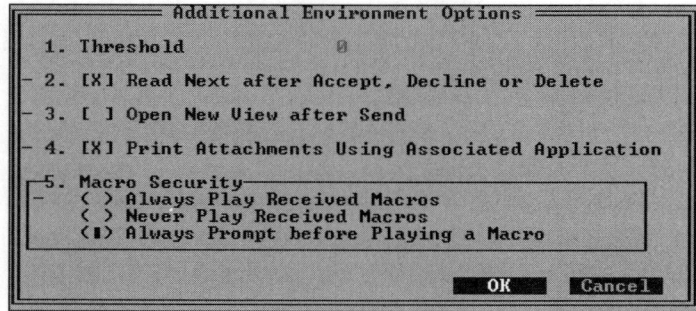

```
╔════════════ Additional Environment Options ════════════╗
║                                                          ║
║   1. Threshold                  0                         ║
║                                                          ║
║ ─ 2. [X] Read Next after Accept, Decline or Delete       ║
║                                                          ║
║ ─ 3. [ ] Open New View after Send                        ║
║                                                          ║
║ ─ 4. [X] Print Attachments Using Associated Application  ║
║  ┌─5. Macro Security─────────────────────────────────┐   ║
║  │ ─  < > Always Play Received Macros                 │   ║
║  │    < > Never Play Received Macros                  │   ║
║  │    <I> Always Prompt before Playing a Macro        │   ║
║  └────────────────────────────────────────────────────┘   ║
║                                                          ║
║                                    █ OK █   Cancel        ║
╚══════════════════════════════════════════════════════════╝
```

Notice that the Threshold setting does not have a dash next to it. This setting cannot be changed by the user, and it is therefore automatically locked.

If you have users in your system who have Pentium machines, you may want to set their Threshold at a higher number than for users of 386 computers. Setting the Threshold for Pentium users higher causes their client application to handle more message-delivery and thus lessens the burden on the post office server.

SECURITY ACCESS

In Chapter 14, you learned how to use the Security Access option to set a password for a user. You can also use the Security Access option to remove a password that has been set by a user. This is very handy if a user has set a password and then forgotten it.

Users can set their own passwords from within the client program and override any passwords that an administrator sets for them in GroupWise Admin.

NOTE

If users choose the Applies Only to Other Users option when setting their passwords, it is very easy for them to forget their passwords because they are never prompted for it.

LOCATION OF FILES—ARCHIVE FILE LOCATION

The most important setting under the Location of Files option (in the Setup dialog box) is the location of the archive directory. GroupWise users tend to become pack rats. Any message that has a modicum of significance—or that provides the least bit of amusement—could end up stored for eternity. One way to prevent mail messages from cluttering your network file servers is to designate users' local hard drives as the archive location.

The Location of Files dialog box is shown in Figure 18.5.

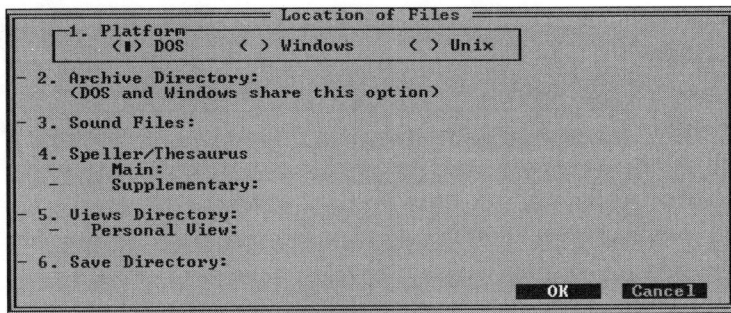

```
================ Location of Files ================
  ┌1. Platform──────────────────────────────────────┐
  │    <■> DOS        < > Windows        < > Unix    │
  └──────────────────────────────────────────────────┘
  2. Archive Directory:
        <DOS and Windows share this option>
  3. Sound Files:

  4. Speller/Thesaurus
  ─       Main:
  ─       Supplementary:
  5. Views Directory:
  ─     Personal View:
  6. Save Directory:

                                    OK      Cancel
```

Notice that this option is set by platform. If you have both DOS and Windows users, you need to set this option for each platform.

There is some controversy among GroupWise administrators about whether it is best to have GroupWise users archive their messages on the network or on their local hard drives. I tend to side with those who opt for archiving on the users' hard drives. Think about how the GroupWise message store works. It is very efficient because a message and its associated file attachments are only stored once per post office, even if that message was sent to every GroupWise user in the post office. An archive directory is a GroupWise user's personal message store. It contains a USER.DB, MSG.DB, and file attachments. When a user archives a message, that message and all of its file attachments are copied to the user's archive directory. If you allow users to specify a directory on the network, in the long run you will be losing network space, even if you are saving space in the post office message store.

For example, if a message has been sent to 50 users in a post office, it is only stored once on the file server that holds the post office message store. However, if all 50 users archive that message, it is then stored 50 times. If the users' archives are on the network, you lose valuable disk space on your file servers. Although you might gain some benefits from archiving on the network, you lose much more when archived messages start taking over your file servers.

If you force users to archive to their hard drives, eventually they will learn to manage their archives wisely—when they see their hard disk space vanishing.

In all fairness, I must also present the argument for archiving on the network, which I'll admit is sometimes a reasonable alternative. Usually, a network drive is backed up quite frequently by network administrators. If something happens to the network directory, the information can be restored from the backup media. On the other hand, if users lose their hard drives, their archived information may disappear as well because there is a good chance they haven't performed regular backups. Sometimes the backing up of the archival directory may be mandated by law or company policy, and in those cases network archival is probably the best solution. You will need to decide, depending on the circumstances, whether data safety is more important than conserving network disk space.

As you make this decision, you can choose different archiving locations on a user or post office basis. For users in company management positions, you may decide to require their messages to be archived on the network for increased data safety.

IMPORTANT

Status-tracking for messages ends when a message is archived.

There are a few other issues you should be aware of relating to archive maintenance. Users often complain that the archive is taking up a lot of space on their hard drives, even after they have deleted their archived messages. When this happens, try the following:

▸ Make sure the users have emptied their archive Trash. Trash has an archive that many people don't know exists. A message deleted from an In or Out Box archive goes to the Trash archive. *The Trash archive is not emptied automatically, even if the Cleanup option is set to Auto-Empty after X Days.* The Cleanup option only affects the Trash in the master mailbox. When I first discovered my own Trash archive, I found over 500 messages dating back 18 months.

▸ Make sure that users check their Out Box archive for old messages. If Auto Archiving is set in the Preferences menu, Out Box items are automatically archived. However, often users don't think about checking the Out Box archive.

▸ Run Check GroupWise against the archive message store. Often you will find that file attachments have been *orphaned* in the Archive message store. In other words, messages have been deleted, but their file attachments have not. OFCHECK will clean out orphaned attachments. (I explain how to use OFCHECK in Chapter 19.)

LOCKING THE OPTIONS

You can lock specific defaults so that users cannot change them. The options can be locked at the domain level, the post office level, or the user level. To lock an option, highlight a domain, post office, or user object in GroupWise Admin, and then:

1 • Select Actions.

2 • Select GroupWise 4.*x* Setup options.

3 • Select the desired category, such as Environment or Location of Files.

A list of the options will appear. Most options will probably have a dash (–) to the left of the option number. A dash indicates an option that can be locked is currently unlocked.

4 • Change the option as desired.

5 • If you are using the mouse, click on the dash next to the option number. If you are using the keyboard, press tab so the cursor moves to the dash and then press the space bar.

A letter will appear next to the option. *D* indicates that the option is locked at the domain level. *P* indicates that the option is locked at the post office level. *U* indicates that an option is locked at the user level. Once an option is locked, the default cannot be changed by a user.

If you do not lock a value, the order of precedence (from highest to lowest) is as follows: user, post office, and then domain. For example, if you select a specific user and specify a certain directory for that user's archive files, the setting for that user overrides any setting for that user's post office. But, because you have not locked the option, it is simply a modifiable default for that user. The user can still change the option in the client Preferences menu.

If you lock a value, the order of preference is as follows: domain, post office, and user. For example, suppose that the mail message cleanup option for all users in a domain is set to delete messages automatically after 90 days. You have established a setting at the domain level and locked it. This setting overrides any settings established at the post office or user level. Once an option is locked, it cannot be changed by the user.

Terminating Users' Accounts

Occasionally, you may need to terminate a user's access to GroupWise while still retaining their information in the message store. There are a few common situations when you might want to do this:

▸ A user takes a leave of absence, and you want to disable the account but not delete it.

▸ A user is a temporary employee and will only be on the job for a certain length of time.

▸ An employee has been terminated, but you need to retain their messaging information (e.g., for legal reasons).

In these cases, you should terminate the user's account but not delete it. To do so:

1 • Highlight the user in the main GroupWise screen.

2 • Choose Actions.

3 • Choose Edit.

4 • Choose Expire Date.

5 • Enter the date on which the user's account should expire.

6 • Choose OK.

To reinstate the user's account, simply repeat these steps and change or delete the date.

To permanently remove the records of a user's whose account has been terminated:

1 • Highlight the user.

2 • Click on Tools.

3 • Click on Purge Expired Records.

Deleting a User's Account

Deleting a user object will cause that user and all of the user's information to be completely removed from the system.

IMPORTANT

You should only delete users when you are sure that they will not need access to their mailboxes again. You should also make sure that a user's information will not be needed for future reference and that you are not legally required to retain the data for a certain length of time.

Deleting a user object is simple. Here are the steps:

1 • In the main GroupWise Admin screen, highlight the user.

2 • Choose Actions.

3 • Choose Delete. (Or simply press the Delete key when the user is highlighted after Step 1.)

The user's master mailbox will be removed from the post office message store, and the change will be replicated throughout the system so that the user no longer appears in the address book.

Renaming Users

Renaming GroupWise users is a common administration task. For example, you may need to rename a user who has recently married. Also, a change in network-ID-naming standards may necessitate changes in GroupWise naming.

When you rename a user, that change is *synchronized* throughout the GroupWise system. Thus, a user in a secondary domain can be renamed either by the primary domain's administrator or by the secondary domain's administrator. (Refer to Chapter 10 for details about how GroupWise handles this process.)

Keep the following principles in mind as you rename users:

▶ Replication is done from the primary domain. If a secondary domain's administrator makes the change, information about the change is sent to the primary domain, and the primary domain notifies all other secondary domains.

▶ When a user in the secondary domain is renamed from the primary domain, the primary domain must follow the request/confirm/replicate model explained in Chapter 11. This generates additional network traffic.

If possible, I recommend that you rename users from the users' own domains. This eliminates the request and confirm processes and therefore reduces network traffic.

Follow these steps to rename a user:

1 • Highlight the user in the main GroupWise screen.

2 • Choose Actions.

3 • Choose Edit.

4 • Change the information as needed.

5 • Choose OK.

WARNING

Do not rename and move a user at the same time. If a user needs to be renamed and moved, rename the user first, let the system replicate the change, and then move the user. Otherwise you risk losing some of the user's data.

Moving Users

Moving users from one location to another in a GroupWise system is also a very common administration task. However, this task is much more complicated than simply renaming a user because it involves actually moving the user's message store from one place to another. Moving a user's message store requires using the message server, two post office servers and, often, an administration server.

You will need to move users in the following situations:

▸ A user has transferred from one department to another.

▸ You are renaming a domain or a post office. Once you have created a domain or post office, you cannot rename simply by editing the name. You must create a new domain or post office with the new name and move users into it. (I explain the steps for renaming a domain or post office later in this chapter.)

PREPARING TO MOVE A USER

You can significantly increase your chances of success if you plan ahead before you actually move users from one domain or post office to another. Here are some guidelines to follow before you move a user:

▶ Decrease the number of messages that need to be moved.

▶ Make sure the user is not running GroupWise or Notify.

▶ If the user is assigned as an owner of a resource, reassign ownership of the resource.

▶ Make sure all post offices involved in the move are open.

▶ Use high-performance GroupWise server processes running on fast machines.

▶ Move only one or two users at a time.

▶ Perform the move at a time when the system is not busy.

I explain each of these general guidelines in more detail in the subsections below.

IMPORTANT

Before beginning the move process, you should also back up the message store—especially if several users will be moved. If a failure occurs during the move, you can restore data from the backup and try again.

Decreasing the Number of Messages

Every time you move a user object, the user's mailbox and associated messages are moved as well. If a user has thousands of messages, it can take hours for every message to be moved to the new message store. If you are moving multiple users, you should first experiment with moving users *one at a time* to get a sense for the average amount of time it will take to move each user.

A user's messages include all of the information in the user's In Box, Out Box, and Trash. The move will be much more efficient if the user first gets rid of all unnecessary messages.

Take these steps to reduce a user's message store before you move the user:

▸ Ask the user to remove any unneeded messages from the In Box and the Out Box and to empty Trash.

TIP

A user can archive messages in an archive message store on his or her computer's hard drive (assuming that the user's computer will also be moving to the new location). The user can later *unarchive* these messages and return them to the message store in the new location.

▸ Run OFCHECK on the user's database and select Check and Fix. OFCHECK is explained in Chapter 17. (Optional: Run OFCHECK and select Expire/Reduce for message and user databases.)

If you move multiple users from one post office to another, you should understand ahead of time how the move will affect storage of messages in the new post office. Suppose you are moving 20 users from a post office named Sales to a post office called Marketing. Also, let's say these 20 users share many messages in the Sales post office. GroupWise moves users one at a time, and the system does not know when you are moving users to the same location. Therefore, a copy of each shared message will moved with each individual user's information. After the move, the messages that were shared in Sales will *not* be shared among the users that were moved to Marketing. All of the formerly shared messages will be stored 20 times in the Marketing post office. This proliferation of messages can cause message stores to expand beyond your initial expectations when you move several users from one post office to another. The same is true for the file attachments directory when files are attached to the messages.

Exiting GroupWise and Notify

Users should exit both GroupWise and Notify before you move them. Both the GroupWise client and Notify access the users' master mailboxes (USERxxx.DB). Accessing a mailbox can interfere with the move process, and data may be lost during the move.

TIP

**Before moving users, tell them that they should not run GroupWise
or Notify during a specific period of time. Allow yourself plenty of time
to complete the move before the users run GroupWise from their
new post office. The end of a workday is typically a good time to
move users. For example, you can ask users that are being moved
not to run GroupWise from 5:00 p.m. one afternoon to 8:00 a.m. the
next morning.**

Changing Resource Assignments

All resource objects must be assigned to an owner that is a user object. If you are
moving a user that owns a resource, reassign ownership of the resource before moving
the user. GroupWise will not allow a user to be moved if the user owns a resource. You
can change a resource's owner by opening the Resource window in GroupWise Admin,
highlighting the resource and then selecting Actions, Edit.

Verifying that the Old and New Post Offices Are Both Open

To successfully move a user, both the old home post office and the new home post
office should be open. This ensures that the user's data will be transferred efficiently. If
the new home post office is closed when a user is moved, GroupWise will store the data
in the message queues until the post office opens. Although data will not be lost, a huge
backlog of messages will be waiting when the post office reopens, causing a delay in
normal message-delivery to that post office.

Using High-Performance GroupWise Servers and Computers

As you might have guessed, using a high-performance NLM or OS/2 message server
and using post office servers on fast machines will greatly speed up the moving process.

IMPORTANT

If you move users with a version 4.1 NLM Message Server Pack, you should disable the receiving post office's OFS process until the receiving domain's ADS process has had a chance to receive the new user-information and add that information to the WPDOMAIN.DB and WPHOST.DB files. If you don't disable the OFS process, it sometimes receives and processes a user's messages before the WPHOST.DB has been informed about the new user. This occurs because OFS polls its input queues much more regularly than the ADS process does. The messages are then lost because they are rejected by the new post office. This problem has been fixed with version 4.1a (and later) NLM Message Server Packs. You can download this fix, which is incorporated in an update to the NLM Message Server Pack, from Novell's online services.

Moving Only One or Two Users at a Time

There are many processes involved when a user is moved, and there are usually many messages to move for each user. Moving users places a heavy burden on a system's GroupWise server processes. For best results, I recommend only moving one user at a time. Trust me on this one.

The GroupWise system allows you to mark multiple users and move them all at once, but the risk of losing data is not worth the shortcut. If you feel you must move multiple users at the same time, start off with one. Then try two at a time. Verify that the two users were moved successfully, and then try three. Don't ever exceed five users at a time. Believe me—if you do, you're asking for trouble.

Choosing a Time When the System Is Not Busy

As I pointed out already, moving users places a substantial load on the GroupWise post office servers and message servers. Obviously, it makes sense to choose a time when moving users will not substantially interfere with message-delivery for the rest of the GroupWise system.

STEPS FOR MOVING A USER

When you move a user from one post office to another within the same domain, run GroupWise Admin for that domain. (Even though it is possible to move users from the primary domain, I recommend that you perform this task from the relevant domain so that you do not unnecessarily increase network and server traffic.) When you move a user from one domain to another, you must run GroupWise Admin from the primary domain. An administrator in a secondary domain cannot move a user to a different secondary domain.

Follow these steps to move a user:

1 • Complete the preparatory steps and follow the guidelines discussed above.

2 • Run GroupWise Admin.

3 • Highlight the user in the User window.

4 • Select Actions.

5 • Select Edit.

6 • Select Domain / PO.

7 • Choose the destination domain and post office.

8 • Choose OK.

If you think the move might have failed, check the message server, administration server, and post office server log files for more information. When you move a user from one domain to another, view the Pending Operations list in GroupWise Admin (select Tools and then View Pending Operations) to see whether the operation is complete.

If the process did fail, verify that the post office to which you are moving the user has sufficient free disk space. You may also need to run the Check GroupWise utility (OFCHECK) on the destination post office. Then try the move again.

IMPORTANT

Do not attempt to rebuild a user's mailbox until the move is complete.

How It Works

There are several different administrative scenarios you may encounter when you move users:

▸ Post office-to-post office in a primary domain

▸ Post office-to-post office in a secondary domain (running GroupWise Admin from the secondary domain)

▸ Post office-to-post office in a secondary domain (running GroupWise Admin from the primary domain)

▸ Domain-to-domain (running GroupWise Admin from the primary domain)

The following diagrams illustrate the process for moving a user from a post office in a primary domain (Domain 1) to a post office in a secondary domain (Domain 2). Because of the complexity of this operation, I have broken it down into three diagrams. Figure 18.6 shows the first stage.

FIGURE 18.6

Moving a User from One Domain to Another (Stage 1)

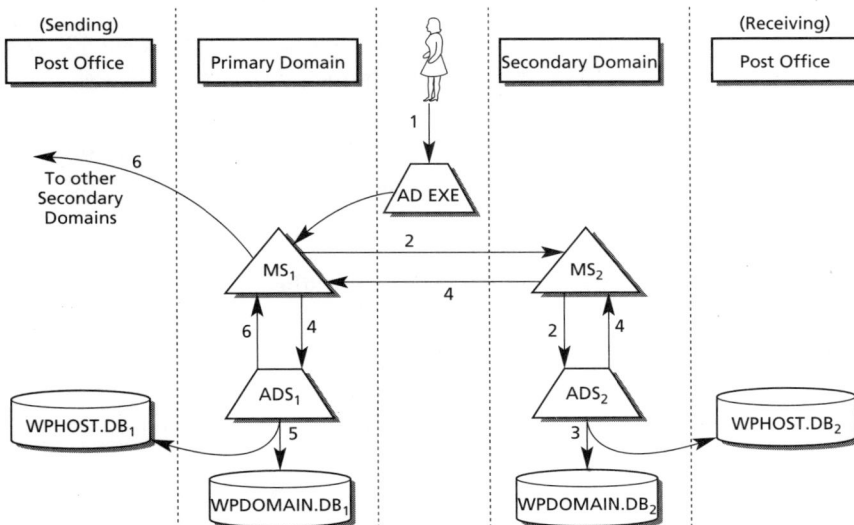

Here is what Figure 18.6 shows:

1 • The system administrator runs GroupWise Admin (AD.EXE) for the primary domain (Domain 1), edits the user information, and changes the domain and post office for the user.

2 • GroupWise Admin creates a request-message addressed to the secondary domain (Domain 2) where the user is to be moved. The request-message asks the secondary domain to verify that a duplicate user does not exist in the domain. Domain 1's message server (MS_1) delivers the message to Domain 2, and Domain 2's message server (MS_2) passes along the message to the secondary domain's administration server (ADS_2).

3 • ADS_2 reads the WPDOMAIN.DB file and the WPHOST.DB file for the post office where the user is to be moved, verifies that a duplicate user does not exist, and adds the information for the new user to the WPDOMAIN.DB and WPHOST.DB files in the secondary domain.

4 • ADS_2 creates a message confirming that a duplicate user does not exist and that the user can be moved. MS_2 delivers the message to Domain 1, and MS_1 passes along the message to ADS_1.

5 • ADS_1 makes the change to the primary domain's WPDOMAIN.DB file and all WPHOST.DB files in the primary domain.

6 • ADS_1 creates a message to replicate the change throughout the system. MS_1 delivers the replication-message to all secondary domains in the system.

Figure 18.7 shows the next stage of the move.

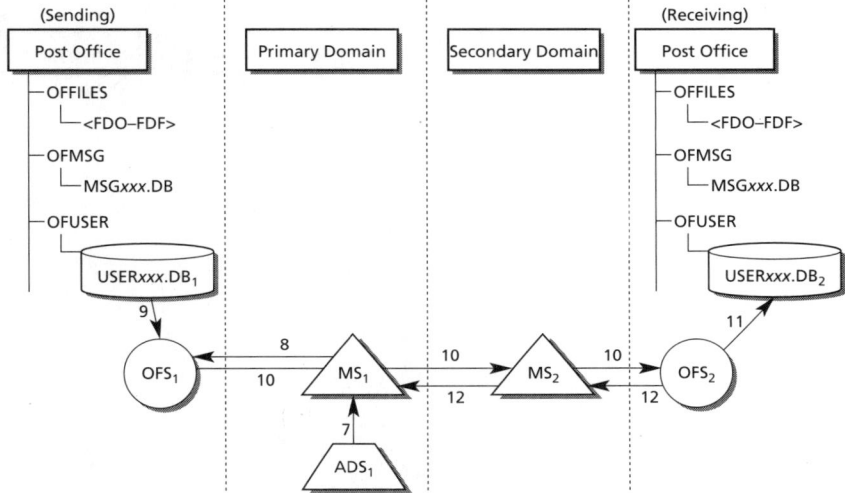

FIGURE 18.7

Moving a User from One Domain to Another (Stage 2)

Here is what you see in Figure 18.7:

7 • ADS_1 creates an administrative message to move the user.

8 • MS_1 delivers the message to OFS_1 directing it to proceed with the move.

9 • OFS_1 reads the user's USERxxx.DB file.

10 • OFS_1 creates a message containing the user's USERxxx.DB information. MS_1 delivers the message to the secondary domain, and MS_2 passes along the message to OFS_2.

11 • OFS_2 assigns a USERxxx.DB file to the user and adds the user information to the new user database.

12 • OFS_2 creates a message confirming that the user database information was received and that the domain is ready for the messages to be moved. MS_2 delivers the message to MS_1.

Figure 18.8 shows the conclusion of the process.

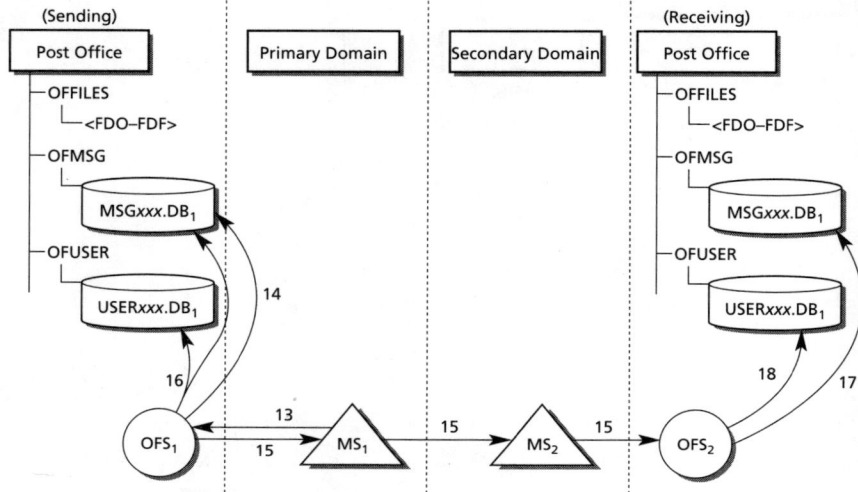

FIGURE 18.8

Moving a User from One Domain to Another (Stage 3)

13 • OFS$_1$ receives a message directing it to proceed with moving the user's messages.

14 • OFS$_1$ reads the user's messages from the message store and creates a series of messages containing the user's messages.

15 • OFS$_1$ delivers the messages to MS$_1$, MS$_1$ passes along the messages to MS$_2$, and MS$_2$ delivers them to OFS$_2$.

16 • OFS$_1$ purges the user information from the original post office.

17 • OFS$_2$ adds the messages to the user's new message database, and it places all file attachments to the OFFILES directory.

As you can see in the steps above, moving a user is a very complex operation involving many different server processes.

THE EASY WAY OUT (FOR ADMINISTRATORS)

Here's a no-nonsense approach to moving users that many administrators swear by. You should consider this alternative if you think you can pull it off without too much resistance. This approach places most of the burden on the users who move instead of on the administrator and the GroupWise system.

1 • Inform users that as of a certain day, their messages will be removed. Tell them to archive, delete, or save all messages.

2 • Terminate the users' accounts using the Expire Account option (but don't delete the users from the system—just in case you need to retrieve their messages later).

3 • Create new user accounts for the users in the new post office and let the users start fresh with new accounts.

4 • Allow users to unarchive messages into the new account if they want their original messages put back into the post office message store.

TIP

If for some reason a user's file ID (FID) changes during the move—in most cases, it shouldn't—a new archive directory is created that does not match the old archive directory name. If this occurs, the user can simply move the contents of the old archive directory to the new archive directory.

The disadvantage of this approach is that the administrator must rely on users to manage their messages, and users are not likely to appreciate having to perform this task if it ends up taking a long time.

Consequences of Renaming or Moving Users

When you rename or move a GroupWise user, there are some significant ramifications for the GroupWise system. The following items are affected when a user is moved or renamed:

- Public and personal groups

- Proxy address lists

- GroupWise Remote settings

- Replies to preexisting messages

- Status information

- Client settings

Public Groups and Personal Groups

GroupWise stores absolute addresses (syntax: *domain.postoffice.userID*) in both personal and public groups; not simple addresses (syntax: *userID*). Groups are used to simplify addressing for the users. Public groups are created by the system administrator in GroupWise Admin. Personal groups are created by the individual users and are stored in the user databases.

A user's absolute address changes when the user's GroupWise ID is changed or when the user is moved to a new location in the GroupWise system because either the post office name changes or the domain name changes (or both). When you rename or move a user, the public groups that contain that user are automatically updated with the user's new absolute address. However, personal groups that contain the user's old address will not be updated. When users send messages using personal groups that contain outdated addresses, the messages are returned marked *Undeliverable*.

The GroupWise Enhancement Pack, available from Novell, contains a feature that automatically incorporates updated user-addresses into personal groups.

TIP

Proxy Address List

If a user's GroupWise address changes, any proxy access lists that contain the user must be updated.

GroupWise Remote

If a GroupWise Remote user's absolute address changes, that user will need to change Preferences in GroupWise Remote. Changes to the user's GroupWise ID, domain, or post office in GroupWise Remote mean that new message and user databases must be created. All messages stored in the GroupWise Remote message store will be lost.

However, this is not as bad as it sounds. Remember: GroupWise Remote works on a database synchronization model. Even if the data in the GroupWise Remote mailbox is lost, the data still exists in the master mailbox (unless the account has expired and or the information has been deleted). The GroupWise Remote user simply needs to download the data from the master mailbox again.

Replies to Preexisting Messages

If a reply is sent to a user who has been renamed or moved, the address in the reply message will be invalid. For example, suppose that a user with the GroupWise name TAWNEE sends a message to several other GroupWise users. Subsequently, Tawnee's absolute address changes because she has been moved in the system or has received a new user ID. If one of the message recipients opens the message and replies, GroupWise will insert the original absolute address in the To: field, but that address is no longer valid. The reply would be returned as undeliverable. In this situation, the person sending the reply needs to enter Tawnee's new GroupWise ID in the To: field or choose her name from the address book, which is automatically updated by the directory synchronization process.

Message Status Information

A status message is similar to a reply. It's a message that is sent back to the sender's message store using an absolute address. Just like a reply, a status message will not be returned to the correct address after a user moves or receives a new ID. When messages are moved along with a user object, the corresponding status messages are lost and no further status updates for those messages will occur.

Client Settings

A moved user's GroupWise client settings may need to be modified after a move. For example, if the user has startup switches pointing to a particular post office, those switches will need to be adjusted to reflect the new post office location.

Renaming a Post Office or Domain

You may wonder what a section called "Renaming a Post Office or Domain" is doing in a chapter about user-related administration tasks. Strange as it may seem, renaming a domain or post office really is a user-level administration task. In essence, when you change the name of a post office domain or, you actually move users *en masse* from the old domain or post office to a new one with a different name.

Unfortunately, renaming a post office or a domain is not quite as easy as renaming a user object. There is no "Rename Post Office" or "Rename Domain" function in GroupWise Admin. You cannot simply edit the post office name or domain name.

In order to rename a post office in GroupWise, you need to follow these steps:

1 • Create a post office in the same domain with the new name.

2 • Move each user from the old post office to the new post office.

3 • Delete the old post office.

Here are the steps for renaming a domain:

1 • Create a domain with the new domain name.

2 • Create post offices in the new domain that correspond to post offices in the old domain.

3 • Move users from their current post offices to corresponding post offices in the new domain.

4 • Delete the old post offices.

5 • Delete the old domain.

These are not simple procedures. You should avoid renaming post offices and domains whenever possible. That is why I warned you earlier to choose post office and domain names wisely.

If you must rename, you should to plan do it over a weekend or during a holiday vacation when the rest of the system won't be affected by the moving.

Summary

In this chapter, you learned how to do many common user-related administration tasks. These tasks are the day-to-day duties of a GroupWise administrator.

Chapter 19 explains how to maintain GroupWise databases using the Check GroupWise utility and other methods of database maintenance.

GroupWise Database Maintenance

In this chapter, I discuss techniques for maintaining GroupWise databases. I explain how to maintain GroupWise databases using the *Check GroupWise utility* (often simply referred to as OFCHECK, pronounced "off-check") and using the *Database Management option* in GroupWise Admin.

GroupWise databases can be divided into two general categories:

▸ Message store databases, which consist of user databases and message databases. These databases exist in the post office, in users' archive directories, and in GroupWise Remote directories.

▸ Directory store databases, which consist of domain databases and post office databases.

The Check GroupWise utility can be used to perform database maintenance on message store databases. Directory store databases are maintained using the Database Maintenance option under the Tool menu in GroupWise Admin.

Using Check GroupWise (OFCHECK)

Understanding how to use Check GroupWise (OFCHECK.EXE) effectively is key to successful GroupWise administration. Check GroupWise has two main purposes:

▸ Checking the structural integrity of the message store databases and fixing problems that it finds

▸ Checking the integrity of database contents and resolving problems that it finds

Other functions of Check GroupWise include:

▸ Resetting user defaults for current users in a system

▸ Deleting items from users' In Boxes and Out Boxes and emptying items from Trash

▶ Generating statistical reports that indicate when users have more than a certain number of items in their In or Out Boxes

NOTE

The OFCHECK utility is updated frequently. You should always try to use the most recent version. You can find OFCHECK in Novell's NetWire forums. Refer to the document on the CD-ROM entitled "Locating GroupWise and NetWare Patch Files" for locations of updated utilities and patches. OFCHECK.EXE version 4.1b is included on the CD-ROM that comes with this book.

You will find the Check GroupWise Files option under the Tools menu in GroupWise Admin. When you choose this option, you get a dialog box allowing you to select various database maintenance operations. This dialog box provides an interface to the OFCHECK.EXE utility. In other words, it lets you select OFCHECK options and run OFCHECK from within GroupWise Admin.

When a user has trouble sending or receiving items (or reading items that have already been received) the problem often lies with either the message databases or with the user database. Various anomalies can occur in a database system. These abnormalities include structural problems in the databases themselves, as well as logical inconsistencies and mismatches in the database contents. OFCHECK will detect and, if possible, repair such problems.

To use OFCHECK effectively, it is important that you understand the following concepts:

▶ Structural problems, as opposed to content problems

▶ Alternative methods for running OFCHECK

▶ Processing options

Database Problems: Structure versus Content

It is important to understand the distinction between problems with the structure of a database (i.e., flaws in its physical aspects) and problems with its contents (i.e., logical errors related to the information stored in the database). Structural (physical) problems relate to the way the database has been stored on a disk. Structural problems occur when the physical aspects of a database have been modified abnormally and in such a way that GroupWise cannot read or write to the database properly.

Content (logical) problems in a database occur when (1) the database contents have been modified in such a way that GroupWise cannot understand the data or manipulate it, and (2) when one part of the data in a database is inconsistent with another part. Content problems can occur even though the database is structurally sound. Often, GroupWise is able to save and retrieve data correctly in spite of a content problem. The majority of the problems reported by users are structural problems.

NOTE **Many errors in GroupWise cause an error number to be displayed. This number can usually be referenced in the ERRORS.TXT file, located in the domain directory. The ERRORS.TXT file lists the error codes, the causes of errors, and the most likely solutions.**

Running Check GroupWise

There are four different ways to run Check GroupWise:

▶ You can launch Check GroupWise from within GroupWise Admin.

▶ You can use GroupWise Admin to dispatch an OFCHECK job to a post office server.

▶ You can run OFCHECK.EXE from the DOS command line using the MENU startup option.

▶ You can run OFCHECK.EXE from the DOS command line in batch mode.

I discuss each of these methods later.

NOTE

The **NLM** and **OS/2** versions of the post office server automatically perform some **OFCHECK** functions. I explain these automated tasks later in the chapter.

RUNNING CHECK GROUPWISE FROM GROUPWISE ADMIN

GroupWise Admin provides an interface for the Check GroupWise program. Follow these steps to run Check GroupWise from GroupWise Admin:

1 • Highlight a user object or post office.

2 • Choose Tools.

3 • Choose Check GroupWise Files. You will see the Check GroupWise screen shown in Figure 19.1.

```
================= Check GroupWise Files =================
Path To Post Office: C:\TESTDOM1\POST1
Post Office Name:    Post1
Object Name:         all
┌1. Action──────────────────────┐
│  <I> Analyze/Fix               │
│  < > Expire/Reduce             │
│  < > Statistics                │
└────────────────────────────────┘
┌2. Parameters──────────────┐  ┌3. Files──────────────┐
│  [X] Structure            │  │  <I> User Database    │
│      [ ] Index Check      │  │                       │
│  [ ] Contents             │  │  < > Message Database │
│      [ ] Collect Stats    │  │                       │
│  [X] Fix Problems         │  │  < > User/Msg Database │
└────────────────────────────┘  └───────────────────────┘
┌4. Logging─────────────────┐  ┌5. Execution──────────┐
│  Log Name:  ofcheck.log   │  │  < > Server           │
│  [ ] Verbose Logging      │  │  <I> Local            │
└────────────────────────────┘  └───────────────────────┘
Options File Name:  chkoff.opt
 Retrieve Options   Save Options          Run    Cancel
```

4 • Select the desired processing options.

5 • Choose Run OFCHECK.

When you use this method, OFCHECK.EXE is launched from the workstation where you executed GroupWise Admin. For this option to work correctly, the workstation that you are using to run GroupWise Admin must have a valid drive mapping to the post office directory, and the drive letter that is mapped must be the same as the drive letter specified in the post office definition in GroupWise Admin. In other words, the post office must be open.

DELEGATING AN OFCHECK TASK TO A POST OFFICE SERVER

You can use these steps to make a post office server perform a Check GroupWise task:

1 • Highlight a user or post office.

2 • Choose Tools.

3 • Choose Check GroupWise Files.

4 • Select the desired processing options.

5 • Select Execution.

6 • Select Server.

The advantage of using this method is that the administrator's machine is not tied up while OFCHECK is running. This allows the administrator to set up a number of jobs to be executed concurrently. The log file from the analyses will be returned to the administrator's mailbox.

RUNNING OFCHECK.EXE WITH THE MENU OPTION

OFCHECK.EXE is located in the *<domain>*\WPTOOLS directory. You can run OFCHECK from the command line by using the MENU startup option. The syntax is shown below:

```
OFCHECK MENU
```

You will see the screen shown in Figure 19.2:

· ◄

FIGURE 19.2
OFCHECK MENU Screen

```
Novell GroupWise - OFCHECK version 4.1    - CURRENT PROCESSING OPTIONS

Path to Host   = x:\office4        │ Current Opts File = ofcheck.opt
   Post Office = All              │   Retrieve new options from file
   User        = All              │

Output Log Name= ofcheck.log       │
Verbose        = No               │
Screen Saver   = Off              │
_____

Action to perform= ANALYZE/FIX DATABASE

   Fix problems  = Check only
   CheckLevel    = Structure
   IndexCheck    = No

   Files         = User & Msg

Enter ID of item to change, <ESC> to quit, <CR> to process:
```

From this screen, select the desired options and press Enter.

RUNNING OFCHECK IN BATCH MODE

You can run GroupWise in batch mode. (In other words, you can set up a set of parameters for OFCHECK.EXE and run OFCHECK from a batch file.) To do so, use this command:

```
OFCHECK BATCH options filename
```

Using this option allows you to bypass the OFCHECK menus and can be used to perform multiple sequential OFCHECK operations on different user objects or on different post offices. You can use the Check GroupWise Files option in GroupWise Admin to create *options files*, or you can create them by running OFCHECK MENU. Options files are files that specify the exact tasks that you want OFCHECK to perform when it is launched. Once you have created options files, you can use the OFCHECK BATCH command in a batch file for overnight or weekend processing.

The batch method is especially helpful in larger systems where there are several post offices to check and you want OFCHECK to run without supervision. When using the batch method, you can specify the post office name and directory by using the /PH and /PO startup switches. A sample batch file is shown below:

```
OFCHECK BATCH OFCHECK.OPT /PH-L:\MIS /PO-MIS
OFCHECK BATCH OFCHECK.OPT /PH-L:\ADV /PO-ADVERTISING
```

This batch file runs OFCHECK for a post office named MIS and a post office named ADVERTISING, using the options found in the OFCHECK.OPT file.

> **NOTE**
>
> **With both the GroupWise Admin and Menu OFCHECK interfaces, saved options files can be retrieved so you don't have to repeat frequently used options. However, each options file must contain a valid /PH-*path to post office* field that corresponds to the current drive mapping. If no options files are specified when you run OFCHECK, the OFCHECK.OPT file is used.**

Each time you run OFCHECK, a log file is created called OFCHECK.LOG. This file provides a summary of the results of the OFCHECK operation.

MONITORING POST OFFICE SERVER CHECK GROUPWISE TASKS

The post office server (OFS) automatically performs certain OFCHECK tasks, such as rebuilding user and message databases when it detects structural problems. When the OFS process attempts to read or modify a database and encounters a structural problem, it automatically initiates a structural rebuild process to correct the error. If problems or errors occur during this process, the post office server sends a message to the administrator for the post office to that effect.

> **NOTE**
>
> **Automatic database rebuilding is not available with the DOS Message Server Pack.**

If you want to disable the post office server's rebuilding capability, you can add the /NOREBUILD switch to the NLM or OS/2 post office server.

> **NOTE**
>
> **Do not count on the OFS process to keep your message store in perfect condition. It is possible for the message store to experience irreparable corruption when there are problems with the network infrastructure (e.g., file-locking problems). If you encounter such problems, it is likely that users will lose some of their messages because the system will have to be rebuilt with the OFCHECK utility. Therefore, you should perform regular backups so you don't lose data if the message store is corrupted. I present a backup strategy at the end of this chapter.**

Check GroupWise Options

You can run the Check GroupWise utility for a post office or for an individual user. When you run Check GroupWise for a post office, the dialog box shown earlier in this chapter at Figure 19.1 appears.

There are five main fields:

▶ Actions

▶ Parameters

▶ Files

▶ Logging

▶ Execution Mode

Actions are the various tasks that can be performed by Check GroupWise. Parameters are the different settings that can be used for each action. The Files field allows you to choose the databases that each action will affect. The Logging option controls how much information will be written to the OFCHECK log file when you perform an action. The Execution Mode option allows you to determine whether OFCHECK will be launched by GroupWise Admin or by the post office server.

ACTIONS, PARAMETERS, AND FILES

I'll first explain the various actions, along with their associated parameters and the files the actions can affect.

There are six actions that can be performed by Check GroupWise. The first three discussed here can be used for both post office (message store) and user-level (user mailbox) database maintenance. The second three can only be used for user-level database maintenance. (If you refer to Figure 19.1 again, you will see that only three actions are listed in the Actions field when OFCHECK is run for a post office.) The six actions are:

▶ Analyze/Fix

▶ Expire/Reduce

▶ Statistics

▶ Reset Preferences

▶ Rebuild User Database

▶ Structural Rebuild

OFCHECK Actions for Both Post Office and User-Level Database Maintenance

The actions that can be performed for either post office or user-level database maintenance are Analyze/Fix, Expire/Reduce, and Statistics.

Analyze/Fix   When you select the Analyze/Fix action, OFCHECK analyzes the databases and reports any problems that are found. Table 19.1 explains the parameters you can specify when you choose the Analyze/Fix option.

TABLE 19.1	PARAMETER	EXPLANATION
Parameters for Analyze/Fix	Structure	Checks the physical structure of the database.
	Index Check	Checks the index within the database.
		This analysis is very time-consuming, but it sometimes finds problems that a structure check alone does not reveal.
	Contents	Checks the contents of the database.
	Collect Stats	Collects database statistics while checking the contents. Some of the stats that can be collected include:
		▶ Total mailbox items
		▶ Distribution statistics
		▶ Item count by message type (mail, appointment, etc.)
		▶ Item count by priority
	Fix Problems	Attempts to correct any problems that are found.

The Analyze/Fix option can be run for a user database, a message database, or both at the same time.

Expire/Reduce The Expire/Reduce option retrieves unused space from the database. In normal operations, the GroupWise database engine does not reduce the database file size when items are deleted. It keeps the unused blocks in an available list for more efficient operation. If disk space is critical on a file server, this option can be very useful. Table 19.2 explains the parameters associated with the Expire/Reduce option.

TABLE 19.2	PARAMETER	EXPLANATION
Expire/Reduce Parameters	Reduce only	Reclaims unused space in the database and reduces the size of the database file.
	Expire and Reduce	Allows you to expire items over a specified age limit and empty items in the Trash that are older than a certain age.
		After the items are expired and the Trash is emptied, this option then reclaims free space in the database and reduces the database file size.

When you select Reduce only, you can specify which files are reduced—a user database, a message database, or both. With the Expire and Reduce parameter, the Files option is not available because Expire/Reduce then affects both user and message databases.

Statistics This option allows you to gather statistical information about user and message databases, such as the number of records in a database and the size of the database. The parameters for this action are shown in the Table 19.3.

TABLE 19.3	PARAMETER	EXPLANATION
Statistics Parameters	Summary Stats	Provides summary information about the contents of the user and message databases.
	Complete Stats	Shows complete stats about the mail system, and allows you to specify a Box Limit. When a Box Limit is specified, a list of users whose mailbox exceeds the limit will be generated.

OFCHECK Actions for User-Level Database Maintenance Only

When you run Check GroupWise for a user, the dialog box shown in Figure 19.3 appears.

F I G U R E   19.3

Check GroupWise for a User

```
═══════════════════ Check GroupWise Files ═══════════════════
  Path To Post Office: C:\TESTDOM1\POST1
  Post Office Name:    Post1
  Object Name:         MCANFIELD
 ┌1. Action──────────────────────────────────────────────────┐
 │   <■> Analyze/Fix          < > Reset Preferences           │
 │   < > Expire/Reduce        < > Rebuild User Database        │
 │   < > Statistics           < > Structural Rebuild          │
 │                                                            │
 ┌2. Parameters──────────────┐  ┌3. Files─────────────────────┐
 │ [X] Structure             │  │   <■> User Database          │
 │     [ ] Index Check       │  │                             │
 │ [ ] Contents              │  │   < > Message Database       │
 │     [ ] Collect Stats     │  │                             │
 │ [X] Fix Problems          │  │   < > User/Msg Database      │
 │                           │  │                             │
 ┌4. Logging─────────────────┐  ┌5. Execution─────────────────┐
 │ Log Name:  ofcheck.log    │  │   < > Server                 │
 │ [ ] Verbose Logging       │  │   <■> Local                  │
 │                           │  │                             │
 Options File Name:  chkoff.opt
  Retrieve Options    Save Options              Run    Cancel
```

You will notice that there are three additional actions that do not appear when you run Check GroupWise for a post office.

The following three OFCHECK actions can be used for user-level database maintenance only.

Reset Preferences   This option allows you to reset a single user's or several users' default preferences when you are not locking the options (i.e., when you are only setting user defaults). Locked options are stored in the WPHOST.DB file and do not need to be updated in the USERxxx.DB. When you set environment options, you should use run OFCHECK with this option to apply the changes to all existing users. I explained how to set environment options in Chapter 16. There are no parameters for this option. The Reset Preferences action affects only user databases.

Rebuild User Database   This option rebuilds a user's database from the information in the message databases. There are no parameters for this option. This option is rarely necessary because most problems are fixed with the structural Analyze/Fix option.

IMPORTANT

Rebuild User Database should only be used when a user's database has been deleted or completely destroyed. Rebuilding a user's database causes all items' folder assignments to be lost and sometimes causes all personal items (e.g., appointments, tasks, notes, and groups) to be lost.

Structural Rebuild   This option performs a complete structural reconstruction of a database. This is the same action that results when a problem is found by the Analyze/Fix action with the Structure parameter selected.

NOTE

Whenever OFCHECK fixes a structural problem, the damaged database is saved for future reference and as a backup. The old database is saved using the same filename with a third letter added to the file extension. For example, a rebuilt user database might be given the file extension .DBA. These files can be deleted if the database reconstruction resolves all problems. When OFCHECK detects a structural problem, another file is created with the same database filename and the file extension .$ER. This file contains a summary of the problems found in the database.

Newer versions of OFCHECK (4.1 and later) allow you to rebuild user and message databases online. With the newer versions of OFCHECK, users do not have to exit the system during database rebuilding. For most of the rebuilding process, users can read from—but not write to—the database. However, during the final phase (when the database is actually reconstructed) users cannot read from or write to the database. Rebuilding databases online is very convenient. You need not worry about removing users from the GroupWise system as you work on databases.

LOGGING

The Logging field in Check GroupWise allows you to specify a log's filename. You can also use this field to determine how much information will be written to the log file. Unless you modify this field, the log file will be named OFCHECK.LOG, and the file will be written to same the directory that contains the OFCHECK.EXE file. (You will recall that the default directory for OFCHECK.EXE is *<domain>*\WPTOOLS.)

If OFCHECK finds an existing log file when it begins processing, it renames the existing file, giving it a numeric tag (for example, OFCHEC01.LOG).

The Verbose Logging option causes additional informational messages to be given when OFCHECK is processing. This option slows down the processing and generates much larger log files. In general, it should not be used. You may need to use this option at the request of Novell customer support technicians when you are trying to resolve a problem.

EXECUTION

The Execution field allows you to dispatch the task of running OFCHECK to the post office server.

Using OFCHECK for Remote and Archive Databases

You can run OFCHECK for GroupWise Remote databases and for users' archive databases. You need the following files to run OFCHECK in those cases:

▸ OFCHECK.EXE (the Check GroupWise executable file)

▸ OFCHECK.MSG (the Check GroupWise message file)

▸ OFUSER.DC (a template for rebuilding user databases)

▸ OFMSG.DC (a template for rebuilding message databases)

To run OFCHECK for a GroupWise Remote database or for an archive database, you need to specify the location of the remote or archive message store with the /PS startup switch. For example, if a GroupWise Remote message store is located in C:\OFWIN40\ROFDATA, the command would be as follows:

```
OFCHECK /PS-C:\OFWIN40\ROFDATA
```

TIP

> You can simply copy the **OFCHECK** files to the **ROFDATA** directory and then run **OFCHECK** from that directory without any switches. If you install **OFCHECK** on a **GroupWise** Remote user's machine, the **ROFDATA** directory may be the best place to put the files. Then the user does not need to worry about using the **/PS** switch.

When you run Check GroupWise for a remote or archive database, you can choose from the list of actions shown in Figure 19.4. (Figure 19.4 shows the menu for Remote databases. When run OFCHECK for an archive database, the word "Archive" would replace "Remote" but the options are identical.)

FIGURE 19.4

OFCHECK Actions for Remote and Archive Databases

```
Novell GroupWise -- OFCHECK  version 4.1
  Copyright WordPerfect Corp., 1993, 1994


"Remote" databases found in current directory

Select action to perform:
  0 - none (exit)
  1 - check structure of databases, repair problems
  2 - check contents of databases, repair problems
  3 - recreate user database from message database
  4 - reduce databases (reclaim free space)
```

Option 1 ("check structure of database and repair problems") checks for structural problems. This is similar to the Analyze/Fix action when you run OFCHECK for a post office database. Option 2 ("check contents of database and repair problems") is very useful because it verifies the contents of a database and makes sure there are no orphaned file attachments. If OFCHECK finds orphaned file attachments—i.e., file attachments without corresponding messages in the database—those files are deleted. Option 3 ("recreate user database from message database") should only be used when the other options do not correct a problem. Just like the Rebuild User Database action for normal user databases, Option 3 causes folder assignments to be lost and sometimes causes all personal items—e.g., appointments, tasks, notes, and groups—to be lost. Option 4 ("reduce database") reduces the amount of disk space used by the message and user databases. The disk space you can recover in an archive or remote message store is usually minimal.

When to Run Check GroupWise

There are no hard-and-fast rules about when to run Check GroupWise for a system. If you are using the NLM or OS/2 message servers, most of the problems with the message and user databases are corrected automatically. However, you should periodically run OFCHECK to make sure that problems are, in fact, corrected by the post office server's automatic checking process. As I mentioned before, periodically running OFCHECK is also important because the post office server only fixes structural problems. The post office server does not automatically detect content problems. Therefore, it is important to run Check GroupWise on a regular basis.

Here are some general guidelines for deciding when to run OFCHECK:

▸ If your system has post office servers that automatically check for database structural problem, you should run OFCHECK at least once a month.

▸ If your system has DOS post office servers (or if you have disabled the automatic checking procedure) you should run OFCHECK for those post offices at least once a week.

▸ If the file server crashes and that server houses a post office message store, you should run OFCHECK to verify that the message store has not been damaged.

▸ If users experience difficulties that are symptomatic of database problems, you should run OFCHECK. Some of the symptoms that indicate database problems are described in the next subsection.

You can automate Check GroupWise procedures by running the program in batch mode. (See the subsection called "Running OFCHECK in Batch Mode" earlier in this chapter.)

COMMON DATABASE PROBLEMS

The key to troubleshooting problems reported by users is to think carefully about how users describe the problems. The information you get from users should help you identify what's causing problems and which databases might be affected. You should ask users which operations they were performing when they encountered difficulties. You should also find out whether a particular error occurs only with specific items or during certain operations.

Here are some examples of common problems and what you should do to address them:

▸ A user is able to perform most operations but cannot send mail. This indicates a possible problem with the message database that the user is assigned to. You should run a *structural check-and-fix* (in other words, the OFCHECK Analyze/Fix action with the Structure option selected) on the message database in question.

▸ A user gets an error when trying to read a specific message. This could indicate a problem with the message database that contains the message. You should run a structural check-and-fix on the message database.

▸ A user gets an error while exiting GroupWise. This type of error usually indicates a problem with archiving. If GroupWise is set to archive automatically after a certain number of days, archiving occurs when the user exits the program. The error could be the result of a simple problem like an incorrect path to the archive directory in the Preferences settings or insufficient rights to the archive directory. On the other hand, the error could indicate a more serious problem with the archive message store. You should check the paths first. If you don't find anything wrong there, you should run a structural check-and-fix on the archive message store.

▸ A user (1) cannot log in to GroupWise, (2) gets an error indicating that a database is invalid, or (3) gets an error indicating that a password is invalid. All three of these problems could indicate that a database header has been modified and the database engine no longer recognizes the database. A structural check-and-fix should correct the problem.

Maintaining Directory Store Databases

Up to this point, I have discussed how to maintain only user databases and message databases. These databases make up the GroupWise message store and can be maintained using the Check GroupWise utility (OFCHECK).

OFCHECK cannot be used to maintain directory store databases, however. Rather these databases must be maintained using GroupWise Admin.

As shown in Figure 19.5, there is a list of options under the heading Database Maintenance in the Tools menu of GroupWise Admin.

*Database Maintenance
Options in GroupWise Admin*

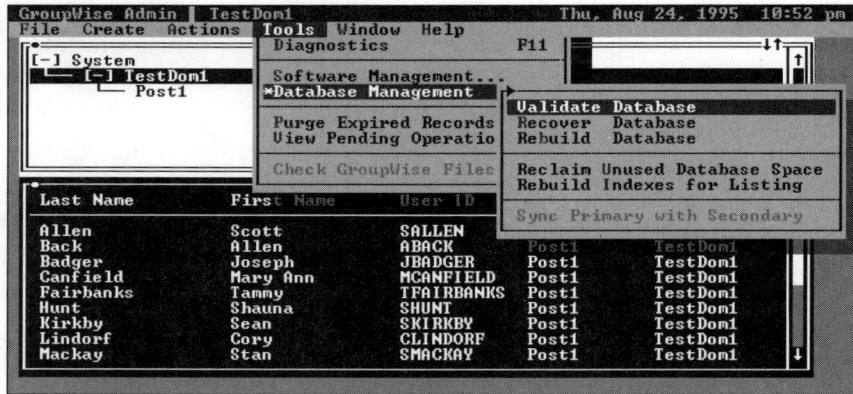

These options can be used to maintain the directory store databases (WPDOMAIN.DB and WPHOST.DB).

IMPORTANT

Remember: Database Maintenance options in the Tools menu apply to *directory store* databases. The Check GroupWise utility (OFCHECK) is used to maintain *message store* databases.

VALIDATE DATABASE (WPDOMAIN.DB OR WPHOST.DB)

The Validate Database option checks the structural integrity of a domain or post office database. GroupWise Admin must have access to the domain or post office database in order to *validate* it (in other words, in order to indicate whether its structure is valid). If a validation is successful, that means GroupWise Admin found no problems. However, if a validation is not successful, you will need to rebuild the database.

RECOVER DATABASE (WPDOMAIN.DB)

When used on a domain database, the Recover Database option recovers as many records as possible from the existing domain database while it is still in use. You can use this option while the message server, the administration server, and gateways are running. In a primary domain, you can use the Recover Database option in the domain database or on any secondary domain database. In a secondary domain, you can only use this option for the secondary domain's own domain database.

When the Recover Database option is used, GroupWise Admin makes a copy of the WPDOMAIN.DB file and names it RECOVER.DDB. Next, GroupWise Admin queries the RECOVER.DDB database to see how many records it contains. GroupWise Admin then reads the WPDOMAIN.DB and rebuilds its contents. (The WPDOMAIN.DB file is never renamed or recreated.) Finally, GroupWise Admin compares the number of recovered records to the total number first reported during the initial query of RECOVER.DDB. If the number of recovered records is less than the original, GroupWise Admin reports that some data has been lost. When data has been lost, you must rebuild the database to restore the lost records. See the subsection "Rebuild Database (WPDOMAIN.DB)" below.

RECOVER DATABASE (WPHOST.DB)

When used on a post office database, the Recover Database option recovers as many records as possible while the database is still in use. You can run the Recover Database option while the post office server, the administration server, and the client software are active.

When you select the Recover Database option, GroupWise Admin makes a copy of the WPHOST.DB file named RECOVER.HDB. GroupWise Admin then queries the RECOVER.HDB to see how many records it contains. GroupWise Admin then reads the WPHOST.DB and rebuilds it using the information in the CREATING.HDB file. GroupWise Admin then compares the number of recovered records to the total number first reported. If the number of recovered records is less than the original, it will report a data loss. The database must be rebuilt to recover the lost records. See "Rebuild Database (WPHOST.DB)" below.

IMPORTANT

The Recover Database option provides only a structural (physical) rebuilding—not a content (logical) reconstruction. Therefore, its uses are limited to some extent. For example, this option will not fix duplicate name-entries in the address book.

REBUILD DATABASE (WPDOMAIN.DB)

When used on a domain database, the Rebuild Database option can restore the database after it has been damaged. Rebuilding can also be used to force directory synchronization to occur or to fix a database index.

IMPORTANT

In cases where the domain database is so severely damaged that not even GroupWise Admin will run for the domain, you can try to start GroupWise Admin with the /REBUILD startup switch. This technique should only be used in the most drastic circumstances.

A primary domain can rebuild itself or any of the secondary domains in a system. A secondary domain can only rebuild itself.

When rebuilding a domain database, GroupWise Admin needs exclusive access to the WPDOMAIN.DB file. You should disable the message server, the administration server, and all gateways before rebuilding a domain database.

TIP

You can make a copy of the WPDOMAIN.DB file, perform the rebuild on that file, and then replace the existing WPDOMAIN.DB file with the rebuilt file. When you choose the Rebuild Database option, GroupWise Admin will prompt you for the path to the WPDOMAIN.DB file. You can specify the path to the copy of the file in the temporary directory.

The following process occurs when a domain database is rebuilt:

1 • GroupWise Admin renames the WPDOMAIN.DB file to RECOVER.DDB.

2 • GroupWise Admin creates a CREATING.DDB file, using the WPDOMAIN.DC file. (The WPDOMAIN.DC file is a template file that is used to rebuild and create domain databases. It is located in the domain directory.)

3 • GroupWise Admin reads the parent database. If the primary domain is being rebuilt, then the parent database is the RECOVER.DDB file. If a secondary domain database is being rebuilt from the primary domain, then GroupWise Admin reads the information from the primary domain database. If a secondary domain is rebuilding itself, then the parent will be the RECOVER.DDB file.

4 • If the reconstruction is successful, GroupWise Admin renames the CREATING.DDB file to WPDOMAIN.DB and then deletes RECOVER.DDB. If the rebuild is unsuccessful, GroupWise Admin renames RECOVER.DDB to WPDOMAIN.DB and deletes CREATING.DDB. This restores the system to the state it was in prior to the rebuilt attempt.

REBUILD DATABASE (WPHOST.DB)

When run on a post office database, the Rebuild Database option can restore the database after it has been damaged. Rebuilding can also be used to force directory synchronization to occur or to fix a database index.

Exclusive access to the post office database is required to rebuild WPHOST.DB. The post office server, the administration server, and all client software should be disabled before you rebuild the database.

TIP

You can make a copy of the WPHOST.DB file, rebuild the database on that file, and then replace the existing WPHOST.DB file with the rebuilt file. When you choose the Rebuild Database option, GroupWise Admin will prompt you for the path to the WPHOST.DB file. You should specify the path to the copy in the temporary directory.

The following processes occur when you rebuild a post office database:

1 • GroupWise Admin renames the WPHOST.DB file to RECOVER.HDB.

2 • GroupWise Admin creates a CREATING.HDB file, using the WPHOST.DC file. (The WPHOST.DC file is a template file that is used to rebuild and create post office databases. It is located in the domain directory.)

3 • GroupWise Admin reads the domain database and enters the necessary records into the CREATING.HDB file.

4 • If the reconstruction is successful, GroupWise Admin renames the CREATING.HDB file to WPHOST.DB and deletes RECOVER.HDB. If the reconstruction is unsuccessful, GroupWise Admin renames RECOVER.HDB to WPHOST.DB and deletes CREATING.HDB. This restores the system to its form before the attempt to rebuild the database.

REBUILD INDEXES FOR LISTING (WPDOMAIN.DB AND WPHOST.DB)

GroupWise uses three different indexes for the address book:

▸ One that lists all users in the entire system

▸ One that lists users in each domain

▸ One that lists users in each post office

The Rebuild Indexes for Listing option can be used for problems with address lists. When information is added to a flawed database, sometimes the data will be added to the database but not to the index.

The clearest indicator of index problems is the address book. Sometimes, a user that is added to a database does not appear in the address book. Occasionally, a user's name appears several times in the address book. The list of users in the address book is merely data drawn from the indexes. If a record is not listed in an index—even though it appears in the database—you will not be able to see it in the address book.

If a user's name appears in the Users Window in GroupWise Admin but doesn't appear in the address book, you should use the Rebuild Indexes for Listing option to rebuild the indexes. GroupWise Admin goes through the database and makes sure that there is an appropriate index listing for each record.

NOTE **Sometimes users do not appear in the client address book because of visibility settings. The visibility setting is the first thing you should check when users cannot be found in the address book.**

RECLAIMING DATABASE SPACE (WPDOMAIN.DB AND WPHOST.DB)

As records are added, modified, and deleted, pockets of wasted space can be left in the databases. This space can be eliminated by using the Reclaim Unused Database Space option for a domain or post office database.

SYNC PRIMARY WITH SECONDARY

The final option available in the Database Maintenance menu is Sync Primary with Secondary. This option should be used when a secondary domain contains information that has not been distributed to the primary domain through the replication process.

When a primary domain lacks records that have been added to a secondary domain's database, go into GroupWise Admin, highlight the secondary domain, and then choose the Sync Primary with Secondary option. This action causes the primary domain to be updated with the most current information from the secondary domain.

MANUALLY SYNCHRONIZING RECORDS

In Chapter 10, I discussed how automatic directory synchronization works when an administrator makes a change in a GroupWise system. You learned that directory synchronization is a matter of sending administrative messages throughout the system and that directory synchronization uses basically the same processes as regular e-mail messages.

Sometimes the automatic directory synchronization process fails, however, and a change is not successfully replicated throughout a system. When this occurs, you can synchronize directories manually by using GroupWise Admin.

The Synchronize option is located under the Actions menu in GroupWise Admin. You can synchronize domain, post office, or user records. Different processes occur depending on where you run the Synchronize option and what you are synchronizing.

If the primary domain is the current domain and you synchronize a record, that record is replicated throughout the system. For example, if a secondary domain for some reason does not contain information about a post office in the primary domain, you can highlight the post office and select the Synchronize option. The secondary domain will then receive updated information about the post office in the primary domain. This option is usually used for synchronizing object records, such as user objects.

If you run GroupWise Admin in a secondary domain and you wish to synchronize an object that is outside your authority (i.e., in another secondary domain or in the primary domain), a message will be sent to the object's owning domain asking for that record to be replicated. The owning domain will then replicate the record throughout the system.

Backing Up GroupWise Databases

As a GroupWise administrator, you should implement a strategy for backing up the critical databases in your system. Your backup strategy should provide methods for backing up the directory store databases (WPDOMAIN.DB and WPHOST.DB files) and the message store databases and file attachments directory (USERxxx.DB, MSGxx.DB, and OFFILES).

PRIMARY DOMAIN DATABASE

The most important database in the GroupWise system is the primary domain database (WPDOMAIN.DB). It stores the configuration information for the entire messaging system, and it is the source file from which all secondary domain databases and post office databases are built. You should carefully guard this database. In most cases, only administrators have access to the domain directory. Users' access should be limited to the post office.

You should back up the primary domain database whenever you make a change in any domain database (such as adding a new post office, domain, gateway, and so forth). It is a good idea to retain the last four or five copies of the primary domain database. This allows you to respond quickly if the database is accidentally deleted or if data becomes critically corrupted. Also, you might not immediately detect inaccurate data in the primary domain database. If you have a backup copy of the last four or five versions of the primary database, you can be reasonably sure that you have a healthy copy somewhere that can be used to get your system running again without a long delay.

NOTE

You can rebuild a secondary domain database from the primary domain database. However, if you lose your primary domain database, your entire GroupWise system will be frozen. It is impossible to administer a GroupWise system properly without a working copy of the primary domain database.

SECONDARY DOMAIN DATABASES

Even though secondary domain databases can be rebuilt from the primary domain database, it is still important that you back up each secondary domain database whenever administrative changes occur. You should keep the last four or five copies of each secondary domain database, too. This helps to minimize the risk of inaccuracies in both the primary and secondary domain databases. If you maintain current backups of your secondary domain databases, you can be confident that you can correct problems with the GroupWise domain databases by restoring data from a backup file.

POST OFFICE DATABASES

Post office databases (WPHOST.DB) can be rebuilt from the domain database that owns the post office. However, it is important that you regularly back up each post office database in the GroupWise system. You should back up a post office database whenever you make changes to it (such as when you add or move users).

Rebuilding a post office database can be time-consuming. It is often faster to restore the post office database from a backup than to rebuild it from the domain database. This is especially true when there are several thousand objects (i.e., users and resources) in the GroupWise system.

It is possible that rebuilding a post office database from the domain database does not correct certain database problems. The domain database could contain incorrect information about the post office. When this is the case, you should first rebuild the domain database and then attempt to rebuild the post office database. If this does not correct the problem, you can restore a backup copy of the domain database and then rebuild the post office database.

THE MESSAGE STORE

The databases and files in the post office message store directories should be backed up regularly. I recommend weekly backups of the message store. Although backing up directory store databases is imperative for smooth operation of your GroupWise system, backing up the message store databases is even more important because it ensures that your users' messages and critical data are not lost.

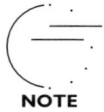

> **Often, there are legal issues related to backing up message stores. Check with your organization's legal department to be sure that your backup procedures accord with legal requirements, as well as with your organization's internal policies.**
>
> **NOTE**

The most important databases associated with a post office are the message databases (located in the OFMSG directory) and the file attachments and message text files located in the OFFILES directory. It is possible to rebuild user databases from the message databases and from the files stored in the OFFILES directory. However, you should regularly back up all files in these three locations.

Backing up an entire message store minimizes the risk of losing data. Backing up files prevents your users from losing important information about their individual GroupWise configurations (such as folder names, personal preferences, and mailbox passwords). An administrator who has a comprehensive backup strategy will be much-appreciated in the event of a major system failure.

BACKUP PROCEDURES FOR ENTERPRISE ORGANIZATIONS

In most large GroupWise implementations, GroupWise domains and post offices are located on many different file servers in the organization. Each file server may be administered by a different person. Thus, it is often difficult to coordinate enterprise-wide GroupWise backup procedures. The situation becomes even more complicated when GroupWise administrators are not the network administrators.

It is important that backup procedures be clearly communicated to everyone who administers a server that contains a GroupWise domain or post office. It is a good idea to make sure that each administrator faithfully follows established backup procedures. Strict attention to backup procedures can save hundreds of hours of database-rebuilding in the long run. At the same time, it can prevent loss of valuable data. It is your responsibility, as a GroupWise administrator, to make sure that adequate and up-to-date backup files exist for your system.

For additional information about backing up your GroupWise system, see these GroupWare Support TechTip documents on the CD-ROM:

▸ "Backup Procedure—Recommended" (filename BACKUP.TT)

▸ "Database Maintenance after a File Server Crash" (filename DBMAINT.TT)

Summary

In this chapter you learned some important techniques for database maintenance. In the next part of the book I discuss additional utilities, add-on products and technologies that can be used to enhance the performance of your GroupWise system.

PART IX

Additional GroupWise Utilities, Add-On Products, and Technologies

In the final part of the book, I briefly explain several additional utilities, modules, programs, and technologies that can be used to add functionality to a GroupWise system.

In Chapter 22, I discuss three utilities that can help simplify GroupWise administration. The first utility is the GroupWise Integration Module (also known as the NWAdmin Snap-In Tool), which allows you to perform several common GroupWise administration tasks from within NetWare 4.*x*'s NWAdmin program. The second utility is the NDS Synchronization NLM, which automatically updates your GroupWise system when you make changes in a NetWare 4.*x* network. The third utility I discuss is the Binder Synchronization NLM, which basically performs the same tasks for NetWare 3.1*x* networks that the NDS Synchronization NLM does for NetWare 4.*x* networks.

In Chapter 21, I explain several add-on products that can add functionality to your GroupWise system. I discuss the additional capabilities provided by the GroupWise Enhancement Pack for the Windows client, the GroupWise ListServer, Collabra Share, the Fax/Print gateway, the Pager gateway, and the Telephone Access Server (TAS).

Chapter 22 covers the connectivity products that are available for connecting your GroupWise system to other e-mail systems (e.g., Lotus cc:Mail) and for connecting your system with other protocols, such as the Internet. I also explain two popular options for setting up your GroupWise system to communicate over the Internet.

In Chapter 23, I introduce two of GroupWise's companion products in the Novell GroupWare product line: Novell InForms and Novell SoftSolutions. InForms provides electronic forms capability for your organization, and SoftSolutions gives you document-management capabilities. I explain how each of these products integrates with GroupWise.

CHAPTER 20

GroupWise Administration Utility Programs

Now that you've learned how to install, configure, and maintain a GroupWise system, here are some additional utilities that can help lighten your administrative workload:

▸ GroupWise Integration Module (NWAdmin Snap-In Tool)

▸ NetWare 4.*x* NDS Synchronization NLM

▸ NetWare Bindery Synchronization NLM

GroupWise Integration Module

The GroupWise integration module (also known as the NWAdmin Snap-In Tool), adds GroupWise administration capabilities to the Windows-based NetWare Administrator program (NWAdmin) for NetWare 4.1 networks.

I believe the GroupWise Integration Module provides a glimpse of things to come. Using this module should give you some indication of what the future of GroupWise administration looks like.

TIP

You can perform these tasks with the GroupWise Integration Module:

▸ Create a NetWare user object and set up a GroupWise account for that user at the same time

▸ Set up a GroupWise account for an existing NetWare user

▸ Create GroupWise resources

▸ Create GroupWise mail distribution lists (public groups)

▸ Perform database maintenance with Check GroupWise

▸ Delete GroupWise accounts

NOTE

The GroupWise Integration Module is available through Novell NetWire on CompuServe and at Novell's World Wide Web site. It is not a product that can be ordered or purchased from Novell on diskettes.

Before you install the module, make sure each of the following is true:

▸ The NetWare 4.1 file server is running.

▸ The workstation that will run NWAdmin has the NetWare 4.1 client software and Virtual Loadable Modules (VLMs) installed and configured. (A VLM is an executable process that runs on DOS workstations to enable communication with the NetWare 4.1 file server.)

▸ You have browse, write, and create rights to the domain and post office directories.

▸ You have system administration rights at the root of the NDS tree (only required for first-time installations of the Integration Module when you extend the NDS schema).

▸ The GroupWise system has been created and the message server, post office servers, and administration servers are running.

IMPORTANT

The NDS Synchronization NLM and the Bindery Synchronization NLM, which I explain later in this chapter, should not be used if you use the NWAdmin Snap-In Tool.

INSTALLATION OPTIONS

You will be presented with three options when you install the GroupWise Integration Module:

- ▸ Extend NDS Schema

- ▸ Install Files

- ▸ Configure Workstation

Extend NDS Schema

NetWare 4.1 uses *NetWare Directory Services* (NDS) to keep track of users and objects in a NetWare 4.1 network. NDS is a global, replicated database that is stored on the file servers in a NetWare 4.1 network. The *NDS schema* is the physical structure of an NDS database.

When you install the GroupWise Integration Module, your NDS schema (the NDS database structure) is extended to include fields for GroupWise. This allows GroupWise options for a specific user to be set from NWAdmin. The Extend NDS Schema option is only available the first time you run the Integration Module installation routine.

IMPORTANT

Before you do anything that affects the NDS schema, it is vital that you back up NDS. Extending the schema is a universal change to your NDS structure. In other words, extending the schema affects the entire network. The schema cannot be restored to its previous form once you have extended it unless you can restore the NDS from backup. You can back up the NDS schema with Novell's DS Standard version 2 or with the SBACKUP program. Also, if you merge two NDS trees with DSMERGE, make sure that the schema is extended for *both* trees before beginning the merge.

Install Files

The Install Files option installs the GroupWise Integration Module files. These files are usually installed in the NetWare server's PUBLIC directory.

Configure Workstation

You can choose this option in order to allow the Integration Module to run from any workstation running NWAdmin. This option adds the required Integration Module parameters to the NWADMIN.INI file.

INSTALLING THE INTEGRATION MODULE

Follow these steps to install the GroupWise Integration Module:

1 • Once you have obtained the GroupWise Integration Module, decompress the files to diskettes or to a directory on a workstation that runs NWAdmin.

2 • Run Windows.

3 • Choose Run from the File pull-down menu.

4 • Type the path and filename of the SETUP.EXE file and then select OK. You will see the dialog box shown in Figure 20.1.

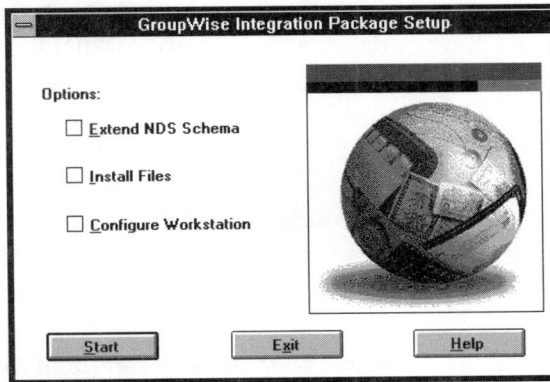

F I G U R E 20.1

*GroupWise Integration
Module Installation Screen*

5 • Select the desired options by clicking on the check boxes.

6 • Choose Start.

7 • From the Make the NDS Adjustments for GroupWise field, choose Make Adjustments. This step extends the NDS schema.

8 • Choose OK when a "Modification to NDS Completed" message appears.

9 • Enter the path to the directory where the GroupWise Integration Module files should be installed.

10 • Choose Start.

11 • Choose OK when the "GroupWise Integration Package has been successfully installed!" message appears.

Once the files have been installed successfully, the routine for configuring the workstation will begin. NWAdmin requires information about the locations of the GroupWise domain directory and the location of the GroupWise Integration Module. This information will be added to the NWADMIN.INI file.

12 • Type the path to the GroupWise domain directory.

13 • Verify that the path to the GroupWise Integration Module is correct.

14 • Choose Start.

15 • Choose OK when the message "The NWADMIN.INI file has been successfully modified" appears.

16 • Choose Exit to return to Windows.

To verify that the installation process was successful, run NWAdmin and look under the Tools menu. You should see a GroupWise option under Tools, and the GroupWise option should have three submenu selections—Delete Account, Check Files, and Preferences.

The Delete Account option allows you to remove users from your GroupWise system. Using this option, you can choose to expire an account and leave the mailbox, delete the user and the mailbox, or simply remove the NDS association. If you remove the NDS association, you break the link between GroupWise and NDS. Subsequent changes in a user's NDS information will not be updated in GroupWise.

The Check GroupWise Files option provides a graphical interface to the Check GroupWise (OFCHECK) utility. This interface is similar to the screen you see in GroupWise Admin when you choose Tools and then Check GroupWise Files. (Refer to Chapter 19 for information on Check GroupWise.) Figure 20.2 shows the Check GroupWise Files dialog box.

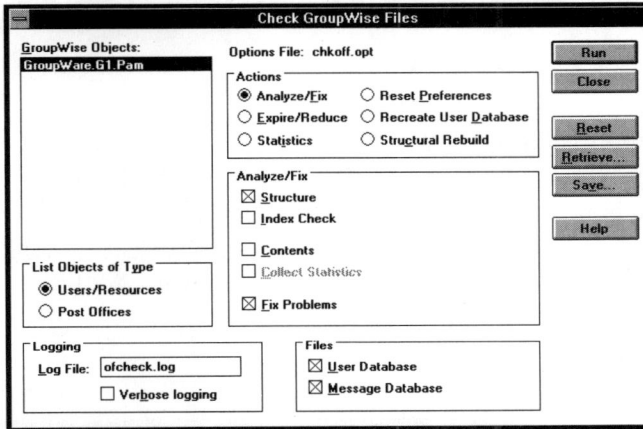

FIGURE 20.2

Check GroupWise Files Dialog Box

The Preferences option allows you to define the defaults for the GroupWise Integration Module. You can use the Preferences option to set or confirm the path to the domain, to set options specifying how the Integration Module handles the Network ID field for the GroupWise user record, and to set options to filter the GroupWise fields to be displayed in the various dialog boxes in NWAdmin.

ASSIGNING NETWARE USERS TO GROUPWISE ACCOUNTS

The GroupWise Integration Module makes it very easy to set up a network user and assign that user a GroupWise account at the same time. Follow these steps to set up a user and assign a GroupWise account:

1 • Run NWAdmin.

2 • Highlight the organization (or organizational) unit that will contain the user you are creating.

3 • Choose Create from the Object menu.

4 • Choose User and then select OK.

5 • Enter the user's information in the Create User dialog box.

6 • Select the Define Additional Properties option.

7 • Choose Create.

When you select the Define Additional Properties option in Step 6, the Properties dialog box will appear after you choose Create. This dialog box allows you to select additional options for the user, including the GroupWise options. The button in the lower righthand corner of the dialog box is labeled "GroupWise." (You may need to scroll to the bottom of the dialog box in order to see this button.) The dialog box is shown in Figure 20.3.

F I G U R E 20.3

User Properties Dialog Box

User : PSchmit	

Identification

Login Name:	PSchmit.GW_EPD
Given Name:	Paul
Last Name:	Schmitman
Full Name:	Paul G. Schmitman
Generational Qualifier:	
Middle Initial:	G.
Other Name:	
Title:	
Description:	
Location:	
Department:	
Telephone:	
Fax Number:	

Buttons: Print Job Configuration, Login Script, Intruder Lockout, Rights to Files and Directories, Group Membership, Security Equal To, Postal Address, Account Balance, See Also, GroupWise

OK   Cancel   Help

When you click on the GroupWise button, you will be allowed to assign the user to a GroupWise domain and post office, and you will be able to set the user's visibility.

When you use NWAdmin to create or change GroupWise options for a user, the Integration Module updates the domain database, and then the administration server (the ADS process) generates an administrative message that replicates the change throughout the GroupWise system using the normal directory synchronization process. (See Chapter 11 for an explanation of the directory synchronization process.)

NOTE

Because ADS may not poll the ADS input queue for several minutes, it may take awhile before you notice the changes in GroupWise Admin.

If you install GroupWise on a NetWare 4.1 network that has existing users, you can use the Integration Module to assign a GroupWise account by editing the user's properties.

NDS Synchronization NLM

As I mentioned earlier, NetWare 4.x systems use NDS to keep track of users. The GroupWise NDS Synchronization NLM monitors changes you make to user objects in an NDS database and automatically updates GroupWise post offices with those changes. For example, if you add a user to an NDS container, that user will be automatically added to the GroupWise post office associated with that container. Each GroupWise post office can be associated with multiple NDS containers, but a single NDS container can only be associated with one post office.

Suppose that your *NDS tree* has two containers for users in two different divisions called Marketing and Sales. (The NDS database organizes objects in a hierarchical tree structure known as the directory tree or NDS tree.) The users in the two containers are all members of the same GroupWise post office—i.e., MKTG. You can configure the NDS Synchronization NLM so that both containers are associated with the MKTG post office. If a user is added to or deleted from either container, the change will automatically be made in the MKTG post office.

The NDS Synchronization NLM can run on file servers that have NDS-tree responsibilities. A file server has NDS-tree responsibilities if any one of the following is true:

▸ Directory Services is enabled on the file server.

▸ The master NDS partition resides on the file server.

▸ A replica NDS partition resides on the file server.

INSTALLING THE NDS SYNCHRONIZATION NLM

Before you install the NDS Synchronization NLM, you should verify that the following requirements are satisfied:

▸ NetWare 4.1 is running on the file server.

▸ The file server has 8MB RAM and 2MB of available disk space.

▸ Directory Services is enabled.

▸ Either a master or a replica NDS database resides on the server.

▸ The GroupWise NGWLIB.NLM is installed and running on the server. If the NGWLIB.NLM is not running, it will be loaded automatically by the NGWSYNC.NLM startup process. The NGWLIB.NLM is a supplemental NLM that is used by GroupWise NLMs. Supplemental NLMs are explained in Chapter 8.

The NDS Synchronization NLM is actually composed of three files: NGWLIB.NLM, STARTUP.SYN, and NGWSYNC.NLM. Here is the recommended procedure for installing the NDS Synchronization NLM.

1 • From the file server console or from an RCONSOLE session, type **LOAD INSTALL**.

2 • Highlight Product Options and press Enter.

3 • Highlight Install a Product Not Listed and press Enter.

4 • Place the diskette with the NGWSYNC.NLM files in the A: drive and press Enter in order to accept the A: drive, or press F3 and enter a different drive location.

5 • Press Escape (Esc) to exit the installation routine after it is complete.

LOADING THE NDS SYNCHRONIZATION NLM

The NGWSYNC.NLM associates users in an NDS container (or multiple containers) with a GroupWise post office. You must define the associations that tell the NGWSYNC.NLM which containers should be associated with the different post offices in your system. The NGWSYNC.DOC file—included with the NGWSYNC.NLM—explains how to configure the associations and the startup parameters.

The startup options and associations can be loaded as command line options (i.e., switches) or in a startup file. The STARTUP.SYN file is a template startup file that you can modify to fit your system. The startup file is limited to 8K in size. You can define any number of associations or startup options up to the 8K limit. I recommend using the startup file instead of typing in the commands at the system prompt.

The required startup switches are explained in Table 20.1.

T A B L E 20.1	SWITCH	EXPLANATION
NGWSYNC.NLM Startup Switches	/HOME-*directory*	Specifies the GroupWise domain directory. You should use the NetWare path syntax. For example: `/HOME-CORP\SYS:\HDQRTRS`
	/ASSOC-*association*	Associates NetWare containers with post offices. The container must be defined in typeless NDS format with no leading periods, and it must be separated from the post office by three periods, as shown in the following example: `/ASSOC=OREM.EDUCATION...HDQRTRS.ACCT` In this example, the organization is OREM, the organizational unit is EDUCATION, the domain is HDQRTRS, and the post office is ACCT.

You must define an association for each NDS container that you want the NGWSYNC.NLM to monitor. Refer to the NGWSYNC.DOC file for the additional switches that you can use. When you are finished and you wish to load the NDS Synchronization NLM, type **LOAD NGWSYNC.NLM @STARTUP.SYN** from the NetWare command prompt.

NOTE

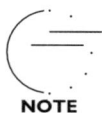

The NDS Synchronization NLM is available through Novell's NetWire forums and at Novell's World Wide Web site. It is not available to be purchased on disk from Novell. This utility can be downloaded as a compressed file, which decompresses into several files. One of the files is NGWSYNC.DOC, which explains the startup switches and associations.

WARNING

If you are using the NWAdmin Snap-In Module, you should *not* use the NDS Synchronization NLM.

Bindery Synchronization NLM

Novell NetWare 3.*x* systems use the NetWare bindery to track information about the users in a network. The bindery resides on each NetWare 3.1 file server and stores network users' IDs and group information.

The GroupWise Bindery Synchronization NLM (NGWBDS.NLM), which is included in the NLM Message Server Pack, automatically updates GroupWise post offices when users are added to or removed from the NetWare bindery.

The Bindery Synchronization NLM runs on the same file server that houses the GroupWise post office. When a user is added to that file server, the Bindery Synchronization NLM detects the change, and adds that user to the post office. This change is then replicated throughout the GroupWise system.

NOTE

To use the Bindery Synchronization NLM, you must have a message server in the domain where the post office is located. The Bindery Sync NLM runs on the file server that holds the post office, and it can service only one post office per file server.

There are different options you can choose from in the Bindery Synchronization NLM to determine how the NLM automatically updates the GroupWise post office:

▸ Add GroupWise users when they are added to the network bindery. (This is the default setting.)

- Add and delete GroupWise users when they are added to or deleted from the bindery.

- Delete GroupWise users when they are deleted from the bindery.

The Bindery Synchronization NLM can run in *Individual mode* or *Group mode*. These different modes are explained below.

INDIVIDUAL MODE

When the Bindery Synchronization NLM runs in Individual mode, changes in the bindery that affect individual users are automatically reflected in the GroupWise address book.

Here is what happens when a change is made:

1 • The Bindery Synchronization NLM detects the change and generates an administrative message for the administration server and sends the message to the message server for the domain.

2 • The message server forwards the message to the administration server.

3 • The administration server adds the user information to the domain and post office database.

4 • If the Administrator option is enabled, the post office server generates a message to the domain's administrator to inform the administrator of the change.

5 • The change is replicated throughout the system by the directory synchronization process explained in Chapter 11.

GROUP MODE

NetWare *groups* can be used to assign multiple users the same rights to certain network resources. If you run the Bindery Synchronization NLM in Group mode, you can instruct the NLM to monitor a specific group in the bindery (e.g., the GroupWise group). Only users added to that group are added to the GroupWise post office.

The benefit of using Group mode is that you can add and delete users in your network without adding or deleting those users in GroupWise. Only users who are added to or deleted from the GroupWise group will be added to or deleted from the GroupWise post office.

The processes involved are the same as for Individual mode, except that only a specified group is monitored instead of all individual user changes.

RUNNING THE BINDERY SYNCHRONIZATION NLM

Like other GroupWise NLMs, the Bindery Synchronization NLM uses a startup file to specify the NLM's operating parameters. The startup file is named STARTUP.BDS, but you can rename it to be more descriptive. The startup switches (both required and frequently used optional switches) are explained in Table 20.2.

T A B L E 20.2	SWITCH	DESCRIPTION
STARTUP.BDS Switches	@*startup filename*	Used to specify the name of the startup file. For example: `LOAD NGWBDS.NLM @STARTUP.BDS`
	/CYCLE-*minutes*	Sets the maintenance cycle interval, in minutes, that the NLM checks for additions or deletions from the specified NetWare group.
	/HOME-vol:\post office directory (Required)	Points the NLM to the post office directory for which the NLM is running. For example: `/HOME-SYS:\HDQTRS`
	/MODE-*operating mode*	Specifies the NLM's operating mode. The settings are: ▸ Add (This is the default.) ▸ Add&Del ▸ Del

Refer to the *NLM Message Server Guide* for a complete listing of switches for the Bindery Synchronization NLM. The *Message Server Guide* also contains a complete explanation of the Bindery Synchronization NLM monitor screen.

NOTE

The Bindery Synchronization NLM can be used on NetWare 3.x file servers and on NetWare 4.x servers that are running in Bindery Emulation mode. You should not run the Bindery Synchronization NLM if you are using the NWAdmin Snap-In Tool or if you are running the NDS Synchronization NLM on NetWare 4.1 servers.

When to Use an NDS or Bindery Synchronization NLM

Like any NLM, the Bindery Synchronization and NDS Synchronization NLMs use file server resources. You should carefully consider whether you need these NLMs. They are only recommended in situations where network changes occur on a regular basis. If changes are made to your network infrequently—and then only one or two at a time—running these NLMs continuously would not be an efficient use of file server resources. However, you might decide to run these NLMs only while network changes are made.

Because these NLMs have very specific functions, you will not need to load them through your AUTOEXEC.NCF files unless your network changes occur regularly.

Summary

The following files on the CD-ROM provide additional information about the GroupWise Integration Module and the NDS Synchronization NLM:

▶ "GroupWise 4.1 Instant Expert Guide—NWADMIN Snap In Module," filename NWADMIN.IE

▶ "GroupWise 4.1 Instant Expert Guide—NDS Sync NLM," filename NDSSYNC.IE

CHAPTER 21

GroupWise Add-On Components

By itself GroupWise is an extremely powerful electronic messaging system that is ideal for organizations of all sizes. However, there are several additional products available that can add even more functionality to your GroupWise system.

In this chapter, I provide overviews of these products:

▸ Enhancement Pack for the GroupWise Windows client

▸ GroupWise ListServer

▸ Collabra Share for GroupWise

▸ GroupWise Software Developer's Kit (SDK)

▸ GroupWise Telephone Access Server

▸ GroupWise Fax/Print gateway

▸ GroupWise Pager gateway

▸ GroupWise API gateway

Technical documents about most of these products can be found on the CD-ROM that comes with this book. The technical documents list the hardware and software requirements for these products and provide technical overviews.

GroupWise Enhancement Pack (Windows Client)

The GroupWise Enhancement Pack is a collection of utilities that have been developed using the GroupWise Software Developer's Kit (SDK). The Enhancement Pack can be used to add functionality to the GroupWise Windows client.

Once installed, the Enhancement Pack can be accessed by users of the GroupWise Windows client from the Tools menu in the client program. The GroupWise Enhancement Pack dialog box is shown in Figure 21.1.

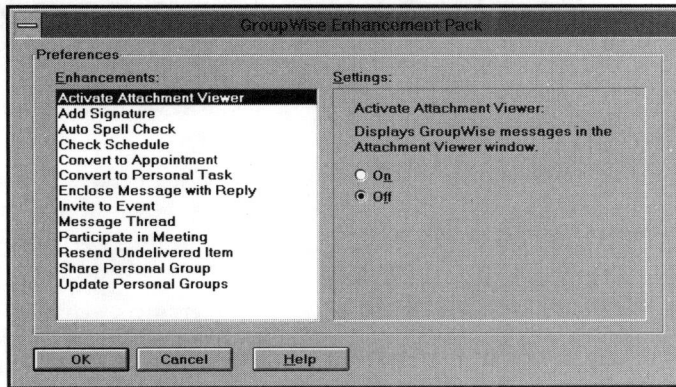

FIGURE 21.1

GroupWise Enhancement Pack

Users can activate or disable each feature individually. Table 21.1 provides a brief description of the features added by the GroupWise Enhancement Pack:

TABLE 21.1

GroupWise Enhancement Pack Features

FEATURE	DESCRIPTION
Activate Attachment Viewer	Allows users to display message text in a resizable windows when message items are opened.
Add Signature	Allows users to compose and add signatures to the end of messages. This feature is also useful for adding custom tag lines and disclaimer statements.
Auto Spell Check	Runs the spell-check feature whenever messages are sent.
Check Schedule	Helps GroupWise users decide whether to accept or decline an appointment by presenting a calendar view for the day of the appointment.
Convert to Appointment	Converts message text into an appointment item by transferring the text to corresponding fields in an appointment view.
Convert to Personal Task	Creates a personal task using the information contained in a GroupWise message.

(continued)

TABLE 21.1

*GroupWise
Enhancement Pack
Features*

(continued)

FEATURE	DESCRIPTION
Enclose Message with Reply	Creates a complete log of messages pertaining to an issue. This feature works best when all relevant correspondents use it.
Invite to Event	Invites others to an event that the recipient has been scheduled for. The person invited receives the appointment just as the recipient did.
Message Thread	Lets users with heavy message traffic view related items at a glance. The chronological organization of items makes reviewing the history of a dialog easier.
Participate in Meeting	Adds the user ID of someone sending an appointment to the To: field. This ensures that originators of appointments will not forget to include themselves.
Resend Undeliverable Item	When a message is returned marked "Undeliverable," this feature automatically checks the address book, attempts to correct the recipient's address, and then resends the message. This feature is particularly useful for GroupWise users who maintain personal groups. Users with personal groups occasionally find that messages addressed to some members are undeliverable because the members' mailboxes have been moved to new post offices.
Share Personal Group	Allows a user to send a personal group to another user.
Update Personal Groups	Checks addresses of GroupWise users in personal groups and updates them as necessary. This is useful when many users have been moved from one post office to another.

Detailed instructions for installing the GroupWise Enhancement Pack are provided in the Instant Expert Guide, EHNPACK.IE, on the CD-ROM.

GroupWise ListServer

The GroupWise ListServer is an Internet-newsgroup-style list server that works within a GroupWise system. ListServer allows users to create structured groups for discussions about specific topics. Users subscribe to lists according to their needs and interests.

For example, a company could create a GroupWise list that deals with safety practices in the workplace. A Safety list would be created, and then users interested in receiving information about workplace safety—or who want to participate in safety-related discussions—could subscribe to this list. Messages posted to a list are received by all users who subscribe to it. Subscribers can then reply to those messages, and their replies will also be posted in the list. Figure 21.2 shows a message generated by ListServer, confirming my subscription to the Scouts list.

GroupWise ListServer
Confirmation Message

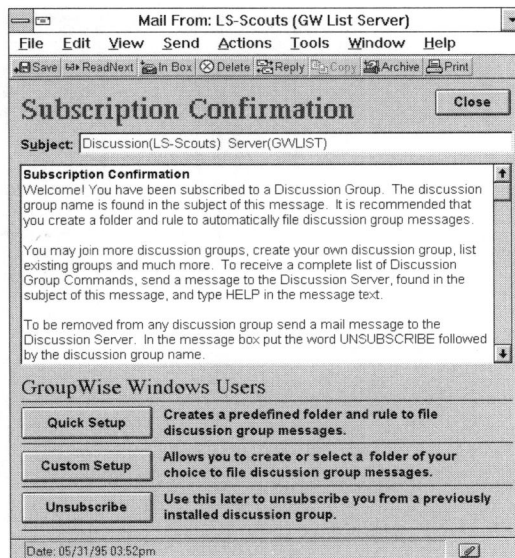

All messages posted to a GroupWise list are distributed by ListServer to all subscribers. GroupWise rules move the list's messages to a folder designated for those messages.

Because ListServer works within a GroupWise system and uses a GroupWise mailbox for ListServer messages, other GroupWise features can be used along with it—including remote access, telephone access, paging, and faxing.

Collabra Share for GroupWise

Collabra Share for GroupWise lets GroupWise users create, access, and share information in discussion forums. Collabra Share for GroupWise enhances traditional GroupWise e-mail by making group discussions possible and offering other collaborative tools.

Collabra Share organizes related information into electronic discussions using a hierarchical structure and concepts such as forums, categories, and threads. This type of communication is familiar to users of online services like CompuServe. You can access a forum on a particular subject. Within that forum, you can post a message, and others who wish to share information or join in the discussion can also add messages to the thread. Figure 21.3 shows a typical Collabra Share for GroupWise screen.

F I G U R E   21.3

Collabra Share Screen

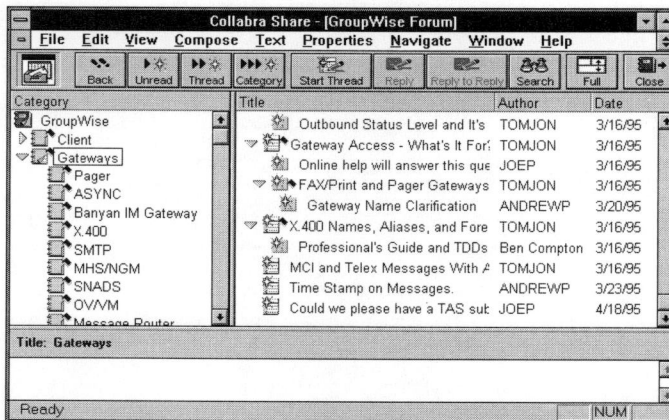

Detailed information about the GroupWise ListServer and Collabra Share can be found in the documents entitled "Collabra Share for GroupWise Product Overview," filename COLLABRA.OVR, and "ListServer and Collabra Share for GroupWise," filename LISTCOLL.TB, on the CD-ROM.

GroupWise Software Developer's Kit (SDK)

The GroupWise Software Developer's Kit (SDK) allows developers to design custom programs that integrate with GroupWise. The features in the GroupWise Enhancement Pack are a good example of the kinds of tools that can be developed using the SDK.

A complete overview of the GroupWise Software Developer's Kit is found in the document entitled "GroupWare SDK," filename GWSDK.WPD on the CD-ROM.

GroupWise Telephone Access Server (TAS)

The GroupWise Telephone Access Server (TAS) allows GroupWise users to send and receive messages remotely using only a standard touch-tone phone.

Users in a GroupWise system equipped with TAS can use a telephone to call in to the GroupWise system. By entering their account code and a password, they can listen to the messages in their In Box. A synthesized voice—sounding a lot like something from *Star Trek*—reads the messages to them over the phone.

Users can also use TAS to fax their GroupWise messages and daily calendars to a fax machine. Suppose you are traveling and you don't want to pack your laptop (which is undoubtedly equipped with GroupWise Remote). Using TAS, you can dial in to GroupWise and have the system fax your calendar and messages to your hotel's fax machine.

A complete overview of the Telephone Access Server, along with the required hardware and software components, is provided in the document entitled "Product Overview—Telephone Access Server," filename TAS.TB on the CD-ROM.

GroupWise Fax/Print Gateway

The GroupWise Fax/Print gateway allows GroupWise users to fax messages worldwide or send them to a printer within a local or wide-area network. This allows users to send messages to recipients who do not have access to a computer. Users can also send messages and scheduled events to a printer. In addition, the Fax/Print gateway allows users to send faxes from GroupWise without leaving their desks. The Fax/Print gateway also supports inbound fax routing.

A complete overview of the Fax/Print gateway, including the required hardware and system components, is provided in the document entitled "Product Overview—GroupWise Fax/Print Gateway," filename FAXPRINT.TB on the CD-ROM.

GroupWise Pager Gateway

The GroupWise Pager gateway lets users send messages directly to alphanumeric or numeric pagers and PCMCIA paging receivers via a Motorola Site Connect Server.

When the Pager gateway is installed in a GroupWise system, a user with a pager can utilize GroupWise rules to forward messages to the pager while away from the office. For example, a user could set up a rule that forwards all messages from a specific individual (or all messages that are sent high priority) directly to the pager.

A complete overview of the Pager gateway, including the required hardware and software components, is provided in the document entitled "Product Overview—GroupWise Pager Gateway," filename PAGER.TB on the CD-ROM.

GroupWise API Gateway

The GroupWise API (Applications Programming Interface) gateway provides access to GroupWise messaging functions from within other applications.

The API gateway uses a keyword–text file interface to access the GroupWise databases. Some of the capabilities of the API gateway include importation of large lists of users, as well as exportation and importation of calendar and schedule information to and from other programs or file formats.

Large companies that have company databases often use the API gateway to transfer information from their databases directly into their GroupWise systems. This limits redundant data entry. For example, when a new employee is hired, that employee's information may be entered into a company database. You can then transfer the new employee's information from the database through the API gateway directly into GroupWise instead of re-entering the data into the system.

A complete overview of the GroupWise API gateway, including the required hardware and software components, is provided in the document entitled "Product Overview—GroupWise API Gateway for OS/2," filename API.TB on the CD-ROM.

GroupWise Connectivity Products

Connecting GroupWise systems to other e-mail products and protocols is a topic that deserves a whole book (or even a set of books) in and of itself. Rather than delving into the intricacies of GroupWise connectivity, in this chapter I provide an overview of current GroupWise connectivity products that are available from Novell. I briefly explain the features of each product. Detailed technical "white papers" and product overviews have been included on the CD-ROM that comes with this book.

In this chapter, I discuss the following products:

▶ GroupWise cc:Mail gateway

▶ GroupWise Gateway to Lotus Notes

▶ Microsoft Mail Conversion utility

▶ GroupWise SMTP gateway

▶ GroupWise MHS gateway

▶ GroupWise OfficeVision/VM gateway

▶ GroupWise SNADS gateway

▶ GroupWise X.25 gateway

▶ GroupWise X.400 gateway

▶ GroupWise Gateway to Banyan IM III

Each of the above gateways connects GroupWise either to another e-mail system or to another e-mail protocol. In the section on the GroupWise SMTP gateway, I also provide an overview of different ways to configure your system to connect with the Internet.

GroupWise cc:Mail Gateway

The GroupWise cc:Mail gateway allows a GroupWise system to connect to a Lotus cc:Mail system. GroupWise users can send messages effortlessly from GroupWise to cc:Mail users, in the same manner the users would address other GroupWise users. Here are some of the key features of the cc:Mail gateway:

► cc:Mail Import/Export utility transfers messages between GroupWise and cc:Mail systems.

► The cc:Mail Automatic Directory Exchange (ADE) utility provides directory synchronization between GroupWise and cc:Mail. (This product is available separately from Lotus.)

► The gateway supports distribution lists, file attachments, scheduling messages, and send options.

► The gateway supports passthrough messaging. This allows a cc:Mail system to act as a transport mechanism between separate GroupWise systems without losing any GroupWise functionality.

► The cc:Mail utility comes with a Migrate utility that can be used to move a cc:Mail user and the user's messages from a cc:Mail system to a GroupWise system.

The cc:Mail gateway runs on the DOS platform. For more details about each of the cc:Mail gateway's features, as well as a complete listing of system requirements and an overview of how the gateway works, see the document entitled "Product Overview—GroupWise Gateway for cc:Mail," filename CCMAIL.TB on the CD-ROM.

GroupWise Gateway to Lotus Notes

The Gateway to Lotus Notes connects GroupWise users to users of Lotus Notes. These are some of the Notes gateway's key features:

▸ Provides directory synchronization that, when enabled, keeps a GroupWise user list and Notes primary address book synchronized. This allows GroupWise users to choose Notes users from the GroupWise address book.

▸ Supports directory exchange. When directory exchange is enabled, each night a full update of the GroupWise address book occurs in Notes, and a full update of the Notes foreign domain and post offices occurs in GroupWise.

▸ Automatically converts GroupWise messages into Notes-message format and then sends them to a Notes domain through the Notes server. All features that are supported in both Notes and GroupWise are preserved in the translation process.

▸ Allows GroupWise users to send file attachments along with messages. The Notes gateway sends the message and the attachments in original formats to the Notes server.

▸ Includes a migration process that takes messages in Notes-users' existing message databases and converts them to GroupWise format.

▸ Supports passthrough or tunneled messages. This allows the Notes system to act as an intermediary transport between two or more physically separate GroupWise system without losing any GroupWise functionality.

▸ Offers numerous send options, such as message priorities and return notifications, for messages sent between GroupWise users and Notes users.

The Notes gateway runs on the OS/2 platform. For more details about the GroupWise Lotus Notes gateway's features, as well as a complete listing of system requirements and an overview of how the gateway works, see the document entitled "Product Overview— GroupWise Gateway for Lotus Notes," filename LNOTES.TB on the CD-ROM.

Microsoft Mail Conversion Utility

The Microsoft Mail Conversion utility is not a gateway, but it deserves mention in this section because it allows a Microsoft Mail user's messages to be converted and moved into a GroupWise system. This utility is available on the Novell Remote Document Server, Novell NetWire CompuServe forum, and the Novell World Wide Web Internet site.

The Microsoft Mail Conversion utility extracts messages from a user's message store and converts them into a format that the GroupWise API gateway can read. The API gateway then converts the user's information into a GroupWise format.

When you extract the Microsoft Mail Conversion files, you should find a file named README.MCU. This file explains the Microsoft Mail Conversion utility in detail. The Microsoft Mail Conversion utility is included on the CD-ROM that comes with this book.

GroupWise SMTP Gateway

The GroupWise SMTP gateway allows GroupWise users to exchange messages with users on networks running TCP/IP protocol. The SMTP gateway translates and sends messages from the GroupWise system to any SMTP (Simple Mail Transfer Protocol) message system through TCP/IP. This is one of the most widely used gateways because it provides a way to connect a GroupWise system to the Internet. The GroupWise SMTP gateway is available for UNIX, DOS, and as a NetWare NLM.

When a GroupWise user sends a message to a user on an SMTP system, the gateway converts the message to SMTP text format and transfers it to the foreign mail system. Binary attachments are automatically uuencoded and uudecoded.

This gateways performs the following services:

▶ Automatically converts appointments, tasks, notes, and telephone messages to text messages.

▶ Offers different message-priority levels (high, normal, and low).

▸ Provides attachment capabilities, even though standard SMTP protocol does not support attachments. The gateway encodes and decodes attached files automatically, using UUENCODING. This encoding system converts non-ASCI files to a 7-bit ASCII character set. This character set can be send across a diverse range of network types.

▸ Allows GroupWise users to exchange messages with other GroupWise users at remote sites or satellite locations. Passthrough messaging facilitates message interchange and provides complete GroupWise compatibility.

If your GroupWise system needs to communicate via the Internet, one possibility is to connect to the Internet through a GroupWise SMTP gateway.

For details about the GroupWise SMTP gateway's features, as well as a complete listing of system requirements and an overview of how the gateway works, see the document entitled "Product Overview—GroupWise SMTP Gateway," filename SMTP.TB on the CD-ROM.

CONNECTING TO THE INTERNET WITH AN SMTP GATEWAY

In organizations that already have a direct pipe to the Internet (or plan to obtain one) the GroupWise SMTP gateway will allow you to exchange messages with Internet users.

Detailed instructions on how to set up a network to access the Internet would be beyond the scope of this book. Nevertheless, you need to make sure that network-level Internet connectivity components are in place before you install and configure the GroupWise SMTP gateway for connection to the Internet.

TIP

To verify that the appropriate network-level requirements are in place for a machine that will run the SMTP gateway, try to *ping* **(i.e., send a test signal and receive a confirmation signal back using the PING utility) another machine to which Internet messages will be sent. If you can successfully ping another machine's IP address, the machine can then be set up to run the SMTP gateway.**

Here are some general steps for setting up a GroupWise system with an SMTP gateway connection to the Internet; however, you should refer to the SMTP gateway documentation for precise details about set up and configuration:

1 • Install the SMTP gateway software to a GroupWise domain.

2 • Configure the SMTP gateway in GroupWise Admin.

3 • Configure the machine that will run the SMTP gateway.

4 • (Optional) Create a foreign domain that will represent the Internet.

5 • (Optional) Create a gateway link between the domain that contains the SMTP gateway and the foreign domain.

6 • (Optional) Create links between the other domains in the system and the foreign domain. These are usually indirect links through the domain that contains the gateway.

Addressing Messages to the Internet

Steps 4 through 6 above are optional. However, I recommend following those steps because they simplify addressing for the GroupWise users.

If these steps are not followed, users will have to use absolute addressing to send messages via the Internet. The syntax for absolute addressing of messages sent via the Internet is *domain.gateway:"user@host"*. For example, if a user wanted to send a message to STEPHANIE@ACME.COM, the addressing syntax might be:

```
HDQRTRS.SMTPGATE:"STEPHANIE@ACME.COM"
```

where HDQRTRS is the name of the domain that contains the gateway, and SMTPGATE is the name of the SMTP gateway. Figure 22.1 illustrates how a GroupWise system would appear if a foreign domain is not configured.

F I G U R E   22.1

GroupWise System with
SMTP Gateway Installed

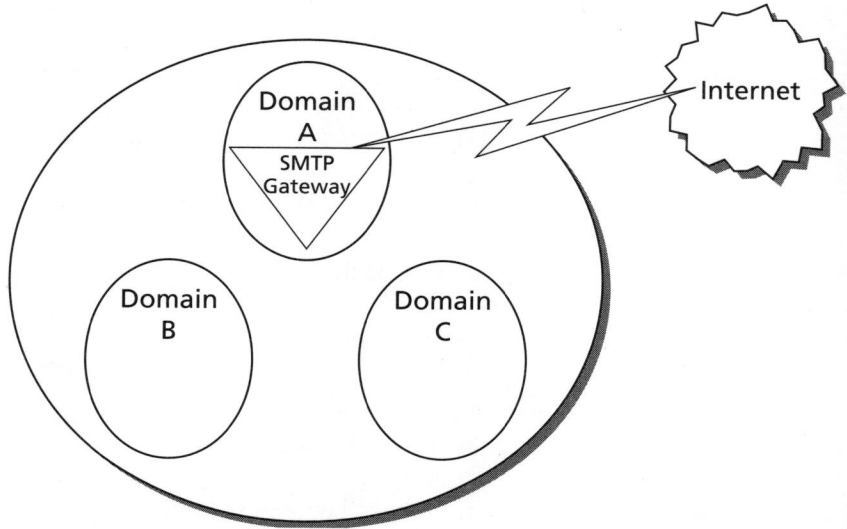

If you use Steps 4 through 6 and configure a foreign domain to represent the Internet, the addressing is much easier because the users can simply enter the domain name followed by the Internet address. The syntax is *domain:user@host*. For example, to send a message to STEPHANIE@ACME.COM, the syntax would be as follows:

```
INTERNET:STEPHANIE@ACME.COM
```

where INTERNET is the name of the foreign domain. Figure 22.2 shows a system that has a foreign domain configured.

The foreign domain is often named INET or INTERNET to simplify addressing for the GroupWise users who send messages via the Internet.

TIP

*GroupWise System with
Foreign Domain*

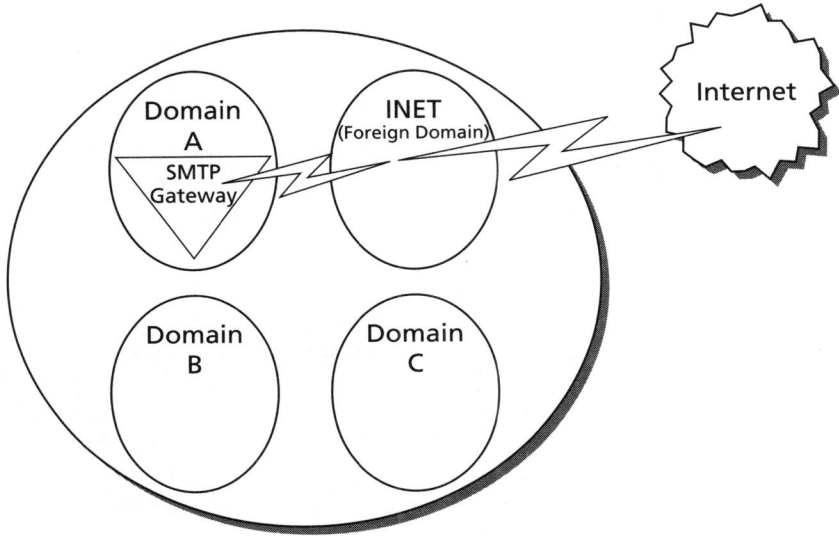

To further simplify addressing to recipients on the Internet, a GroupWise administrator can create user-information for the Internet recipients. An administrator must create a foreign domain with post offices and users and then link the domain to the gateway. Internet users are created using the same information required for GroupWise users on a LAN. By creating users in the foreign domain, GroupWise users can select Internet users directly from the address book.

TIP **GroupWise users can simplify addressing to Internet recipients by creating a personal group for each Internet recipient. The public group stores the complete addresses for those recipients. An alternative way to simplify addressing is to use the QuickCorrect feature in the Windows client and define a QuickCorrect entry that automatically types out the recipient's Internet address in the TO: field.**

Receiving Messages from the Internet

Once the SMTP gateway has been installed, every GroupWise user in the system automatically receives an Internet address through which they can receive Internet mail. If a user's ID is unique within the entire GroupWise system, the address will become the user's Internet address. The syntax is user *ID@host name*. The host name must be a fully qualified domain and host name for the gateway machine. User IDs that are not unique must include a post office name in the address (*post office user ID@host name*) or the administrator must create an alias for that user.

USING AN INTERNET MESSAGING PROVIDER

In organizations where obtaining a direct pipe to the Internet is not feasible (for example, because of administrative issues or cost) contracting with a public GroupWise hub service can be a good alternative. This option is often used in smaller GroupWise systems with between 5 and 500 users, where messaging traffic to and from the Internet is not expected to be extremely high.

A GroupWise hub service provides these advantages:

▸ No need to up a security firewall to prevent intruders from accessing your system. All communication goes through an asynchronous connection between your GroupWise system and the hub service.

▸ You pay only for the hub service and your long-distance phone charges. (Some hub service providers offer reduced long-distance rates.)

▸ Hub service can easily be defined as an external domain and linked to your system with an Async gateway.

▸ You only have to administer the Async gateway, instead of worrying about Internet administrative issues.

▸ Most hub services register companies' names with the Internet.

A drawback to using a hub service is that the users in your system will not have "surfing privileges" to browse the Internet. A hub service only provides a message passthrough solution. Also, heavy Internet traffic may necessitate installation of expensive hardware to support the Async gateway. For example, if several users decide to subscribe to high-volume Internet mail lists, the Async gateway could quickly become overloaded. Some mail lists generate hundreds of messages per day.

How It Works

When you use a public GroupWise hub service, you contract with the service, and they worry about all of the Internet administrative issues, such as maintaining the Internet connection, providing security, etc. The service usually takes care of the paperwork involved with registering a company's name with the Internet. Basically, you pay the service to take care of the steps outlined in the previous section. The service sets up and maintains the Internet connection and the SMTP gateway in its own system.

At your site, you define the hub service as an external domain and then install and configure an Async gateway in your system (if you don't already have one). You then define a Remote Domain Profile for the hub service's Async gateway and link to the external domain with a gateway link.

Because you can configure calling schedules and intervals for the Async gateway, you can control how often your system calls the hub service to pass messages to the Internet. As you learned in Chapter 15, you can configure the Async gateway to call when a certain number of high, medium, or low priority messages are waiting to be sent. Therefore, you can set up the gateway to connect quickly when high priority messages are waiting. You can also configure the calling schedules to take advantage of discount calling periods.

In most cases, the hub service will not initiate calls to your site for incoming Internet messages unless you provide the hub service with a toll-free telephone number to your gateway.

NOTE

Once you have established a connection to the hub service, users can send messages to the Internet by using standard Internet addressing (e.g., JOHN@ACME.COM), preceded by the name of the external domain. For example, on the TO: line, a user would might type:

```
INTERNET:JOHN@ACME.COM
```

where INTERNET is the name of the external domain.

Users in your system will have their own Internet IDs, which also include the names of their post offices (unless your system only has one post office). For example, if NoCWACs were to use an Internet hub service, the Internet ID for a user named Burke in the MGMT post office would be BURKE@MGMT.NOCWACS.COM.

To use a hub service, you must make sure all users in your system have unique GroupWise user IDs.

IMPORTANT

To get recommendations for public GroupWise hub services that can provide Internet messaging services in your area, you should post a message on any of the GroupWise-related online services.

GroupWise MHS Gateway

The GroupWise MHS gateway is a message handling service (MHS) gateway that provides compatibility with MHS networks. The gateway provides connectivity to MHS-compatible message systems, such as X.400, Da Vinci, SMTP, Wang, TELEX, PROFS/OfficeVision/VM, CompuServe, X.121, DEC, MCI Mail, and AT&T EasyLink.

The MHS gateway translates message files from GroupWise format to the Standard Message Format (SMF-71 or -70) and then transfers the file to the MHS mail system.

The MHS gateway is available for the DOS platform and as an NLM. For more details about the MHS gateway—including how the gateway interacts with MHS systems—and a complete listing of system requirements, see the document entitled "Product Overview—GroupWise MHS Gateway for NLM and DOS," filename MHSGATE.TB on the CD-ROM.

GroupWise OfficeVision/VM Gateway

The OfficeVision/VM (PROFS) gateway connects GroupWise users with users on IBM mainframe OfficeVision/VM or PROFS systems.

This gateway provides cross-calendar checking, directory synchronization, and a user migration tool from PROFS to GroupWise.

The OfficeVision/VM gateway is available for OS/2. For more details about the OfficeVision/VM gateway, as well as a complete listing of system requirements and an overview of how the gateway works, see the document entitled "Product Overview—GroupWise OfficeVision/VM Gateway for OS/2," filename OVVMGATE.TB on the CD-ROM.

GroupWise SNADS Gateway

The SNADS gateway transports and converts GroupWise information to other systems that use SNADS (Systems Network Architecture Distribution Services). These systems include OfficeVision/400, OfficeVision/MVS, Verimation MEMO/VM, MEMO/MVS, and IBM's Message Exchange (collectively referred to as *hosts*).

The GroupWise SNADS gateway gives GroupWise and host users the ability to exchange messages transparently. The SNADS gateway provides a directory exchange process that facilitates administration and allows users to select GroupWise and host recipients from native address lists.

The SNADS gateway is available for OS/2. For more details about the SNADS gateway, as well as a complete listing of system requirements and an overview of how the gateway works, see the document entitled "Product Overview—GroupWise SNADS Gateway," filename SNADS.TB on the CD-ROM.

GroupWise X.25 Gateway

The GroupWise X.25 gateway connects GroupWise and remote sites together through an X.25 network. The X.25 gateway also supports wireless users with RAM Mobile Data's wireless data network.

The X.25 gateway is available for OS/2. Two documents on the CD-ROM provide details about the X.25 Standard and the GroupWise X.25 gateway:

▸ "GroupWise 4.1 OS/2 X.25 Gateway," filename X25GATE.IE

▸ "GroupWise 4.1 X.25 Gateway—X.25 Basics," filename X25BASIC.WPD

GroupWise X.400 Gateway

The GroupWise X.400 gateway allows GroupWise users to send GroupWise messages to users in an X.400 messaging standard system. The GroupWise X.400 gateway provides access to electronic mail systems that support the X.400 specification.

The X.400 gateway is available for OS/2. For more details about the GroupWise X.400 gateway, including an overview of the X.400 standard and the gateway's features and a complete listing of system requirements, see the document entitled "Product Overview—GroupWise X.400 Gateway for OS/2," filename X400GATE.TB on the CD-ROM.

GroupWise Gateway to Banyan IM III

The GroupWise 4.1 Gateway to Banyan IM III allows GroupWise users to communicate with Banyan IM users (i.e., users of any e-mail package that utilizes IM). It allows Banyan network sites to implement GroupWise e-mail, calendaring, and scheduling on their existing enterprise network infrastructures.

The gateway is a DOS-based program that can run on a GroupWise message server or on a separate, dedicated DOS workstation. (The workstation should be connected to the file server storing the GroupWise domain directories and to the server running VINES Intelligent Messaging.) In addition to the DOS-based gateway, a VINES service (Proxy) component must be installed to provide connection to Intelligent Messaging.

This gateway provides directory synchronization with Banyan STDA, conversion of GroupWise messages to and from Banyan Intelligent Messaging, and Passthrough Messaging (tunneling) via Intelligent Messaging.

For more details about the GroupWise 4.1 Gateway to Banyan IM III features, as well as a complete listing of system requirements and an overview of how the gateway works, see the document entitled "Instant Expert Guide—GroupWise 4.1 Gateway to Banyan IM III," filename BANGATE.IE on the CD-ROM.

Novell GroupWare Products: InForms and SoftSolutions

In addition to GroupWise, there are two other programs in Novell's GroupWare product line—Novell InForms and Novell SoftSolutions. In this chapter, I provide an overview of these products and explain how they integrate with GroupWise.

Novell InForms

Novell InForms is a tool to help organizations collect and distribute data. It solves many of the bureaucratic problems associated with paper forms in the business world. For example, it eliminates the need to enter data manually into databases from paper forms, and it checks to make sure that the data collected is accurate.

InForms can also act as a front end to a wide range of desktop and SQL databases. This capability allows data to be collected and queried so that reports can be generated automatically.

InForms has five main components:

▶ InForms Designer

▶ InForms Filler

▶ Security Module

▶ Database Services

▶ Workflow Services

The first three are actually separate programs that ship with InForms. Database services and workflow services are structural components of InForms. I discuss workflow services later in this chapter, in the section where I explain how InForms integrates with GroupWise.

INFORMS DESIGNER

InForms Designer is used to create and edit electronic and printed forms. InForms Designer provides a variety of tools for creating sophisticated forms, including a variety of data-entry and lookup fields, calculations, drawing tools, tables, and viewers. These tools can be used to create simple single-page forms, as well as complex multiple-page forms.

Data Fields A data field in a form is linked to a field in one or more databases. A data field can be used to display information already in a database, or an end user can input information to be added to a database.

Calculations Calculations can be embedded in forms to process data automatically and perform a variety of functions. InForms Designer supports arithmetic, attribute, database, date/time, financial, statistical, text, and other types of data-manipulation that can be used to automate work processes.

Drawing Tools InForms Designer includes a large set of drawing tools that can be used to make forms both attractive and easy to use. You can use the form creator to create design elements from scratch, or you can import graphics (such as backgrounds and logos). InForms also supports common of bar-code types.

Tables InForms Designer's tables feature can be used to create entry fields quickly in a column-and-row format. Cells in a table can then be linked to databases just like an entry field. Table cells can also hold spreadsheet and other calculations to process information automatically as soon as it is entered.

Viewers InForms Designer can also insert a file viewer within a form so that end users can preview files—such as word processing documents, graphics, and other forms—without actually bringing the files into the form. The viewer can be sized and placed anywhere in the form, and its uses are varied. For example, an end user could view a document and drag selected text from the document to a form field, or display photographs in a personnel file, or display floor plans to prospective real estate customers.

INFORMS FILLER

Once forms have been created in the designer, they can be viewed and filled in using InForms Filler, which is available for DOS, Windows, and Macintosh. Forms can be used to gather information, as well as to distribute information to users. Each user in a network who needs to fill in or view a form must access to the filler program. The features of Informs Filler are:

Query   To locate specific information, an end user can use the filler's query function to query databases linked to a form. Using the query feature, a user indicates which fields should be searched and then specifies search keys (or criteria) for each field. When data satisfying the query is displayed in InForms Filler, it can then be brought into a form. The information can then be modified and saved back into databases. Records satisfying the query can also be printed or saved as a new database.

Find   The find feature is similar to the Query feature, except that it is used from within an actual form. After filling in one or more form fields, a user can utilize this feature to find records that match the information already entered into the form. For example, if a user has already filled in the First Name, Last Name, and City fields in a form, the user can then use Find to search for occurrences of records in the database that match the values entered.

SECURITY MODULE

When you design a form, you can use the Security Module included with InForms to make sure that sensitive information is not compromised by people filling in forms and querying databases while using InForms Filler. Once created, the security database can be used to add safeguards, such as electronic signatures, TamperSeal, and RSA encryption to selected forms.

Security Database   The InForms administrator adds user names, user IDs, user passwords, user departments, and approval groups to the security database. The combination of user name and user ID uniquely identifies each user. Approval groups are similar to e-mail distribution groups, except that they are used to assign the same approval authority to a group of people. For example, a certain group of people may have authority to approve amounts listed in an electronic expense report form. Only users who need to "sign" the electronic forms are included in the security database.

Signature Fields   When designing a form that needs to be secured, you can create a signature field on the form. This signature field is then linked to an approval group in the security database. You choose which approval groups are valid for a particular form and then specify which users can sign the form to complete it. Multiple signature fields can be included in a single form, allowing for multiple levels of approval.

TamperSeal   InForms uses TamperSeal technology to ensure that forms are not modified by unauthorized users.

RSA Encryption   RSA is both a company, RSA Data Securities, Inc., and an algorithm called RSA Public/Private Key Cryptogram. Novell has licensed this technology from RSA Data Securities, Inc., to provide security for forms created in InForms. The public and private keys used in the security databases described above are created with RSA.

Database Services

Novell InForms provides extensive database support. InForms provides access to these desktop databases:

- ASCII Delimited
- dBase
- Btrieve
- FoxPro
- Clipper
- Paradox
- DataPerfect
- WP Secondary Merge

InForms provides access to these SQL databases:

- DB2
- Informix
- Microsoft SQL Server
- Lotus Notes
- Oracle
- OS/2 DBM

- NetWare SQL
- XDB
- ODBC
- SQLBase
- Sybase

Database Linking   When creating a form in InForms Designer, fields within the form can be linked to fields in any of the databases listed above. InForms also supports multiple links to multiple databases within a single form. Each field can be linked to one or more databases, and one or more fields in the database. This multiple linking is transparent to a user viewing or filling in the form.

Database Creation and Conversion   InForms incorporates the ability to create many popular desktop database structures, including dBase, Clipper, FoxPro, and Btrieve. For example, a person creating a form in InForms Designer can create a data link and select Paradox as the database type and then actually create a Paradox database at the same time. The user does not need to own Paradox to accomplish this task, and the database can then be accessed by Paradox users who do not own InForms.

NOTE   **This database creation capability currently applies only to certain desktop databases. To link with or create SQL databases, the designer must have the appropriate SQL database software.**

InForms also provides the ability to convert information from one database format to another. Users can query any database, or set of databases, and save the resulting data in a completely different database format.

Integrating InForms and GroupWise

Forms created using InForms can be accessed and filled in directly from a network file server. However, using InForms in conjunction with GroupWise dramatically extends your form-distribution capabilities.

> **NOTE**
>
> **InForms also supports some other e-mail systems, including WordPerfect Office 3.1 and 4.0, cc:Mail, Microsoft Mail, and Windows for WorkGroups. However, Novell GroupWise gives you the fullest range of InForms functionality.**

When using InForms in conjunction with GroupWise, a user simply selects GroupWise from the Mail menu. The user then fills in the GroupWise fields and the form is sent as an attachment to the message. This allows the form to travel anywhere in the GroupWise system, including to GroupWise Remote users and through gateways that support binary file attachments.

GroupWise also allows forms to be routed to a list of users in sequential order. For example, if you have a form that must be signed by several people with different levels of authority, GroupWise can route the form to the appropriate individuals in the appropriate order, thereby providing workflow services for form-routing.

Forms can be sent from GroupWise to several users at once, using two different methods. The first is known as a *broadcast message* (or *parallel routing*). Using this method, you simply add multiple users to the To: field. The second method involves using a GroupWise *routing slip*. The Routing Slip is found under the Send menu in the GroupWise client. When recipients of a routed form do not change, the route can be hard-coded into the form.

Another advantage offered by using GroupWise and InForms together is that a form's routing status can be checked by using the GroupWise Out Box.

There are two ways to send a form—as a form transport file (.ML) or as a data-only file (.DO). A form transport file is essentially the same as a regular form file, except that an .ML file itself only holds data (as opposed to linking directly to a database). An .ML file should be used when a recipient does not have network access to the database that the form is linked to. A data-only file should only be used when you know that the recipient has access to the database that the form is linked to.

When a user fills in a form that has been sent as a form transport file, the data entered is not immediately saved to the database; it is saved with the form transport file. When the user mails the form back to a person who has access to the database, that person then copies the data from the .ML file to the database.

Two documents on the CD-ROM provide extensive information about Novell InForms:

▸ "InForms Product Overview," filename INFORMS.WPD

▸ "InForms Architecture," filename INFRMARC.WPD

Novell SoftSolutions

SoftSolutions is a document manager that offers both system administrators and users several tools to solve network information overload. SoftSolutions offers six basic services and functions for document management:

▸ Searching and retrieval services so users can quickly find and access documents

▸ Library services that automate the filing, retrieval, withdrawal and profiling of documents on a network

▸ Security services to protect data (SoftSolutions enforces document security at the management systems level, the file level, and the network level.)

▸ Version control that tracks multiple versions of documents

▸ Archival and deletion control

▸ Integration with applications, as well as networks

Two documents on the CD-ROM provide extensive information about SoftSolutions and Novell's document management strategy:

▶ "SoftSolutions Product Overview," filename SOFTSOL.WPD

▶ "SoftSolutions Document Management Architecture," filename SSOLARCH.WPD

Integrating SoftSolutions and GroupWise

SoftSolutions and GroupWise integrate in two ways:

▶ ODMA (Open Document Management Architecture)

▶ RDS (Remote Document Server)

ODMA

ODMA (Open Document Management Architecture) is a standard API specification that document management vendors and many application vendors have agreed to use.

When you use ODMA with GroupWise, the Open, Attach, Save, and Save As dialog boxes are customized to allow you to control where a document is stored and how it can be retrieved.

REMOTE DOCUMENT SERVER (RDS)

A SoftSolutions Remote Document Server makes documents stored on a LAN available to users who are not connected to the LAN. The RDS accomplishes this by using an e-mail system, such as GroupWise, as the transport agent.

With RDS, users can send search requests and other commands to SoftSolutions in e-mail messages. The RDS, which is running on a workstation connected to the LAN, receives and processes these messages and then responds to users by sending return messages with the documents or search results requested.

With RDS, remote users can perform full-text or profile searches, retrieve copies of documents, check out documents for editing, check in documents, add new documents, and forward existing documents to other users.

To try out an RDS for yourself, send an e-mail message to PUBLIC@NOVELL.COM with the word "Help" in the subject line. You will receive a reply message that contains instructions for using Novell's GroupWare RDS, along with a list of the GroupWare-related documents and utilities that you can receive through this service.

Overview of Some GroupWise Client Features

Appendix A provides an overview of the GroupWise client features that have been mentioned in this book. These are the features that directly affect GroupWise administrative decisions and tasks.

Proxy

The *proxy* feature allows a GroupWise user to access another GroupWise user's mailbox. The user who accesses another's mailbox must have access rights to that mailbox. The access rights must be granted by the mailbox owner. A system administrator cannot give access rights to a user.

The proxy feature only works within post offices. When planning a GroupWise system, administrators need to be aware of this limitation so that users who must have proxy access to other users' information are located in the appropriate post offices. For example, if an administrative assistant needs to read a supervisor's calendar, the assistant needs to be placed in the same post office as the supervisor.

Users in the same workgroups often grant to each other the Read proxy right to calendar information. This allows each member of the workgroup to check the other members' schedules.

IMPORTANT

Users should be very careful about which access rights they grant to other users. Users should be especially wary about granting the Write privilege because that privilege allows other users to write and send GroupWise messages in someone else's name.

Send Options

When you send an e-mail message with GroupWise, the Send options you select can affect how the message is sent. For example, you can choose to send the message high priority, reply requested, and with a return mail receipt.

Use the following steps to access the Send options:

1 • Double-click on a message icon (mail, appointment and so forth).

2 • Choose Send and then select Send Options. You will see the dialog box shown in Figure A.1.

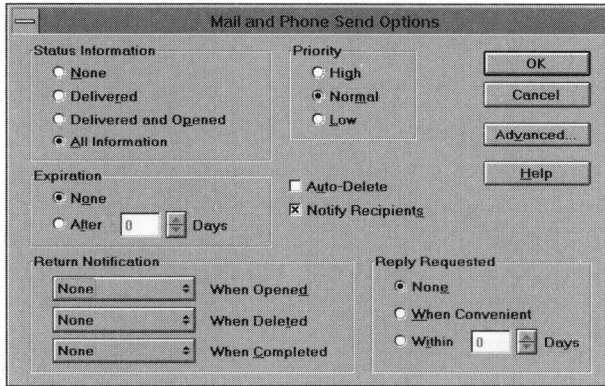

F I G U R E A.1

Send Options Dialog Box

3 • Select the desired options.

4 • Choose OK.

A message's priority determines which queue directories are used when the message moves through the GroupWise system. Table A.1 shows the message types that are processed through each queue directory:

T A B L E A.1

Queue Directory Uses

DIRECTORY	PRIMARY USE
0	Busy searches
1	GroupWise Remote requests
2	Admin messages and high-priority GroupWise messages
3	High-priority status messages
4	Normal-priority messages

(continued)

DIRECTORY	PRIMARY USE
5	Normal-priority status messages
6	Low-priority messages
7	Low-priority status messages

Views

If you are using a graphical GroupWise client (Windows, Macintosh, or UNIX), each of the message types and the day-calendar have different *views*. A view is simply a different visual layout of a message item. For example, a mail item has three views: Mail, Small Mail, and Expanded Mail. The Small Mail view is shown in Figure A.2.

F I G U R E A.2

Small Mail View

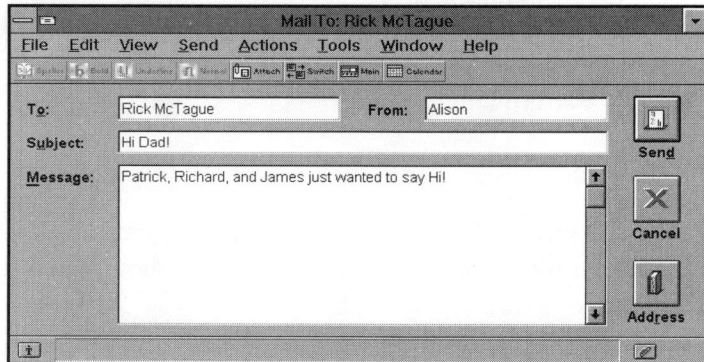

Notice that the Small Mail view does not contain a Carbon Copy or Blind Copy field. GroupWise comes with a utility program called *View Designer*. With View Designer, users can create custom views for each message type and for the calendar. Views can contain colors, different fonts, graphic images, embedded objects, etc. An example of a custom view is shown in Figure A.3.

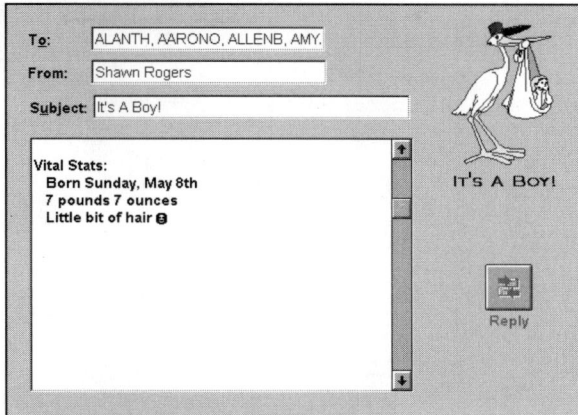

When a view is used to send an item, it is transported along with the message. GroupWise users who are using a client that supports a graphical interface see the view created by the sender.

> **Views that contain colors, fonts, graphics, etc., increase the size of the message that is sent and therefore increase network traffic.**

IMPORTANT

Address Book

The address book is a directory of GroupWise objects (users, resources, groups, etc.) that is available from the GroupWise Main Window or from within any of the message types. The address book displays the information contained in the post office's WPHOST.DB file. The address book for the Windows client is shown in Figure A.4.

F I G U R E A.4

Address Book

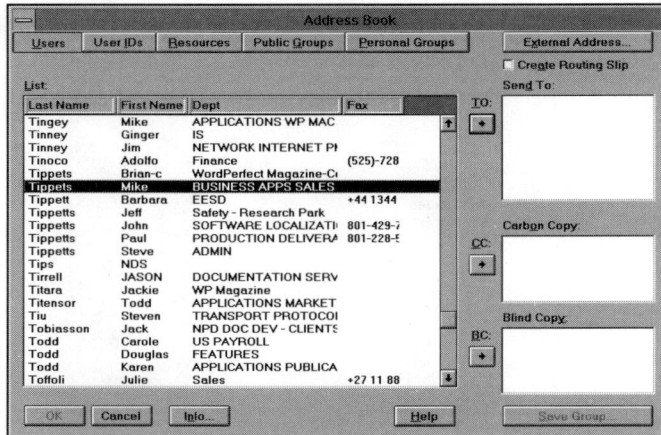

The following parts of the address book are defined by the system administrator:

- ▸ Sort-order for user names

- ▸ Public groups

- ▸ Resources

Personal groups are defined by the user and are stored in the user's master mailbox (USER*xxx*.DB).

The visibility setting that is established for a user determines which address books in the system display the user's information. A GroupWise user with system visibility is listed in all address books in the system. A GroupWise user with domain visibility is only listed in the address books in that domain, and a GroupWise user with post office visibility is only listed in the address books of users in that post office. If you have a certain group of users who need to be visible to each other but should not be visible anywhere else in the system, you need to put all of those users in their own post office.

User Preferences

The system administrator has the ability to use the GroupWise Administration program to set default user preferences for the client software. Preferences are accessed by clicking on File and then choosing Preferences.

The following are some of the default preferences you may want to set for GroupWise users:

▶   Mail and Appointment Send options

▶   Location of files

▶   Cleanup options

▶   Security access

Chapter 18 explains how to set user options from GroupWise Admin.

Rules

A rule is an action or series of actions performed on a GroupWise message when certain conditions are met. GroupWise users define both the conditions that are required and the actions that occur.

The Create Rule dialog box is shown in Figure A.5. Notice that the rule named "Rick's Messages." This rule watches for any incoming mail, notes, tasks, or appointments from Rick, and automatically empties the item from the Trash.

Create Rule Dialog Box

Create Rule		
Rule Name: Rick's Messages		**Save**
When Event Is		**Cancel**
Event: New Item ⬥ ⦿ Incoming ◯ Outgoing ◯ Personal		**Users...**
If Item Type Is		**Help**
☒ Mail ☒ Appointment ☒ Task ☒ Note ☐ Phone **Misc Values...**		
If Item Contents Are		
From: Rick McTague **Subject:**		
To: **Message:**		
CC:		
Then Actions Are		
Empty Item	**Add** ▾	
	Edit	
	Delete	

Here are a few common uses of GroupWise rules:

▸ Automatically reply to the sender of a message stating that you are out of the office and will return on a certain date.

▸ Automatically move certain items to a specified folder. This is very helpful if you subscribe to Internet mailing lists and would like all messages from a list automatically placed in a folder for future reference.

▸ Forward high-priority messages to a pager (if paging is supported in the GroupWise system).

Rules are stored in the user's database (USERxxx.DB).

Novell Education GroupWise Courses

Novell Education offers the following certification programs for GroupWise:

▸ CNA (Certified Novell Administrator)

▸ CNE (Certified Novell Engineer)

▸ CNI (Certified Novell Instructor)

The following GroupWise courses are available from Novell Authorized Education Centers (NAECs) worldwide:

Course 325: GroupWise 4 Administration

Overview   Learn how to plan, configure, maintain, and troubleshoot GroupWise systems of low to moderate complexity.

Target Audience   Experienced network administrators, CNA and CNE candidates.

Type of Course   Instructor-led

Course Length   3 days

Key Topics   The following topics are covered:

▸ GroupWise messaging system structure

▸ Responsibilities of the GroupWise administrator

▸ Single post office administration

▸ Multiple post office administration

▸ Multiple domain systems

Courses 326 and 327: GroupWise 4 Async Gateways and Remote Client Support

Overview   Learn how to add Async Gateway capability to an existing GroupWise system and provide support for GroupWise Remote users. Course 326 teaches you haw to set up and configure the DOS and OS/2 Async Gateway versions. Course 327 teaches you how to set up and configure the OS/2 and NLM Async Gateway versions.

Type of Course   Instructor-led

Course Length   2 days

Key Topics   The following topics are covered:

▸   GroupWise Async gateway overview

▸   DOS and OS/2 Async gateways (326)

▸   NLM and OS/2 Async gateways (327)

▸   MS Windows Remote client

▸   Remote client support

▸   Monitoring and troubleshooting Async gateways and remote clients

Course 328: GroupWise 4 Advanced Administration

Overview   Learn how to perform advanced GroupWise administration tasks in a multiple domain GroupWise system. Course 328 teaches you how to perform advanced client administration techniques, how to administer users, how to set up advanced message server configurations, and how to use the GroupWise Integration Module (NWAdmin Snap-in Tool).

Type of Course   Instructor-led

Course Length   2 days

Key Topics   The following topics are covered:

- ▸ Advanced client administration

- ▸ User administration

- ▸ External domains

- ▸ Consolidating GroupWise systems

- ▸ Advanced message server configurations

- ▸ GroupWise Integration Module

- ▸ GroupWise technologies

In addition to the above-listed system administration courses, Novell Education also offers a GroupWise client course—Course 321a: Introduction for New Users Module.

Course 321a teaches the basics of using the GroupWise messaging system. It introduces new users to the different types of GroupWise messages, including electronic mail, telephone messages, group and personal appointments, group and personal tasks, and group and personal notes.

For additional information about Novell Education's certification programs and courses, call 1-800-233-3382 (within the United States only), or 1-801-429-5508.

Setting Up a GroupWise Test System on a Single PC

In this appendix section, I explain how to set up a multiple-domain GroupWise system using a single PC. This exercise can be used as a training tool to familiarize yourself with GroupWise Admin and to help you understand the procedures for setting up domains, post offices, users, and the GroupWise client.

As you set up you test system, you can try some of the optional activities I present throughout this appendix. Additional optional activities are listed at the end of the appendix.

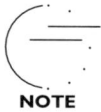

NOTE

Some of the steps in this appendix apply only to setting up a test system and would not be performed if you were actually installing GroupWise on a network. I indicate which steps those are with the words "Simulation Only."

In order to set up a test system, you need to have the following:

- ▶ 386/33 computer or faster (I recommend a 486 computer.)

- ▶ 100MB free hard disk space minimum

- ▶ Windows 3.1 installed

In addition to these requirements you need to load the DOS program SHARE.EXE, found in the DOS directory. You should put the command to load SHARE.EXE in the AUTOEXEC.BAT file.

TIP

This simulation works best if you can run Windows in a high-resolution display mode, such as SVGA 1024x768.

You need the following software:

- ▶ GroupWise 4.1 or 4.1a Administration diskettes

- ▶ GroupWise 4.1 or 4.1a Windows client

- ▶ GroupWise 4.1 or 4.1a DOS Message Server Pack

NOTE

These procedures have been tested on Windows 3.1. If you are familiar with OS/2 or with Windows 95, you can adapt these procedures to your operating system by simply using the OS/2 or Windows 95 conventions instead of the Windows 3.1 conventions explained here.

This appendix is divided into sections that correspond to the chapters in this book.

Chapter 4: Installing GroupWise and Configuring a GroupWise System

Materials needed:

- GroupWise Administration diskettes

- GroupWise Windows client diskettes

INITIAL INSTALLATION

1 • Go to the DOS prompt.

2 • Insert the GroupWise Admin Disk 1 into drive A:.

3 • Type **A:INSTALL** and press Enter.

4 • When prompted to continue installation, choose Y.

5 • The Install From option should list the current directory (A:). Accept this option when it is listed.

6 • Specify the domain directory to which the files will be installed. Type **C:\ DOMAIN1** and answer Y when prompted to create the directory.

NOTE

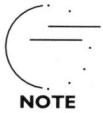

In these instructions, I use the **DOMAINx** and **POSTx** convention for the domain and post office directories, and I use generic names for the domains and post offices. You can use any names you want, just remember to substitute your names consistently.

7 • Select the Files to Install option, mark Administration and Windows Client, press F10 to continue, and press Enter on the Start Installation option.

8 • Choose Y when prompted to continue with the installation. The Administration files will be installed to C:\DOMAIN1. This will become the GroupWise primary domain directory.

9 • Insert each GroupWise disk as prompted by the installation program. When the installation is completed, follow the prompts to exit back to DOS.

10 • (Optional) Run Windows File Manager and look at the directory structures and files that have been installed under C:\ DOMAIN1. Look at the files in C:\ DOMAIN1\WPOFFICE\OFWIN40\SETUP. Notice that they are the compressed Windows client files. They are not decompressed in the domain directory. Also, notice that the Windows client views files have been installed in the C:\DOMAIN1\WPOFFICE\OFVIEWS\WIN subdirectory.

You have now installed the GroupWise Administration files and the Windows client files to the domain directory.

CREATING THE INITIAL DOMAIN, POST OFFICE, AND USER OBJECTS

The following steps guide you through the process of using the Assisted Setup program to create a domain, a post office, and users.

1 • Go to the C:\DOMAIN1 directory, type **AD**, and press Enter. GroupWise Admin will automatically launch the Assisted Setup routine because there is no domain database file (WPDOMAIN.DB) in the domain directory.

NOTE

You may need to load SHARE.EXE for GroupWise Admin to load. This program should be found in your DOS directory.

2 • Using the information in Table C.1, follow the Assisted Setup prompts to set up the primary domain, the post office, the Windows client, and users.

TABLE C.1	**FIELD**	**INFORMATION**
Assisted Setup Information	Domain Name	DOMAIN1
	Network Type	Novell NetWare
	Time Zone	Use the time zone for your region.
	Post Office	POST1
	Post Office Directory	C:\POST1
	Copy Software	Copy the Windows client software to the post office.
	Users	Create at least 5 users, using names of your choice.

3 • After adding several users, choose Continue, review the information presented about enabling the clients, and then choose Done to exit the Assisted Setup routine.

4 • (Optional) Run AD.EXE again. Notice that the Assisted Setup routine does not run. Add several more users manually using the Create menu.

5 • (Optional) Run Windows File Manager and look at the files and subdirectories in the C:\POST1 directory. Look at the files in the C:\POST1\OFWIN40\SETUP subdirectory. Notice that they are the compressed Windows client files, identical to the Windows client files in the domain directory structure.

6 • (Optional) Run a text editor program and open the README.AD file. Familiarize yourself with the contents of this file, especially the section about required network rights.

7 • (Optional) Open the ERRORS.TXT file in a text editor. Notice that it contains a detailed listing of GroupWise error messages and their possible causes and solutions.

You have now you created and named your domain and post office, created several GroupWise users, and copied the Windows Client software to the post office directory structure.

Chapter 5: Enabling the Client Software

In this part of the simulation, you will enable the GroupWise Windows client on the PC. Here are the steps for enabling the client in the post office and for performing a workstation installation.

1 • Run Windows.

2 • Click on File and then click on Run.

3 • Type **C:\POST1\SETUPWIN /A** and then click OK.

4 • (Simulation Only) Notice that the dialog box is entitled "GroupWise Server Install." These options are for enabling (decompressing) the Windows client files at the post office level. To conserve disk space in this simulation, choose Exit after you have looked at the options. *Do not install the software at this point.*

5 • From Windows Program Manager, click on File and then Run.

6 • Enter **C:\ POST1\ SETUPWIN** and then click on OK. The GroupWise Install dialog box will appear. These options install the GroupWise files to the workstation hard drive.

7 • Select the Standard Install option.

8 • Specify drive C: as the destination drive, and select OK. The Windows client will be installed to the C:\OFWIN40 directory, and a program group and program icons will be created for GroupWise in Windows Program Manager.

9 • (Optional) View the README file.

The Windows client has now been enabled. You can run the client for one of the users you created by using these steps:

1 • Highlight the GroupWise icon, and click on File and then Properties.

2 • Add the /@U-*user ID* switch to the command line.

3 • Double-click on the icon to run GroupWise for the user you specified in Step 2.

4 • (Simulation Only) When prompted, enter the network ID for the user. GroupWise should then open for that user. The network ID should be the same as the user ID.

TIP

You can put also put the /LA-*network ID* switch in the command line in the icon's properties to avoid the network ID prompt. This is necessary in the simulation because the simulation machine is not logged in to a network, therefore GroupWise cannot detect a valid network login ID upon startup.

TIP

You can also use the /@U-? switch on the command line, and GroupWise will prompt you for the user ID upon startup.

5 • (Optional) Send a message to another user in the post office.

6 • (Optional) Create another GroupWise icon for the user to whom you sent the message.

7 • (Optional) Modify the icon's properties using Step 2 above.

8 • (Optional) Run GroupWise for the recipient and verify that the message was received.

NOTE

The simulation works because the default post office security is set to Low. Otherwise, a password would be required on the master mailbox to allow the user of the /@U-userID switch. Also, the message can be sent to another user because the default message delivery mode is Server Never. Therefore, the client handles all message delivery.

Chapter 6: Managing a GroupWise Post Office

Chapter 6 discusses post office management issues. None of the tasks in this chapter will change the simulation PC's configuration. However, you can complete these optional activities on the simulation PC to solidify your understand the concepts presented in Chapter 6.

▶ Run GroupWise Admin for the domain and locate the post office security setting. Don't change it to High, or the simulation will not work.

▶ Use the File Manager program and find the message databases and the user databases that have been created in the post office. Identify which message database is used when a certain user sends a message. Match the user databases with the corresponding users by using the file IDs.

▶ Send several messages between users in the same post office using the steps listed in the simulation for Chapter 5. Send some messages with file attachments over 2K. Locate the file attachments in the directory store.

Chapter 7: Implementing a Multiple Post Office GroupWise System

Additional Software Needed   DOS Message Server Pack (1 disk)

In this portion of the simulation, you will install the DOS message server to the domain, create a second post office and users in your test system, run the DOS message server, and send messages between users in the two post offices.

INSTALL THE DOS MESSAGE SERVER PACK

1 • Go to a DOS prompt.

2 • Insert the DOS Message Server disk into drive A:.

3 • Type **A:INSTALL** and press Enter.

4 • Select Install To and specify your domain directory (C:\DOMAIN1).

5 • Select Files To Install, mark Message Server, press F10, and then choose the Start Installation option.

6 • Answer Y to the Continue with Installation prompt.

7 • Follow the prompts to return to DOS.

These steps installed the DOS message server files to the *<domain>*\WPCS directory.

CREATE ANOTHER POST OFFICE AND ADD SOME USERS

1 • Run AD.EXE from the domain directory.

2 • Click on Create and then choose Post Office.

3 • Enter a name for the post office (e.g., POST2).

4 • Enter a directory for the post office (C:\POST2). You can accept all other default options as they are listed.

5 • (Simulation Only) When you see the Copy Software to Post Office dialog box, unmark the Windows client, and choose OK. You will use the Windows client already installed when you run it for users in POST2. This will minimize the amount of disk space used by this simulation.

6 • Add three or four users by using the Create menu and selecting the User option.

Ctrl-U is a shortcut keystroke for creating users.

TIP

CONFIGURE THE MESSAGE SERVER DELIVERY MODE

Currently the message server delivery mode is set to Server Always. This mode will not allow messages to be sent between the two post offices. Use these steps to change the message delivery mode:

1 • Highlight the domain in GroupWise Admin and press F6.

F6 is a shortcut keystroke to edit the highlighted domain, post office, or object.

TIP

2 • Choose Message Server Configuration.

3 • Choose the Execution option.

4 • Choose Message Delivery.

5 • Choose Use App Thresholds.

6 • (Optional) Set the Logging Level to Diagnostic. This will allow you to watch the details of the message delivery process later when you run the message server.

7 • Choose OK to exit back to the main GroupWise Admin screen.

8 • Exit GroupWise Admin.

(SIMULATION ONLY) SETTING UP THE MESSAGE SERVER TO RUN IN A WINDOW

These steps set up an icon for the message server so that it will run in a window within Windows and allow you to watch message delivery occur between the two post offices.

1 • Run Windows.

2 • Open the Main program group.

3 • Double-click on the PIF Editor icon to open the PIF editor.

4 • Type **CS.EXE** in the Program Filename field.

5 • Type **DOS Message Server (DOMAIN1)** in the Window Title field.

6 • Type **/PH-C:\ DOMAIN1** in the Optional Parameters field.

7 • Type **C:\ DOMAIN1\WPCS** in the Start-up Directory field.

8 • Select the Windowed option in the Display Usage field.

9 • Mark the Background Execution check box.

10 • Select File and then select Save.

11 • Name the file CS1.PIF and then select OK.

12 • Select File and then choose Exit to exit the PIF Editor.

You have now created a custom PIF file that will allow the message server to run in a window. The next steps will create an icon to launch the DOS message server.

1 • Open the program group that contains your GroupWise icons.

2 • Choose File and then select New.

3 • Choose Program Item and then choose OK.

4 • Type **DOMAIN1 Message Server** in the Description field.

5 • Type **C:\WINDOWS\CS1.PIF** in the Command Line field.

6 • Choose OK to close the dialog box.

7 • Double-click on the DOMAIN 1 Message Server icon to launch the message server.

The message server will launch in windowed mode, and you will see it initializing the post offices. Once the post offices are initialized, they will show as Opened in the Status window. You will then notice that the message server starts polling the message queues.

SENDING MESSAGES BETWEEN USERS IN DIFFERENT POST OFFICES

Create a new GroupWise icon for a user in POST2 with these steps.

1 • Highlight an icon that you created for a user in POST1, hold down the control key, click and drag the icon away from the first icon, and then release the mouse button. This makes a copy of the first icon.

2 • Highlight the new icon and press Alt-Enter. This will take you to the icon properties screen.

3 • Add these switches to the command line:

/ PH-C:\ POST2

/@U-*user ID*

LA-*network ID*

The / PH switch tells the client to look at the post office files in the POST2 directory.

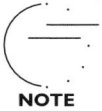

> **NOTE**
> **The network ID will usually be the same as the user ID unless you specifically modified the network ID field for that user in GroupWise Admin.**

4 • Choose OK.

5 • Run GroupWise for the user in POST2.

> **NOTE**
> **You can leave the message server running. Either minimize the message server to an icon, or move it to an out-of-the-way location on the screen.**

6 • Create and send a mail message to a user in POST1.

7 • Watch the message server process the message.

8 • After you have seen the message server process the message, check the message status in the Out Box. It should show a Delivered status.

9 • Run GroupWise for the message recipient and verify that the message was received.

You have now created a multiple post office GroupWise test system on your PC.

> **NOTE**
> **The DOS message server automatically launches the administration server (ADS.EXE) and the post office server (OFS.EXE) as they are needed. This is a unique characteristic of the DOS message server. If you watch the message server screen, you will see it launching OFS to deliver the message to the recipient and to process the status messages.**

Chapter 10: Setting Up a Multiple Domain System

In this part of the simulation, you will create a secondary domain, create one or more post offices in the domain, establish direct links between the domains, and send messages between users in the two domains.

CREATING THE SECONDARY DOMAIN, A POST OFFICE, AND USERS

Complete these steps to create the secondary domain:

1 • Run GroupWise Admin for the primary domain.

2 • Click on Create and then select Domain.

3 • Enter the name for the domain (DOMAIN2).

4 • Enter the directory for the domain (C:\DOMAIN2).

5 • Choose OK to create the domain.

6 • (Simulation Only) *Don't copy any software to the domain.* Make sure all options are unselected.

Because the administration, message server, and client are already installed on the hard drive for the primary domain, this simulation will use these same files with startup switches to point to the secondary domain when these processes are run for the secondary domain. This conserves disk space on the simulation PC's hard drive.

7 • Exit GroupWise Admin.

8 • Launch GroupWise Admin for the secondary domain. Because GroupWise Admin was not copied to the secondary domain, run AD.EXE from the primary domain directory with the /PH-*domain directory* switch, as follows:

AD /PH-C:\DOMAIN2

Notice that the secondary domain is listed as current.

9 • Create a post office in the secondary domain (POST3).

> **Because you did not copy archive software to the secondary domain directory, you will get an error message indicating that the archive software is not found. Choose OK to bypass this message.**
>
> **NOTE**

10 • Add two or more users to the post office.

LINK THE TWO DOMAINS WITH DIRECT LINKS

At the end of the previous steps, you were still in the secondary domain. Create a direct link to the primary domain by using these steps:

1 • Highlight the secondary domain.

2 • Click on Actions and then choose Edit.

> **F6 is a shortcut keystroke to edit a domain, post office, or user in GroupWise Admin.**
>
> **TIP**

3 • Select Message Server Configuration.

4 • Select Execution and change the Message Delivery option to Use App Threshold.

5 • Select Logging and change the Level to Diagnostic.

6 • Select the Network Links option. Notice that a link is not defined for DOMAIN1.

7 • Highlight DOMAIN1 and choose Edit Link.

8 • Choose Link Type and select Direct.

9 • Choose OK, choose Close, and then choose OK to return to the Domain Information Screen. Then choose OK to return to the main GroupWise Admin screen.

10 • Exit GroupWise Admin.

11 • Run GroupWise Admin for the primary domain.

12 • Use the previous steps to create a direct link from the primary domain to the secondary domain.

At this point you are ready to send messages between the users in both domains. However, for this simulation, you will need to create icons for the secondary domain's message server and a GroupWise icon for a user in the secondary domain. Here are the steps to do this.

1 • Run Windows.

2 • Open the Main program group.

3 • Double click on the PIF Editor icon to open the PIF editor.

4 • Type **CS.EXE** in the Program Filename field.

5 • Type **DOS Message Server (DOMAIN2)** in the Window Title field.

6 • Type **/ PH-C:\ DOMAIN2 / SW-C:\ DOMAIN2** in the Optional Parameters field.

> **The /SW-C:\DOMAIN2 switch tells the message server to create the message server swap file in the C:\DOMAIN2 directory. This allows both message servers to run at the same time. Both message servers cannot use the same working directory for the swap files.**

NOTE

7 • Type **C:\ DOMAIN1\WPCS** in the Start-up Directory field.

NOTE

> **The CS.EXE file is located in DOMAIN1's directory, because you didn't copy the message server to DOMAIN2 in the previous steps.**

8 • Select the Windowed option in the Display Usage field.

9 • Mark the Background Execution check box.

10 • Select File and then select Save.

11 • Name the file CS2.PIF and then select OK.

12 • Select File and then Exit to exit the PIF Editor.

You have now created a custom PIF file that will allow the message server to run in a window. The next steps will create an icon to launch the DOS message server.

1 • Click on the program group that contains your GroupWise icons.

2 • Choose File and then select New.

3 • Choose Program Item and then choose OK.

4 • Type **DOMAIN2 Message Server** in the Description field.

5 • Type **C:\WINDOWS\CS2.PIF** in the Command Line field.

6 • Choose OK to close the dialog box.

7 • (Simulation Only) Using a file manager program, create a directory named WIN under the C:\ POST3\ OFVIEWS directory. Copy the files in the C:\POST2\OFVIEWS\WIN directory to the C:\POST3\OFVIEWS\WIN directory. This step is necessary to make the Windows client run correctly for the users in POST3.

8 • Create a GroupWise icon for a user you added to domain 2. Use the /PH-*post office* switch to point to the correct post office, use the /@U-*user Id* switch to specify the user, and use the / LA-*network ID* switch to specify the network ID.

9 • Double-click on the DOMAIN1 Message Server icon to launch DOMAIN1's message server.

10 • Double-click on the DOMAIN2 Message Server icon to launch DOMAIN2's message server.

11 • Run GroupWise for a user in DOMAIN1 and send a message to a user in DOMAIN2.

12 • Run GroupWise for the user in DOMAIN2 who received the message to verify that the message was received.

Optional Activities for Chapter 10

▸ Configure a transfer pull directory in DOMAIN1 and configure DOMAIN2's message server to retrieve messages destined for DOMAIN2 from the transfer pull directory.

▸ Create a third domain in your system called DOMAIN3. Configure indirect links between DOMAIN2 and DOMAIN3 by using DOMAIN1 as the routing domain.

▸ Shut down the message server processes. Run GroupWise Admin for a user in DOMAIN1 and send a message to a user in DOMAIN2. Use Windows File Manager to locate the message file in the message queue directories. Then run the message server for DOMAIN1, let it process the message, and shut it down.

Use Windows File Manager to find the message file. Run DOMAIN2's message server to finish delivery of the message. Repeat this activity with a high-priority mail message and note the different directories that are used.

Optional Activities for Chapter 11

▶ Run GroupWise Admin for DOMAIN1 (primary domain) and add a user in DOMAIN1. Launch both message server processes and watch the message servers and administration servers process the change. Run the client program for a user in each domain to verify that the new user appears in the Address Book. Open the message server log files and look at the directory synchronization processes that occurred.

▶ Run GroupWise Admin for DOMAIN1 and add a user to a post office in DOMAIN2 (centralized administration model). Run the message servers and watch the directory synchronization processes. Compare the log files with the log files from the previous activity. Identify the request /confirm /replicate directory synchronization phases.

Optional Activities for Chapter 17

▶ Release DOMAIN2 from your system so that it becomes an external domain by using the steps listed in Chapter 17. Send messages between the two domains.

▶ Merge DOMAIN2 back into the system.

Optional Activities for Chapter 18

▶ Use the steps in Chapter 18 to move a user from POST1 to POST2. Run the DOS message server and watch the processes that occur.

▶ Use the steps in Chapter 18 to move a user from DOMAIN1 to DOMAIN2.

Optional Activities for Chapter 19

▶ Run GroupWise Admin and experiment with using Check GroupWise on the message store databases in the system.

▶ Run GroupWise Admin and experiment with the Database Management options.

Message Queues Used with Various Thread Settings

TABLE D.1

Message Queues Used with Thread Settings

PRIMARY USE	PRIORITY DIRECTORY	DEFAULT OPERATION	WITH /FAST0	WITH /FAST4	WITH BOTH /FAST0 AND /FAST4
Busy Searches	WPCSIN0	High Priority Thread	High Priority Thread One	High Priority Thread	High Priority Thread One
GroupWise Remote Client Requests	WPCSIN1		High Priority Thread Two		High Priority Thread Two
Admin and High Priority Messages	WPCSIN2		Low Priority Thread	Low Priority Thread One	Low Priority Thread One
High Priority Status	WPCSIN3				
Normal Priority	WPCSIN4	Low Priority Thread		Low Priority Thread Two	Low Priority Thread Two
Normal Priority Status	WPCSIN5				
Low Priority	WPCSIN6				
Low Priority Status	WPCSIN7				
Total Number of Threads in Use		2	3	3	4

Worksheet for End Users Setting Up the GroupWise Remote Client

Here are the instructions for installing GroupWise Remote for Windows:

1 •   Run Windows.

2 •   Insert the GroupWise Remote disk 1 in the A: drive.

3 •   Click on File.

4 •   Click on Run.

5 •   Enter **A:\SETUP** and click on OK.

6 •   Insert the disks as prompted.

7 •   After installation is complete, double-click on the GroupWise Remote icon to launch GroupWise Remote.

8 •   Use Table E.1 to fill in the required user settings:

*GroupWise Remote User
Settings Information Sheet*

OPTION	SETTING
Full Name	Enter your full name as it should appear in the From: field on your messages.
User ID	Enter your GroupWise user ID <or ID provided by administrator>
Master Mailbox Password	Enter the password you have set on your master mailbox <or password provided by administrator>
Domain	<Provided by administrator>
Post Office	<Provided by administrator>
Modem	Select your modem from the list.
Time Zone	Enter the time zone in your area.

CONNECTION DEFINITION INFORMATION		
Modem Connection	**Connection name**	Enter a name describing this connection.
	Phone Number	<Provided by administrator>
	Gateway Login ID	<Provided by administrator>
	Password	<Provided by administrator>
	Modem Script	Leave blank <or Script provided by administrator>
Network Connection	**Connection Name**	Enter a name describing this connection.
	Path to Post Office	<Provided by administrator>

GroupWise Remote User
Settings Information Sheet
(continued)

OPTIONAL	
Adminstrator Phone Number	\<Provided by administrator\>
Copy all files on diskette labeled \<supplemental\> to C:\OFWIN40.	

NOTE

A softcopy of this file is located on the CD-ROM that comes with this book. The filename is REMWRKS.WPD. It is in WordPerfect 6.1 format.

Index

Notes

Notes

IDG BOOKS WORLDWIDE LICENSE AGREEMENT

Important — read carefully before opening the software packet(s). This is a legal agreement between you (either an individual or an entity) and IDG Books Worldwide, Inc. (IDG). By opening the accompanying sealed packet(s) containing the software disk(s), you acknowledge that you have read and accept the following IDG License Agreement. If you do not agree and do not want to be bound by the terms of this Agreement, promptly return the book and the unopened software packet(s) to the place you obtained them for a full refund.

1. **License.** This License Agreement (Agreement) permits you to use one copy of the enclosed Software program(s) on a single computer. The Software is in "use" on a computer when it is loaded into temporary memory (i.e., RAM) or installed into permanent memory (e.g., hard disk, CD ROM, or other storage device) of that computer.

2. **Copyright.** The entire contents of this disk(s) and the compilation of the Software are copyrighted and protected by both United States copyright laws and international treaty provisions. The individual programs on the disk(s) are copyrighted by the authors of each program respectively. Each program has its own use permissions and limitations. You may only (a) make one copy of the Software for backup or archival purposes, or (b) transfer the Software to a single hard disk, provided that you keep the original for backup or archival purposes. To use each program, you must follow the individual requirements and restrictions contained in the Installation Instructions. Do not use a program if you do not want to follow its Licensing Agreement. None of the material on this disk(s) or listed in this Book may ever be distributed, in original or modified form, for commercial purposes.

3. **Other Restrictions.** You may not rent or lease the Software. You may transfer the Software and user documentation on a permanent basis provided you retain no copies and the recipient agrees to the terms of this Agreement. You may not reverse engineer, decompile, or disassemble the Software except to the extent that the foregoing restriction is expressly prohibited by applicable law. If the Software is an update or has been updated, any transfer must include the most recent update and all prior versions. Each shareware program has its own use permissions and limitations. These limitations are contained in the individual license agreements that are on the software disks. The restrictions include a requirement that after using the program for a period of time specified in its text, the user must pay a registration fee or discontinue use. By opening the package which contains the software disk, you will be agreeing to abide by the licenses and restrictions

for these programs. Do not open the software package unless you agree to be bound by the license agreements.

4. Limited Warranty. IDG Warrants that the Software and disk(s) are free from defects in materials and workmanship for a period of sixty (60) days from the date of purchase of this Book. If IDG receives notification within the warranty period of defects in material or workmanship, IDG will replace the defective disk(s). IDG's entire liability and your exclusive remedy shall be limited to replacement of the Software, which is returned to IDG with a copy of your receipt. This Limited Warranty is void if failure of the Software has resulted from accident, abuse, or misapplication. Any replacement Software will be warranted for the remainder of the original warranty period or thirty (30) days, whichever is longer.

5. No Other Warranties. To the maximum extent permitted by applicable law, IDG and the author disclaim all other warranties, express or implied, including but not limited to implied warranties of merchantability and fitness for a particular purpose, with respect to the Software, the programs, the source code contained therein and/or the techniques described in this Book. This limited warranty gives you specific legal rights. You may have others which vary from state/jurisdiction to state/jurisdiction.

6. No Liability For Consequential Damages. To the extent permitted by applicable law, in no event shall IDG or the author be liable for any damages whatsoever (including without limitation, damages for loss of business profits, business interruption, loss of business information, or any other pecuniary loss) arising out of the use of or inability to use the Book or the Software, even if IDG has been advised of the possibility of such damages. Because some states/jurisdictions do not allow the exclusion or limitation of liability for consequential or incidental damages, the above limitation may not apply to you.

7. U.S.Government Restricted Rights. Use, duplication, or disclosure of the Software by the U.S. Government is subject to restrictions stated in paragraph (c) (1) (ii) of the Rights in Technical Data and Computer Software clause of DFARS 252.227-7013, and in subparagraphs (a) through (d) of the Commercial Computer—Restricted Rights clause at FAR 52.227-19, and in similar clauses in the NASA FAR supplement, when applicable.

CD-ROM Installation Instructions

To install the 2-user versions of GroupWise, In Forms, and SoftSolutions on your hard disk, go to the APPS subdirectory and:

1 • For GroupWise, go to the GRPWISE4*language* directory (where *language* corresponds to the country code you desire, for example, US), run the SETUP.EXE program and follow the installation prompts to install the GroupWise components to your hard drive.

2 • For InForms, go to the INFORMS directory, run SETUP.EXE, and follow the installation prompts to install InForms to your hard drive.

3 • For SoftSolutions, go to the SOFTSOLS directory, run SETUP.EXE, and follow the installation prompts to install SoftSolutions.

To view or to copy technical documents to your hard disk, go to the **TECHDOCS** subdirectory. An index of the technical documents' filenames appears in the file named README.WPD. The documents are in WordPerfect 6.1 format. You can copy the documents to your hard drive, or retrieve them directly into WordPerfect (or into another word processing program that supports the WordPerfect file format) from the CD-ROM directory.

To install the GroupWare Software Developers' Kits to your hard disk, go to the **SDKS** subdirectory, run SETUP.EXE, and follow the command prompts to install the software to your hard disk.

To install the GroupWare Support Center Shared Code Troubleshooting utility (GSC), the GroupWise Integration Module (NWADMIN Snap-In Module), the Check GroupWise utility (OFCHECK), and the Microsoft Mail Convert utility (MSMAIL), go to the **UTILITY** subdirectory and:

1 • For the GroupWare Support Center Shared Code Troubleshooting utility, copy the files in the GSC directory to a subdirectory of your choice on your hard drive, run Windows, then run GSC.EXE from the directory where the GSC files are located.

2 • For the GroupWise Integration Module, run Windows, then run SETUP.EXE from the UTILITY\NWADMIN directory on the CD-ROM. Follow the installation prompts to install the utility to the NetWare 4.x server.

3 • For the Check GroupWise utility, you can replace the Check GroupWise files in the WPTOOLS directory in the GroupWise domain with the Check GroupWise files on the CD-ROM in the OFCHECK directory. (The Check GroupWise utility on the CD-ROM is an updated version of the Check GroupWise program that comes with the GroupWise Admin program.)

4 • For the Microsoft Mail Convert utility, go to the MSMAIL directory on the CD-ROM, copy the MMCONV.EXE file to a directory on your hard drive, and then run MMCONV.EXE to decompress the files. After the files are decompressed, run Windows, and then run SETUP.EXE to launch the installation routine for the Microsoft Mail Convert utility.

IDG BOOKS WORLDWIDE REGISTRATION CARD

RETURN THIS REGISTRATION CARD FOR FREE CATALOG

Title of this book: Novell's Groupwise 4 Administrators Guide

My overall rating of this book: ❑ Very good [1] ❑ Good [2] ❑ Satisfactory [3] ❑ Fair [4] ❑ Poor [5]

How I first heard about this book:

❑ Found in bookstore; name: [6]

❑ Advertisement: [8]

❑ Word of mouth; heard about book from friend, co-worker, etc.: [10]

❑ Book review: [7]

❑ Catalog: [9]

❑ Other: [11]

What I liked most about this book:

What I would change, add, delete, etc., in future editions of this book:

Other comments:

Number of computer books I purchase in a year: ❑ 1 [12] ❑ 2-5 [13] ❑ 6-10 [14] ❑ More than 10 [15]

I would characterize my computer skills as: ❑ Beginner [16] ❑ Intermediate [17] ❑ Advanced [18] ❑ Professional [19]

I use ❑ DOS [20] ❑ Windows [21] ❑ OS/2 [22] ❑ Unix [23] ❑ Macintosh [24] ❑ Other: [25]_____
(please specify)

I would be interested in new books on the following subjects:
(please check all that apply, and use the spaces provided to identify specific software)

❑ Word processing: [26]

❑ Data bases: [28]

❑ File Utilities: [30]

❑ Networking: [32]

❑ Other: [34]

❑ Spreadsheets: [27]

❑ Desktop publishing: [29]

❑ Money management: [31]

❑ Programming languages: [33]

I use a PC at (please check all that apply): ❑ home [35] ❑ work [36] ❑ school [37] ❑ other: [38] _____

The disks I prefer to use are ❑ 5.25 [39] ❑ 3.5 [40] ❑ other: [41]_____

I have a CD ROM: ❑ yes [42] ❑ no [43]

I plan to buy or upgrade computer hardware this year: ❑ yes [44] ❑ no [45]

I plan to buy or upgrade computer software this year: ❑ yes [46] ❑ no [47]

Name: _____ Business title: [48] _____ Type of Business: [49]

Address (❑ home [50] ❑ work [51]/Company name: _____)

Street/Suite# _____

City [52]/State [53]/Zipcode [54]: _____ Country [55] _____

❑ **I liked this book!** You may quote me by name in future
IDG Books Worldwide promotional materials.

My daytime phone number is _____

IDG BOOKS

THE WORLD OF
COMPUTER
KNOWLEDGE

☐ YES!

Please keep me informed about IDG's World of Computer Knowledge.
Send me the latest IDG Books catalog.

SECRETS™

...FOR DUMMIES™
COMPUTER
BOOK SERIES
FROM IDG

MACWORLD MW AUTHORIZED EDITION

AUTHORIZED PC WORLD EDITION